A THEORY OF
EVOLVING TONALITY

Da Capo Press Music Reprint Series

A THEORY OF

EVOLVING TONALITY

BY

JOSEPH YASSER

DA CAPO PRESS • NEW YORK • 1975

Library of Congress Cataloging in Publication Data

Yasser, Joseph.
  A theory of evolving tonality.

  (Da Capo Press music reprint series)
  Reprint of the ed. published by American Library of
Musicology, New York, which was issued as v. 1 of Con-
temporary series.
  Includes index.
  1. Tonality. 2 Musical intervals and scales.
  I. Title.
  ML3811.Y2T4   1975   781'.22   74-34376
  ISBN 0-306-70729-2

This Da Capo Press edition of *A Theory of Evolving Tonality* is an unabridged
republication of the first edition published in New York in 1932. It is reprinted
from an original in the collections of the Memorial Library, University of
Wisconsin.

Published by Da Capo Press, Inc.
A Subsidiary of Plenum Publishing Corporation
227 West 17th Street, New York, N.Y. 10011

AMERICAN LIBRARY OF MUSICOLOGY

CONTEMPORARY SERIES : VOLUME ONE

A THEORY OF
EVOLVING TONALITY

BY

JOSEPH YASSER

NEW YORK

AMERICAN LIBRARY OF MUSICOLOGY

1932

FOREWORD

A number of readers, I presume, have already familiarized themselves with the new theory evolved in this book, through two fairly extensive articles written by me, one of which, entitled *The Supra-Diatonic Scale as the Organic Basis of the Music of the Future,* appeared in the *Pro Musica* Quarterly (March-June, 1929), and the other, *The Future of Tonality: Tonality and Atonality as syn-thesised by Supra-Tonality,* was published by the LEAGUE OF COMPOSERS as a special supplement to the Quarterly *Modern Music* (November–December, 1930). I have found it expedient to reprint both these articles, with a few changes, at the end of this volume, as unquestionably they will be of great assistance for a better understanding of the subject. The first of these articles, which will be found under the heading of *Addendum I,* represents a series of synoptic extracts from the most important sections of this book, arranged in such a way as to form one unbroken sequence and to convey the general idea of the entire treatise in a coherent manner and in a form readily grasped; thus, it fills the purpose of a "Retrospect" and as such will be of service to the reader after the book is read through. The second of these articles *(Addendum II),* while dealing virtually with the same subject and containing all the essential points of this work (intentionally without the aid of mathematical calculations and acoustical diagrams) represents, nevertheless, more than a mere summary. It will be at once noticed, in the first place, that the basic idea of the new theory is worked out in this article according to the principles of the dialectic method (in the philosophico-historical sense), absent in the book proper. In connection with this a somewhat modified viewpoint is offered with regard to the evolutionary phases of musical psychology in Western Europe during the Middle Ages and the period immediately following it. Consequently, the article in question may be regarded, to a certain extent, as a further and special elaboration of the main theme—an elaboration far from complete, however, and for this very reason purposely separated from the main body of this work whose principal idea, therefore, will not necessarily break down in case the application of the above "dialectic" method and all that follows from it are found so far insufficiently substantiated by historical facts. This article touches but one of a great many "particular" problems connected with the new theory developed herein and which have yet to be worked out by years of study and experiment. The theory submitted, therefore, though quite definite in its fundamental idea, cannot be regarded as unalterable and "final" in every detail. No science ever speaks in terms of finality; accordingly, the author is inclined to view his work not so much as a finished task than as a preliminary theoretical foundation, as the cornerstone of a huge edifice yet to be erected.

I think it also necessary to add that this theory and its deductions are in no way evolved in accordance with my personal likes and dislikes, in so far as any particular music or school of composition of the day is concerned, and the reader will certainly make the gravest mistake if he draws any conclusions in this respect. Were I, then, asked to express the attitude taken in this work towards contemporary composers and certain creative trends in modern music, I could not find a better way than to repeat with Spinoza: "None do I praise or condemn, I merely study."

In conclusion I wish gratefully to acknowledge the assistance of Miss Lucile Gillet who collaborated with me in editing my own English translation of the original Russian manuscript.

J. Y.

New York, 1932.

TABLE OF CONTENTS

PRELIMINARY PART

PAGE

CHAPTER I. PROBLEM OF THE RESEARCH 3

On the threshold of a new tonal system. Tonality as an organic phenomenon. Its slow and continuous evolution. Increase of tonal material through quarter tones and other "mechanical" divisions unjustified. New scale to be organically and historically evolved. Definition of "modern music" adopted in this work.

CHAPTER II. THE DIATONIC, INFRA-DIATONIC AND SUPRA-
DIATONIC SCALES 5

The universality of the pentatonic scale. Its complete and incomplete forms. Different functions of its regular and auxiliary degrees. Grounds for its determination as an infra-diatonic scale. Possibility of forming a new or supra-diatonic scale on a principle similar to that of diatonic and infra-diatonic scales. Mutual interrelation of the three scales discussed. Supra-Tonality to supplant Tonality and Atonality in the course of historical evolution.

CHAPTER III. PLAN OF THE WORK 9

The two principal parts respectively dealing with the scales of the past and of the future. Theoretical and practical feasibility of an independent infra-diatonic system. Elaboration of a supra-diatonic system, its relation to modern tendencies in musical art and its possible use for practical purposes.

CHAPTER IV. RELATIVITY OF SOME STABILIZED MUSICAL
NOTIONS 11

Proper selection of musical terms. Lack of adequate nomenclature in music and acoustics. Relativity of diatonicism and chromaticism and of various designations with reference to intervals, modes, tonalities, intonations, harmonic combinations, etc. Necessity of additional terminological formations.

CHAPTER V. THE DECIMAL SYSTEM APPLIED TO MUSICAL
INTERVALS 13

Simplified method for acoustical calculations. Requires no more than a knowledge of ordinary arithmetic. Equally tempered whole tone as a basic measuring unit. Decitones, Centitones and Millitones representing its decimal subdivisions similarly to those of the Metric System. Advantages of this method as compared with the one dealing with vibration-fractions for the same purpose. Both methods described. Historical forerunners of the simplified method.

TABLE OF CONTENTS

FIRST PART   (*Infra-Tonality*)

PAGE

CHAPTER VI. HISTORIC SURVEY OF CHINESE SCALES   .   .   .   25

Ancient musical system and its two contradistinctive scales functionally supplementing each other. The basic acoustic principles and computations of the Chinese. Numerous and complicated systems suggested throughout the ages for the sole purpose of obtaining greater freedom in transposition. Principle of Equal Temperament discovered after long search but barred from practical use for religious considerations. Manifold phases of the Chinese pentatonic scale in the course of historical development. The invariably subordinated functions of the two auxiliary tones added to the principal five. Foreign influences and the resulting amalgamated scales. Restoration of the original constructions with slight modal changes.

CHAPTER VII. THE INFRA-DIATONIC SYSTEM   40

The organic nature of the infra-diatonic scale. Functional distinction between its regular and auxiliary degrees among the peoples of Celtic origin similar to that of the Chinese. Divergencies in their present tendencies. Characteristic qualities of the infra-diatonic scale. Seven-tone Equal Temperament of the Siamese. Semi-sesquitone Temperament of the Scotch bagpipers. Relativity of terms *whole step* and *half step*. System of musical notation for the infra-diatonic scale. Five principal infra-modes (Tonal pentatonic). The variety of altered infra-modes (Semitonal pentatonic, Japanese scales, archaic Greek pentatonic, etc.). Cycle of seven keys for each inframode. Convenience of the Siamese infra-tempered intonation. A few psycho-physiological considerations regarding the practical use of Equal Temperament. Intervals of the infra-diatonic scale. Their specific division into consonances and dissonances.

CHAPTER VIII. INFRA-DIATONIC HARMONY   62

Harmonic constructions and harmonic sense of the Orientals. Interrelation of harmony and scale. Data on Chinese Harmony. Resemblance to Occidental harmonic formations of the Middle Ages. The modern scientific approach to the origin of Harmony in European music. Principles of harmonic construction in Occidental and Oriental countries. Signs of harmonic evolution among the Chinese. Chord-formations "by infra-Thirds" similar to the principle of Occidental chord-formation "by Thirds." *Dyad* as a common (consonant) chord in the infra-diatonic system. Theoretical elaboration of infra-diatonic Harmony in all its principal branches. New method for harmonization of pentatonic melodies.

INTERMEDIATE PART   (*Tonality*)

CHAPTER IX. RUDIMENTS OF THE DIATONIC SYSTEM   .   .   107

Brief data on modes, keys, intervals, chords and three principal intonations of the diatonic scale; inserted for reference only.

SECOND PART   (*Supra-Tonality*)

CHAPTER X. FORMATION OF THE SUPRA-DIATONIC SCALE   .   113

Structural interrelation of the diatonic and infra-diatonic scales leading to the solution of the problem. Pythagorean intonation in the capacity of a provisional "common denominator." Quantitative and qualitative acoustic structure of the supra-diatonic scale. Methods of Equal Temperament for all three scales. Artificial circles and natural spirals of Fifths. Theoretically infinite chain of organically interconnected scales.

PAGE

SUPPLEMENT TO CHAPTER X. THE SUB-INFRA-DIATONIC

SYSTEM   140

The primitive sub-infra-diatonic (pre-pentatonic) scale. Its place in the general chain of organic scales. Its natural and tempered intonation. Its musical notation. Principal and altered sub-infra-modes. Cycle of five keys for each principal sub-infra-mode. Intervals of the sub-infra-diatonic scale. *Monad* as complete consonant chord. A miniature harmonic system. Historical data. The ancient Greek Dichord, Trichord and Pentachord. The Javanese *Salendro* scale. Need of further research in this direction.

CHAPTER XI. THE SUPRA-DIATONIC SYSTEM   .   .   .   154

The supra-diatonic scale as historically legitimate successor of the diatonic scale. Its essential properties analyzed. An expanded musical notation. Modal characteristics of the supra-diatonic scale. Its incongruity with the duodecuple or atonal scale. Formation of twelve supra-modes, each transposable into nineteen keys. Classification of intervals of the supra-diatonic scale and their division into consonances and dissonances. *Hexad,* formed by "supra-Thirds" as a common (consonant) chord of the new system. A tangled knot of imaginary paradoxes. Scales constructed up to this point upon the spiral of Fifths and Fourths retuned from Pythagorean to Just Intonation. Various groups of overtones comprised within the consecutive octaves of the Natural Harmonic Series used as basic "nuclei" in this procedure. Practicability of supra-tempered intonation.

SUPPLEMENT TO CHAPTER XI. NORMS AND ODDITIES OF

JUST INTONATION   .   .   195

Two versions of Just Intonation for the supra-diatonic scale. Their advantages and disadvantages. The proper interbalance of consonances and dissonances as mutually "opposite forces" within the supra-diatonic system. Relativity of Just Intonation. Harmonic and melodic aspects of the principle. Their theoretical norms. Acoustic "flaws" of purely tuned scales. Didymus and Ptolemy. Modern discrepancies. Tonality and Just Intonation.

CHAPTER XII. SUPRA-TONALITY VERSUS ATONALITY .   .   .   225

Further deductions with regard to supra-diatonic harmony, particularly those concerning the tonal functions of various chordal formations, restricted at present by practical obstacles. Inadequacy of the twelve-tone tempered scale in relation to any intonation of the supra-diatonic scale. Initial flashes of modern music. Whole-step harmonic combinations of Debussy as intuitive, though not quite adequate anticipations of the supra-diatonic Hexad. Subconscious attempts of Scriabin to rectify these anticipations. Inconsistencies of the so-called "Scriabin theory." Harmonic monism and dualism. Principle of harmonic polarity as a "categorical imperative" of musical consciousness. Consonances, dissonances and falsonances—three indispensable, though relative divisions of intervals in any music. Causes of hypertrophic harmonic complexity in the period of Atonality. Melodic creation hindered by the artificial structure of the duodecuple scale. Unconscious efforts of modern composers to break through to the melodic plane of the supra-diatonic scale. Scriabin's use of his "synthetic" chord in the capacity of a scale foundation. On Schönberg's melodic design. Polytonality, at bottom, a fictitious phenomenon. Relation between chords formed "by Thirds" in one system and "by whole steps" in another. Neutral intervals of the atonal scale inadequately reflecting the genuine intervals of the supra-diatonic scale. Stravinsky's "anti-emotional" theory. Mechanical subdivisions of existing tempered intervals—the shortest cut but an improductive one for creative purposes. Constructive and destructive properties of Equal Temperament. The principle requires periodical re-adjustment in consecutively consolidated stages of musical development. Twelve-tone Temperament system used by modern composers on the strength of historic inertia. Necessity of averting any break between different periods of musical art based on acoustically incongruous scales.

CONCLUSION

PAGE

CHAPTER XIII. FROM THEORY TO PRACTICE   277

Actual introduction of the supra-diatonic scale in music to be preceded by exhaustive experimental tests in all branches of acoustics. Flexibility of the human ear as regards its accommodation to different intonations. Two acoustically contradistinctive systems of the Javanese. Nineteen-tone Equal Temperament for music based on diatonic and supra-diatonic scales. Preservation of the original "modal" characteristics of the chromatic scale, one of its many advantages over the twelve-tone Equal Temperament. Chromatic modes structurally identical to supra-modes. Modern chromaticists unconsciously becoming supra-tonalists. Various types of uniform keyboards for diatonic and supra-diatonic music. Problem of new Harmony and Counterpoint. Inevitable historical factors behind the present atonal anarchy. Necessity of restrictions for creative purposes. Decorative tendencies in modern musical art resulting from limitations and inadequacies of the old tonal system. Supra-diatonic scale reconciles tonal complexity satisfying the modern way of musical thinking with firm basic principles derived from innately unchangeable laws of the musical mind.

ADDENDUM I.

The Supra-Diatonic scale as the Organic Basis of the Music of the Future .   .   295
(Reprinted from *Pro Musica* Quarterly)

ADDENDUM II.

Tonality and Atonality as synthesized by Supra-Tonality   329
(Reprinted from *Modern Music* Quarterly)

PARALLEL TABLE OF CENTITONES AND THEIR EQUIVALENT VIBRATION-RATIOS FOR ALL INTERVALS ENCOUNTERED IN THE PRESENT VOLUME   355

GLOSSARY OF TECHNICAL TERMS   363

INDEX   377

PRELIMINARY PART

CHAPTER I

PROBLEM OF THE RESEARCH

Whatever one's attitude toward the radical musical tendencies of to-day, and whatever the absolute artistic value of modern musical compositions may be (most of them, unquestionably, mere "creative experiments"), yet considering all the manifold historic, theoretic and acoustic data accumulated up to the present time, one can hardly doubt that those radical tendencies are signs or reflections or at least anticipations of some profound and volcanic process in musical art which will ultimately lead to the practical adoption of a new, tonally more complicated and, consequently, more subtle scale.

From a historical point of view, this adoption of a new scale need not surprise us, for we know that our diatonic scale, and later the chromatic scale, were not established in music at one stroke either, but were preceded by less complex scales which, as a rule, have now been abandoned. And from another angle there are no reasonable grounds whatever for supposing, as some theorists and musicians are inclined to do, that with these two present-day scales (diatonic and chromatic) the general evolution of tonal foundations in music has reached its final stage or, still worse, has come to an *impasse* from which there is no possible way out. Neither the physico-acoustical possibilities, nor the psycho-physiological faculties of our auditory apparatus and its corresponding brain centers favor in the very least such an assumption.

We should not lose sight of the fact that a genuine musical scale (or *tonality*, in a more fundamental sense) is, in a way, an organic phenomenon, a material-ized product of our inmost psychic functions, which, like everything else live and organic, is bound to grow, to expand, to evolve continuously. It is essen-tially an *evolving*, not a *static* phenomenon. As a given musical scale unfolds in this continuous manner, nothing more natural, therefore, than its gradual trans-formation into another scale of a more complicated and subtle type which, after acquiring a definite pattern, takes a dominant position over its predecessor for a certain historical period, and ultimately replaces it almost entirely; the whole process then begins anew, but each time on a comparatively higher plane.

The process itself of replacement of different scales by others gradually increasing in complexity, went on, it is true, very slowly and almost impercep-tibly in the course of historical evolution, and not only took many generations, but was accompanied by parallel psychological, perhaps also biological, muta-tions within the races themselves. Deliberateness, however, is characteristic of every live and genuine organic process; it would be rash, therefore, to believe that our present musical scale, for instance, will be replaced in the future by a more complex one, as soon as such a scale has been theoretically found and is accessible practically. Even granting that the conditions of modern civilization are able in some way to accelerate the evolutionary process, we are forced to admit that much time will probably elapse before there can be created, besides the new scale and new theory of composition connected with it, new music sufficiently convincing to profoundly alter the musical psychology of mankind and thereby overshadow the grandiose musical achievement of past centuries.

It was probably due to the natural leisureliness of the evolutionary process indicated and to the resultant meagerness of corresponding records that the inherent laws which govern this slow, though continuous, structural development of scales and which could thus give us a clue to the structure of the scale of the future, have not been revealed so far. And it is ignorance of these laws often coupled with scientifically undisciplined speculation that makes some modern composers, who earnestly long for increased tonal material, lean to a "short-cut" solution of this problem, namely, to a purely mechanical division of the equally tempered intervals of our present system into quarter tones or sixth tones or even smaller fractions. However, aside from the fact that such a naïve method is historically unjustified and acoustically absurd, it also proves to be, in spite of the temptation it offers, utterly uncertain and unstable. This is because, starting from the principle of a mechanical and arbitrary splitting of a whole tone, there are no reasons whatever for preferring one of its possible divisions to another. Thus, quarter tones have no essential advantages over eighth tones, and the latter are in no way better or worse than sixth tones or sixteenth tones, etc.

It is, then, apparent that the problem of increasing our present tonal material within the limit of an octave (and, incidentally, of obtaining intervals smaller than a semitone) requires, not a mechanical, but rather a sort of organic and, in any case, more convincing method which, being justified by historic experience, would subsequently lead to only *one* and not to several solutions.

Through the application of such an "organic" method, which in this case is but another name for the *historical* method, the author's aim is to discover the objective laws to which the structural changes of scales in musical evolution are subject, and with these laws as a basis, to form a new and more complex scale whose properties could explain, at least in rudimentary fashion, the most characteristic creative currents and trends in modern music. It should be remembered, however, that the expression *modern* will here invariably refer only to those musical manifestations which show a perfectly unambiguous tendency to break away from the existing diatonic system. And if a composer displays but a partial tendency of this sort (as is most often observed), then his music will be considered modern only as regards that particular portion.

CHAPTER II

THE DIATONIC, INFRA-DIATONIC AND SUPRA-DIATONIC SCALES

Of all the various scales which in music preceded our present diatonic scale, the particular attention of theorists has always been attracted to the so-called pentatonic scale, whose structure may be very closely expressed by the notes C-D-F-G-A of the generally accepted tempered musical system. Some of these theorists have repeatedly advanced the hypothesis that the pentatonic scale indicated does not seem to be the exclusive musical appanage of a given nation or group of nations or even of an entire race, but simply represents a certain stage of the musical development of mankind in general. The soundness of this hypothesis is corroborated nowadays, with ever-increasing evidence, by a gradually more extensive study of the world's musical folk-lore, which step by step establishes the fact of past or present use of the pentatonic scale in almost every quarter of the globe. Not to mention most of the Asiatic nations that are using the pentatonic scale to this day with particular tenacity, or the numerous aborigines of the American, Australian and African continents among whom this scale, although occasionally in veiled form, may be found without any especial effort, it is interesting to note that in many parts of Europe also, if not in every one of them, the past, and sometimes present use of the pentatonic scale now becomes more and more certain.*

---

* Somewhat more detailed information regarding the use of the pentatonic scale in European countries will be found in *Addendum II* of this book. (See page 335).

An additional remark here will be timely in order to make our standpoint perfectly clear with regard to the universal use of the pentatonic scale as outlined in the text. This, of course, is to be taken in a *comparative* sense and is not to be misinterpreted as in any way implying *exclusion*. The universal use of the pentatonic scale, therefore, does not preclude, by any means, the existence of other primitive scales which, as a matter of fact, are sometimes found in certain localities either alone or side by side with the former. But there is a radical difference—in essence and in general use—between the pentatonic scale, as well as its easily recognizable variations, on the one hand, and the rest of the more or less primitive scales, on the other. Of these two roughly divided classes, only the pentatonic scale, like our diatonic scale, may be regarded as an *inwardly*

organized tonal system, the readily grasped acoustic interrelation of its component units forming what is usually termed *Tonality* in the fundamental sense of the word. From this point of view all the other primitive scales are rarely more than arbitrary aggregations of acoustically unrelated tones, or, rather, related in such a complicated manner, that were we to take them at their face value and venture on an explanation, we would be driven to questionable overestimations and paradoxical assumptions with regard to the artistic subtlety of their originators, who scarcely went beyond the lowest stages of musical development. These characteristic and contradistinctive features of the two different kinds of scales indubitably predetermined their dissimilar musical destinies, the pentatonic scale with its direct appeal to the natural sense of "tonal organization" having been independently formed and adopted to an unparalleled extent in different parts of the world, while the other primitive scales gained hardy more than purely tribal recog-

The above indicated structure of the pentatonic scale, everywhere identical with the exception of the basically immaterial "modal" changes and the usual slight acoustic incongruities, does not represent, however, its final and complete form, since in some localities where this scale is most firmly established (for instance in Scotland and Ireland as well as in some countries of the Orient situated at a great distance from them), there has frequently been observed a tendency to extend its tonal material, and consequently its musical resources, by the sporadic application of two additional notes, E and B. But from this it must not be hastily inferred that such a tonal extension inevitably transforms the pentatonic scale into the diatonic scale, for in those recorded cases where the two degrees (E and B) are added, their functions differ profoundly from the functions of the *regular* degrees (C-D-F-G-A) of the pentatonic scale. In contradistinction to these regular degrees, the notes E and B merely play the rôle of *auxiliary* degrees of the pentatonic scale, serving as a basis for melodic embellishments, and they can always be omitted at will without essential detriment to the melody itself.

In other words, the functions of these two auxiliary degrees, interpolated between the five regular degrees of the pentatonic scale, are similar to the functions of five chromatic (likewise "auxiliary") degrees interpolated between the seven regular degrees of our diatonic scale.* And just as the latter is not transformed into an independent twelve-tone scale as long as the functions of its diatonic and chromatic degrees have the familiar demarcations, so the pentatonic scale is not necessarily transformed into an independent seven-tone scale as long as the functions of its regular and auxiliary degrees have similar demarcations.

This characteristic co-existence of two functionally different groups of degrees in the diatonic as well as in the pentatonic scale suggestively inclines

---

nition. We must bear in mind that it is quite unimportant, for our purpose, whether the pentatonic scale is, or has been used, in a given region, exclusively, or predominantly, or even subordinately, and what percentage of folk songs is based on this scale, as compared to others, in any of these instances. The crucial point of the matter is that this inwardly "organized" scale, irrespective of the frequency of its application, will actually be found in an immense number of practically disconnected localities, while other scales, no matter how faithfully adhered to within the places of their origin, have not been traced beyond their home boundaries, as a rule.

In making the above statement, we disregarded, for the time being, another and similarly universal scale which, preceding the pentatonic scale in the course of evolution, covers a number of *pre-pentatonic* formations and is extensively discussed in the Supplement to Chapter X of this volume. This scale, naturally, falls in the class of those tonal systems which, like the pentatonic and diatonic scales, are characterized by the prin-

ciple of Tonality determining their structure. We have left entirely aside, however, the question of the esthetic potentialities of various folkloristic scales (whether "universal" or not), which may give rise to widely different opinions and which, at any rate, precludes a purely scientific approach. This question is entirely beyond the scope of the present work, which has been intentionally limited to the problem of the evolutionary interrelation of strictly "organized" scales, with the ultimate object of expanding the possibilities of an equally "organized" creative musical art based on such scales.

* This has already been observed once in a similar way by Carl Engel (*The Music of the most ancient nations,* page 143, London, 1909) who literally expresses himself in the following manner: "These two intervals [i.e. the intervals formed by two auxiliary degrees of the Chinese pentatonic scale—J. Y.] they employed only in exceptional cases, or rather nearly in the same way as we introduce chromatic intervals into our diatonic scale."

one to recognize a certain similarity in the structural plan of these two scales. Such a recognition is further supported by many other conforming features, which I shall discuss later, and especially by the little-known fact that in Siamese musical practice the five regular degrees of the pentatonic scale jointly with its two auxiliary degrees, *while strictly retaining their functional distinctions*, are incorporated in one closed equally tempered system, thus forming a set of seven equidistant tones within an octave. Which is similar to our Occidental scale whose seven diatonic and five chromatic degrees are jointly incorporated in a larger but likewise closed equally tempered system forming a set of twelve equidistant tones within an octave.

In this way, considering the similar qualitative characteristics and the dissimilar quantitative constitution of the two scales in question, we may regard the pentatonic scale as a smaller diatonic scale, or rather as a diatonic scale of a "lower order," and we shall therefore term it henceforth the *infra-diatonic scale*. In those instances where it will be desirable to indicate or to emphasize the complete form of this scale, combining its two functionally distinguished, although doubtless in some way organically connected groups of degrees, we shall designate it, or supplement its name, by the formula "5 + 2." Accordingly, the diatonic scale will be designated, or its name supplemented, under similar circumstances, by the formula "7 + 5."

The existence in the musical history of mankind of two scales differing quantitatively in tonal complexity, and at the same time possessing a number of similar structural features, substantiates the forecast advanced above regarding the possible and probable adoption in the future of a new and still more complicated scale, as far as quantitative constitution is concerned, and yet—we may now add—structurally similar to the former. Such a possibility will subsequently become more plausible, especially when further examination of the diatonic and infra-diatonic scales discloses that besides their many-sided similarity there also exists a quite definite interrelation between the number and arrangement of their regular and auxiliary degrees—an interrelation which contains latently a leading clue to the construction of the new scale with the same characteristic opposition of its two functionally different groups of degrees. This new scale, bearing the same relation to the diatonic scale ("7 + 5") as the latter does to the infra-diatonic scale ("5 + 2") will obviously represent a sort of diatonic scale of a "higher order," and will therefore be termed henceforth *the supra-diatonic scale*.*

* In using the word "diatonic" in such a relative sense we do not commit any sin against the literal meaning of this ancient Greek term which in itself is rather vague because its etymological root *(tone)* has two entirely different meanings, namely:

1. a musical sound of definite pitch, this

being the original meaning derived from the Greek word *tonos, stretching*, i.e., in a figurative sense something resulting from a stretched string.

2. an interval equal to a major Second, this being obtained by the subtraction of a natural Fourth from a natural Fifth.

(OVER)

Judging from numerous and convincing characteristics of the supra-diatonic scale constructed in this manner, it is the very next one that lies in the path of continuous musical evolution and which, obeying infallible historic laws, slowly and gradually draws nearer to us, eventually to replace the diatonic scale. Moreover, this new scale, as we shall see, is the one which, despite the present insufficient appeal of its characteristics, is subconsciously anticipated by many modern composers in the course of creation, although this scale naturally finds but a limited application and very inadequate representation in their compositions.

Two of the most essential and, for modern composers, least attractive characteristics of the supra-diatonic scale are—by virtue of its structural similarity with the two antecedent scales—a clearly expressed mode and tonality which, of course, in accordance with the increased complexity of the new scale acquire here a somewhat altered meaning and will therefore be termed henceforth *supra-mode* and *supra-tonality,* respectively. These two notions are radically opposed to the now predominant principle of atonality, which signifies no more than a transitory stage in the course of replacement of the old diatonic scale by the new supra-diatonic one. Such an intermediate stage is quite unavoidable and readily explained, not only in this particular instance but in any other similar replacement of some closed musical system (in no small part due to artificial equal temperament) by another and more complicated musical system, as will be shown later in the proper place.

In this way, supra-tonality which is to supplant existing diatonic tonality as well as transitory atonality, will appear not as a conservative reverting to past media of musical expression (as it may seem from a superficial glance) but simply as the result of an *extended* application of old principles invariably corresponding to the requirements of the human psyche, and for this very reason producing an organically evolved and tonally enriched musical scale.

It is quite apparent that with neither of these definitions will the word "diatonic"—which literally means "through tones" *(dia tonos)*—adequately express what is usually implied by this term. Indeed, if we take the term *tone* as a *sound,* then any scale, inasmuch as it is composed of sounds, may be named "diatonic," which is absurd. On the other hand, should we take the term *tone* as an *interval,* then only one scale, namely the whole-tone scale, as being exclusively composed of major Seconds, could be considered "diatonic," which is equally absurd. Again, if (as is often the case) we attach the term "diatonic" to a scale *mostly* composed of whole tones (major Seconds), even then such a definition will include many scales which cannot in any way be regarded as diatonic.

It seems more logical, therefore, to revert to the original meaning of the term *tone* (i.e. a sound) when using it as the root of the word "diatonic," but to limit it, in this instance, to the notion of a *regular* tone or regular degree of a given scale in contradistinction to the latter's *auxiliary* or chromatic degrees, the existence of which is automatically assumed with this newly adopted notion of a (regular) tone. The term "diatonic" would then have to be applied to a scale whose *main body* is composed of regular tones or degrees (irrespective of the intervals they form within an octave) but which also contains—actually or potentially—a set of auxiliary degrees specifically interpolated between the former. Such a new and enlarged definition will not only successfully cover our modern conception of the diatonic scale but will also wholly justify the two new terminological formations ("infra-diatonic" and "supra-diatonic") derived from it and applied for the first time in this book.

CHAPTER III

PLAN OF THE WORK

The foregoing pages being necessarily only a concise and abridged exposition of the central idea of the present work, it cannot of course be claimed that they possess the clarity that is supposed to result from a more extensive and careful elaboration of the subject. Such an elaboration is given in the two subsequent and main parts of this book.

Of these two parts, the first deals with our newly adopted point of view regarding the pentatonic scale, for the first time considered here as an infra-diatonic scale (i.e. the diatonic scale of a lower order), with all the characteristics implied in such a designation. Since, strictly speaking, this point of view is the main premise on which rests the solution of the fundamental problem of this work, its substantiation calls for a maximum of thoroughness, and must be carried through not only as regards theoretic possibility but also as regards the practical viability of an entirely independent infra-diatonic musical system.

Looking for authentic material to form a background for this first part, I naturally came across the music and theoretic speculations of the Far East, particularly China, as almost the sole source capable of revealing, at least in part, the true nature of the pentatonic scale. Some information corroborating the above viewpoint in regard to this scale is to be found in numerous and exhaustive Chinese musical treatises which, however, by reason of their great intricacy and purely external details often obscure the true intent of the theoretical structures they contain.

In order to impart and to elucidate to the reader the real and, by the way, somewhat rudimentary nature of these structures—rudimentary at least in that portion which has a direct bearing on our subject—I have found it expedient to present them in the form of a compact historical survey of Chinese scales, preceding the chapter which deals with the nature and properties of the infra-diatonic scale. Similarly, I shall preface my own elaboration of infra-diatonic Harmony with the most essential historical data regarding Chinese Harmony. The former will represent but the logical development of what is potentially contained in the semi-embryonic Chinese musical material and will be subjected to a practical test by actual harmonization of genuine infra-diatonic melodies.

Omitting now the intermediate portion of the book which is inserted merely for purposes of reference, we come to the second part, entirely devoted to the theoretic elaboration of the supra-diatonic musical system. It begins with the formation of the supra-diatonic scale, then turns to an analytical examination of its nature and properties, and ends with an investigation, in that light, of the most important and characteristic tendencies of modern musical art. In conclusion I have lightly touched upon some essential problems in connection with a possible transition to the practical application of the supra-diatonic scale in the music of the future.

CHAPTER IV

RELATIVITY OF SOME STABILIZED MUSICAL NOTIONS

One of the most perplexing points encountered by the author was the selection and appropriate application of musical terms the meaning of which, hitherto regarded as quite stable and constant, becomes very elastic here in view of the somewhat unconventional treatment of the subject, and particularly of the extremely "relative" views on the notions of diatonicism and chromaticism. This flexibility or relativity of musical notions is apt to mislead the reader, especially when they have to be applied in association with some definite acoustic magnitudes (intervals). The latter, as is known, have no *independent* nomenclature in music or in acoustics, and are expressed either by mathematical ratios or— in the few instances where this is feasible—by numerical designations of the various degrees of the diatonic scale in which some of all the generally conceivable intervals may be found. Thus, for instance, an interval which is scientifically expressed by the mathematical ratio $\frac{3}{2}$ is called not only in music but often in pure acoustics, a "Fifth," for the sole reason that the interval of the same dimension is formed by the fifth regular degree of the (justly intoned) diatonic scale and its Tonic (C-G).

To borrow these numerical designations (e.g. Prime, Second, Third, etc.) for the purpose of indicating certain tonal relations is, of course, quite admissible, but only as long as they always convey the very same acoustic meaning, i.e. as long as every one of these numerical designations invariably expresses some definite and constant interval. In this book, however, we shall have to deal for the first time with scales in which, owing to the comparatively increased or decreased number of their "regular" degrees, the numerical designations of the latter will have their own acoustic meaning, incompatible with those of the diatonic scale. Thus, for example, the interval formed by the fifth regular degree of the infra-diatonic scale and its Tonic (C-A), i.e. the interval which by etymological determination is a "Fifth" of this scale, will be much wider than the "Fifth" of the diatonic scale (C-G), the difference between them being exactly a whole tone (G-A). Similarly, the interval formed by the fifth regular degree of the supra-diatonic scale and its Tonic, i.e. the "Fifth" of this scale, will be much smaller than the "Fifth" of the diatonic scale, this being quite obvious since the greater the general number of degrees in a scale, the smaller the intervals between them and, consequently, the smaller the intervals formed by every one of those degrees and the common (for all scales) Tonic.

In this way, the "Fifth" which until now was considered a sufficiently stable notion, from an acoustic point of view, here acquires a decidedly relative meaning which varies with the general tonal constitution of one scale or another.

Hence it is not difficult to foresee that this "relativity" will likewise involve the rest of the numerical denotations of the degrees of all three scales. Moreover, it will also extend to many other musical concepts which, being directly connected with the similar structure of these scales and having within every one of the latter a musically similar, although acoustically quite different meaning, should, in consequence, be identically termed. Such are, besides intervals, the notions of mode, tonality, intonation, whole step and half step, diatonic succession, chromatic alteration, etc. This also applies to many notions in the field of Harmony, each of which loses here its absolute stability and acquires a relative meaning.

To avoid inextricable confusion or, to say the least, continual explanations, which would be needed under the above conditions, I have found it advisable to introduce certain additional terminological formations, using exclusively for that purpose the, to the reader, already familiar prefixes "infra" and "supra," as direct indications that a given term refers to one or the other scale. For instance, the usual nomenclature of the regular degrees for which, in the diatonic scale, a consecutive numerical series is accepted, viz. Prime, Second, Third, etc., will become, in the infra-diatonic scale, the following series: infra-Prime, infra-Second, infra-Third, etc., and in the supra-diatonic scale: supra-Prime, supra-Second, supra-Third, etc.

A similar procedure will be followed when necessary for other terms for which the corresponding indications will be found in their proper place. To further facilitate an understanding of all these additional terminological formations, as well as of some entirely new terms introduced in this book, a special glossary is given at the end.

CHAPTER V

THE DECIMAL SYSTEM APPLIED TO MUSICAL INTERVALS *

The expanded musical terminology adopted above not only will prevent the confusion that threatens to overtake musical notions, but will also permit, as heretofore, an unobstructed application of the customary acoustic terms, borrowed from the numerical denotations of the various degrees of the diatonic scale, even in those instances where the argumentation touches upon something having no direct connection with this scale at all. We shall constantly avail ourselves of this possibility, so that wherever the terms *Prime, Second, Third,* etc. are subsequently encountered, even if the diatonic scale is not specifically mentioned, they will invariably express acoustic magnitudes equalling the intervals of this particular scale. It is essential to bear this in mind in order to avoid further confusion.

For all that, however, the utilization of these customary and convenient terms will by no means liberate us from the "arid language of figures," from mathematical expressions, since these terms, being strictly limited in number (i.e. limited exactly by the tonal constitution of the diatonic scale), do not cover that mass of intervals with which we shall have to deal in numerous acoustic calculations in this book. At the same time it is the author's earnest desire that this work should be understood not only by theorists and acousticians but also by practical musicians and even by musical students whose knowledge of mathematics, not to mention acoustics, is confined—as a rule—to very elementary notions.

Taking this into consideration, the author found it practical to adopt in all calculations and measurements a very simple method, which does not require from the reader more than a knowledge of ordinary arithmetic. In contradistinction to the abstruse, though scientifically most accurate, method of dealing with vibration-fractions, it consists in expressing the dimension of any interval in simple numbers, for which some conventional interval, as a basic measuring unit, is assumed. The principle of the method is in essence by no means new, its various versions differing only in the basic measuring unit assumed.

For reasons which will be discussed later, I have found of greater practical value the assumption, for such a unit, of an *equally tempered whole tone,* (i.e. one-sixth part of an octave), or, to be more explicit, of the interval which is equal

* This chapter is a revised version of a separate article entitled *Decitones—Centitones—Millitones,* published by the writer in *Pro-Musica Quarterly* (New York), March, 1928. The section of this article dealing with the practical necessity of acoustic knowledge is omitted here entirely.

to the major Second of our tempered scale as expressed on the modern pianoforte. To designate the fractional divisions of this unit I have followed the principle of terminological formation used in the metric system, and adopting the term "tone" as the root, I have called one-tenth of a tone *Decitone,* one-hundredth of a tone *Centitone,* and finally one-thousandth of a tone *Millitone.**

The application of any of these designations depends, of course, only on the degree of accuracy desirable for various measurements. For general purposes, however, expression in terms of centitones is the most practical and may be considered as sufficiently exact.

For the sake of convenience, I have also found it advisable to borrow from the metric system the method of forming abbreviations for these three terms, viz. *dtn,* instead of decitones, *ctn,* instead of centitones and *mtn,* instead of millitones.

Thus, the equally tempered whole tone will contain:

10 dtn. or 100 ctn. or 1000 mtn.

Accordingly, the equally tempered semitone will contain:

5 dtn. or 50 ctn. or 500 mtn.,

and the equally tempered quarter tone:

2.5 dtn. or 25 ctn. or 250 mtn. etc.

On the other hand, two equally tempered whole tones, i.e. the tempered major Third, will contain:

20 dtn. or 200 ctn. or 2000 mtn.,

two and a half tempered tones, i.e. the tempered Fourth, will contain:

25 dtn. or 250 ctn. or 2500 mtn.,

three and a half tempered tones, i.e. the tempered Fifth, will contain:

35 dtn. or 350 ctn. or 3500 mtn. and so on, adding 5 dtn. or 50 ctn. or 500 mtn. for every additional semitone and twice that number for every additional whole tone.**

* This principle would make the name "tonometric" appropriate for this system. Such a name, however, is intentionally avoided here, as the same word, with an entirely different meaning, could be coined from *tonometer* (sometimes called *sonometer* and even *phonometer*), an instrument for measuring the pitch of sounds and not the intervals between them, with which we are dealing. Confusion would obviously arise from the twofold meaning of the term *tone* as discussed above (see Footnote on page 7).

**In order to distinguish the two different meanings of the term *tone*—sound and interval —in the latter instance it will be almost always accompanied by the adjective *whole.* Consequently the term *tone* will from now on signify "a sound of definite pitch" and the term *whole tone*—an interval equal to a (tempered) major Second. Hence, expressions like "a scale composed of six tones" and "a scale composed of six whole tones" would create no confusion, as the former would obviously signify a six-tone scale (irrespective of its component intervals) and the latter, the familiar whole-tone scale. There will be exceptions to the above rule of omitting the adjective *whole* only in those instances where the dimension of an interval cannot be exclusively expressed in whole tones. We shall say, for example, that a perfect Fifth contains 3½ tones (not 3½ whole tones), which will not be misunderstood since a tone, in the sense of a sound, cannot be expressed in fractional quantities.

All other tempered as well as non-tempered intervals are expressed in relation to this standardized table.

For those who are not very familiar with acoustics, I shall briefly explain the essentials and practical advantages of this method of representing the dimension of musical intervals, as compared with the one dealing with vibration-fractions for the same purpose.

The latter method expresses the interval between two sounds by a mathematical ratio, for instance $\frac{3}{2}$, in which the upper figure represents the number of sound-vibrations per second (the vibration-number) of the upper note of a given interval, while the lower figure represents the vibration-number of the lower note of the same interval. The dimension of an interval remains unchanged as long as the proportion between the vibration-numbers of its two notes is preserved, so if, for instance, the vibration-number of the upper note of any given interval is one and a half times that of the vibration-number of the lower note, as is the case in the above example, $\frac{3}{2}$, then this interval, irrespective of the absolute value of these two numbers, will produce on our ear the impression of a natural Fifth. Another example: 60 is one and a half times as large as 40. Accordingly, two sounding bodies (two strings, let us say), one of which produces 60 vibrations per second, while the other produces 40 vibrations in the same time, will impress our ear as the interval of a natural Fifth, which in this case will be expressed by the fraction $\frac{60}{40}$.

The very same interval, but at a different pitch, will be formed by any other pair of vibration-numbers having the same ratio, i. e. any one in which the upper number is one and a half times the lower number. Hence, the fraction $\frac{96}{64}$, for example, will express a natural Fifth just as much as $\frac{120}{80}$ or $\frac{144}{96}$ etc. But in every instance this interval will be found at a different pitch, raised with the proportionate increase of its two vibration-numbers and lowered with their proportionate decrease. This will become still clearer if we substitute for all the vibration-numbers in the last three fractions the corresponding notes, viz. $\frac{C}{C}$ instead of $\frac{96}{64}$, $\frac{B}{E}$ instead of $\frac{120}{80}$ and $\frac{d}{G}$ instead of $\frac{144}{96}$. *

The conclusion easily drawn from the above is that the ordinary arithmetical difference between the two numbers of any given vibration-fraction does not give any indication of the dimension of the interval expressed, for this difference is not a constant quantity in the very same interval taken at various pitches. Thus, in the vibration-fractions $\frac{96}{64}$, $\frac{120}{80}$ and $\frac{144}{96}$, every one of which expresses with absolute accuracy, but at a different pitch, the interval of a natural Fifth, this difference (subtracting the lower numbers from the upper ones) will be equal to 32, 40 and 48 vibrations, respectively. Apart from the fact that these numbers are not alike and could be varied infinitely, according to the pitch of the interval, they may also occur in many vibration-fractions that express entirely different intervals. For instance, the difference between the two numbers of the vibration-fraction $\frac{160}{128}$ is equal to 32 vibrations, and the same is true of the interval $\frac{C}{C} = \frac{96}{64}$. The fraction $\frac{160}{128}$, however, will by no means express the interval of a natural Fifth, for its upper vibration-number is *not* one and a half

*The so-called philosophic or arithmetical pitch, assuming that C = 64 vibrations, is applied in these particular examples.

times as large as the lower one, i. e. the ratio of these two numbers (160 and 128) does not meet the sole and essential requirement for the production of a natural Fifth, as explained above.*

Consequently, the constant characteristic of a vibration-fraction expressing the very same interval appears to be solely the ratio of its two vibration-numbers and nothing else. This ratio, however, sufficiently obvious in such a simple interval as a natural Fifth, is infinitely more complex in less familiar intervals and, therefore, can no longer be grasped as quickly in these cases, especially when the same interval is being transposed into a different pitch, thereby invariably (although proportionately) changing the numbers of its vibration-fraction. But all these disadvantages are entirely eliminated by the simplified method of representing intervals, which assumes the equally tempered whole tone (or any other conventional interval) as a basic measuring unit. For in the latter case every interval, irrespective of the pitch at which it is taken, will be unalterably expressed by one and only one identical and easily grasped number. A natural Fifth, for instance, at any pitch, will be invariably expressed (in centitones) by the number 351, which immediately shows that this interval exceeds the tempered Fifth (equal, as we know, to 350 ctn.) by one centitone, i.e. by one-hundredth of an equally tempered whole tone, which is understood by every musician.

Should we compare with these definite numbers the vibration-fractions respectively expressing the intervals of a natural and tempered Fifth, viz. $\frac{3}{2}$ and $\frac{433}{289}$, we shall not find anything in them *explicitly* indicating the degree of their dissimilarity. Even to reduce these two fractions to a common denominator, viz. $\frac{867}{578}$ and $\frac{866}{578}$, will be of little or no help, as far as direct explicitness is concerned, since the obvious difference between their numerators, equal to one vibration, is not a constant quantity, and, as we know, depends wholly on the actual position of these two intervals, i.e. on the pitch at which they are taken. The matter is not greatly facilitated, in this regard, by the fact that when dealing with an interval *irrespective* of its actual position in a scale, the generally adopted practice is to express it by the smallest possible vibration-fraction. The reason is that such a fraction does not necessarily consist of small vibration-numbers, even in instances of musically very ordinary (though acoustically complex) intervals. The above example of a tempered Fifth which cannot be expressed with sufficient accuracy by a fraction smaller than $\frac{433}{289}$, may serve as one of the best illustrations of this fact. Only natural intervals with the simplest acoustic relations may be expressed by comparatively small vibration-fractions, although, even then, their relative dimension in comparison with other intervals is not obvious to a musician, who can hardly grasp it from the too great and unescapable variety of fractions that preclude any common and convenient ground for comparison.

Another difficulty in the matter of dealing with intervals expressed in vibration-fractions is rooted in the general law governing *addition* and *subtraction* of intervals whose vibration-fractions have to be *multiplied* and *divided* respectively in order that the combined dimension of two or more intervals or the difference between them may be obtained. It is, of course, easy to multiply a simple fraction like $\frac{3}{2}$ by $\frac{3}{2}$, i.e. a natural Fifth by itself, the result being $\frac{9}{4}$, a natural major Ninth. But suppose one

* The two numbers of the vibration-fraction $\frac{160}{128}$ are obviously in the ratio $\frac{5}{4}$, which cor- responds to the interval of a natural major Third C-E.

has to multiply such a fraction as $\frac{433}{289}$ by $\frac{433}{289}$ i.e. a *tempered* Fifth by itself, and the difficulty of obtaining the tempered major Ninth, viz. $\frac{187489}{83521}$ or about $\frac{449}{200}$, will at once increase to a considerable degree. Similarly, the division of one vibration-fraction by another, like $\frac{3}{2} : \frac{4}{3} = \frac{9}{8}$, which is a requisite for the subtraction of a natural Fourth from a natural Fifth, and gives a natural major Second, may be a simple matter. But one needs merely to substitute tempered intervals for the natural ones in this instance, i.e. divide a vibration-fraction expressing the tempered Fifth by the one expressing the tempered Fourth, which gives a tempered major Second, and the difficulty of the corresponding mathematical operation, viz. $\frac{433}{289} : \frac{303}{227} = \frac{98291}{87567}$ or about $\frac{449}{400}$, will again increase many times.

Nothing of this kind, however, will occur if the decimal system above set forth is used, since the adding of one interval with another will merely require an addition (not a multiplication as before) of their respective figures. Similarly, the subtracting of one interval from another will require a subtraction (not a division) of the smaller figure from the larger. Thus, in the case either of two natural or two tempered Fifths added together, one has merely to add 351 ctn. to 351 ctn. in the former instance and 350 ctn. to 350 ctn. in the latter, and the respective totals of 702 ctn. and 700 ctn. will not only indicate the dimension of a natural and tempered Ninth, but will also immediately disclose the difference between them: 2 ctn. Just as simple would be the subtraction of 249 ctn. from 351 ctn., a natural Fourth from a natural Fifth, and of 250 ctn. from 350 ctn., a tempered Fourth from a tempered Fifth. The two results, 102 ctn. and 100 ctn., will indicate the dimension of a natural and of a tempered major Second, and, as in the instance of intervals added together, will disclose the difference between them: 2 ctn.—an advantage which is not even remotely possible when one deals with intervals expressed in vibration-fractions.

Speaking of the various difficulties arising in the latter case, it is also opportune to point out that the acoustic computations become still more complicated when one is confronted with the necessity of multiplying a considerable number of identical intervals or of dividing a certain interval into a number of smaller and equal parts. This is because the multiplication of intervals requires an "involution" of their vibration-fractions, which have to be raised to the power equalling the general number of these intervals. On the other hand, the division of a certain interval into equal parts calls for the reverse operation, that is, for the extraction of a root (evolution) from the original vibration-fraction, with an index equalling the number of these smaller parts. Thus, the multiplication of a natural Fifth twelve times, let us say, will require the consecutive multiplication of its vibration-fraction by *itself* ($\frac{3}{2} \times \frac{3}{2} \times \frac{3}{2}$ etc.) as many times, which is equivalent to raising this fraction to the power of twelve, i.e. $(\frac{3}{2})^{12} = \frac{531441}{4096}$. Conversely, the division of an Octave, for instance, into twelve equal parts, will require the extraction of a twelfth root from $\frac{2}{1}$, the vibration-fraction of that interval, i.e. $^{12}\sqrt{\frac{2}{1}} = 1.05946$ or about $\frac{89}{84}$,—a complicated procedure and already a difficult one without the aid of logarithms. The same two operations will appear incomparably simpler when expressed in terms of the decimal system, since the latter requires merely the multiplication of 351 ctn. by 12, in the former instance, which gives 4212 ctn., an enormous interval comprising twelve natural Fifths, and just as simple a division of 600 ctn. (interval of an Octave) by 12, in the latter instance, which gives 50 ctn., an interval of a tempered semitone.

The simplicity and convenience of the decimal system in dealing with musical intervals is explained by the fact that it represents, strictly speaking, only a sort of logarithmic system adapted for musical purposes and, above all, in such a specific manner that even a knowledge of logarithms is not required for its use. And it is hardly necessary to add that the significance and characteristic function of any logarithmic system is the simplification of mathematical operations through the substitution of multiplication and division for involution and evolution (raising to powers and extraction of roots), and of addition and subtraction for multiplication and division. It is in this very kind of simplification, therefore, and, particularly, in the change of *proportions* into *differences* that lies the purely practical advantage of the decimal system over that dealing with vibration-fractions. This advantage will be still better grasped from the two following diagrams (Ex. 1, *a* and *b*) showing our present equally tempered scale ("7 + 5") with the indication of its intervals in terms of vibration-fractions (approximative) and centitones, respectively:

EXAMPLE 1:

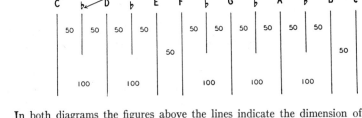

In both diagrams the figures above the lines indicate the dimension of intervals formed by every note and the common Tonic, while the figures between the lines indicate the dimension of the tempered whole tones and semitones.* The long lines represent the "regular" degrees of this scale and the short lines its "auxiliary" (chromatic) degrees.

To facilitate an understanding of all the manifold acoustic relations which will be met with at every step, I shall henceforth also represent all other calculations by means of similar diagrams.

* Should one wish to express the scale in terms of *decitones* or *millitones*, it will be sufficient, of course, to divide every figure of the lower diagram by 10 in the former case, and to multiply them by 10 in the latter.

As already stated, the idea of converting the mathematical ratios expressing musical intervals into comprehensible and constant magnitudes has been advanced more than once by different theorists, but of the systems concretely proposed so far there are only two that deserve attention from the point of view of practical utility and they may as well be described here for the sake of completeness.

The first of these systems was originated by John Herschel (1792-1871) who adopted the octave, consisting of one thousand units, as a fundamental measuring interval. In the equally tempered scale ("7 + 5") these thousand units (which subsequently acquired the name of "millioctaves") would be distributed in the following manner among the twelve semitones contained in every octave:*

EXAMPLE 2:

[The slight inequality of the figures representing equal intervals, like 83 and 84, also 166 and 167, is an imaginary one and is the result of the intentional avoidance of fractions.]

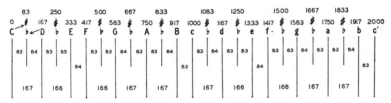

*A brief description of Herschel's system (which was apparently never published by Herschel himself) is to be found in a book entitled *On sound and atmospheric vibrations with the mathematical elements of music*, by George Biddel Airy (London, 1871), page 222. The term "millioctave" was probably introduced for the first time by Arthur v. Oettingen in *Das duale Harmoniesystem* (Leipzig, 1913), page 250, although Riemann (*Akustik*, p. 113) seems to ascribe to him the millioctave system itself, which is obviously erroneous. At any rate it should be noted here that this system represents a development of the principle applied long ago by Leonard Euler in his treatise *Tentamen novae theoriae musicae ex certissimis harmoniae principiis delucide expositae* (Petropoli, 1739), i.e. the principle of binary logarithms which, when applied to musical intervals, designates an Octave as a unit and smaller intervals as fractions thereof. Thus, an interval of a tempered semitone is represented, according to this principle, by the fraction 0.083333, a tempered whole tone by the fraction 0.166666 and so on. It is at once evident that in order to render these values into the terms of the millioctave system, it is sufficient to multiply them by 1,000, i.e. simply to shift the decimal point three digits to the right. The remaining fractional figures are entirely omitted if they do not equal half of a millioctave and taken as *one* millioctave if they equal or exceed that quantity. Therefore, if Euler's figures represent the logarithms of interval-ratios on the base of 2 (binary logarithms),

then the figures of the millioctave system may evidently be regarded as logarithms on the base of $\sqrt[1000]{2}$.

Another writer who availed himself of Euler's principle and merely changed the logarithmical base from 2 to $\sqrt[100]{2}$, i.e. assumed an Octave as a fundamental measuring interval (Meter) consisting of one hundred units (Oktavenzentimeter), was Karl Laker, the author of *Das musikalische Sehen; anschauliche Darstellung von Begriffen und Gesetzen der Musiklehre* (Graz, 1913). It will be opportune, in connection with the above, to point out a decidedly inaccurate statement in Riemann's *Lexikon* (under the heading of "Logarithmen," edition of 1922 and 1929), in which the introduction of binary logarithms for musical purposes is attributed to M. W. Drobisch, the author of *Ueber musikalische Tonbestimmung and Temperatur* (1852), while L. Euler is held responsible for the introduction of common logarithms (on the base of 10) for the same purposes. The truth is, however, that although Drobisch did avail himself of binary logarithms in his book, priority in this respect belongs to Euler (see the seventh chapter of his treatise, in which he first introduces the principle of binary logarithms, and the ninth chapter, in which the pure and equal intonation of the chromatic scale is represented in logarithmic values on the base of 2). Regarding the initial introduction of common logarithms in music, see the Footnote which follows the next.

This system, of little convenience for measuring intervals within the limit of an octave, is more advantageous than other systems in comparatively rare calculations involving more than one octave simultaneously dealt with. This is because all the figures representing compound intervals (i.e. greater than an octave) will be the same as their corresponding simple intervals (i.e. not exceeding an octave) but increased by a thousand units for every subsequent octave. Thus, for instance, if the major tempered Third (c'—e') is represented, according to this system, by the figure 333, then the major tempered Tenth (c'—e'') will be represented by the figure 1333 and the major tempered Seventeenth (c'—e''') will be represented by the figure 2333, etc. Likewise, the numbers representing all other intervals will be increased by a thousand units for every subsequent octave.

The second system was evolved by Alexander J. Ellis (1814-1890) and being much used by him in his extensive acoustic research work, gained considerable recognition in England and some in Germany.*

A. J. Ellis adopts as a fundamental measuring unit the interval of a tempered semitone, which is divided into one hundred equal parts called *Cents*. The following diagram is formed by analogy with the preceding ones and shows the figures of our equally tempered scale according to this writer:

EXAMPLE 3:

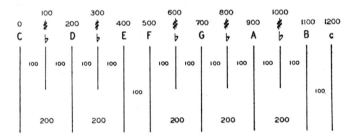

Comparing this diagram with the one represented in Example 1, *b*, it is immediately seen that all its figures are exactly double those of the diagram referred to. This, of course, is quite natural, since in our previous diagram (Example 1, *b*) the intervals are expressed in hundredths of a tempered whole tone (centitones) while in the above diagram they are expressed in hundredths of a tempered semitone (Cents).

From this viewpoint the decimal system herein proposed and applied for measuring musical intervals very closely approximates the one evolved by A. J. Ellis and, strictly speaking, may be regarded as a development of the latter.**

---

* *The musical scales of various nations* by A. J. Ellis, in the Journal of Society of Arts for March, 1885 (London). This system was republished by A. J. Ellis in his additional notes to the English edition of Helmholtz's *Sensations of Tone*, of which he is the translator.

** Ellis's system itself, however, virtually represents no more than an interpretation of a principle applied some years before him by Heinrich Bellermann in his book *Die Grösse der musikalischen Intervalle* (Berlin, 1873), page 89, etc. Bellermann was the first who assumed the tempered semitone as a fundamental measuring unit, but he expressed all its fractions either in eight place decimals, when great accuracy was desired, or in integral numbers, as Ellis did, when hundredths

The decimal system has the following advantages over the system of A. J. Ellis (and consequently better chances for universal acceptance).

1. In contradistinction to a semitone, a whole tone as a basic measuring unit permits the rational formation of fractional and homogeneous terms—decitones, centitones and millitones—directly indicating the various degrees of division (tenths, hundredths and thousandths) in regard to their common unit as well as the name of the latter (tone).

Objection to the term "cent" lies in the fact that it is a fraction of a term (semitone) which to a musician's mind is fractional in itself, representing but a portion of a larger unit (whole tone). Furthermore, the term "cent" can be used to designate the hundredth part of any other unit, in any other field—as, for instance, in American currency.

2. All the figures expressing any larger interval (exceeding a whole tone) in deci-tones, centitones or millitones, give direct indication of the number of whole tones and fractions thereof it contains (thus, the figures expressing, say, a tempered Fifth, viz. 35 dtn. or 350 ctn. or 3500 mtn. at once show that this interval consists of $3\frac{1}{2}$ tones) —hence they will more readily convey an idea of its dimension than in Ellis's system, in which the figures disclose the number of *semitones* and fractions thereof the same interval contains (thus, 700 cents will show that the tempered Fifth consists of 7 semi-tones). This is because we usually think of the larger intervals in terms of whole tones

---

parts of a semitone would suffice. In the latter case he assumed a semitone to contain 100 millimeters and, therefore, an Octave 1200 millimeters, which perfectly corresponds to Ellis's 100 Cents in a semitone and 1200 Cents in an Octave. Thus, he expressed the natural major Third $(\frac{5}{4})$ either as 3.86313714 or as 386 m/m, the latter figure being obviously a hundred times greater than the former. Therefore, mathematically speaking, the figures of Bellermann's "milli-meters," as well as of Ellis's "Cents," represent nothing but logarithms on the base of $^{1200}\sqrt{2}$, while Bellermann's figures with fractional values are logarithms on the base of $^{12}\sqrt{2}$.

In the latter connection it may perhaps be of some interest to musicologists to know that the New York Public Library possesses a very rare and original manuscript, to which—after a thorough investigation made at my request—no references could be found in any of the existing bibliographies, or obtained from other available sources, and which, therefore, may turn out to be a generally unknown and unique work on acoustical subjects. The manuscript is entitled *The Geometrical Scale in Musick; or Gam-Ut reduced to Geometrical proportions,* and, according to the statement of its author (whose name, GAUDY, is merely guessed from indirect indication), was written some time be-fore the year 1705 and revised about the year 1735 (the date of the preface). The particular interest of this work lies in the fact that it overthrows the commonly accepted opinion in regard to the initial introduction, in music, of the logarithmic method to express musical inter-vals, the priority of which, in a general sense, has been heretofore attributed to Euler (born in 1707; published his famous treatise, as

already stated, in 1739). The manuscript in question expresses all the intervals it deals with in common logarithms as well as in logarithms on the base of $^{12}\sqrt{2}$ (both with twelve-place decimals), although the latter technical expres-sion does not appear. But the author of this manuscript gives a very broad explanation of this principle (Chapter 9), according to which an Octave is supposed to equal one Foot, all the intervals being expressed in inches and fractions thereof. One readily understands, of course, that the figures expressing various in-tervals in terms of inches, of which there are twelve to a Foot, must be (in fact, are) abso-lutely identical with those expressed, by Beller-mann, in terms of tempered semitones, of which there are twelve to an Octave. Furthermore, the author of that manuscript gives the rule for the rendition of intervals expressed in common log-arithms into the terms of his "Geometrical Scale," as he calls the measuring standard of 12 inches to an Octave, and is surprised that such a simple method of representing musical intervals, as he says, "either in numbers that might represent them to the mind or in Geomet-rical distances that might represent them to the eye, had been so long sought in vain." The rule, as will be instantly seen, is a plain formula of transformation of logarithmical values of interval-ratios on the base of 10 into those on the base of $^{12}\sqrt{2}$, and reads as follows: "Divide 12 by the logarithm of Octave and multiply the Quotient by the logarithm of every other ratio whose measure you want in inches" (page 54 of the MS.). The manuscript also contains a severe criticism of Mersenne's method of ex-pressing musical intervals by means of the number of commas they contain (p. 48-49).

rather than of semitones, which may be proved by questioning a number of musicians as to the dimension of any of these intervals. One may be sure that in the instance of a perfect Fifth the majority will answer 3½ tones—not 7 semitones.

The final remark that seems necessary to conclude this chapter concerns the two general drawbacks of the simplified method of representation of musical intervals, the application of which requires a certain caution, at least in some instances.

One of these drawbacks resides in the fact that acoustic expressions in terms of the decimal system do not convey any idea of the *character* of the intervals dealt with, so far as their acoustic simplicity or complexity is concerned. Thus, one could never judge from the mere numbers expressing the just major Third and the Pythagorean major Third, viz. 193 ctn. and 204 ctn. respectively, that the former is acoustically much simpler than the latter. But this very difference in character of the two intervals becomes instantly evident when they are expressed in terms of vibration-fractions, namely, $\frac{5}{4}$ and $\frac{81}{64}$. Therefore, whenever the *character* of intervals (in the above sense) represents one of the most important issues, it is more advantageous to express all acoustic values in vibration-fractions than in terms of the decimal system.

The other drawback resides in the *approximate* accuracy of the figures of the simplified method, as compared with the scientifically accurate figures of the method dealing with vibration-numbers and their ratios. The minute errors that follow are negligible in all ordinary cases but they are apt to increase considerably when the simplified method is applied to more complicated and lengthy calculations. In the latter case, therefore, to avoid perceptible errors, it is advisable first to make all calculations in terms of vibration-fractions, rendering only the final results in the easily understood terms of the decimal system.

Although a knowledge of these operations is not required of the reader, yet a very simple rule for the rendition of musical intervals, expressed in vibration-fractions, into decitones or centitones or millitones, may be of some use or, at least, of some interest to those who possess an elementary knowledge of logarithms. This rule is as follows: The (common) logarithm of a given vibration-fraction (obtained through the subtraction of the logarithm of the lower vibration-number from that of the upper vibration-number) is multiplied by a constant factor which may be expressed with sufficient accuracy by the number 19931. The product will immediately show the dimension of the interval, whose logarithmic value has been multiplied, in terms of *millitones*, which may then easily be also expressed into *centitones* or *decitones*, as desired, by shifting the decimal point one or two digits to the left. Thus, if one wishes to express the interval of a natural Fifth ($\frac{3}{2}$) in the terms of the decimal system, one has merely to subtract the logarithm of 2 from the logarithm of 3, viz. 0.47712 — 0.30103 = 0.17609, and to multiply the difference by 19931. The product, after the decimals are dropped, will be 3509 mtn. or 350.9 ctn. (351 ctn. in round numbers) or 35.1 dtn. (cannot be expressed in round numbers with sufficient precision). Considering the fact that the number 19931 is obtained by dividing 6000 (interval of an Octave in millitones) by 0.30103 (logarithm of the vibration-fraction of an Octave, i.e. $\frac{2}{1}$), one will readily understand that values expressed in terms of decitones, centitones and millitones represent simply the logarithms of vibration-fractions on the bases of $\sqrt[60]{2}$, $\sqrt[600]{2}$ and $\sqrt[6000]{2}$ respectively.

FIRST PART

INFRA-TONALITY

CHAPTER VI

HISTORIC SURVEY OF CHINESE SCALES

The musical system of the Chinese, as it was established by them in antiquity, * comprised two contradistinctive scales functionally supplementing each other, namely:

    1. The familiar pentatonic scale or, as we termed it above, infra-diatonic scale, only five regular tones of which, in the modal arrangement F-G-A-C-D, have been used as a basis for their musical creation.

    2. The twelve-tone scale (resembling our Occidental chromatic scale) which *exclusively* served for the transposition of the former—and, consequently, of all Chinese music in general—into different keys.

It is unknown to-day to which note exactly corresponded the fundamental tone of the ancient Chinese musical system, but some writers arbitrarily assume it to be F, which will also be adopted in this book, in the same capacity, as possessing certain practical advantages for our further constructions.

In spite of the fact that both scales were evolved by Chinese scholars in a purely theoretical way, to which were often added different symbolic speculations, it can scarcely be doubted that the infra-diatonic scale, on which the entire Chinese song-lore is based, existed in practice long before its official canonisation by Chinese musical science. The latter *a posteriori* merely placed a theoretical foundation under this scale and then by means of singular numerical calculations linked it to characteristic religious, philosophic, cosmological and other symbols. In order to find a strict theoretical justification for the tonal basis of their music, already in existence, it was sufficient for the Chinese to familiarize themselves empirically with the most rudimentary acoustic laws to discover very soon that the musical sounds produced by five pipes,** each of which is

---

* Over 2800 years B. C., according to some Chinese sources. This generally accepted date, however, is given with a certain reservation, as modern sinology seems inclined to consider as unquestionably authentic only those written Chinese documents which do not relate to any period prior to the eighth century B. C., when dealing with the history of China.

**Unlike the ancient Greeks who experimented in acoustics with the aid of a monochord, the Chinese used bamboo pipes for the same purpose. These pipes—their origin being, by the way, associated with various native legends—were cut from bamboo reeds in such a way as to have a knot as the natural closing of one of the ends. The sound was produced by simply blowing into the pipe, similarly to whistling into a key. It is quite probable that the accessibility of this plant, as well as the simplicity of producing sounds of different pitch depending merely on the length of the pipes, turned the Chinese to the initial acoustic experiments which ultimately led to the construction of their entire musical system. At later historical periods, these pipes were made of copper, sometimes even of different sorts of stones, in order to withstand atmospheric changes.

successively shortened by one-third, form a series of natural Fifths (Example 4ᵃ), which being subsequently brought within the compass of an octave, constitute the infra-diatonic scale used by them. (Ex. 4ᵇ.) The grouping together of all five sounds within an octave presupposed, of course, doubling the length of two pipes when transposing their respective tones (g″ and d″) an octave lower, and quadrupling the length of one pipe when transposing its tone (a‴) two octaves lower: *

EXAMPLE 4:

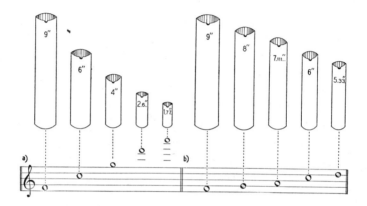

As soon as the principle of construction of the infra-diatonic scale was found, it only remained to extend its application to the aims dictated by musical practice.

It is quite evident that further ascending by natural Fifths, together with their duplication in the adjoining octaves, would open a wide field for transposition of the fundamental infra-diatonic scale (F-G-A-C-D) into different keys. Thus, for instance, the addition to the above series (Ex. 4ᵃ) of one more Fifth (E)

---

*There are some data stating that SZE-MA-CH'IEN (or CHE-TSI), a celebrated Chinese historian of the second century B. C., found a very simple method (according to other sources, he merely refers to its real discoverer by the name of Ling-Lun, one of the ministers of the Emperor HUANG-TI, who reigned about 2697 B. C.) by which immediate construction of these five pipes could be effected, i.e. without the additional procedure of doubling or quadrupling their length in order to comprise all their tones within the compass of an Octave. This method calls for the alternating subtraction and addition of one-third the length of the pipes involved in this operation, which will produce the following series, if it is assumed that the fundamental tone is expressed by the figure 81, for the purpose of avoiding fractional numbers (as probably intended by the Chinese): F = 81; subtracting one-third (27) we shall obtain C = 54; adding thereto one-third (18) we get G = 72; next subtracting one-third (24) gives us D = 48; and the final addition of one-third (16) makes A = 64. The same rule could be applied, of course, to the numbers of our example which show the actual length of pipes when the open C pipe of the Great Octave is assumed to be eight feet, thus bringing the stopped F pipe of the Middle Octave to nine inches. According to the method described, the five pipes represented in the above example (4b) would be constructed in the following sequence: F = 9″; C = 6″; G = 8″; D = 5.3333″; A = 7.111″.

would make it possible to form an identical infra-diatonic scale a Fifth higher, i.e. composed of the notes C-D-E-G-A; the next Fifth (B) would transpose the same scale, if necessary, to the key G-A-B-D-E, etc.

The nature of sound permits a continuation of the chain of natural Fifths *ad infinitum*. The Chinese, however, confined themselves, for practical considerations, to twelve tones of this series as a medium for transposition. They figured at the time that, in point of fact, the thirteenth tone E♯ so closely approximates the fundamental note F (their difference is equal to 12 ctn.) that if necessity arose to transpose the infra-diatonic scale to a key in which the tone E♯ occurred, the latter could be replaced, allowance being made for a certain auditory strain, by the note F. For the same reasons the next tone of the series of Fifths, i.e. B♯, could be replaced in further transpositions by the note C, and the tone F♯♯ by the note G, etc.

Accordingly, the Chinese constructed their standard set of twelve bamboo tubes (the Chinese for such a "tube" is "lü"), and while they followed the above principle of natural Fifths they immediately doubled the length of those tubes which exceeded the octave of the fundamental note (F), transposing them thereby an octave lower and obtaining, as a result, the following series of tones: *

EXAMPLE 5:

These notes, when arranged in "stepwise" order, constituted the Chinese twelve-tone scale, which upon being repeated in the upper and lower octaves formed three consecutive series of grave, middle and acute "lüs." [See Ex. 6.]

The division of all the degrees of this scale in *odd* and *even* or positive and negative degrees, as shown in Example 6, had a purely symbolic meaning for the Chinese, corresponding to their conception of primordial Chaos, supposedly divided, in like manner, into two mystic principles—Male and Female—or perfect and imperfect.

---

* The formation of scales upon the principle of consecutively arranged natural Fifths was also practiced, as is known, in ancient Greece, and since it was first introduced there by Pythagoras (circa 6th century B. C.) the resulting intonation is called "Pythagorean" in musical acoustics, in spite of the fact that priority probably belongs to Chinese theorists.

EXAMPLE 6:

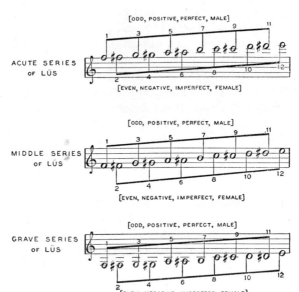

Similar symbolic speculations permeate the entire Chinese musical system to such an extent that a detailed description of them would at least double the length of the present survey. However, since this particular subject is absolutely foreign to the purpose of this book, we shall touch upon the speculations in question chiefly as it may sometimes be indispensable to consider them in some of the Chinese theoretical constructions whose musical incoherence is more than evident, as a result of the direct intervention of this symbolism.

Returning to the structure of the Chinese twelve-tone scale, it is necessary to add that it was only approximately and inadequately represented above by the notes of the Occidental chromatic scale. This is because, apart from the fact that each of the twelve tones (in contradistinction to the Occidental scale) has an entirely separate appellation * and, consequently, independent significance, the two scales also differ in intonation. This is illustrated by the following diagram in which the Chinese scale is represented by the lower set of lines and the Occidental scale by the upper set of lines. The numbers between the lines indicate

---

* These acoustically constant appellations in the twelve-tone Chinese scale simply represent the first syllable of the names of the tubes ("lüs") which produce them, and are solely applied in practice to indicate the key-note of a musical composition, which is quite indispensable in Chinese notation. These abbrevi- ated names seem to be of a much later origin, having been substituted for the complete names of the "lüs" used in ancient times for the twelve-tone scale as well as for the indication of the key. (The complete names of the "lüs" are given in Ex. 5 of the text).

the dimensions of intervals formed by the adjacent degrees in every scale, and the numbers above and below the lines show the intervals formed by every note and the Tonic common to both scales:*

EXAMPLE 7:

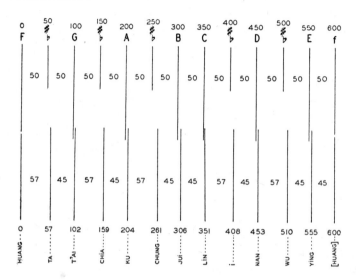

The difference in intonation of these two scales results from the artificial equalization (Temperament) in Occidental musical practice, of all the twelve component intervals, the principle of which will be described at length in a subsequent chapter. For the present we shall confine ourselves to indicating that it was only through this principle of Temperament that the possibility of unimpeded transposition of the Occidental diatonic scale into twelve different keys was attained.

This full freedom of transposition had no place, however, in ancient Chinese musical practice, because the infra-diatonic scale, transposed by means of twelve non-tempered "lüs," preserved its original acoustic structure only in those keys in which not a single note was encountered, starting with E♯ along the series of natural Fifths. The reason is that these particular notes (i.e. E♯, B♯, F♯♯ etc.) were absent in the twelve Chinese "lüs" and, as already stated, had to be replaced by more or less approximative notes (i.e. F, C, G etc.) intoned almost a quarter of a semitone lower.

* In this as well as in all the following diagrams and tables every number represents the dimension of intervals in *centitones*, unless otherwise indicated.

The following diagram will show in what keys the infra-diatonic scale preserves its original structure and to what degree it deviates acoustically in all the rest of the keys. The notes produced by those Chinese "lüs" which replace the tones E♯, B♯, etc. absent in the fundamental set of twelve tubes, are represented in black:

EXAMPLE 8: *

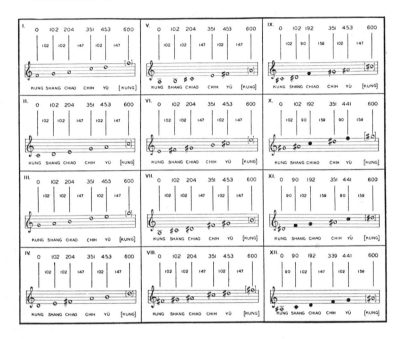

This illustration proves that the original acoustic structure of the infra-diatonic scale remains constant only in the initial eight keys (F, C, G, D, A, E, B, F♯) formed by the aid of the twelve "lüs" and is altered in each of the remaining four keys (C♯, G♯, D♯, A♯).

These slight and at first tolerable acoustic deviations were sufficiently obvious, however, to the Oriental musical ear, so that the problem of avoiding them was studied by the Chinese almost from the inception of their musical system. There are vague indications that as early as the reign of Emperor SHUN (2255 B.C.) there existed (though probably only in theory) an Equal Temperament

* The Chinese designations *Kung, Shang, Chiao, Chih* and *Yü* represent the names of the regular degrees of the infra-diatonic scale (similarly to the Occidental *Tonic, Supertonic,* *Mediant,* etc.) and, consequently, indicate their position irrespective of the absolute pitch of the scale itself. These five names, as usual, had a certain symbolic meaning with the Chinese

system which is said to have been lost, subsequently, during the barbaric period of destruction of books (circa 213 B.C.)*

The same problem was not taken up again until the latter period of the HAN dynasty (206 B. C.–220 A. D.) when two Chinese scholars proposed avoiding these acoustic deviations by an entirely different method which consisted in a further prolongation of the adopted series of natural Fifths and, consequently, in an increase of the number of keys preserving the original acoustic structure of the infra-diatonic scale.

The first of these scholars, TSIAU-YEN-SHIAU (circa 200 B.C.), applied the principle of natural Fifths to the construction of a system containing 64 tones within an octave with the object, however, of using in practice only 60 different keys of the infra-diatonic scale.** In this intentional inclusion within his system of a greater number of tones, as compared with the number of keys ordained for musical practice, this scholar probably relied upon the rule that none of the last four notes of any series of natural Fifths can serve as a Tonic for the infra-diatonic scale without detriment to the latter's acoustic structure. The system of 60 different keys, none of them acoustically affected, thanks to the four additional tones, was developed so as to be used in its entirety during each period of five years,*** since according to the ritual code of the Chinese, their sacred music must be performed in a different key every month and, consequently, takes up twelve keys in the course of a year.

The second of these scholars, KING-FANG, applying the same principle as his predecessor and teacher, constructed a system of 53 tones within the compass of an octave. He computed that as the difference between the 54th tone of the series of natural Fifths and the fundamental note F (within the same octave) is less than 2 ctn. (about 18 mtn.), it represents an interval that is scarcely perceptible to the ear,**** and permits, therefore, the transposition of the in-

---

(they corresponded to the notions of *Emperor, Minister, Nation, State* and *material objects,* respectively) and served as actual musical notation until about the fourteenth century of our era.

Exposé de la musique des Chinois par J. A. van Aalst (*L'écho musical,* 12 Octobre 1890, Bruxelles). This information is not given in his well-known and earlier book (in English) on Chinese Music. (See Footnote on page 64).

**Compare with *The Chinese Theory of Music* by E. Faber (*China Review,* 1873, page 388)—the only study in which one may find a reference to the 60-tone system "extended" to 64 tones, as illustrated by the original Chinese diagram, which apparently was examined by this writer.

***The figure 5 is one of the most significant in Chinese symbolism. Thus, it applies to:

Five planets—Mercury, Mars, Venus, Jupiter, Saturn.

Five elements—Water, Fire, Metal, Wood, Earth.

Five directions—North, South, East, West, Center.

Five colors—Red, Yellow, Blue, Black, White.

Five organs of the body—Heart, Lungs, Stomach, Spleen, Liver.

Five gustatory qualities—Sweet, Bitter, Salted, Sour, Piquant.

Five virtues—Benevolence, Righteousness, Propriety, Wisdom, Sincerity.

With this figure, the pentatonic scale, of course, is also associated.

****This approximation of 53 natural Fifths to 31 Octaves served, as is known, for the creation of a 53-tone tempered system by Nicholas Mercator (a Danish mathematician of the seventeenth century), which was probably never pub-

fra-diatonic scale in all 53 keys without noticeable detriment to its acoustic structure in the last four keys.

To this scholar are also attributed some still more cumbersome, though scientifically less interesting systems which, like those just described, could not be used in practice on account of their utter complexity. This is equally true of those "straight" Chinese systems, which required a construction of quite independent series of pentatonic and later also heptatonic scales from each of the twelve standard "lüs," this leading up to the necessity of dealing with exaggeratedly large sets of 60 (i.e. 5×12) and 84 (i.e. 7×12) tones, respectively.

The impracticability of all these systems was probably the cause of increasing attempts, side by side with them, to return to the ancient and more rational idea of Equal Temperament. This idea was advanced at a considerably later period and in more concrete form by HO-TCHENG-TIEN, the noted astronomer (370-447 A. D.) who, in the language of the Chinese scholars "did violence to figures" when by slightly lengthening each of the eleven "lüs" (i.e. all except the one producing the Tonic) he altered their intonation in such a way as to bring the thirteenth "lü" (E♯) to the pitch of the fundamental tone (F) and thus form a closed circle of twelve equal intervals. His figures showing the length of the tempered "lüs" are not quite accurate, however, and from all evidence are only computed tentatively.

At a still later period, and inaccurate too, came the calculations of LIEOU-TCHO (543-610 A. D.), a well-known historian, and of WANG-FO (died 959), probably a physician. These not quite successful experiments continued more or less sporadically until the sixteenth century when, at last, the learned prince TSAI-YU (of the MING dynasty) who, as he said himself, "meditated for days and nights before the light of Truth was revealed to him," found the exact formula for the equally tempered tuning of the twelve "lüs," presenting the final calculations for their respective lengths in his famous treatise on Music, published in the year 1596.

Thus, the problem which through the ages had puzzled the minds of Chinese scholars was ultimately solved, the theory of transposition taking the form of a most comprehensible and easily applied system. Through the strange irony of things, however, not even this convenient system was destined to be used in practice, at least not to its fullest extent, since after the downfall of the MINGS (1664) the official musical authorities of the new dynasty rejected the principle

---

lished but was briefly described from the original manuscript by William Holder in his *Treatise of the Natural Grounds, and Principles of Harmony* (London, 1694, pp. 104-106). This system did not receive any practical application, however, although a special musical instrument in accordance with it (harmonium) was built by R. H. M. Bosanquet in the 80's of the past century. This instrument is described in his book entitled *An Elementary Treatise on Musical Intervals and Temperament.* (London, 1875) and is now owned by the South Kensington Museum.

of Equal Temperament and in 1712 definitely reverted to the original intonation of twelve natural Fifths which formally exists to this day.*

It is difficult to believe that these new authorities should have failed to realize the practical expediency of TSAI-YU's Temperament system and to grasp the musical significance of this marvelous innovation, the achievement of which had required the efforts of generations of scholars.

But such a state of affairs is very characteristic of the Chinese who, besides musical considerations, always have equally if not more important consider- ations of a religious and, especially, symbolic order which take precedence over purely musical matters. From the standpoint of Chinese symbolism, Equal Temperament, consisting of an artificial untuning of the natural Fifths, rep- resents, as stated above, actual "violence done to numbers," for it alters the original acoustic relation between the tones expressed, in each instance, by the formula 3:2, i.e. the very one possessing the most profound significance for the Chinese, and which is consecrated in their music by immemorial tradition. In their ancient doctrines the figure 3 symbolizes Heaven while the figure 2 symbolizes the Earth, and since between Heaven and Earth there exists, they claim, perfect harmony, this must also be true of two sounds whose relation is 3 to 2. According to their speculations, therefore, when the length of the funda- mental "lü" was first established in ancient times, two-thirds of it (which is equivalent to the ratio $\frac{3}{2}$ in terms of vibrations expressing the interval of a natural Fifth) constituted the length of the second "lü," then two-thirds of the latter constituted the length of the third "lü," etc., this "sublime" principle being adopted for the construction of the entire musical system and thus laid down as the basis of their Music.

Among the old sacred musical instruments with fixed and unchangeable intonation, which are preserved in China to the present day, there is said to be none tuned according to the calculations of prince TSAI-YU. It is impossible, therefore, to decide to what extent the principle of Equal Temperament was used in the musical practice of his time. One may surmise that on the strength of tra- dition that illustrious scholar left untouched all instruments of this type, as being exclusively used in formal religious ceremonies, and confined himself to the practical application of his calculations merely for the correction of intervals while playing the *Ch'in,*** this correction being a specific art which, according to his own statement, was already known to educated Chinese musicians in the re- motest antiquity. Such a supposition is still more plausible if one considers

---

* None the less there seem to be indications that isolated attempts to construct more com- plicated tonal systems have not entirely ceased in China even at the present time.

**Ch'in,* a sort of seven-stringed lute, is con- sidered the most aristocratic and poetic musical instrument by the Chinese. According to tradi- tion it is allowed to play it only in a special chamber or in a beautiful garden, with incense burned and appropriate dress worn.

that even to-day the Chinese avail themselves of the correction of intervals in transposition as a favorite effect when playing the *Ch'in*.

Thus, the musical practice of the Chinese departs from the rigid and tardy official theory, and one may observe more than once in their musical history how the former sometimes eludes the guardianship of the latter, obeying, in such cases, solely the inner dictates of the artistic conscience.

*   *   *

Up to this point we have devoted our attention almost exclusively to a survey of those manifold phases presented in the history of Chinese music by the problem of a practical basis for transposing the infra-diatonic scale into different keys. In the meantime this scale itself did not always remain unaltered in its original version but underwent an independent evolution which, in the long run, somewhat changed its appearance.

In its initial form, as represented above (Ex. 4^b), the infra-diatonic scale officially existed from the day of the foundation of the Chinese musical system until the CHOU dynasty (1122 B. C.). Almost at the beginning of the latter's reign (circa 1116 B. C.) certain considerable musical reforms were made throughout the Celestial Empire. As part of these reforms new ritual music was composed which, however, it has been observed, could not be played upon the five regular degrees of the infra-diatonic scale, the reason being that this music sometimes filled the two large gaps of the old scale (i.e. the intervals A-C and D-F) by two tones, formerly absent.

It was therefore resolved, in conformity with the new music, also to change the scale officially by introducing the two missing degrees among those already in existence. Their two corresponding tones, B and E, were easily found in the series of natural Fifths as they immediately followed those from which the five regular degrees of the infra-diatonic scale were generated. Thus, as a result of this transformation the Chinese scale acquired the following appearance (the two new degrees are designated by small notes):

EXAMPLE 9:

An obstinate struggle arose over this innovation between the partisans of the old musical system on the one hand and the musical reformers of the new dynasty on the other. The former insisted that the two new tones ought to be ruled out for being just as useless, in their judgment, as "two extra fingers on a hand." They ironically termed "new fabrication" this reform which overthrew the entire order of religious ceremonies symbolically linked to the original number of degrees (5) of the infra-diatonic scale, and which, as a consequence, broke up all the established relations between Philosophy, Music and Religion.

The innovators, on the contrary, proved in the first place that the two new tones were not arbitrarily "fabricated" since they were found long before in the folk songs of some of the Northern provinces (whence their name "Northern tones") * and therefore could be utilized for the renewal of ritual music that had become dull. As for the symbolic relations which must justify every reform, these are found in the well-known formula which combines three forces of nature (Heaven, Earth and Man) with the four seasons of the year, thus constituting the figure 7, i.e. the one that corresponds to the general number of degrees of the new scale.

Besides this, it has been further explained that this reform does not basically change the structure of the old scale, since the two new tones are introduced not on a par with the five regular degrees but solely *as auxiliary degrees adorning the melodic line proper,* and, as such, they do not even have independent names but borrow them from adjacent regular degrees, prefixing to the latter, for distinction, the term *pien.*

This Chinese term literally means "altered" or "deviated," but in musical practice it exclusively indicated the lowering of the regular degrees similarly to our Occidental "flat." Therefore, the derivative *pien-Kung,* for instance, signified "lowered or flatted first regular degree," i.e., taking the original Chinese scale, it corresponded to our note F♭ or approximately to the tone E. In like manner, the term *pien-Chih* signified "flatted fourth regular degree" of the same scale, i.e. it corresponded to our C♭ or B.

There did not exist in the Chinese musical system any special term indicating the raising of regular degrees, similar to our "sharp," both auxiliary degrees of the infra-diatonic scale being always designated as *flats;* and it is a significant fact that from the purely theoretical point of view (independently evolved by the author further on), this designation is quite correct when the scale in question is built up by *ascending* natural Fifths, as was actually done by the Chinese.

---

* *Instructions sublimes* de CHENG-TZU-QUO-GEN-HOANG-TI, translated from the Chinese in *Mémoires concernant les Chinois,* Tome IX, page 223. A Chinese song-book is said to have been published in 1792 in which all its tunes, 456 in number, are divided into Northern and Southern, the former using the entire seven degrees of the infra-diatonic scale, and the latter only its five regular degrees. According to more recent information, however, the two supplementary degrees of the scale "5 + 2" are chiefly used, at least nowadays, in Southern China (see, for instance, *Some aspects of Chinese Music* by G. P. Green, London; page 43). Still another opinion regarding this matter is found in the book entitled *The Middle Kingdom* (New York, 1883; page 95) by S. Wells Williams, who holds that only the theatres and the more cultured circles of Southern China avail themselves of the complete infra-diatonic scale, while the rural population resort to its five regular degrees exclusively.

Judging from certain indications, the prefix *pien* is of later origin, having been substituted for two ancient terms, distinctive for each flatted degree, and translated as "auxiliary" for the first flat, (i.e. F♭) and as "different" for the second (i.e. C♭).

MAURICE COURANT calls the two newly introduced degrees "supplementary" as distinguished from the five "principal" degrees.*

PÈRE AMIOT qualifies them as auxiliary degrees "deviating" from the regular ones.**

LOUIS LALOY regards them as slightly noticeable embellishments in a musical composition, as "irregularities" which appear suddenly and as suddenly vanish.***

The subordinate character of the two newly introduced degrees of the infra-diatonic scale was later on confirmed in practice by the fact that it was allowed to omit them at will in the course of a musical performance, as such an omission was not detrimental to the general melodic line. Chinese musicians, therefore, usually jotted down beforehand, at the beginning of their music, those notes to which the two auxiliary degrees corresponded in a given composition, according to its key, and then played them *ad libitum*.

The practical use of these auxiliary degrees throughout the later periods of Chinese Music fluctuated continuously, depending on the personal views of the musical authorities of the reigning dynasties, but their subordinate position in relation to the five regular degrees of the infra-diatonic scale did not change. That is why, notwithstanding the fact that from the time of the CHOU dynasty the general number of degrees of the Chinese scale was equal to *seven,* it was never called a seven-tone scale but only a *five-tone scale with two supplementary or auxiliary degrees,* this exactly corresponding to our formula "5 + 2" adopted above.

The expression "seven principles" referring to seven scale-tones, often encountered in Chinese musical treatises, most probably seeks to stress the *method* of scale formation according to the series of natural Fifths, since the acoustic relation between every pair of contiguous tones in this series was called "a principle," which symbolized the relation, already pointed out, between Heaven and Earth. Later Chinese commentators often explained that in a series of seven tones constructed by this method the two groups of regular and auxiliary degrees must be definitely distinguished.

As for the actual use of the infra-diatonic scale in Chinese music, it practi-

---

* *Essai Historique sur la musique classique des Chinois* par Maurice Courant (dans *l'Encyclopédie de la Musique,* par Albert Lavignac, Paris, 1914, pages 92 and 93).

**Mémoires concernant l'histoire, les sciences, les arts, les moeurs, les usages, etc. des Chinois,* par les missionnaires de Pékin,* Tome VI (De la musique) par M. Amiot (page 249, under the heading "pien"), Paris, 1780. The most extensive, although somewhat antiquated, work on Chinese Music in a European language.

***La musique chinoise* par Louis Laloy (Paris), page 58.

cally never ceased, with the exception of a few short periods under external influences. The latter merely brought a certain temporary confusion in the established musical norms of the Chinese, when foreign scales were amalgamated with their own to form peculiar combinations which, however, never gained general recognition and in the course of time were invariably dropped.

Hindu music, introduced into China by Buddhist monks in the seventh century of our era, represents one of the earliest influences of this sort recorded in Chinese documents. To foreign influences which in every conceivable way penetrated into China (especially in conjunction with military invasions and dynastic downfalls) should be ascribed, perhaps, that intricacy and well-nigh inexplicable character of some Chinese scales which have come down to us with certain musical instruments on which they were fixed.

A curious combination of the Chinese and the Mongolian scales was established in the fourteenth century by KUBLAI-KHAN (the founder of the YÜAN dynasty), who in order to reconcile the musical tastes and customs of the Mongols and the conquered Chinese united these two scales in the following manner:

EXAMPLE 10:

This amalgamated scale with the new Mongolian notation * was in use until the MING dynasty (1368-1644) which in course of time restored the infra-diatonic scale, merely changing the arrangement of its degrees which, in Occidental music, is equivalent to a change of the mode.** The new notation, however, introduced by *Kublai-Khan,* remained untouched:

---

* The independent names of the two auxiliary degrees in this newly adopted notation (which is used, by the way, up to the present day) do not speak in favor of their *musical* independence, for entirely distinct names are sometimes given in this notation even to one and the same tone, for the sole and obviously groundless reason that it is found in different octaves.

** It would be impossible for the reader to understand, at this point, the real cause behind this change before he is acquainted with the principles of harmony connected with the infra-diatonic scale. The explanation of this change will therefore be given after the latter subject is discussed (see the last Footnote to Chapter VIII on Infra-diatonic Harmony).

EXAMPLE 11:

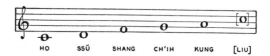

This arrangement of degrees of the infra-diatonic scale assumed a central place in the new musical system of the Chinese, but side by side with it, certain other arrangements, perhaps in a sense of "relative modes," have also been used by them in musical practice. One of these modal arrangements (D-F-G-A-C) which seemed to be quite a favorite, serves as a basis for the majority of hymns to Confucius—that show, by the way, great musicianship—as well as for many monastic chants.

At a later period of the MING dynasty (or, according to some, during the CH'ING dynasty that followed) the two auxiliary degrees of the infra-diatonic scale were again re-introduced and conformably to the new order of the regular degrees were arranged as follows:

EXAMPLE 12:

In this form the Chinese scale exists up to the present time. Its two auxiliary degrees are used nowadays with the utmost discretion and are therefore only encountered sporadically in ritual music. They are far more frequently found in folk songs but even so not everywhere—only in some provinces of China and of Indo-China in which the same scale is constantly used.*

*   *   *

In summing up the above discussion, it will be sufficient to call the attention of the reader to two principal theses which it has been the author's endeavor to prove as having an important place in the formation of the historical background for the infra-diatonic system.

The *first* of these theses consists in the assertion that the well-known complexity and extraordinary cumbersomeness of the musical theory of the Chinese

---

* The fact that these two auxiliary degrees are used in the folk songs of the Annamites (Indo-China) is mentioned by Gaston Knosp (*Mercure Musical*, IIIe année, No. 9, pages 898-956).

are in great part the natural result of their numerous and repeated attempts to build up a musical system without the aid of Equal Temperament, despite their being long familiar with it; the *second* thesis is that the entire actual musical creation of the Chinese has never gone beyond the boundaries of the infra-diatonic scale which at different historical periods was merely either supplemented by the two auxiliary degrees (E and B) or freed of them for various reasons. Special note should be taken of this second thesis as it leads up to an essential deduction, i.e. that the two auxiliary degrees of the infra-diatonic scale have *never* been used by the Chinese on a par with its five regular degrees and that, consequently, there has *never* existed in their music (even theoretically) a heptatonic scale in the sense of an independent tonal basis containing seven "regular" scale-degrees.

CHAPTER VII

THE INFRA-DIATONIC SYSTEM

The preceding survey shows with fairly convincing conclusiveness that the infra-diatonic scale which passed the acid test of the ages in the history of Chinese music, and which has remained, in its innate substance, unchanged to our day, has its roots deep down in the subconscious human mind at a certain stage of musical development, and probably represents one of the organic forms of musical perception and musical thought in general. In no way "arbitrary," therefore, is the structure of this scale with its characteristic division in two functionally demarcated groups of regular and auxiliary degrees, since no speculative computations, no outside influences and no artificial formations could undermine its foundation or pervert its nature over such a long period of time.

The organicalness of its structure is furthermore proved by the fact, among others, that Far Eastern music is not the only one which, based on the infra-diatonic scale ("5 + 2"), rigidly distinguishes the functions of its two component groups of degrees. A perfectly identical distinction is found in innumerable ancient songs of the Celtic races, in which it sprang quite independently and, in any case, outside of any external connection with the music of the Far East.

To this demarcation of five regular and two auxiliary degrees of the infra-diatonic scale in Celtic music, attention has been called many a time by different writers, particularly by Helmholtz, who points this out as follows:

> ". . . in the popular melodies (of the Gaels and Erse) the missing tones [from the standpoint of the diatonic scale—J. Y.] are sometimes just touched as appoggiature or passing notes. . . . . It is usually possible to omit the notes which do not belong to the scale of five tones without impairing the melody." *

Another account is found in a book on Irish folk songs by R. Mason, who says:

> ". . . In many (Irish) songs the half tones, even when employed, are of such secondary importance that they may be omitted without prejudice to the character of the tune. They are often mere connecting links—'passing notes,' theorists would call them—or used for ornament." **

---

* *Sensations of Tone,* page 258 (Fourth English edition, 1912).

** *The Song Lore of Ireland* by Redfern Mason, New York, 1910. Something similar is stated in the book by Carl Engel already quoted, *The Music of the most ancient nations,* (page 172) with reference to an Irish tune, analyzed by him, in which the twice recurrent major seventh (i.e. one of the auxiliary degrees of the infra-diatonic scale) does not constitute, in his opinion, an essential note of the melody.

A. H. Fox Strangways expresses virtually the same idea in the following statement:

> "A song may be in a pentatonic scale although more than five distinct notes are touched in it, if it has only five *substantive* notes and the other one or two are used as passing notes."*

It must be added, however, that the infra-diatonic scale being the *only* one on which the most ancient songs of Celtic tribes were based, became the *principal* one used by their descendants, who settled chiefly on what is now geographically known as the British Isles. This is proved by their songs of a much later period (scarcely before the end of the twelfth century), many of which are partly, sometimes wholly, based on the diatonic scale.

Unfortunately, there is no direct historic information referring to the birth of these new songs, which show a certain evolutionary move in the musical consciousness of the Celts, and still less are there any scientific data explaining in general the psychological motives as well as the various external causes which lead one race or another to the adoption of a new and more complicated musical scale. We are therefore compelled to confine ourselves to a plain statement of this new orientation of the Celts (in spite of the fact that their old pentatonic songs have been preserved to the present time), which apparently took place long before the musical resources of the infra-diatonic scale had been sufficiently utilized by them.

In this connection entirely different tendencies are observed among the Far Eastern peoples, who have not only remained faithful until now to the infra-diatonic scale, but who display a quite unambiguous desire to delve into its musical depths by means of the most expedient method of Equal Temperament, which consists in dividing the octave into seven equal parts conformably to the general number of degrees of their scale ("5 + 2"). This sort of Temperament, so far applied only in the musical practice of the Siamese, in no way alters the essential characteristics of the infra-diatonic scale.** At the same time it offers

---

* *The music of Hindostan* by A. H. Fox Strangways (Oxford, 1914), footnote on page 126 referring to the scale foundation of Scotch and Irish folksongs.

**There is one more and rather unusual method of Temperament known to be applied with regard to the infra-diatonic scale. This "semi-sesquitone" method, as it may be called, found its embodiment in the Scotch bagpipe, which at any rate shows that the idea of applying the principle of Temperament to the infra-diatonic scale has not been entirely foreign even to Europeans. As a number of measurements proved, the notes which correspond to the two auxiliary degrees of the infra-diatonic scale are artificially placed in the chaunter of the bagpipe between their respective regular degrees (these being all left untouched), in such a way as to form two *equal* three-quarter tones in each case instead of a whole tone followed by a half tone, as the natural structure of this scale calls for. This peculiar tuning which, according to D. J. Blaikley (Grove's Dictionary, V. I page 195), has been traditionally maintained by Scotch pipers, may serve as additional proof of the radical distinction which exists between the two groups of regular and auxiliary degrees of the infra-diatonic scale, and in particular, of the purely "embellishing" functions of the latter group as they have evidently long been regarded by peoples of Celtic origin. Further considerations concerning the possible reason for the introduction of the *Semi-sesquitone Temperament* are given in the Footnote to Ex. 109 of this volume.

in exchange for a certain acoustic compromise, the greatest freedom in exploitation of the inherent resources of this scale, similar to the freedom allowed by
that Equal Temperament which has already been applied for over two hundred
years in Occidental musical art and which consists in dividing the octave into
twelve equal parts conformably to the general number of degrees of the diatonic
scale ("7 + 5").

It would not be, therefore, totally unjustified to surmise that similarly to
this Equal Temperament which, in its time, laid a solid technical foundation
under Occidental music, the Equal Temperament of the Siamese may also
some day place on secure ground the music of the Far Eastern peoples which in
fact still remains in a but little developed state, especially from the point of
view of Harmony. The backwardness of these people in music must also be
ascribed to a considerable extent to the fact that they lack a correctly evolved
musical theory which would point the way to the most advantageous utilization
of the infra-diatonic scale and which would thus guard them from the creatively
sterile arbitrariness of bare intuition, no less dangerous in any art than bare
intellectualism.*

The rudimentary evolution of such a theory is closely connected with the
matter of disclosing the nature and properties of the infra-diatonic scale as well
as its inherent harmony, which constitute the subject of these two consecutive
chapters and upon which we will now immediately enter.

To facilitate an understanding of the following discussion, it seems practical
to preface it with a clear keyboard illustration of the infra-diatonic scale, the
latter's five regular degrees being therein represented by white keys and its two
auxiliary degrees by black keys. [See Ex. 13 opposite page.]

This drawing requires explanation. First of all it must be borne in mind that
the infra-diatonic scale is shown here in its Siamese version already mentioned,
i.e. in the equally tempered intonation which, as we know, does not acoustically
coincide with the equally tempered intonation of the diatonic scale (since the
octave is divided into seven equal portions in the former case and into twelve
equal portions in the latter) and which, therefore, will hereafter be termed, for

---

* From the point of view of general musical
culture, the importation of acoustical and theoretical knowledge into the Far-Eastern
countries, pertaining to native musical art, would
be far more essential than the present importation of "ready-made" Western music, foreign
in every sense to the Oriental people. From the
personal observation of the author the propa-
gation of this Music—and incidentally not
always of the best—is rather encouraged by the
Europeanized elements of China and Japan, who
unfortunately do not seem fully to realize the
great value of their own national musical treas-
ures. Should the involuntary inoculation of
the diatonic scale, caused by the importation
of foreign music, ever meet with marked success
among the Orientals (which is doubtful so far),
it would certainly be a bad thing for musical
art in general, as it would deprive the latter
of its most vital source of "infra-diatonic"
music which, thanks to the existence of Siamese
tempered intonation, has every chance of an
original and promising development. The
foundation of special "creatively stimulating"
centers among the people of the Far East, for
the purpose of theoretically and practically
cultivating everything that bears any relation
to the infra-diatonic scale and to music based
on it, would of course, be the best possible solution of the problem.

EXAMPLE 13:

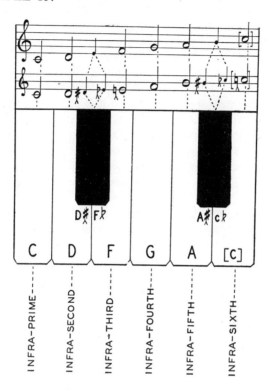

the sake of distinguishing it, *infra-tempered intonation.* This Siamese version preserving the specific characteristics of the infra-diatonic scale, will at the same time greatly simplify its description.

Affixing the new numerical terms (infra-Prime, infra-Second, etc.) to the regular degrees of this scale, I have retained, however, for practical reasons, the conventional literal denotations (C-D-F-G-A) borrowed from the diatonic system, although this inevitably results in something of a departure from their more accurate alphabetical order.

As for the two auxiliary degrees of the infra-diatonic scale, for which the two letters E and B have been used up to this point, having no independent significance in this scale they should no longer be independently denoted. Similarly to the chromatic degrees of the diatonic scale, these two auxiliary degrees therefore borrow their literal denotations from their adjacent regular degrees, to which one of the two signs of alteration is correspondingly added. For the sake of differentiation these two signs will be termed here *infra-sharp* and *infra-flat,* their graphic form being slightly modified as compared with the conventional chromatic accidentals of the scale "7 + 5," as will be easily noticed from their representation as follows:*

$$\text{INFRA-SHARP} = \sharp \qquad\qquad \text{INFRA-FLAT} = \flat$$

The infra-sharp and infra-flat respectively raise and lower the pitch of the regular degrees of the infra-diatonic scale a half step. However, since by *half step* is implied, in this work, merely the minimum interval in every scale, it is apparent that the actual dimension of a half step is not a constant quantity but is expanded or contracted depending on the general number of the minimum intervals in a given scale. Any pair of adjacent half steps forms *one whole step* which for the same reason will be acoustically different in scales of dissimilar complexity.

Here is the very point from which the relativity of these two notions ensues. A *half step* and a *whole step* coincide with the more or less acoustically constant notions of half tone and whole tone only in the diatonic scale,** but have an entirely different acoustic meaning in the infra-diatonic scale, where they are of a greater dimension than a half tone and a whole tone, as well as in the supra-diatonic scale where, for obvious reasons, they must be of a smaller dimension, as will be seen later.

The infra-tempered intonation equalizes all the half steps as well as all the whole steps of the scale "5 + 2" and therefore also actually identifies, in every instance, an infra-sharp with an infra-flat respectively derived by raising and lowering the two neighboring regular degrees, as indicated in front of every black key which serves for both those "infra-chromatic" alterations. It is understood that the auxiliary degrees of the scale "5 + 2" which are represented by the two black keys could never fill this twofold function in any other intonation but the infra-tempered one; and in this connection we again find a similarity between them and the auxiliary degrees of the scale "7 + 5," which only in the tempered intonation may likewise be used either as sharps or flats.

The inequality of some half steps as well as of some whole steps in any *non*-tempered intonation is characteristic of both these scales and is only more per-

---

* It will not be amiss to note here that this graphic modification of the signs of alteration would be unnecessary in actual practical use, since their very presence in the three-line system (which will be explained later) is sufficient to distinguish them from the same signs used in the five-line system. But in a theoretical discussion simultaneously dealing with different systems of notation, the absence of the indicated modification might lead, in some instances, to a confusion of quite incongruent musical conceptions.

** This coincidence, however, should not be taken to mean a *natural* advantage of the diatonic scale, since the terms of whole tone and half tone have no absolute meaning, and are but *conventionally* given to the whole step and half step of this scale (historically, through the diatonic Tetrachord). We might equally assimilate these two pairs of terms in any other scale with the result that they would no longer coincide in the diatonic scale.

ceptible in the scale "5 + 2" than in the scale "7 + 5"; this latter circumstance, however, does not essentially change their structural similarity. A considerable part of this greater "perceptibility" is probably also due to the fact that the conventional *literal* designations of degrees which we used for the infra-diatonic scale involuntarily evoke within us habitual conceptions of diatonic intervals musically quite incongruent to the infra-diatonic intervals. Thus, for instance, the infra-diatonic half step designated as C-D involuntarily evokes within us the idea of a diatonic whole step, which, even if acoustically equal to the former, has, in comparison with it, an entirely different musico-psychological meaning. Likewise there will be no affinity, in this latter sense, between the whole step of the infra-diatonic scale and the sesqui-step (minor Third) of the diatonic scale expressed in both cases by the notes D-F, etc. And should even one of these scales be equally tempered, the discrepancy between the above intervals will crop out, above all, on the plane of their actual dimensions. Thus the interval C-D, equal to 102 ctn. when considered as a *natural* diatonic whole step, and equal to 100 ctn. when tempered, will be expressed, when regarded as an infra-tempered half step, by 85.7 ctn. Again, the intervals D-F and F-A being unequal in any intonation of the scale "7 + 5" (since one of them consists of a sesqui-step and the other contains two whole steps), will coincide in dimension, when considered in the light of the infra-tempered intonation of the scale "5 + 2" in which each of them turns out to be a whole step, equal to 171.4 ctn.

The nature of the *infra-tempered intonation* will be visually elucidated by the following diagram in which it is plotted with the lower set of solid lines exactly corresponding to the present-day Siamese scale ("5 + 2"). The upper set of solid lines shows the *natural intonation* of the infra-diatonic scale ("5 + 2") as now used in Chinese musical practice; the dotted lines indicating the equally tempered intonation of the diatonic scale are given here for the sake of comparison. [See Ex. 14 following page.]

It appears from this diagram that the familiar series of notes of the diatonic scale placed at the top of the preceding keyboard illustration expresses but approximately the natural intonation of the scale "5 + 2" and very inaccurately its infra-tempered intonation. Furthermore it should be observed that the five-line stave is also formally incorrect for the notation of the infra-diatonic scale, since the latter's two auxiliary degrees occupy, within each octave of this stave, two separate places, being represented thereon by independent notes (E and B), which is in conflict with the principle of their "derivation" from the regular degrees.

The correct notation of the scale "5 + 2" would then obviously call for an abbreviated stave, eliminating the number of lines which, in the diatonic five-line system are used for notes E and B. Their approximate equivalents (D♯—F♭

EXAMPLE 14:

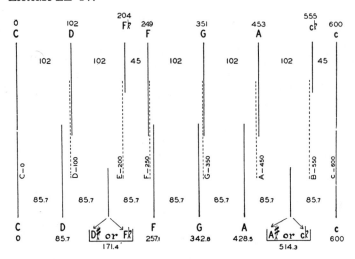

and A♯—C♭), indicating but the infra-chromatic alterations of the regular degrees, should be placed on the same lines (or between the same lines) as the latter.

It is not difficult to figure out that according to this principle our five-line stave should be replaced by a three-line stave in which, similarly to the former, two full octaves of its corresponding scale are evenly distributed in each Clef, and incidentally the two terminal notes (C and c' in the Bass Clef, as well as c' and c''' in the Treble Clef) are retained in their notation, as will be seen from the following representation:

EXAMPLE 15:

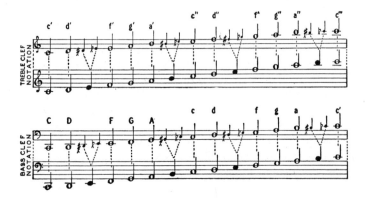

In accordance with the preceding considerations, the correct three-line notation of the infra-diatonic scale is placed just above its keyboard illustration (the regular degrees, as heretofore, being designated by white notes and the auxiliary degrees by small black-faced notes) and parallel to the five-line stave which is added there merely for elucidation. We shall also avail ourselves of the three-line system in all the examples that follow, inasmuch as notation on it has the advantage of theoretical correctness. But it will be accompanied everywhere by the five-line notation, which will help us to read the visually unconventional three-line notation.

Proceeding with our examination of the same keyboard illustration, we find that the series of the regular degrees (white keys) of the infra-diatonic scale forms a chain of definitely arranged whole steps and half steps, reminding one of a more complex and, of course, differently arranged chain of whole steps and half steps of the diatonic scale. And as the principle of this characteristic arrangement of intervals bears the name of *mode* in the diatonic scale, it will be appropriate to give this principle the name of *infra-mode* in reference to the infra-diatonic scale.

I have already had occasion to mention in the last chapter that the Chinese avail themselves of various "modal" arrangements of the infra-diatonic scale in their ritual as well as in their popular music, i.e. that they use various "phases" of this scale or "infra-modes," as one may call them in the appellative sense of the word. It will now be opportune to add that various infra-modes are applied also by other peoples of the Far East, the Siamese, in particular, and that some of these infra-modes are likewise used in folk songs of Celtic origin.*

As a rule, the infra-modes, in common with the diatonic modes, are formed on the various regular degrees of their corresponding infra-diatonic scale, and consequently differ from each other merely in the formula of arrangement of the very same number of whole steps and half steps. Hence, assuming in turn every one of the five regular degrees of the infra-diatonic scale as the Tonic, we shall obtain five infra-modes, as demonstrated in Ex. 16. [The various infra-modes will be named after the two terminal notes that occur when the former are constructed exclusively upon the "white keys," like "C-c," "D-d," etc.]

Besides these five principal infra-modes, a number of their "variations" could of course be easily formed, should we avail ourselves, for this purpose, of the two auxiliary degrees of the scale "5 + 2," substituting them in different combinations for its regular degrees, and each time limiting to *five* the general number of tones in such altered infra-

---

* Les premières gammes celtiques et la musique populaire des Hébrides, par Maurice Duhamel (Annales de Bretagne, Paris, Tome 31, pages 1-18). Also The distinctive characteristics of ancient Irish melody: the scale, by James C. Culwick, (Dublin, 1897). Both these studies contain, besides, some information regarding the evolution of the pentatonic into the heptatonic scale or—to apply our new terminology—of the infra-diatonic into the diatonic scale.

EXAMPLE 16:

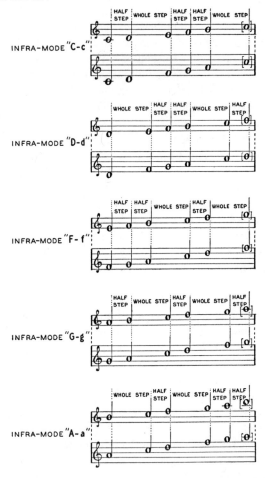

modes. As a matter of fact, several of the "variations," or altered infra-modes of this kind, are being occasionally used in different countries, including some of the Chinese and Indo-Chinese provinces.

From a purely structural point of view (and we are not dealing here with any other) some of these "variations," at least, could be regarded as bearing the same relation to the principal infra-modes, as do the similarly derived "variations" (like the well-known harmonic and melodic minor modes, for instance) to the principal diatonic modes. It is needless to stress the fact that the fundamental laws of tonal organization which govern the construction of infra-modes in one case, and of diatonic modes in another, remain essentially the same for their respective variations. The latter, in other words, represent nothing else but particular instances of the principle of infra-Tonality and of diatonic Tonality, which they manifest virtually to the same extent as the original scale-constructions from which they derive.

No less than fifty altered infra-modes, in the author's estimation, may be formed through various substitutions of the auxiliary degrees for the regular degrees of the infra-diatonic scale. Such an estimation is made in regard to the prevailing *non-tempered* form of this scale, which requires a separately tuned infra-sharp and infra-flat representing the double aspect of each auxiliary degree, and which, furthermore, reverses their respective positions, depending on whether harmonic or melodic intonation of the scale is taken into consideration. We shall not dilate, at present, upon these particular acoustic technicalities which will gradually become clearer in the course of subsequent discussion. (See the text following Ex. 89^a, and the Footnote to Ex. 109.) Suffice it to remember, for the time being, that an infra-chromatic alteration raises or lowers a regular degree of this scale 45 ctn. (about a semitone of our piano) in its harmonic intonation, and 102 ctn. (about a whole tone) in its melodic intonation. Therefore, when representing the altered infra-modes in the familiar notation of our diatonic system, we shall designate the infra-chromatically lowered *C*, for instance, by the note *B* in the case of harmonic intonation, and by the note *B♭* in the case of melodic intonation, the usual reservation being made for the slight discrepancy in the tuning adopted for our instruments. Similarly, the infra-chromatically raised *D* will be designated by the notes *E♭* and *E,* respectively, etc.

The fifty altered infra-modes, which we have referred to, may be conveniently arranged in ten groups, the five infra-modes within each group appearing as mere "inversions" of each other, similarly to the five principal modes demonstrated above. Of these ten groups, two are of exceptional musical interest, inasmuch as they represent the so-called *semitonal* pentatonic scales which are being actually used with and without the *tonal* pentatonic scales (Ex. 16) in various countries, and which have long puzzled certain theorists who failed to realize the proper and very evident structural connection between these two salient types of pre-diatonic scales. These theorists, apparently, never took into account the existence of the two auxiliary degrees organically embodied in the scale "5 + 2," and thus unwittingly put themselves in the position of persons trying, for instance, to find a connection between the principal and altered diatonic modes without considering the five auxiliary degrees organically embodied in the scale "7 + 5." Such an attitude would give them equal reason to be perplexed by the harmonic minor mode, let us say, which would probably have to be regarded by them as an "independent" scale, and not as a variation of the diatonic scale—an obvious absurdity.

As will presently be seen, all the widely known forms of the semitonal pentatonic scale are most naturally explained and covered by the various types of the altered infra-modes which we have built up according to a principle similar to that used for the construction of the altered diatonic modes. The reader will easily recognize, among them, one of the two archaic Greek Pentatonics (the other is a tonal pentatonic and corresponds to the principal infra-mode "C-c"), the entire set of Japanese scales (one of them identical with the semitonal pentatonic of Southern India), and, probably, many others which have been considered up to the present time as "independent" scales, and which have seemingly challenged the very possibility of any unifying classification in regard to primitive scales in general.

The first of the ten groups represents a series of altered infra-modes in which the note *F* of the regular series (C-D-F-G-A) is transformed into *F infra-flat*. According to the rules of melodic intonation this note is designated in the five-line notation as E♭.

EXAMPLE 16ᵃ:

JAPANESE "KUMOI"

In the second group, the notes *F* and *C* of the regular series are similarly transformed into *F infra-flat* and *C infra-flat*. They are designated in the five-line notation as E♭ and B♭, respectively.

EXAMPLE 16ᵇ:

ARCHAIC GREEK   JAP. "HIRAJOSHI"   JAP. "IWATO"

For the sake of comparison both these groups can be transposed to the "white keys" of our piano, being expressed by the series D-E-F-A-B (and its inversions) in the former instance, and by the series C-E-F-A-B in the latter.

We shall now confine ourselves, for brevity, to a single series of notes in our representation of all the other groups of altered infra-modes, with the understanding that each of these series may be similarly inverted, giving, as a result, five infra-modes in each case.

The third group has the note *A* transformed into *A infra-sharp* (B in the diatonic notation) and will produce the series C-D-F-G-B.

The fourth group with the notes *A* and *D* transformed into *A infra-sharp* and *D infra-sharp* (B and E) will give the series C-E-F-G-B.

In the remaining six groups many scales gradually lose their specific "pentatonic" characteristics and begin to approach those of the diatonic scale. Thus, with the note *C* transformed into *C infra-flat* (diatonic B♭) we obtain the fifth group based on the series B♭-D-F-G-A. Next comes the sixth group with the note *D* transformed into *D infra-sharp* (diatonic E) and producing the series C-E-F-G-A. A "mixed" variation with the note *C* lowered and *D* raised, leads to the series B♭-E-F-G-A of the seventh group. Another "mixed" variation with the note *F* lowered and *A* raised produces the series C-D-E♭-G-B of the eighth group.

The ninth and tenth groups are built according to the principle of *harmonic* intonation and produce the series B-D-F-G-A (*C* lowered) in the former instance, and B-E♭-F-G-A (*C* lowered, *D* raised) in the latter. All the other possible alterations will merely repeat in different keys those already demonstrated.

We shall limit ourselves to the above data and will not revert to the question of altered infra-modes, since the latter occupy a very secondary place in our general scheme and are quite unimportant for further constructions. In the following discussion, therefore, whenever any reference to infra-modes is made, the *principal* infra-modes (Ex. 16) will be implied exclusively.

The keyboard illustration of the infra-diatonic scale represented above (Ex. 13) is made in accordance with the infra-mode "C-c" which is found a Fifth above the fundamental infra-mode "F-f," and is, as we know, one of those now predominant in China. It will be recalled that for the fundamental infra-mode we assumed the one on which the ancient Chinese scale is based, and which is constructed of five tones arranged by ascending natural Fifths

$$F\text{-}C\text{-}D\text{-}G\text{-}A$$

i.e. the infra-mode

$$F\text{-}G\text{-}A\text{-}C\text{-}D$$

Hence it is easy to infer that the infra-mode

$$C\text{-}D\text{-}F\text{-}G\text{-}A$$

which we find a Fifth above the fundamental one, is constructed of four tones arranged by ascending Fifths

$$C\text{-}G\text{-}D\text{-}A \text{ plus one descending Fifth C-F}$$

Were we to start from the same principle when constructing the diatonic scale and assume for the fundamental mode the one that is exclusively formed by ascending Fifths

$$C\text{-}G\text{-}D\text{-}A\text{-}E\text{-}B\text{-}F\sharp$$

we would obtain, *not* the generally accepted major mode, but the so-called Lydian mode

$$C\text{-}D\text{-}E\text{-}F\sharp\text{-}G\text{-}A\text{-}B$$

or, which is the same (when transposed to the "white keys"),

$$F\text{-}G\text{-}A\text{-}B\text{-}C\text{-}D\text{-}E$$

Hence it is clear that our conventional major mode, being found a Fifth above the former, is built not only by means of a series of ascending Fifths but also includes, like the contemporary Chinese infra-mode, one descending Fifth namely:

$$C\text{-}G\text{-}D\text{-}A\text{-}E\text{-}B \text{ and } C\text{-}F$$

This similarity in structure between the contemporary Occidental major mode and the Oriental infra-mode is demonstrated here for the reason that in accordance with it we shall subsequently build up the new supra-diatonic scale.

Every one of the five infra-modes (Ex. 16) may be transposed into different keys of the infra-diatonic scale, and here is where the advantage of the Siamese Equal Temperament system over the natural but cumbersome system of the Chinese is particularly evident. Contrarily to the latter, the Siamese do not at present need, for this purpose, the special twelve-tone scale which, among other drawbacks, only permits the infra-diatonic scale to be transposed in *some* keys, preserving its original acoustic structure (See Ex. 8). The full set of seven degrees of the Siamese infra-tempered scale ("5 + 2") permits (in exchange for a certain acoustic compromise) its unhampered transposition into seven different keys just as the full set of twelve degrees of the Occidental tempered scale ("7 + 5") easily permits the latter to be transposed into twelve different keys. And as these twelve keys of the diatonic scale, being consecutively arranged a (tempered) Fifth apart, form a complete and closed system, likewise the seven keys of the infra-diatonic scale (without counting, of course, the enharmonically equivalent keys) form a complete and closed system, being consecutively arranged a (infra-tempered) Fifth apart, as shown in Ex. 17.

The keys with the "infra-flat" signature are represented on the left, and those with the "infra-sharp" signature on the right of this example. The maximum number of signs of alteration is contained in the keys with five infra-flats and five infra-sharps (i.e. equalling the number of regular degrees of this scale) similarly to the diatonic scale in which the maximum number of signs of alteration falls on keys with seven sharps and seven flats (i.e. also conformably to the number of its regular degrees), if, of course, we exclude the practically useless, though theoretically possible keys beginning with the double sharp and double flat signature, etc.

Should anyone try to play this example (17) on the seven white digitals of our piano, he will instantly discover—at first, perhaps, unexpectedly—that some of the keys of the infra-diatonic scale represented do not preserve their original "modal" structure, in spite of the fact that this scale is formed in all keys according to one identical formula, viz.:

HALF STEP	WHOLE STEP	HALF STEP	HALF STEP	WHOLE STEP
I	II	III	IV	V	[I]

The reason for the discrepancies thus made manifest between some keys of this scale is that its infra-tempered "tuning" dealing with but seven tones equally

EXAMPLE 17:

[The enharmonically equivalent keys are indicated by arrows.]

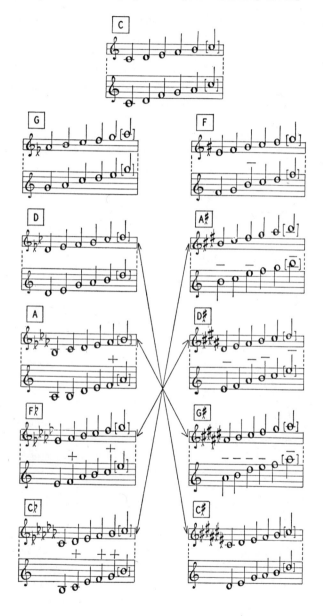

distributed within an octave, leads up to entirely different acoustic relations as
compared with the equally tempered "tuning" of the diatonic scale ("7 + 5")
which deals with twelve tones within the same interval of an octave, and this difference sometimes crops out too conspicuously in some keys of the former scale
when they are played on our "equally tempered" pianoforte.

It is therefore necessary, in the latter case, to mentally correct the pitch of
some tones of the infra-diatonic scale and for this purpose additional designations (+ and —) are introduced in the five-line notation of Example 17 showing
the very tones which one must imagine respectively sharped or flatted, in
some degree; although, properly speaking, all the tones of this scale ought to be
more or less corrected in piano Temperament. A more exact idea of the extent
of these corrections may be gathered from the diagram represented in Ex. 14.

The cycle of keys of the infra-diatonic scale, as represented above, only refers to a single infra-mode "C-c." It is quite understood, however, that similar
cycles may be formed with regard to all the remaining infra-modes of this scale.

The following Table includes the complete set of such cycles containing seven
different keys for every one of the five infra-modes of the modern Siamese
scale. The enharmonically equivalent keys, as well as the guiding five-line
notation, have been eliminated this time:

EXAMPLE 18:

Existing literature on the music of Siam, which incidentally is very scarce,
contains no data referring to the historical period and to the circumstances in
which the infra-tempered intonation was first introduced in the musical practice
of that country. Neither is it known how the Siamese in general turned to the use

of seven keys of the infra-diatonic scale, instead of twelve keys (obtained by the aid of the "special" twelve-tone scale), the latter number playing such an important part in Chinese as well as Indo-Chinese ritualistic ceremonies.

Among the manifold systems which sprang up at various epochs of Chinese musical history—inseparate, in early periods, from the musical history of the Siamese, who belong to the same Sinean branch of the Yellow race*—there is only one which may be regarded as a precedent. It is a "straight" system constructed in the twelfth century of our era and based on the (natural) infra-diatonic scale ("5 + 2") which was supposed to be transposed only in those seven keys whose Tonics formed its entire body. Inasmuch as every key of this scale required a separate series of seven tones, the whole system represented a complicated set of 49 (i.e. 7 × 7) tones within an octave. One may be assured that this, probably unique, instance of departure from the "duodecimal" principle had some symbolic justification among the Chinese, perhaps similar to the one which we had occasion to mention in the last chapter (page 35).

As far as our principal subject is concerned, the most important point in this case, however, is not so much the strict authenticity of historic information—and still less the Oriental symbolism relating to music—as the fact of present practical application of the principle of Equal Temperament with regard to the infra-diatonic scale.

This fact, besides the significant part it plays in revealing similarity between two quant·'atively different scales (diatonic and infra-diatonic), permits one to draw a few deductions, or, at least, plausible conjectures, regarding some properties of the musical ear in its physiological and psychological aspects, namely:

1. The practical use of the principle of Equal Temperament in the Orient in addition to the application of the same principle (though to a different scale) in Occidental countries, carries a conviction that the human ear adjusts itself with comparative ease to artificial intonations even if their deviations from Just Intonation are very perceptible, as occurs especially in the Siamese "infra-tempered" system. The explanation of this adjustment by insufficient discrimination of tonal relations on the part of the Asiatic peoples, which might be, and in fact has been occasionally advanced, falls to the ground in the light of the results of the special experiments which were made with a group of Siamese court musicians sent by their King to

---

* This racial relationship is pointed out by F. Dawes in his *Six essays on the ancients, their music and instruments* (London, 1893). For additional, though indirect proof of kinship between the musical cultures of China and Indo-China, or, at least, of the influence of the former over the latter, there may be cited the following details from a description referring to one of the bas-reliefs of an ancient Cambodian temple in Ongcor, on which are . . . . "portrayed a combat and processions, with drums, flutes, trumpets, tam-tams, and organs said to be *Chinese.*" See *Travels in the Central Parts of Indo-China (Siam), Cambodia and Laos*, by M. Henri Mouhot, Vol. I, p. 296 (London, 1864).

the Exhibition of Inventions in London (1885), where they gave evidence of a quite surprisingly accurate musical ear with respect to the infra-tempered scale.* It seems opportune to add here that the problem of accommodation of the human ear to various acoustic deviations has so far been merely touched upon by musical science, although there are grounds for believing that this auditory faculty greatly exceeds the demands made by any of the artificial intonations ever used in the musical practice of all nations.**

2. The widespread recognition of Equal Temperament inclines us also to the admission that musical intervals are perceived by the human ear, not through their absolute acoustic value (or, at least, not *always* so) but

---

* Appendix to Mr. Alexander Ellis's paper on *The Musical Scales of Various Nations* in the Journal of Society of Arts, October 1885, Vol. XXXIII, page 1103 (London).

** I would especially refer, in this respect, to an interesting and valuable passage in an article entitled *The possibility of quarter-tone and other new scales* by Leonid Sabaneev (*The Musical Times*, June 1, 1929, London) which reads as follows:

"We know that our ear has the faculty of the psychological corrective. We *hear* one thing and *feel* or are conscious of it as something else. The accuracy of intonation in our musical performances is often approximate, the expressional and casual deviations from purity frequently exceeding two or even three commas. Furthermore, measurements made by me at the Academy of Art sciences, Moscow, showed that every sound—by which I mean a musical and not an acoustic sound—has a certain breadth; it is never an isolated sound of an exact pitch, with a definite number of vibrations, but a more or less compact group of sounds having an approximatively similar number of vibrations. A sound which, acoustically, is absolutely pure is to us simply unpleasant, smacking of the dry and the abstract. It appeared from my measurements that with singers the breadth of a note is often as much as a *semitone*. Our ear orientates these notes, and refers them to a certain centre, a certain pitch, being guided therein by the structure of the musical tissue. One and the same note will seem to us to vary in pitch according to the context in which it is presented to us."

This passage, besides its important and experimentally verified data in regard to the faculty of ear-accommodation in general, incidentally is also of interest in another connection. The fact that every tone, musically speaking, must have—and, indeed, usually has—a certain breadth in musical performances (unless pro-

duced on instruments with fixed intonation), may explain how it is that the folkloristic musical material collected in a given region with what would appear to be scientific accuracy does not seem always to adhere to the fundamental scale on which this material is ordinarily based, but occasionally manifests various acoustical deviations from it, which some theorists are even inclined to view as independent scales. It is very likely that the breadth of the *same* tones, when reaching the limit at some points of the melodic line, is responsible for the impression that *entirely different* tones, absent in the fundamental scale, are struck by the performer, or even—on the strength of custom in interpreting certain compositions—by a great number of performers. Should this factor be taken into account, when it comes to the determination of scales used in the manifold musical folklore, far less variety would be found by theorists in this respect,—all the "deviating" forms, which result from artistic interpretation, being reduced to a few definitely established types of scales. And this factor *has* to be taken into account, since we usually judge folkloristic scales by the actual performance of musical compositions based on them, the scales to which the native musical instruments are tuned not being always reliable in this respect on account of their technical imperfection, and particularly, of their inability to resist atmospheric conditions with regard to their "fixed" intonation.

It would not be too daring to assume that Mr. Sabaneev's ingenious theory of the "breadth" of a tone applies, generally speaking, not only to melodic constructions, but—naturally to a much lesser extent—also to harmonic formations. As a matter of fact, it is easily observed that a well trained *a cappella* choir sings the very same harmonies—even such an obvious chord as a major Triad—with acoustically varied intonations, depending on the polyphonic context in which they appear, and this variety of intonation perceptibly increases with the complexity of chords in a musical performance.

through their relative position in one scale or another. An interval does *not* intrinsically change in character for the sole reason that it is tempered or infra-tempered (i.e. being virtually "false") as long as the ear understands it as the correlation between two definitely and internally sensed degrees of a given scale.

3. Equal Temperament in no way impairs the inherent qualities of a scale which we perceive through the prism of its various phases (i.e. modes and infra-modes) provided its most characteristic feature—the chain of specifically alternating, even if somewhat acoustically changed, whole steps and half steps—is preserved. The innocuousness of Equal Temperament, under the latter condition, can be easily verified with regard to the infra-diatonic scale, by playing some very familiar "pentatonic" tune on a Siamese musical instrument with fixed infra-tempered intonation.* Such tests with very typical Scotch tunes have been made independently by A. J. Ellis and C. Stumpf, and also by the latter alone with the well-known Wagnerian theme from *Feuerzauber* (See Ex. 57), which, when unaccompanied, requires no more than the five regular degrees of the infra-diatonic scale for its performance. None of these melodies lost their intrinsic character when played on the Siamese *Ranat,* and their acoustic deviations from Occidental intonation proved to be fully tolerated by the ear.** There have also been observed a few cases of the utilization of some popular Irish and Scotch tunes by Siamese musicians, who probably caught these melodies by ear from British sailors whistling them on the streets of Bangkok. These European tunes, usually based on the infra-diatonic scale, evidently preserve their character when played on Siamese musical instruments, if they are easily recognized by foreigners who sometimes make reports of this sort while visiting that country.***   It is understood, of course, that no melody for which the seven *regular* degrees of the diatonic scale are required could be similarly recognized (especially if it progresses "stepwise") when reproduced by *all* seven tones of the Siamese scale ("5 + 2"). The reason is that

---

* The principal infra-tempered instruments in Siam to which all the rest are tuned represent a series of *Ranat's* furnished with metallic or wooden bars, from 16 to 21 in number. These instruments are built in different registers jointly embracing $3\frac{1}{4}$ octaves, beginning from *c* of the small octave up to *e♭* of the thrice accentuated octave. They are employed as important orchestral instruments and are also widely used in private life by the Siamese, similarly to our piano.

***Tonsystem und Musik der Siamesen* von Carl Stumpf (*Beitrage zur Akustik und Musikwissenschaft,* Leipzig, 1901, Heft 3). Incident-

ally, to the fact (already attested a number of times) of demarcation between the regular and auxiliary degrees of the infra-diatonic scale by various nations, may be added that according to this writer, the Siamese when they perform their own music distinctly employ only five notes of their scale for the body of the melody, the remaining two notes being used merely as "passing points" (*Durchgangspunkte*). Stumpf classifies the former as "essential" *(wesentliche)* and the latter as "unessential" *(unwesentliche)* tones of the Siamese scale.

*** See, for instance, *Siam's musical heritage* by A. G. Beaumont *(Inter-Ocean,* v. 8, 1927, Batavia, Java).

the Siamese scale preserving (despite being tempered) the chain of whole steps and half steps characteristic of "pentatonic" melodies, is deprived, however, of the chain of whole steps and half steps which is a feature of diatonic melodies and which, of course, profoundly differs from the former. Instead of this diatonic chain, the Siamese scale is in a position to offer only an absolutely inadequate series of seven equal intervals. [It would be quite appropriate, by the way, to give the name *infra-chromatic scale* to the latter series, similarly to the series of twelve equal intervals known under the name of *chromatic scale* in Occidental music.]

4. Finally, there seems to be room for the probability that acoustic deviations from just intonation of the infra-diatonic scale are not only tolerated by the ear, but that they are capable, at times, of becoming a positive artistic factor in musical art based on this scale—this being true, as we know, with reference to musical art based on the equally tempered diatonic scale. Indeed, it has been frequently observed, for instance, that the major and minor modes of this scale are much more strongly demarcated in character under the condition of the equally tempered rather than just intonation. This stronger demarcation resulting from the greater acoustic difference between the major and minor tempered Thirds, which is unquestionably desirable in "diatonic" music, should thus be regarded as an artistic advantage of Equal Temperament. Something similar to these acoustic deviations in Music may be found in painting—where even in presence of the most realistic style, some deviation from absolute "photographic" accuracy is most desirable. Special experiments made by E. H. Pierce with two different intonations of the diatonic scale, led him to compare equally tempered intonation to good, wholesome, cold spring water as opposed to the very insipid, though chemically pure, distilled water which, in his judgment, is the simile called to mind by a mathematically just intonation. * Of course we cannot at present fully realize all the positive artistic qualities of Equal Temperament with reference to the infra-diatonic scale (aside from its indisputable and, after all, most essential practical advantages), but the postulation of a certain similarity, also in this connection, between it and the diatonic scale, will not be too risky.

The definition of intervals of the infra-diatonic scale—to which our discussion now turns—will simultaneously conclude our analysis of its structure and serve to introduce the further exposition of its inherent harmony.

Let us then again refer to the keyboard illustration of this scale (Ex. 13) for the purpose of compiling a Table of its intervals showing, in the first place,

* *A Colossal Experiment in Just Intonation* by Edwin H. Pierce (*Musical Quarterly*, July, 1924, New York).

their dimension in terms of whole steps and half steps. Reckoning the number of these units in all the intervals taken from each regular degree, we shall obtain the following results (this Table does not include the infra-Primes and infra-Sixths which of course will be everywhere equivalent to Primes and Octaves of the diatonic scale):

INFRA-SECONDS		
I. C-D	½	step
II. D-F	1	"
III. F-G	½	"
IV. G-A	½	"
V. A-c	1	"

INFRA-THIRDS		
I. C-F . . .	1½	steps
II. D-G . . .	1½	"
III. F-A . . .	1	"
IV. G-c . . .	1½	"
V. A-d . . .	1½	"

INFRA-FOURTHS		
I. C-G	2	steps
II. D-A	2	"
III. F-c	2	"
IV. G-d	2	"
V. A-f . . .	2½	"

INFRA-FIFTHS		
I. C-A . .	2½	steps
II. D-c . . .	3	"
III. F-d	2½	"
IV. G-f	3	"
V. A-g	3	"

It will be seen that every group of this Table contains intervals of two different dimensions which obviously require additional designations, indicating what is known in Music as the *quality* of intervals. In the diatonic scale we use for this purpose different "pairs" of terms (like *major* and *minor*, etc.) chiefly depending on the class of intervals—consonant or dissonant—to which a given group belongs.

However, *consonances* and *dissonances* again appear to be, not absolute but relative notions in different scales; therefore, the opposition of intervals as consonant and dissonant is not identical, for instance, in the diatonic and infra-diatonic scales. Hence it is apparent that the qualitative determination of intervals of the infra-diatonic scale must be preceded by a separate investigation of their satisfactoriness or unsatisfactoriness *for an ear well accustomed to the structure of this scale.*

We will have occasion to return later, and more than once, to the basic problem of consonances and dissonances, when our viewpoint concerning this matter—especially with regard to the relativity of these two notions and the resulting specificalness of harmonic laws in each scale—will be more definitely explained. It will be sufficient for the present to point out the commonly established and repeatedly verified fact that the only consonant intervals recognized as such by those who avail themselves of the infra-diatonic scale appear to be (besides Primes and Octaves) pure Fourths and their inversions—pure Fifths—which, under the newly introduced terminology of the infra-diatonic scale, acquired the names of *infra-Thirds* and *infra-Fourths* (see the above Table). To these intervals the two remaining groups of *infra-Seconds* and *infra-Fifths* (the latter representing only inversions of the former) are naturally opposed as dissonances.

Thus, the simplified structure of the infra-diatonic scale, as compared with the diatonic scale, and the lesser number of various intervals it contains, exclude the existence in it of a group of intermediate (imperfect) consonances. Applying now the terms adopted in the diatonic scale for the qualitative designation of intervals, we shall name all the consonances of the infra-diatonic scale *perfect,* and, when they are expanded or contracted by a half step (which transforms them into dissonances) *augmented* and *diminished.* In respect to the two different magnitudes in the groups of dissonant intervals we shall apply the terms *major* and *minor.* As a result of this nomenclature, the complete Table of intervals of the infra-diatonic scale will appear as follows:

EXAMPLE 19:

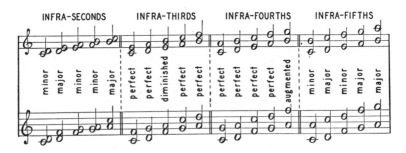

or, if we build it similarly to the familiar Table of intervals of the diatonic scale with the indication of the number of whole steps and half steps each interval contains:

	I	II	III	IV	V
INFRA-PRIMES	perf. 0	perf. 0	perf. 0	perf. 0	perf. 0
INFRA-SECONDS	minor $\frac{1}{2}$	major 1	minor $\frac{1}{2}$	minor $\frac{1}{2}$	major 1
INFRA-THIRDS	perf. $1\frac{1}{2}$	perf. $1\frac{1}{2}$	dim. 1	perf. $1\frac{1}{2}$	perf. $1\frac{1}{2}$
INFRA-FOURTHS	perf. 2	perf. 2	perf. 2	perf. 2	augm. $2\frac{1}{2}$
INFRA-FIFTHS	minor $2\frac{1}{2}$	major 3	minor $2\frac{1}{2}$	major 3	major 3
INFRA-SIXTHS (octaves)	perf. $3\frac{1}{2}$	perf. $3\frac{1}{2}$	perf. $3\frac{1}{2}$	perf. $3\frac{1}{2}$	perf. $3\frac{1}{2}$

It should be noted, incidentally, that the diminished infra-Third (F-A) is equal to a whole step of the infra-diatonic scale—a fact which theoretically substantiates the view that this interval is a dissonance, held by those races who use that scale exclusively in their music. In this connection, the diminished infra-Third is apparently governed by a certain principle common to all "organic" tonal systems, according to which every interval not exceeding a whole step of its respective scale must be regarded as a dissonance in it.

There are two more technical points to add to the above Table of intervals which will conclude this chapter. *First,* the general number of whole steps and half steps of any "infra-diatonic" interval plus its inversion will always be equal to the number comprised in an infra-Sixth (equivalent to the "diatonic" Octave), i.e. to $3\frac{1}{2}$ steps, and *Second,* the rule of inversion of intervals in the infra-diatonic system is similar to the well known rule found in the diatonic system, according to which consonances, when inverted, remain consonances, dissonances remain dissonances, minor intervals become major, major become minor, diminished become augmented and augmented become diminished.

CHAPTER VIII

INFRA-DIATONIC HARMONY

Turning now to the problem of determining the basic laws on which infra-diatonic harmony rests, we enter a field of musical knowledge entirely unexplored so far. Genuine musical material and theoretical data, found almost exclusively in the musical treatises of the Far East and by which one has to be guided in dealing with the above subject, are extremely scarce.

As a natural result, the documentation and findings of Western musical scholars regarding this matter are somewhat superficial and, at times, even erroneous. These scholars, as a rule, not only do not seem to grant a thoroughly specific mode of musical thought in terms of Harmony to the Orientals who avail themselves exclusively of the infra-diatonic scale, but rather, they are inclined to favor the popular opinion which denies the very existence of harmonic constructions to these people and refuses them even a harmonic sense.

To fail to recognize harmonic constructions in Oriental music is an error that is contradicted by the facts, and as such it can easily be refuted. As for the absence of a harmonic sense, it is an error of principle, since not only harmonic constructions but also the primary process of scale-formation among any people are based (to a great extent at least) on a subconscious perception of these or other harmonic relations, according to which the relations of scale-degrees are intuitively sought and then firmly established.

If harmony is not applied or *scarcely* applied in the musical practice of certain peoples, it is nevertheless sensed by them in the depths of their being— perhaps in the form of vaguely stirring emotions—and its laws, so far unformulated, are at work in their music. The scale rests, as it were, on the periphery of these emotions, being therefore discovered before the laws of its harmony. And it is only long after the scale has been definitely established that these laws slowly and gradually rise to the surface of consciousness, although their inherent existence in a scale, even before their actual manifestation, is felt at every step. The tones which constitute a scale may be compared to the tips of an aquatic plant which emerge above the surface of the water and seem to have no connection with each other, but both in their limited range of motion and in their orientation towards some invisible center, we divine the presence of a common root: divided on the surface, the tones of a scale are joined in the depths of their harmony.

Harmony, therefore, not only determines the functions and the interrelation of all the scale-degrees, as is generally known, but is also one of the most important factors which pre-establishes the number of tones in a given scale and specifically distributes them within an Octave. In other words, harmony is something that helps to transform a series of disconnected tones into a completed system whose elements, similarly to the particles of a crystal, become, in a manner, subject to some inner law of cohesion.

Thus, we may fully support the belief * that although the scale *historically* precedes harmony in the tangible aspect of musical evolution, yet *psychologically* harmony precedes the scale whose very existence and properties derive in many respects from harmony and its laws. Without the recognition of this psychological primacy of harmony neither the characteristic distribution of scale-tones nor their mutual tendency to each other and to their common Tonic can be properly grasped.

Schopenhauer's ingenious definition of the Thorough-bass as the "logic of Music" is in the fullest measure applicable to harmony and its engendered scale, inasmuch as harmony is wholly determined by the Thorough-bass, and the scale lies at the foundation of any music and in itself represents an elementary musical idea. A series of tones does not produce music unless it can be explained by harmony, just as a group of words have no sense unless they can be explained by logic. Thus, *harmony is the logic of the scale.*

From this viewpoint the laws of its basic harmony are intrinsically contained in every scale, but, inasmuch as the specific number and arrangement of degrees in each scale presupposes a particular "logic" as regards their interconnection, these laws cannot be identical in different scales. And consequently this distinction must also be true of the harmonic formations based on these laws, as well as of their cardinal opposition as consonances and dissonances, together with all the variety of their interrelation ensuing therefrom. This specificalness of harmonic laws in every scale does not preclude, however, the possibility of their being united by some single and broader acoustic principle, which actually does take place in reality, as we shall see later.

What are, then, these harmonic laws in the infra-diatonic scale and what are the means at our disposal for finding them?

In order to answer this question, let us first examine step by step all existing and noteworthy material which, with a few exceptions, has for its sole source—directly or indirectly—the musical theory and practice of the Chinese.

In the mass of Occidental literature on Chinese music there is very little that contains any information at all on Chinese Harmony and still less that has any

---

* See *The Elastic Language* by Ernest New-man, reprinted in a collection of studies under the general title of *A Musical Motley* (New York, 1925), page 84.

concrete musical material relating to this particular problem.   The authors, although they have acquired a reputation, in some instances, through extensive research in Chinese music in general, confine themselves to the most superficial aspects of Chinese Harmony.   The passages are so brief that we may well quote them in full:

> "In the accompaniment on the *Ch'in*, two strings are always played at the same time. In the *Ch'in* set up for the five tones, the lower chords are formed by what the Chinese call *ta-kiuen-keou*, that is, the *wide interval*, which is a Fifth, and the upper chords are formed by the *chao-kiuen-keou*, that is, the *small interval*, which is a Fourth. So here is a sort of harmony among the Chinese, and it is the only one they know."—M. AMIOT.*

> "The Chinese have nothing like our Harmony, taken in the sense of chords, counterpoint, etc. The only collection of different but simultaneous sounds recognized by them is that produced by playing two strings (at a distance of a Fourth, a Fifth, or an Octave) together on the *Ch'in*, the *Sê*, or the guitar."—J. VAN AALST.**

> "Harmony and polyphony (among the Chinese) have not been studied and reduced to written formulae. The musical taste of the performer is his rule for counterpoint or harmony. The violins, however, often embroider the theme given by the singer. The guitars always play motifs that are true accompaniments. Chinese musicians, therefore, have definite feeling and taste, on the one hand for concomitant sounds and on the other for the simultaneous progression of the two different parts. In any case, when I was thoroughly familiar with the melody played, I could always perceive in the violence of the accompaniments and deafening mass of rhythmic sounds, numerous harmonies, infinitely delicate and varied."—G. SOULIÉ.***

> "There is no such thing as part-singing in China, nor have we met tunes harmonized in any book; only the melody is written. But the *rudiments* of harmony are to be found in a book published as early as 1525; how much earlier they were

---

* *Mémoires concernant les Chinois* par M. Amiot, Tome VI, pages 165, 171, 183 and 245.

** *Chinese Music* by J. van Aalst (Shanghai, 1884), page 24.

*** *Théatre et Musique Modernes en Chine* par Georges Soulié de Morant (Paris, 1926), page 79. In a somewhat earlier but more special work on Chinese Music, the same author does not give any information on Chinese Harmony, confining himself to the single remark that ". . . . methods of harmony are still to be created for all the music of the Far East." *(La musique en Chine* par G. Soulié, page 23, Paris 1911). A supplementary essay to the former of these works, entitled *Etude technique de la Musique Chinoise* by M. André Gailhard, contains the following rather interesting description of a Chinese musical performance with a reference to their Harmony (page 109):—

> "The principal themes are generally rendered by a singer or a solo instrument.

After the theme has been rendered, it is repeated in unison by the instruments. Little by little embellishments are introduced and sometimes other melodies are grafted to the leading theme. Sometimes, too, the singer and instruments have each their own theme. As all the themes are written on the five note scale (the other degrees being merely embellishments or passing notes) a subconscious system based on a single chord possessing the five degrees of the scale is evolved. This chord corresponds to our common chord with the addition of a second and a sixth degree. When a temporary modulation occurs, we find the same single chord corresponding to the new key. In spite of the many liberties taken by the performers, the ensemble remains perfectly consonant. It is curious to note, moreover, that if counterpoints are established haphazard on the Chinese five note scale, consonance is always respected."

in possession of those rudiments we cannot tell. Their various instruments in the various keys are tuned in Fifths and made to respond to one another in Fifths. The *Sung* (or *Shêng,* a sort of Chinese Reed-Organ. J. Y.) is often played in Fifths and Octaves. The Lama priests in *Wutai-Shan* intone their prayers in very deep notes a Fifth apart or an Octave apart. When they began to do this we have no means of knowing . . . Our harmony, however, is utter confusion to the Chinese; doubtless they think it barbarous. The only harmony they think of is the harmony of different sounds of their eight kinds of instruments, that is, using only the instruments that sound well together and are appropriate to be used on any given occasion."—T. RICHARDS.*

"First and foremost in the consideration of Chinese music is the fact that the Chinese have no care for our harmony: they will have none of it. Neither will they take to our diatonic scale: it offends their sense of art. Unisons and concords of two notes (as Fourths and Thirds and their inversions) satisfy their sense of the harmonious."—H. SMITH.**

"The larger *Shêng* leads and the smaller *Shêng* harmonises (accords) whence the smaller is called *Ho,* i.e. the *Concord* . . . The *Hong She ki* says: 'three reeds make one harmony [the third reed is obviously the octave of the first one. J. Y.] and that is perfect harmony' . . . Peculiarly adapted to chords the Chinese never go beyond using the Octaves, Fifths and Thirds."—F. EASTLAKE.***

There is no doubt whatever that the cursory views of these authors were based on utterly fragmentary material and random observations, for besides their obvious incompleteness, they sometimes err in point of accuracy. Thus, for instance, with reference to the intervals which are admitted to be used, when playing the *Ch'in* (Aalst), a rectification has to be made to the effect that Fourths, Fifths and Octaves are *preferably* admitted on the *Ch'in,* since certain other intervals are also encountered, though rarely, in music written for this instrument.

Again, the assertion that "concords of two notes satisfy the Chinese sense of the harmonious" (Smith) is true only as regards Fourths and their inversions, since Thirds, mentioned in the quotation, are proscribed in the sacred music of the Chinese, and are but sporadically found in their popular music.

As for the statement of another writer (Richards) who has not found tunes harmonized in any of the Chinese books, it can hardly have any significance after a number of melodies harmonized by the Chinese, even though in a primitive way, were discovered in some of their musical treatises and partly rendered into

* *Chinese Music* by T. Richards (Shanghai, 1907), page 17. This brief study represents a somewhat extended reprint of an article published in the *East of Asia Magazine,* December 1902 (Shanghai), Part IV, Vol. I, page 301. Regarding part-singing in Chinese monasteries, some details worthy of note will be found in a descriptive sketch entitled *Putoshan* by Arthur

Stanley (Journal of the North China Branch of the Royal Asiatic Society, Vol. 54, 1915, page 18).
** *The World's Earliest Music* by H. S. Smith (London, 1904), page 159.
*** *The Chinese Reed-Organ* (Shêng) by F. W. Eastlake (*China Review,* Hongkong, 1882) pages 37-40.

Western notation, now available to everybody. A considerable portion of these, mainly sacred, melodies are found in the essay already referred to, by M. Courant who, by the way, also inclines to the opinion that Harmony is of secondary importance in Chinese music, being mostly represented in uniform progression by perfect Fourths. A similar judgment on Chinese Harmony is passed by E. Fischer, who analyzed several popular tunes harmonized by Chinese musicians (discussed further on) and recorded by certain explorers with the aid of a phonograph.

There only remains to be added regarding the essay which is exclusively devoted to the Chinese reed-organ (Shêng) that its author (Eastlake) makes no mention whatever of the simultaneous tonal combinations which are indicated on the pipes of this instrument as a guide in harmonization for the performer. In the meantime, in view of such an obvious lack of information in the field of infra-diatonic harmony, these indications have rather an important value.

Now, summing up the above data in their entirety, we may acknowledge that the harmonic formations of the Chinese are still primitive and that they possess nothing resembling our Occidental harmony, which is foreign to them, but this is hardly sufficient ground for denying the existence of harmonic constructions in their music and still less for refusing them any harmonic sense.

The primitiveness of harmonic formations in the music of Far-Eastern nations and, particularly, the abundance of Fourths—mostly in parallel progression—which have a place in their harmonizations, lead certain theorists to see an analogy between these formations and the first steps of harmonization in Western medieval music, known under the name of *Organum* or *Diaphony*. And inasmuch as the latter deals with ecclesiastic chants based almost exclusively on the *diatonic* scale, the postulation of such an analogy FIRST rules out— though by inference only—the possibility of a *specific* feeling for harmony among the people whose music is entirely based on the infra-diatonic scale, and SECONDLY, it similarly prognosticates a path of harmonic evolution for Orientals absolutely identical with the one Occidentals have already left behind them.

However, the comparatively recent investigations (with which the names of Combarieu, Hughes, Lederer, Riemann and a few others are associated) regarding the genesis and birthplace of harmony and polyphonic art in Western medieval music, furnish us with a fairly reliable clue to an understanding of the circumstances which caused the harmonic principles of that time to be identical with those still applied in Far-Eastern countries, and which, we may say, are far from being favorable to the opinion that denies the actual existence of a quite specific "infra-diatonic" perception of Harmony.

As a matter of fact, these investigations established with reasonable certainty that primitive harmonic constructions made their initial appearance in the Western world among the Celtic peoples, and having developed towards the middle of the ninth century, or thereabouts, into a definite system (*Organum*), subsequently spread in this form all over Europe. * But the Celts, as we know, at that time availed themselves exclusively of the infra-diatonic scale; therefore there is nothing surprising in the analogy between their principles of harmony and those applied until now by the Far East. It was only when the principle of *Organum* was carried to the continent (towards the close of the ninth or perhaps even in the early part of the tenth century), that it was dogmatized by

* Of the early use of some very primitive harmonic combinations by the Celts we are informed, *first*, through their specifically constructed ancient musical instruments (such as the Welsh Crowd—a fiddle with six strings, four played with a bow and two with the thumb as accompaniment—mention of which is made by Venantius Fortunatus [530-609], Bishop of Poitiers; then the Organistrum or Lyra rustica dating from the beginning of the eighth century, and the Bagpipe, to enumerate but the principal ones), and, *second*, through a number of highly suggestive linguistic expressions, encountered in their oldest literary documents. An interesting philological excursion into the latter subject is found in *Old Irish Folk Music and Songs* by Patrick Weston Joyce, page XVII (London, 1909), being reprinted from the same writer's extensive work entitled *A Social History of Ancient Ireland*, page 587 (London, 1903). The first mention of the Organum, as a certain principle of Harmony, is made by Scotus Erigena, the Irish philosopher, in his famous treatise, *De divisione naturae*, which was written some time between 865 and 870, according to Henry Bett (*Johannes Scotus Erigena; a study in medieval philosophy*, Cambridge University Press, 1925). Exhaustive information regarding the musical ideology of this philosopher is given in an article bearing the title *Die Musikanschauung des Johannes Scotus (Erigena)* by J. Handschin (*Deutsche Vierteljahrsschrift für Literaturwissenschaft und Geistesgeschichte*, Halle, 1927, Heft II, Seite 316). Erigena is not only occupied with various speculations on the Organum, so characteristic of medieval scholasticism, but he also states the existence of a sort of polyphonic music *(organicum melos)* and of the art of "organizing" *(ars organandi)*, governed by certain rational musical rules, among his contemporaries. Which, considering the pedantic accuracy of expression of medieval scholars and the slow rate of cultural development in those days, leads us to suppose that this method of harmonization made its *initial* appearance among the Irish and other Celtic peoples at a much earlier historical period. Dom Anselm Hughes claims (*Worcester Medieval Harmony*, 1928, page 12) that "the non-existence of harmony before the year 750 may be taken as axiomatic," which is probably true if we exclude the occasional use of the simplest simultaneous combinations of tones played on the ancient Celtic instruments mentioned above, that may have occurred as early as in the sixth century, i.e. during the flourishing period of the Bardic art. We come across a very valuable description of the later polyphonic music of the Celts in the works of Gerald de Barri, a Welsh scholar of the twelfth century, known under the Latinized name of *Giraldus Cambrensis* who, among other things, points out the fact that the principle of "organizing," called by him *organica cantilena*, is firmly rooted and has long been practiced by the inhabitants of Ireland, Scotland and Wales. In his *Irish Topography* this writer only mentions the use of Fourths and Fifths, as far as harmony is concerned, these combinations probably being still predominant, though not exclusive, at that time in the Northern countries. But in the *Description of Wales* he states that, besides these harmonic combinations, the natives avail themselves of more complicated polyphony, so much so that in Welsh chorus singing one may sometimes hear "as many parts as there are performers" (Giraldi Cambrensis Opera edited by James F. Dimock [London, 1867]: Vol. V, *Topographia Ibernica*, Distinctio III, Cap. XI, pages 153 and 154; Vol. VI, *Descriptio Kambriae*, Liber I, Cap. XII, pages 186, 187, 189 and 190; see also *Gerald the Welshman* by Henry Owen [London, 1904], pages 43 and 79, for general information on this writer's texts referring to Music). The above description of polyphonic music in the twelfth century naturally puzzled all the later European theorists, particularly Hugo Riemann, who in his *Handbuch der Musikgeschichte* (Vol. I, part 2, page 145; Leipzig, 1905) advanced the hypothesis that this "polyphony" probably never went beyond the boundaries of the pentatonic scale, then still in use, its structure, incidentally, also explaining the "puzzle" of the predominant position of the Fourth in all early harmonizations in general. This hypothesis becomes even more plausible if one compares the above passage of Giraldus with the description of Chinese "polyphony" (based, naturally, on the same pentatonic scale) by M. André Gailhard, as quoted above (see Footnote on page 64), not to mention the fact that our entire discussion in this chapter thoroughly substantiates Riemann's theory.

learned monks who "discovered" in it some sort of concordance with the basic principle of ancient Greek music, highly authoritative to them, in which the central position, as known, is occupied by the interval of a perfect Fourth.* This far-fetched connection apparently satisfied the casuistic bent of most medieval scholars who found in it sufficient background for theoretical justification of the "imported" *infra-diatonic* method of harmonization—predominantly by parallel Fourths—and, consequently, for the practical application of this method also to the existing *diatonic* church chants, intrinsically subject, however, to their own (diatonic) laws of harmony, entirely different from the former.**

Thus we see that the analogy between Oriental and primitive Occidental harmonizations, as observed by some modern theorists, is a real fact, but this analogy is *genuine* only in relation to the music in which this harmonization was the result of the intuitive perception of harmony by the people who used the infra-diatonic scale and not that of the artificial intervention of scholastically speculating monks.

The question then arises why is it that the Celts, among whom this harmonic perception itself was natural, did not further develop, as might have been expected, any specific infra-diatonic system of Harmony, but subsequently moved along harmonic lines common to all the rest of the Western world? The answer—as a matter of fact it has been partly given in the preceding chapter—is that before such a system could be thoroughly developed the Celts gradually and imperceptibly began to depart from the *exclusive* application of the infra-diatonic scale in their musical creation, and sometimes to avail themselves also of the diatonic scale. To the latter they did not, of course, come at one bound, but probably first contacted it in the way of a more or less "independent" and casual application of the two auxiliary degrees of the infra-diatonic scale, i.e. the very ones which, when used "independently," may easily be regarded as regular degrees of the diatonic scale. This was followed by further

---

* Although the interval of a Fourth was recognized by the ancient Greeks as a consonance (the two others being the Fifth and the Octave), yet none of the authentic documents collected up to the present time gives any trace of evidence regarding the practical application, at that time, of Fourths and Fifths in some sort of progression that can be regarded even as a remote precedent of the Medieval Organum and still less resembling it (See *The Oxford History of Music* by H. E. Wooldridge, V. I. page 6; Oxford, 1901; also *Histoire de la Musique* par J. Combarieu, Tome I, page 94; Paris, 1920). Thus, the only imaginable chance of the possibility that the scholars of the Middle Ages availed themselves of external sources outside of those imported from the Northern

"Celtic" countries, when building up the theory of Diaphony, automatically falls to the ground.

** Should we accept Riemann's viewpoint (*Folkloristische Tonalitätsstudien*, L e i p z i g, 1916), with regard to the true nature of, at least, some Gregorian chants supposed to represent a "Zwischenstadie" between the pentatonic and the diatonic scale, we would be bound to admit that besides theoretical considerations, some medieval scholars of the European continent were also guided by a certain inner sense (evidently still retained at that time) of the basic laws of infra-diatonic harmony, as crudely embodied in the *Organum*. This viewpoint, which only confirms our theory, is adopted and developed by the author in a supplementary article at the end of this book (see Addendum II).

and similarly intuitive steps, little by little including more definite diatonic motives, phrases and complete sentences in their songs, and finally Celtic composers began to create compositions that were frankly diatonic.

This was, possibly, the historic moment when the inborn harmonic intuition of the Celts suggested to them the parallel progression of Thirds and Sixths, characteristic of the diatonic scale, and which at the threshold of the thirteenth century found united embodiment in the principle of the *Faux-bourdon.* * The gradual way in which the above transition from the infra-diatonic to the diatonic scale was effected in Celtic music certainly was true also with respect to the two different principles of harmony corresponding to these two scales. In the latter case, as it appears, the gradual transition from the *Organum* to the *Faux-bourdon* was facilitated by the fact that the progression of Fourths, formally abolished in the Faux-bourdon, actually remained between its two upper parts which accompanied the lower fundamental melody in Thirds and Sixths respectively.

In this way, notwithstanding the profound psychological distinction between these two principles of harmony, there did not exist, so to speak, any outward structural break between them, and this circumstance makes it possible to establish a certain evolutionary connection between the Organum, the Faux-bourdon and the subsequently developed system of Triads (in their four-part Harmony form) of which the latter absorbed the two former principles, just as the Organum first merged into the Faux-bourdon. [See Ex. 20.]

The principle of chord-formation by Thirds being solidly laid down through the system of Triads in European music, further harmonic complication was effected by means of superimposition of new diatonic Thirds upon the dominant Triad (G-B-D), as a result of which the chords of the dominant Seventh (G-B-D-F), Ninth (G-B-D-F-A), Eleventh (G-B-D-F-A-C) and Thirteenth (G-B-D-F-A-C-E) were successively obtained. With the latter chord all the seven regular degrees of the diatonic scale had been completely exhausted, and further superimposition upon it of diatonic Thirds did not form any new chords but began anew the same cycle of intervals by which all the chords enumerated were built.

Reverting now to the harmonic constructions of the Far-Eastern nations, we shall readily observe that while their initial attempts (predominantly progression by Fourths) were, for known reasons absolutely identical with those of the Celts, their further evolution not only fails to show any signs of shifting to diatonic harmony but, on the contrary, manifests a very original, though not quite conscious, tendency towards the formation of a perfectly independent

---

* In spite of the French origin of the term *Faux-bourdon,* English priority of use of the harmonic principle it implies is now established beyond any doubt (see, for instance, *The Mys-* *tery of Faux-bourdon solved,* by Charles van den Borren, published in *The Musical Times,* April 1, 1929; London).

EXAMPLE 20:

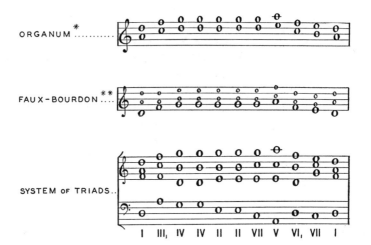

I   III,   IV   IV   II   II   VII   V   VI,   VII   I

(infra-diatonic) harmonic system. This tendency is naturally connected with their persevering use of the infra-diatonic scale, which has been especially

* As the harmonizations of the old Celtic (infra-diatonic) melodies, according to the principle of strict Organum, did not come down to our times, we are compelled to use here the "diatonic" example from the well known Medieval treatise entitled *Musica Enchiriadis*—once ascribed to Hucbald, the learned Flemish monk (840-931), but now recognized to be a work dating, at the earliest, from the second half of the tenth century (see *Hucbald's echte und unechte Schriften* von Hans Müller, 1884) probably by Otger or Odo, abbot of St. Pons de Tomières in Provence—and published in the *Scriptores ecclesiastici de musica sacra potissimum* by Martin Gerbert (1784, Vol. I). The modern notation of this example is given here according to H. Riemann *(Geschichte der Musiktheorie im IX-XIX Jahrhundert,* Seite 29) and is merely transcribed in the Treble Clef. Musical manuscripts with *strict Organum* as applied to Celtic melodies being lacking, its practical use in those days and in association with these very melodies is indirectly proved by a somewhat later document—one of the Oxford Bodleian library manuscripts dating back to the eleventh century (according to Wooldridge, p. 91) and having for its text a part of the Hymn of St. Stephen—which was published by the Plainsong and Medieval Music Society in England (*The Musical Notation of the Middle Ages,* 1890, and *Early English Harmony,* V. I. 1897, v. II 1913, under the heading *Ut tuo propiciatus*). This piece of music has been carefully analyzed by Oscar Fleischer (*Vierteljahrsschrift für Musikwissenschaft,* v. VI, page 424, Leipzig, 1890) who not only opines that it is based on the pentatonic (infra-diatonic) scale despite a few digressions from the latter but who, moreover, believes it to be a sort of adaptation of a Gaelic folk song for ecclesiastic purposes—a method not infrequently resorted to, as is known, by church composers of that and even of much later periods. The two-part harmonization of this composition, representing a specimen of the so-called *experimental* or *irregular Organum,* is infra-diatonic to the same extent as the melody itself, about half of all its harmonic combinations consisting of Fourths and Fifths, sometimes in characteristic parallel progressions, the rest of them—Thirds, Sixths and even Seconds —already showing a certain digression towards diatonic harmony in accordance with the melody occasionally tending towards the diatonic scale.

** This example represents the strictest form of Faux-bourdon, which consists of a chain of chords of the Sixth ensuing from and returning to a common chord in its root position with the Third omitted. However, in the very earliest examples of Faux-bourdon recently discovered by Dom Anselm Hughes (work quoted above on page 67) and belonging to the thirteenth century, one may already observe the occasional use of a few regular Triads in their root positions and without any omissions, showing a latent tendency towards the next stage of harmonic development, as outlined in our text.

stressed by the introduction of Equal Temperament among the Siamese, and it is chiefly expressed by the fact that the interval of a Fourth (infra-Third)— strictly speaking the sole consonance in this scale besides its inversion and the Octave which is the inversion of the Unison—tends to become the formative unit of their more complex harmonic constructions, in the same manner as the Third became the formative unit of all harmonic constructions in the diatonic system.

   True, the actual process of harmonic complication proceeds very slowly among the Far-Eastern peoples, and it cannot be doubted that this is chiefly due to their general predilection for constant symbolic canonisation of once established rules. This negative factor is so significant and powerful among the Orientals that it must always be taken into account in those departments of their many-sided culture where leisureliness in development gives the impression that matters are at a standstill.

When the earliest signs of harmonic combinations appeared in Chinese music—first, probably, in the form of sporadically encountered intervals of perfect Fourths (infra-Thirds)—the chief anxiety of Chinese scholars was to find for them an appropriate symbolic justification. This was easily done, in that the tones constituting the interval of a perfect infra-Third (C-F, for instance) belong to two opposite mystic principles—Male and Female—according to which the twelve Chinese "lüs" are distinguished (See Ex. 6); therefore they figured that the blending of these two tones must be recognized as natural and harmonious.

But, as is usually the case, the Chinese did not confine themselves to the mere symbolic justification of the interval indicated and to the simple recognition of its naturalness and harmoniousness, but set up a dangerous precedent by proclaiming this primitive harmonic combination as an *inviolable principle,* to be used by musicians as a permanent and undisputed guide for all harmonizations.

It is immediately evident, however, that the systematic application of this principle in musical practice was instantly confronted by a certain difficulty, since the structure of the infra-diatonic scale precludes the possibility of continuous accompaniment of all its degrees by intervals of perfect infra-Thirds. The Table of Intervals given in the preceding chapter (Example 19) clearly shows that when harmonizing the infra-diatonic scale by consecutive (parallel) infra-Thirds, one of its five (regular) degrees forms the interval of a diminished infra-Third F-A. This interval, apart from its undoubted unsatisfactoriness for the Chinese musical ear,* could not be admitted in their music for the reason alone

---

  * As is known, the major Third was considered a dissonance also in Western Medieval music, when *Organum,* which originated with the Celts, was exclusively in use. This interval was accepted as an imperfect consonance towards the close of the twelfth century and was theoretically formulated as such by Franco of Cologne in his treatise published under the title *Compendium Magistri Franconis.*

that its two component tones embody only one and the same mystic principle (See Ex. 6) and therefore do not fulfill the indispensable symbolic requirements for a legitimate harmonic combination.

In order to overcome this difficulty and avoid the forbidden interval, the Chinese resorted to a quite original method of harmonization (at least for that time), which consisted in the simultaneous performance of the melody and its accompaniment in two different keys a perfect infra-Third apart. In this way, every degree of the original key, in which the melody moved, was accompanied by the very same degree of another key in which, therefore, this melody constantly proceeded a perfect infra-Third below, as will be seen from the following example representing a fragment from the Hymn to Confucius, harmonized by the Chinese:

EXAMPLE 21:

Should the same fragment be harmonized within the boundaries of a single key, as musical logic dictates but Chinese symbolism precludes, it would form the following series of consecutive infra-Thirds (perfect and diminished):

EXAMPLE 22:

It is impossible to establish at present how long the "bi-infra-tonal" method of harmonization (demonstrated in Ex. 21) was applied by the Chinese, but there is reason to believe that the simultaneous tending of one and the same melody to two different Tonics did not fully satisfy them, for in some other and apparently later harmonizations they endeavored to avoid the proscribed interval of a diminished infra-Third without leaving the boundaries of a single key.

In these new harmonizations the Chinese, it appears, took as their starting point that if one of the degrees (A) of their scale forms the forbidden interval F-A, when accompanied by infra-Thirds from *below*, then the same degree (A) would form the requisite and "legitimate" interval A-D if accompanied by infra-Thirds from *above*. It is obvious, however, that with the continuous accompaniment of the melody from below, the latter interval could be used only in its inverted form (D-A) i.e. as a perfect infra-Fourth.

The following fragment from the Hymn in honor of Ancestors, published like the preceding one in M. COURANT's work, exemplifies such a "mono-infra-tonal" harmonization in which, instead of the interval of a diminished infra-Third F-A, prohibited by the Chinese, the above inversion of a perfect infra-Third, i.e. the interval D-A, is used throughout, incidentally giving a certain variety, as compared with the inevitable parallel progressions continuously applied heretofore. To facilitate the comparison of different musical examples, they are all transposed here into keys containing no sharps or flats:

EXAMPLE 23: *

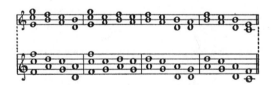

An attempt at further harmonic complication in Chinese music may be illustrated by a fragment of the Hymn to Confucius in which the melody is

---

* There can hardly be any doubt that the initial infra-diatonic harmonizations of the Celts, which we can now merely conjecture from their vague medieval descriptions, must have followed very closely the principle of harmonization given in this example, since this principle is unavoidably determined by the very structure of the infra-diatonic scale which, as explained, precludes the continuous progressions "by Fourths" characteristic of the early "continental" Organum.

identical with the one demonstrated above (Ex. 21 and 22) but which is apparently harmonized by a different Chinese author. This fragment is rendered into Western notation by G. E. MOULE, who published it full-scored as a supplement to his article describing a certain religious festival in China.* I have, however, grouped together within one stave all that sounds in unison:

EXAMPLE 24:

This example immediately attracts attention because of the fact that, at first glance, it seems simultaneously to embody both principles of harmonization analyzed above. Indeed, note A of the melody (second measure) which would form the forbidden interval F-A if harmonized by consecutive infra-Thirds (Ex. 22), is accompanied by note E in the part of the first lute (accentuated time) as well as in the part of the organ (an octave down), that is, just as is required by the "bi-infra-tonal" harmonization (Ex. 21). In the meantime, the very same note (A) is accompanied, in the part of the second lute, by the inversion of the *upper* infra-Third (D), i.e. in the manner prescribed by "mono-infra-tonal" harmonization (Ex. 23). In reality, however, this entirely new and supposedly "mechanical" aggregation of three different notes D-E-A (e) simply represents one of the inversions of a quite organic and somewhat complicated chord formed by infra-Thirds, E-A-D, with its Root doubled an Octave higher.

This single example would, of course, be insufficient for any positive conclusions regarding the harmonic tendencies of the Chinese, were it not for the fact that the very same chords are found among the simultaneous tonal combinations indicated on the pipes of the modern Chinese organ (*Shêng*) which, as is known, belongs to the sacred musical instruments and is secure, therefore,

---

* *Notes of half-yearly sacrifice to Confucius* by G. E. Moule (Journal of the China Branch of the Royal Asiatic Society, 1899-1900).

from individual arbitrariness on the part of its manufacturers. These "harmonic indications" on the *Shêng* were not always the same and, to all appearance, have been varied by the Chinese at different musical periods in accordance with the general evolution of their harmonic "flair." Thus, in the comparatively early period of their harmonized music (scarcely prior to the sixteenth century of our era), the indications on the *Shêng*—containing, at that time, twelve pipes within each octave—consisted practically of perfect Fourths and Fifths (infra-Thirds and infra-Fourths):

EXAMPLE 25:

In this, as well as in the next two examples, the heavy notes indicate the full set of tones produced by the instrument while the small notes represent the tones with which the former ought to be harmonically combined.

At a later period the construction of the *Shêng* was considerably simplified, the number of its pipes, within an octave, being reduced to seven or eight. But its "harmonic indications" became slightly more complicated, as may be seen from the following example in which, besides the previously absent Octave duplications (added to a Fourth or a Fifth) there is found one entirely new combination C-A (major infra-Fifth) which we shall discuss later:

EXAMPLE 26:

These indications of chords are taken down from a *Shêng* acquired in 1901 by A. C. MOULE, the author of a very substantial work on Chinese musical instruments,* but the same harmonic combinations were already given on the instruments of the eighteenth century.

The *Shêng* which I personally purchased in China in 1922, and which is almost identical, in technical structure, with the one described by the above writer, lacks the newly introduced infra-Fifth C-A but, on the other hand, it

---

* *Chinese Musical Instruments* by A. C. Moule (Journal of the North China Branch of the Royal Asiatic Society, 1908).

contains, besides usual Fourths and Fifths (infra-Thirds and infra-Fourths), indications of chords consisting of three different notes, similarly to the chord found in a harmonization already examined (Ex. 24), viz.:*

EXAMPLE 27:

The existence of these chords in Chinese music, aside from any sort of theoretical premises, already tells us that not only the primitive interval of a perfect Fourth (infra-Third), but also the more complex harmonic formations arranged in their root position by Fourths (infra-Thirds), respond to some innate need of the Chinese musical mind.

However, the practical application by the Chinese of all their harmonic constructions lacks a solid basis, for they have not yet worked out a true system of Harmony with a firmly established correlation of chords and rules governing the progression of parts. That is why they avoid the simplest infra-diatonic dissonances in their harmonizations (partly, as stated, for religious considerations), and very seldom use their more complicated three-tone chords (Ex. 24 and 27) which, in these cases, seem always to have a uniform disposition of parts, probably the one that is physiologically least "dissonant" to their ear.

It is difficult, at present, fully to picture the form which the Chinese system of Harmony will acquire in the future, but some outline of it can be gathered even from the scanty data which foretell its advent and which predetermine its development.

We may, for instance, state as fairly probable that the interval of a Fourth (infra-Third) will remain, for the Chinese, the formative unit of all their chords. This follows not only from their practical tendencies but no less from the very structure of the infra-diatonic scale which, within the limit of its regular degrees, precludes the formation of most intervals except Seconds and Fourths (infra-Seconds and infra-Thirds) and their inversions. It is evident that of these two simple intervals of the infra-diatonic scale—not counting their inversions—only the Fourth (infra-Third) has a chance of filling the above function.

* The author thinks it necessary to add that at his request these indications were carved on the pipes of the Shêng in intelligible notation— as a matter of fact in Arabic figures showing the numbers of pipes subject to harmonic blending —and, above all, the chords themselves were played through, for verification, by the seller of this instrument. Incidentally, all this was possible through the courtesy of Mr. N. J. Moosa, Shanghai resident and musician, who took the trouble to accompany the author to the Chinese slums of that city and to explain to the Chinaman in his native language (the only one he knew) what was required of him.

Thus, in the field of chord formations we come across additional evidence of similarity between the diatonic and infra-diatonic musical systems. Indeed, as the Third fills the function of a formative unit with reference to the chords of the former of these systems, so does the infra-Third fill an analogous function with reference to the chords of the latter. And although these two intervals are acoustically incongruent, yet in both instances they invariably cover the space occupied by *three* contiguous regular degrees of their respective scales. Hence, it is clear that the chords of these scales having no affinity in their tonal constitution, but being constructed of Thirds in one instance and of infra-Thirds in the other, are similar in their *formal* structure.

Adopting, as a starting point, this general principle of harmonic formations of the infra-diatonic scale, let us first try to determine the structure of its common (consonant) chords.

Should we formally construct them like the common chords of the diatonic scale, i.e. taking three tones arranged by infra-Thirds from each regular degree of the infra-diatonic scale, we would obtain a series of five chords, three of them comprising—in consecutive order and between their extremes—the intervals D-C, G-F and A-G, which even in the more complicated diatonic scale are undeniably considered as dissonances. Hence we may conclude without undue risk that the harmonic combinations of three tones arranged by infra-Thirds cannot serve as consonant chords in the infra-diatonic scale, since these chords must contain no dissonant intervals.

Much more probable, therefore, will be the supposition that the harmonic combinations of two notes at an interval of a perfect Fourth (infra-Third), so frequently encountered in the music of the Far East, represent the already *complete* consonant chords of the infra-diatonic scale in which, conformably to its smaller tonal constitution as compared with the diatonic scale, a less complicated harmonic basis would seem quite normal, that is, a *Dyad* instead of our Western *Triad*.

In accordance with this, we shall now form a series of Dyads and their inversions from every regular degree of the infra-diatonic scale. These Dyads, being governed as regards formal structure by the general and already known principle of chord-construction, will evidently coincide with the previously demonstrated intervals of infra-Thirds (Ex. 19) while their inversions, one only for each chord, will coincide with the intervals of infra-Fourths encountered on the different degrees of this scale. [See Ex. 28.]

Of these five chords, four have a perfectly identical structure and, in accordance with the intervals they form, may be named *perfect Dyads*. The one remaining chord should accordingly be named *diminished Dyad*.

Perfect or consonant Dyads have the same musical meaning in the infra-

EXAMPLE 28:

TABLE OF DYADS

diatonic scale as have consonant Triads in the diatonic scale, while the diminished Dyad corresponds, in the same sense, to our dissonant diminished Triad. Unlike the consonant Triads of the diatonic scale, distinguished as major and minor, the consonant Dyads of the infra-diatonic scale have no equivalent subdivision because of the uniformity of their component perfect infra-Thirds.

We can now more readily understand the unfavorable attitude of the Chinese towards the interval F-A, expressed under the guise of a symbolic dogma in their primitive rules of Harmony. For, inasmuch as this interval represents a dissonant diminished Dyad, its avoidance in their initial and simplest harmonizations cannot be regarded otherwise as most natural. And it was only the original *method* of this avoidance ("bi-infra-tonality") which of course was entirely wrong.

As to the preferred way of replacing this dissonant Dyad (F-A)—at a later period—by an inversion of one of the consonant Dyads, viz. by the interval D-A, it not only appears to be theoretically quite proper but it can also somehow be justified from a purely musical point of view. Indeed, owing to the fact that this substitution was practiced exclusively in the sacred music of the Chinese, in which the length of each note of the melody is approximately equal to a full Western note in a slow tempo, the harmonization even of a single note by the chord F-A, dissonant to Chinese ears, would give the impression of being utterly illogical, for the resolution of this chord into a consonant Dyad would actually occur too late to allow one to guess at an harmonic connection between them.

But in popular Chinese music which, unlike sacred music, is characterized by unusual mobility, the dissonant diminished Dyad is sometimes encountered among the multitude of perfect Dyads. As an example of such harmonization we shall refer to a brief fragment from one of the phonograms found in the aforementioned work by E. Fischer.* In the following representation it is furnished only with additional three-line notation, the diminished Dyad being marked by an arrow:

*Beitrage zur Erforschung der Chinesischen Musik von Erich Fischer (Leipzig, 1910).

EXAMPLE 29:

In citing this fragment, it may not be amiss to make a reservation to the effect that the popular music of the Chinese represents—as a rule—too uncertain a material to be used for any positive conclusions in regard to Chinese Harmony. The reason is that in this music the Chinese are as slipshod as they are scholastically pedantic in their sacred music. It is not surprising, therefore, that besides the diminished Dyad, one finds in their harmonized popular music (recorded with the aid of a phonograph) other dissonant but obviously fortuitous intervals.

Incidentally, this slipshod and, to a considerable extent, even arbitrary character of Chinese popular music, has not a little in common with the arbitrariness and fortuitousness of tonal combinations which once dominated in Western music in the form of a so-called "florid descant," virtually a free and often utterly inharmonious improvisation rendered by different vocal parts to a given fundamental "Tenor." And just as this form of composition, despite its looseness, subsequently had considerable influence upon the development of Western polyphonic music, in the same manner it is highly probable that the arbitrariness of Chinese popular music will some day acquire an orderly form and jointly with the development of theoretical knowledge, will in the long run lead to certain positive results.

This historical prognosis, however, has no very great significance for us at present. The salient point of this discussion lies solely in the theoretical determination of the principle governing the construction of chords of the infra-diatonic scale, in other words, the principle of chord-formation by infra-Thirds, which is justified by the sacred as well as by the popular music of the Chinese, notwithstanding the arbitrariness of the latter.

This basic principle being firmly established, the formation of more complicated chords is simply a matter of imposing, upon the common chord, new infra-Thirds, similarly to the familiar imposing of Thirds upon the common chord of the diatonic scale. Thus, the chord which immediately follows the Dyad in order of complexity will be composed of three notes arranged by infra-

Thirds and will correspond, in musical significance, to the chord composed of four notes by diatonic Thirds, just as the Dyad and the Triad musically correspond to each other in their respective scales. And as the diatonic chords composed of four notes borrow their names from the intervals comprised between their extremes and are accordingly called *Seventh-chords,* in like manner the infra-diatonic chords, composed of three notes, will borrow their names and will then obviously have to be called *infra-Fifth-chords.* Constructed from every degree of the infra-diatonic scale these new harmonic combinations will form the following series:

EXAMPLE 30:

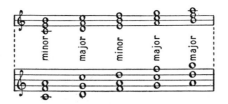

Depending on the *quality* of the infra-Fifths found between the extremes of these chords, the latter must be subdivided into major and minor *infra-Fifth-chords.*

Attention should also be paid to the fact that the minor infra-Fifth-chords formed on different degrees are distinguished from each other by the arrangement of the Dyads they comprise. Thus, for instance, the minor infra-Fifth-chord C-F-A contains the diminished Dyad (F-A) at the end, while the minor infra-Fifth-chord F-A-D contains the very same Dyad at the beginning. In this respect their structure bears a certain resemblance to the diatonic dominant Seventh-chord (G-B-D-F) and the Seventh-chord on the leading note (B-D-F-A), of which the former ends and the latter begins with the diminished Triad (B-D-F).

We have already had occasion to observe that so far the major infra-Fifth-chords are used by the Chinese only in a single and more or less permanent inverted form (Ex. 24 and 27). As to the minor infra-Fifth-chords, one of their very rare instances, at least in the sacred music of the Chinese, is found among the chords of the Shêng demonstrated above (Ex. 26), where it is represented in the form of an harmonic combination C-A. This may be considered as an incomplete minor infra-Fifth chord with its middle note (F) omitted, the latter circumstance being explained by the rejection, in Chinese sacred music, of the interval F-A, which would be automatically formed by this note. Such an explanation is all the more plausible since the notes C-A, constituting the above minor infra-Fifth-chord in its incomplete form, belong to two different mystic principles (see Ex. 6); their simultaneous blending, therefore, does not conflict with the musico-symbolic code of the Chinese.

With the innumerable and customary infra-Thirds and infra-Fourths which are used in music written for solo performance on the lute *Ch'in*, one occasionally finds the above incomplete form of the minor infra-Fifth-chord, although in a greatly extended position (c'-a'''). Quite as rarely the extended inversion of this incomplete chord (a'-c'') is also encountered. Besides these harmonic combinations one sometimes comes across the interval of a minor infra-Seventh (c'-d'') which may be taken as an incomplete form of the already familiar inversion of the major infra-Fifth-chord with the middle note (g') omitted, and, finally, one finds the intervals of a diminished infra-Third (f'-a') and of a diminished infra-Eighth (f'-a''), proscribed in the early sacred music of the Chinese, which simply represent one and the same diminished Dyad in its close and extended positions, respectively.* All these dissonant infra-diatonic chords (some of them probably used merely in the form of natural harmonics or "flageolets") are found in musical fragments rendered into Western notation by M. Courant, and in all likelihood were introduced in music for the *Ch'in* in the nineteenth century.

If we now group together all the harmonic combinations ever used in the sacred and semi-sacred music of the Chinese—the latter refers to music for the *Ch'in*—and barring, for the reasons given, the entire material furnished by their popular music, we shall obtain the collection represented in a classified form on the following page (Ex. 31).

This collection of harmonic combinations is witness to the fact that infra-Fifth-chords represent the apex of harmonic complexity at present accessible to the musical mind of the Chinese who, through sporadic and specific use of these chords, intuitively grope for the hitherto barely tapped musical resources of the infra-diatonic scale. But theoretically it is of course possible to build up, within this scale, still more complicated chords which in time may perhaps also find practical realization in the music of the Chinese, although this is hardly to be expected before a scientifically evolved system of Harmony is mastered and adopted by them.

To these more complex harmonic constructions first belong the *infra-Seventh-*

---

* It may be opportune to add here that although music for the *Ch'in* is not considered quite sacred among the Chinese, yet its conservatively aristocratic origin guarantees us to a great extent from elements of fortuitousness and arbitrariness as regards the theoretical data we are interested in and that are found in this music. As is known, the amateurs from the aristocratic class represent the most highly educated and cultured group of musicians in China, while the vast majority of professional musicians, with but few exceptions, are rated as artisans, in the worst sense of the word.

EXAMPLE 31:

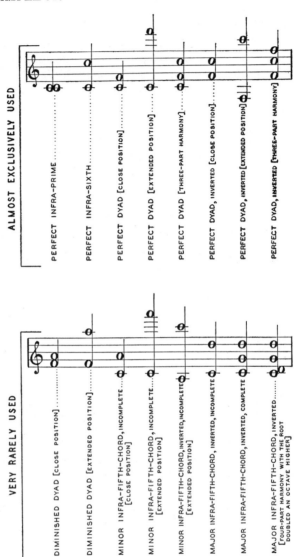

chords which are formed by the imposition of an infra-Third upon every one
of the infra-Fifth-chords and which, like the latter, borrow their name from
the interval found between their extremes:

EXAMPLE 32:

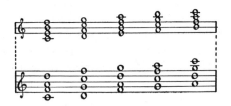

—and finally, the *infra-Ninth-chords* which cover all the five regular degrees of the infra-diatonic scale:

EXAMPLE 33:

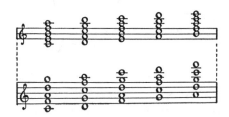

The imposition of one more infra-Third upon any one of these chords will not produce any new harmonic constructions but will merely recommence the cycle of intervals forming the chords of the infra-diatonic scale, as takes place with the chords of the Thirteenth in the diatonic scale.

With a knowledge of the formal structure of the infra-diatonic chords as well as of the principle of their fundamental classification as concords and discords, it is now possible also to lay down with a fair amount of certainty the elementary rules of harmonization of infra-diatonic melodies.

The reservation must be made, however, from the very beginning, that for this particular purpose no use whatever can be made of the Chinese musical material which stood us in good stead before. The reason for this is that the harmonic intuition of the Chinese, which so far correctly suggested to them merely the *structure* of certain chords characteristic of the infra-diatonic scale, is still too primitive to reveal to them the much more complicated *laws of their interrelation and of their functions,* this being an indispensable condition of any strictly substantiated harmonization.

But inasmuch as these laws are potentially contained within the infra-diatonic scale, they may be disclosed in another way. We have already had occasion to observe that the very structure of this scale predetermines to a great extent the formal structure of its chords. Let us now try then—bearing this in mind—to discover the laws of this scale that predetermine the progression of its chords.

In this respect, of great assistance to us is a very valuable property of the infra-diatonic scale (which the diatonic scale also possesses), namely, the undeniable tonal gravitation of its component degrees towards a common center, known as the Tonic. This property obviously extends also to the chords of the scale in question that are based on its different degrees. Thus, for instance, the central position of the Tonic *C* will be shared by the *tonic Dyad* C-F-(c) to which, therefore, all the rest of the Dyads must tend.

Furthermore it will be realized that the two degrees of the infra-diatonic scale (A and D) which are immediately adjacent to the Tonic (C) and which consequently represent the upper and lower leading notes of this scale, will tend to that Tonic more strongly than the rest of the degrees. Hence the chord A-D-(a), comprising both these degrees, is evidently the one which will tend to the tonal center in a most definite way, and which must occupy, therefore, the position of the *dominant Dyad*. In strict progressions of chords, it will naturally resolve into the tonic Dyad.

Before proceeding with our discussion on this particular subject, it is now necessary to digress slightly and to give, somewhat belatedly, a technical nomenclature of the regular degrees of the infra-diatonic scale—which was impossible, however, until the Dominant had been established—so as to be able to designate from now on the Dyads that are based on them. And since two of these degrees have already acquired the names of Tonic and of Dominant, only three degrees are left to which appropriate names have to be attached.

According to its position the degree found immediately above the Tonic will be called *Hypertonic* (I have purposely replaced the customary Latin prefix "super" by its Greek synonym "hyper"). The name of *Subdominant* will be assigned to the degree which is found immediately below the Dominant. Finally the name of *Mediant* will be given to the degree which lies half-way (whence the name) between the Tonic and the Dominant, i.e. actually between the Hypertonic and the Subdominant.

This conventional nomenclature applied to the degrees of the infra-diatonic scale and to the corresponding chords based on them, will be properly understood in connection with the following musical representation, provided with Roman numerals which will also be used, as indicators of degrees, in all the subsequent examples of this chapter:

EXAMPLE 34:

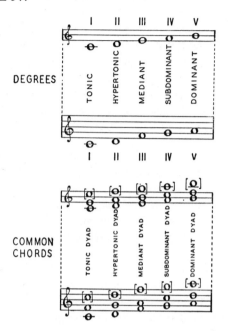

The tonic Dyad jointly with the dominant Dyad comprises four notes (C,D,F,A) of the infra-diatonic scale and, consequently, may be used as a medium for their harmonization. The only remaining note (G) should be harmonized either by the hypertonic Dyad or by the subdominant Dyad, both of which include it. Each of these two Dyads may precede, and resolve into, the dominant Dyad which, in turn, resolves, as we know, into the tonic Dyad.

By means of the chords enumerated, exhausting all the perfect (consonant) Dyads, any infra-diatonic melody could of course be harmonized in an elementary way, just as any diatonic melody could be similarly harmonized by means of the consonant Triads. At the same time it should be well understood that this possibility does not exclude, from infra-diatonic harmonizations, the dissonant chords as well as the whole set of additional and commonly known means that diversify and embellish the harmonic tissue. In fact, the writer has availed himself of all these potentialities in harmonizing two genuine infra-diatonic melodies which are offered for judgment at the end of this chapter. These harmonizations are only preceded by a series of isolated examples demonstrating the progression of parts of the various infra-diatonic chords as they are being connected in different combinations.

There is no doubt that many fundamental principles of part-progression established in the diatonic system of Harmony ought to be adopted for (strict) harmonizations of infra-diatonic melodies. Thus, for instance, it follows as a matter of course that the rule of holding the common notes of different chords within the same parts, as well as that of smooth and preferably "stepwise" progression of the rest of the parts, will apply to both these systems. The progression of *all* the parts in one direction (similar motion) must likewise be carefully avoided, while the distance exceeding an Octave (infra-Sixth) between all the contiguous parts, exclusive of the Bass, should be allowed only in exceptional cases.

As to the consecutive (parallel) progression of perfect consonances, their exclusion concerns here only the infra-Primes and infra-Sixths (Primes and Octaves) but not the infra-Fourths (perfect Fifths), since the latter merely represent inverted infra-Thirds for which parallel progression is as much a characteristic as it is for the Thirds of the diatonic scale and their inversions.

The lesser tonal constitution of the infra-diatonic Dyad, in comparison to the diatonic Triad, makes *three-part harmony* normal in the infra-diatonic system just as *four-part harmony* is normal in the diatonic system. However, the preferable duplication of the root, though desirable within the chords of both systems, cannot be carried out with extreme rigidity with respect to the Dyad, on account of the too limited tonal constitution of this chord. The latter circumstance also greatly reduces the number of the various positions and inversions of the Dyad, which are practically exhausted by the following combinations:

EXAMPLE 35:

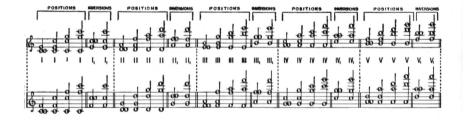

In this as in all subsequent examples, the inversions of chords are designated by small Arabic figures to the right of the Roman numerals which, in turn, indicate, as already stated, the degrees of the infra-diatonic scale.

Entering now upon that part of our subject dealing with the progression of Dyads taken from different degrees of this scale, let us avail ourselves of the following general scheme visually distributing all these chords in the order of their mutual contact through common notes:

EXAMPLE 36:

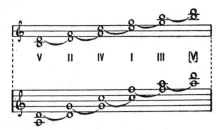

This example readily shows that the tonic and dominant Dyads (I and V)—representing, by the way, in their root position, the main material for the full and half cadences—have no common notes. Accordingly, they will permit, the above rules being observed, the following instances of proper chordal progressions:

EXAMPLE 37:

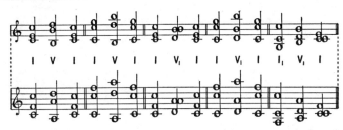

The tonic and subdominant Dyads (I and IV) have one common note which, however, greatly limits the number of acceptable progressions, when the inversions of these chords are used:

EXAMPLE 38:

The subdominant and dominant Dyads (IV and V) have no common notes and allow the following instances of quite good progressions:

EXAMPLE 39:

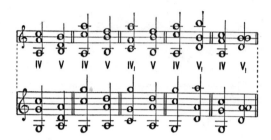

The succession of subdominant, dominant and tonic Dyads (IV, V and I), jointly covering all five tones of the infra-diatonic scale, will rather definitely reveal the character of the infra-mode applied:

EXAMPLE 40:

The hypertonic Dyad (II) is not a "secondary" one in the infra-diatonic system, and therefore is of no less importance than the subdominant Dyad (IV) in the matter of characterization of one infra-mode or another. It is connected with every one of the foregoing Dyads in the following manner:

EXAMPLE 41:

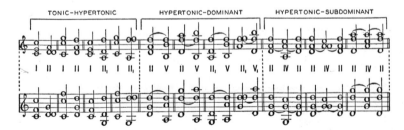

Being used instead of the subdominant Dyad (IV) in the cadence-like conclusions, similarly to the ones demonstrated in Ex. 40, the hypertonic Dyad
(II) will give somewhat different versions of these passages:

EXAMPLE 42:

But the character of any given infra-mode will be revealed with *emphasized*
precision if the two Dyads (II and IV) are used in either succession before the
full cadence:

EXAMPLE 43:

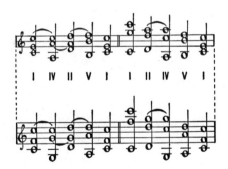

A certain variety in harmonization may be obtained through the occasional
and discreet insertion of the dissonant diminished Dyad which, however, similarly to the diminished Triad of the diatonic scale, should be used preferably
in its inverted form. The following example represents the best manner of
connecting this dissonant Dyad (which, by the way, is a mediant Dyad in the
infra-mode "C-c" analyzed herein) with every consonant Dyad:

EXAMPLE 44:

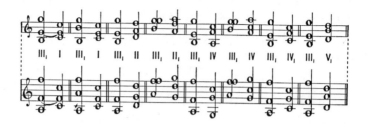

In addition to the various chordal progressions shown in the above set of examples, we shall give a few in which all five Dyads of the infra-diatonic scale are represented:

EXAMPLE 45:

As to the more complicated harmonic formations within the infra-diatonic scale, the most essential of them will be the chord of the dominant infra-Fifth ($\overset{5}{V}$) whose significance here will be similar to the dominant Seventh-chord of the diatonic scale. This new chord ($\overset{5}{V}$) being composed of three different notes (arranged by infra-Thirds), it is clear that none of them will be duplicated in normal three-part harmony. Furthermore, because of such a constitution, this chord ($\overset{5}{V}$) will give two inversions ($\overset{5}{V_1}$ and $\overset{5}{V_2}$) instead of one, as produced by a Dyad. The following example shows the chord of the dominant infra-Fifth together with its two inversions in various positions:

EXAMPLE 46:

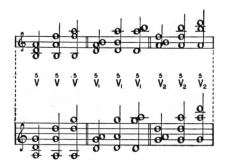

Inasmuch as this chord represents a clearly expressed dominant harmony, it will in most cases precede the tonic Dyad with which the following forms of connection would be feasible:

EXAMPLE 47:

It is noteworthy that the second inversion of the chord of the dominant infra-Fifth ($\overset{5}{V}_2$) resolves not into the root position of the tonic Dyad but into its first inversion (I_1), and, in this respect, it recalls the last inversion of the dominant Seventh-chord of the diatonic scale (chord of the Second) which resolves into one of the inversions of the tonic Triad (chord of the Sixth).

The Subdominant Dyad (IV), when preceding the chord of the dominant infra-Fifth ($\overset{5}{V}$) — oftenest in concluding passages — will permit a "preparation" of the dissonant interval of an infra-Fifth. The same preparation may be effected with the similar utilization of the hypertonic Dyad (II) which has two notes in common with the chord of the infra-Fifth ($\overset{5}{V}$):

EXAMPLE 48:

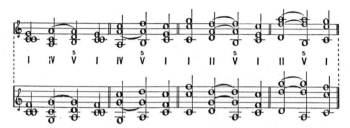

The chords of the infra-Fifth formed on other degrees are subject, when connected with various Dyads, to the same rules of part-progression as is the chord of the dominant infra-Fifth:

EXAMPLE 49:

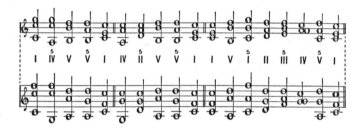

Different chords of the infra-Fifth may also connect between themselves, thereby forming sequence-like passages, similarly to the Seventh-chords of the diatonic scale:

EXAMPLE 50:

As regards the still more complex chords of the infra-diatonic scale, i.e. the chords of the infra-Seventh ($\overset{7}{V}$) and of the infra-Ninth ($\overset{9}{V}$), composed of four and five notes respectively, it is understood that under the conditions of three-part harmony, one note in the former of these chords and two notes in the latter must be omitted. In the chord of the infra-Seventh ($\overset{7}{V}$) the most characteristic intervals of the infra-Fifth and of the infra-Seventh should remain untouched and, consequently, the infra-Third left out. In the chord of the infra-Ninth ($\overset{9}{V}$), for the same considerations, the intervals of the infra-Fifth and of the infra-Ninth should likewise remain untouched and, consequently, the infra-Third and the infra-Seventh left out.

It is advisable, before resolving any of these chords into the tonic Dyad, first to transform them into the chord of the dominant infra-Fifth ($\overset{5}{V}$). This will only require moving one of the three parts a half step up with reference to the chord of the infra-Seventh ($\overset{7}{V}$) and a whole step down where the chord of the infra-Ninth ($\overset{9}{V}$) is concerned.

EXAMPLE 51:

Suspension and Anticipation as practiced in our diatonic Harmony could also be applied to the chords of the infra-diatonic system, as shown in the following progressions:

EXAMPLE 52:

The generally known principles of the simplest modulation which are based on the community of chords belonging to different keys may be equally applied to infra-diatonic Harmony. In the following example, demonstrating an infra-diatonic modulation from *C* to *G,* the connecting link is represented by the chord a'-d'-(a'') which simultaneously appears as a dominant Dyad (V) in the former of these keys and as a hypertonic Dyad (II) in the latter:

EXAMPLE 53:

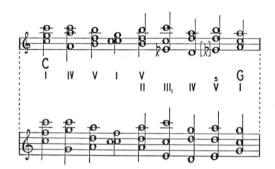

All the rules of part-progression and chordal connections illustrated above on detached examples will suffice perfectly for the practical harmonization of a pair of genuine infra-diatonic tunes, which will bring our general theory of Infra-Tonality to a logical close.

The first of these represents an example of ancient Celtic melody, a sort of "Liebestod-Gesang," whose literary content relates to the early part of the Middle Ages, being associated with certain semi-legendary names mentioned in the Fionn Saga. This song is supposed to be performed by a female voice and in very slow tempo. [The numeral indications of chords in this example are given even in those instances where the harmony evidently appears to be the result of passing notes. In the other example which follows it such notes are occasionally designated by small circles above them. The application of passing notes is too well known to be demonstrated on preliminary examples.]

EXAMPLE 54:*

* The "diatonic" harmonization of this song (with which it would be of some interest to compare our *"infra-diatonic"* harmonization) is found, under the title *The Lay of Diarmad,* in the following collection: *Songs of the Hebrides and other Celtic songs from the Highlands of Scotland,* some collected and all arranged for voice and piano by Marjorie Kennedy-Fraser (Bosey & Co., London, 1909, page 112).

The second harmonization has for its melodic material one of the most lively and popular tunes of China, which is performed all over that country in rather manifold versions but, naturally, in one and the same infra-mode "C-c":

EXAMPLE 55:

This Chinese song (in all its versions the text is invariably associated with "a fresh beautiful flower" or with a "bouquet of flowers" etc.) has been harmonized many a time—in a diatonic way of course—by different European

musicians, among them by Ambros * whose effort in this respect it is particularly worth while to present for comparison; the last few measures of this song,
left unaccompanied by the famous historian, are completed here in accordance

EXAMPLE 56:

---

* *Geschichte der Musik* von A. W. Ambros (Breslau, 1862), page 35. Another similar "diatonic" harmonization of this song may be found (under the title of *The Mou lee Flower*) in the *Characteristic Songs and Dances of all Nations* by J. D. Brown (London, 1901).

with the general style of his harmonization, and the entire composition transposed a whole step down (Ex. 56).

The suggested method of harmonization of the infra-diatonic melodies (Ex.
54 and 55) could of course be given in much greater detail and the subject considerably developed (especially with regard to the rest of the infra-modes*

* It is appropriate to make an important remark here, however, regarding the infra-mode "F-f" which, as compared to other infra-modes, has a disadvantage in that its tonic common chord (F-A) is a *diminished* (dissonant) Dyad instead of a perfect (consonant) Dyad, apparently indispensable for the purpose. It is, then, evident that this "imperfect" infra-mode, as it may be called, can hardly have any but a purely theoretical existence, similarly to the diatonic mode "B-b" which practically has no application, because its tonic common chord is a diminished Triad. Therefore, all the pentatonic tunes which are usually considered as written in the infra-mode "F-f" (for the sole reason that while having no "accidentals," they begin and, especially, end with the note F) belong, in reality, to the infra-mode "C-c," in which the note F serves as an infra-Third. It is no more unnatural for a pentatonic tune to begin and to end with an infra-Third, than it would be for a diatonic tune to begin and to end with a Third or with a Fifth in its respective mode. Indeed, should we find a diatonic tune which begins and ends with the note B and at the same time contains neither sharps nor flats, we would rarely consider it as written in the mode "B-b" (Locrian) but either in the mode "G-g" (Mixolydian) or "E-e" (Phrygian), the note B serving as a Third in the former instance and as a Fifth in the latter. We can then readily understand at this point how it happened that, when the infra-diatonic scale with the music based on it was restored by the Chinese towards the fifteenth or sixteenth century of our era, after it had been blended with the Mongolian scale during the Yüan dynasty, its ancient infra-mode "F-f" was unexpectedly changed to "C-c." The explanation is that the infra-mode "F-f" was probably never actually used, as such, in the musical practice of the Chinese, its existence in their musical system having merely a theoretical significance, since it is the very one which was originated by them in a purely acoustic way, as demonstrated at the beginning of Chapter VI. It is quite natural that before any harmonic combinations were introduced in their music, the Chinese could not realize that the tunes supposedly written in the infra-mode "F-f" belonged, in reality, to the infra-mode "C-c"; and after realizing this fact (during the Ming dynasty) they did not change, strictly speaking, one infra-mode for another but merely rectified, in an official manner, the erroneous conception of the one and the very same infra-mode which intrinsically was always "C-c," of course. The most evident proof of this theory is the original Chinese two-part harmonization of their Hymn in honor

of Ancestors (its opening verse is given in Ex. 23 of the text), whose melody more than others is suggestive (especially to an Occidental musical mind) of the infra-mode "F-f." This harmonization clearly shows, however, that the Chinese attributed it to the infra-mode "C-c." The three-part ("normal") harmonization of this Hymn by the author, which follows, will demonstrate better still that there is nothing unnatural in regarding the opening and the closing note of such a melody as a Mediant and not as a Tonic. And the fact that the melody of the third and last verse of this Hymn ends with the note C, and not F, as in the two preceding verses, may serve as additional proof of our theory. The Chinese harmonization of this concluding note by the subdominant, instead of the tonic Dyad, is easily explained by their avoidance of inverted chords at the close of a composition, which would be inevitable under the condition of two-part harmony as it was applied by them. However, under the condition of three-part harmony the use of a tonic Dyad in its root position is not only possible but is most natural and logical. [The complete Chinese harmonization of this Hymn is found in Maurice Courant's work, already quoted].

FIRST
VERSE

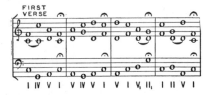

I IV V I V IV V I V I V₁ II₁ I II V I

I₁ V I V₁ I IV₁ II I₁ V I V₁ IV II₁ IV V I

CLOSING MEASURE
OF THE
THIRD VERSE

I IV V₁ I

and, most of all, to the infra-chromatically altered chords which have not been discussed in any way), but the writing of an *exhaustive* manual on infra-diatonic Harmony is somewhat outside the range of the present work. This subject has been touched upon here only in so far as was necessary, in the course of general exposition, to prove the theoretical and practical validity of a harmonization not going beyond the tonal limits of the infra-diatonic scale and, therefore, preserving the psychological unity between harmony and melody.

It would not be exaggerated to state that all existing harmonizations of Chinese and Celtic (pentatonic) tunes sin against this very unity, as they invariably represent an adaptation of diatonic harmony to the infra-diatonic melody which, practically, is an artificial combination of two fundamentally different musical principles, as is very evident from the above example (56). As a matter of fact, all the arrangers who are responsible for these unsuitable harmonizations are repeating the grave mistake (but in reverse order) formerly admitted by medieval theorists who used to adapt infra-diatonic harmony—though in the primitive form of an *Organum*—to diatonic melodies.

It is beyond all doubt that Chinese and Celtic tunes lose their characteristic qualities considerably, if not entirely, in the garments of diatonic harmony, as the latter radically changes our perception of the infra-diatonic scale on which these tunes are based, transforming it into a "diatonic scale with two semitones omitted," which, of course, psychologically does not come to the same thing. There can be found in Western music a good many melodies unquestionably diatonic in which the two semitones are not encountered and which, consequently, could be played upon the five basic notes of the infra-diatonic scale. Nevertheless, these melodies, as a rule, are not perceived as if they were based on this scale. The reason is that although both semitones are actually absent in such melodies, yet they are, so to speak, potentially present, being suggested by the diatonic harmony which accompanies them.

As one of the best examples in this respect, we may cite Wagner's motif from "Feuerzauber," already mentioned on a former occasion, in which the two absent notes (F and B)—from the standpoint of the diatonic scale—are most evidently manifest in the accompanying harmony (Ex. 57^a). On the other hand, the very same melody has but to be harmonized according to infra-diatonic rules, and its original character will instantly change, acquiring a certain primitive touch not in the least typical of Wagner's music (Ex. 57^b).

Other diatonic melodies of this kind (i.e. with the two semitones omitted), when similarly treated, not only fall into primitiveness but, in many cases, also acquire a rather marked Chinese character. The well-known theme from Tschaikowsky's *Pathetic* Symphony re-harmonized in infra-diatonic fashion (Ex. 58^b) and placed side by side with its original diatonic version (transposed

EXAMPLE 57:

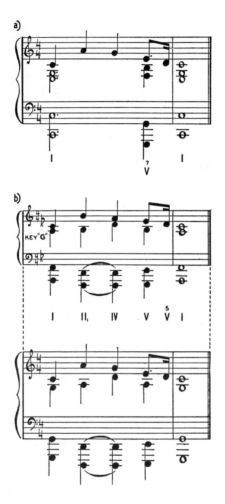

for convenience in Ex. 58ᵃ) may serve as a good illustration of such transformation. [See following page].

From what has been said it is clear that an adequate comprehension of Chinese or ancient Celtic songs is possible to Western nations, at present, only by
padding the contours of the infra-diatonic scale—which underlies these songs
and which is rather alien to our ear—with a harmonization organically ensued
from it. Otherwise, these songs, even if performed in unison, will inevitably be
perceived by us (partly through force of habit) on the harmonic plane of the

EXAMPLE 58:

diatonic scale. But Chinese or Celtic melodies within the diatonic harmony are approximately the same thing as, let us say, the melodies of Palestrina in the "whole-tone" harmonic treatment of Debussy.

INTERMEDIATE PART

TONALITY

CHAPTER IX

RUDIMENTS OF THE DIATONIC SYSTEM

This part of the book sets forth, in schematic form, rudimentary facts regarding our existing diatonic system which, from the standpoint of the basic idea underlying the present work, occupies an intermediate place between the infra-diatonic and supra-diatonic musical systems evolved herein. These rudiments are inserted at this point merely for reference and, demonstrating the diatonic system (familiar to every reader, we assume) in diagrams similar to those accompanying the description of the two other systems, they may, at times, be of some assistance for a better grasp of the entire subject.

1. Keyboard illustration of the Diatonic Scale ("7 + 5"):

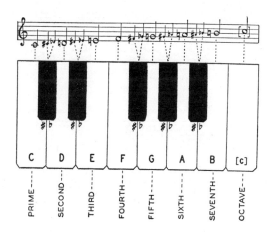

2. Diagram showing the Diatonic Scale in three different intonations: *Just Intonation* (heavy upper lines) which results from a tuning of the three principal Triads—tonic, dominant and subdominant—according to the Natural Harmonic Series (discussed later), *Pythagorean Intonation* (heavy lower lines) which results from the formation of a series of natural Fifths subsequently comprised within the compass of an Octave, and *Equally Tempered Intonation* (dotted middle lines with figures in brackets) which results from a division of the Octave into twelve equal intervals:

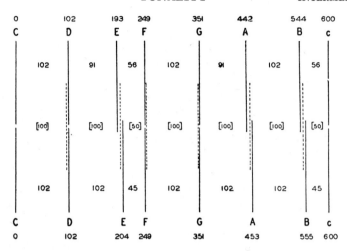

3. The seven principal modes of the Diatonic Scale:

4. The seven cycles of keys (one cycle for each mode) of the Diatonic Scale:

	KEY "C"	KEY "G"	KEY "D"	KEY "A"	KEY "E"	KEY "B"	KEY "F#"	KEY "C#"	KEY "A♭"	KEY "E♭"	KEY "B♭"	KEY "F"
MODE "C–c"												
MODE "D–d"												
MODE "E–e"												
MODE "F–f"												
MODE "G–g"												
MODE "A–a"												
MODE "B–b"												

5. Table of Intervals of the Diatonic Scale (Mode "C-c"):

	I	II	III	IV	V	VI	VII
PRIMES	0 perf.	0 perf.	0 perf.	0 perf.	0 perf.	0 perf.	0 perf.
SECONDS	1 major	1 major	$\frac{1}{2}$ minor	1 major	1 major	1 major	$\frac{1}{2}$ minor
THIRDS	2 major	$1\frac{1}{2}$ minor	$1\frac{1}{2}$ minor	2 major	2 major	$1\frac{1}{2}$ minor	$1\frac{1}{2}$ minor
FOURTHS	$2\frac{1}{2}$ perf.	$2\frac{1}{2}$ perf.	$2\frac{1}{2}$ perf.	3 aug.	$2\frac{1}{2}$ perf.	$2\frac{1}{2}$ perf.	$2\frac{1}{2}$ perf.
FIFTHS	$3\frac{1}{2}$ perf.	$3\frac{1}{2}$ perf.	$3\frac{1}{2}$ perf.	$3\frac{1}{2}$ perf.	$3\frac{1}{2}$ perf.	$3\frac{1}{2}$ perf.	3 dim.
SIXTHS	$4\frac{1}{2}$ major	$4\frac{1}{2}$ major	4 minor	$4\frac{1}{2}$ major	$4\frac{1}{2}$ major	4 minor	4 minor
SEVENTHS	$5\frac{1}{2}$ major	5 minor	5 minor	$5\frac{1}{2}$ major	5 minor	5 minor	5 minor
OCTAVES	6 perf.	6 perf.	6 perf.	6 perf.	6 perf.	6 perf.	6 perf.

6. Triads and their inversions from each degree of the Diatonic Scale:

7. Chord of the dominant Seventh and its inversions with their respective and simplest resolutions:

8. Chords of the dominant Ninth, dominant Eleventh and dominant Thirteenth with their respective resolutions:

All the chromatically altered modes, intervals and chords, as well as many other (and no less important) parts of the diatonic system are omitted here as unnecessary for immediate reference.

SECOND PART
SUPRA-TONALITY

CHAPTER X

FORMATION OF THE SUPRA-DIATONIC SCALE

The many points of similarity between the infra-diatonic and diatonic scales, as disclosed above, already inspire a certain preliminary conviction that the supra-diatonic scale being formed according to the same principle, with a proportionate increase in complexity, will display those common characteristics which will permit us to consider it as an "organic" scale to the same extent as the two former.

The common constructive schema to which the *basic* formation of the infra-diatonic and diatonic scales may be reduced is, as we already know, a series of consecutively arranged natural Fifths (see page 51). The very nature of these scales is such that, when using a similar schema for their *complete* formation, first the group of their regular degrees is (or, under certain conditions, *can* be) generated, in every instance, and only after that the group of their respective auxiliary degrees is produced, as shown by these two rows of notes:

1. Series of natural Fifths which forms the infra-diatonic scale ("5 + 2")

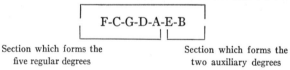

Section which forms the   Section which forms the
five regular degrees   two auxiliary degrees

2. Series of natural Fifths which forms the diatonic scale ("7 + 5")

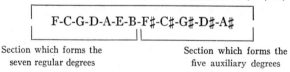

Section which forms the   Section which forms the
seven regular degrees   five auxiliary degrees

It was not difficult, of course, to find these two series of natural Fifths in regard to the infra-diatonic and diatonic scales, since we knew *beforehand* the number and arrangement of their component regular and auxiliary degrees within an octave. But obviously the same cannot be said with regard to the supra-diatonic scale, the determination of its tonal constitution within an octave being our very next problem.

This problem would be automatically solved, however, should we succeed in finding by some other way the series of natural Fifths which corresponds to the supra-diatonic scale. Of this new series of Fifths now sought we know nothing, save the fact that by virtue of its predetermined similarity with the preceding series it has to produce, in analogous sequence, first all the regular degrees of the new scale, then all its auxiliary degrees. But how find the *number* of degrees contained in each of these groups?

The answer to this pivotal question of our problem is given by the quite definite interrelation between the sections of the two above series of natural Fifths which form different groups of degrees of the infra-diatonic and diatonic scales. This interrelation is twofold and may be expressed as follows:

1. The number and arrangement of tones (by Fifths) comprised in the section which forms the group of regular degrees of the infra-diatonic scale is identical with the number and arrangement of tones comprised in the section which forms the group of auxiliary degrees of the diatonic scale (the difference in the absolute pitch of these two sets of tones is at present immaterial).

2. The general number and arrangement of tones of the entire series of natural Fifths which forms the infra-diatonic scale ("5 + 2") is identical with the number and arrangement of tones comprised in the section which forms the group of regular degrees of the diatonic scale.

Inasmuch as it is at the core of this very interrelation that lies the root of all those characteristics of both scales that make so many of their aspects similar notwithstanding their different tonal constitution, it is apparent that the principle of analogical interrelation used for the formation of the new scale will solve the above problem.

In order to apply this principle to such a formation it will be necessary to adopt the complete series of natural Fifths which forms the scale "7 + 5" as a basis for the group of regular degrees of the supra-diatonic scale, and then to adopt the initial section of this series which forms the group of regular degrees of the scale "7 + 5," as a pattern for that new section of natural Fifths (disregarding the difference in absolute pitch) which is destined to constitute the group of auxiliary degrees of the supra-diatonic scale. This entire operation is shown in the following schema:

Series of natural Fifths which forms the supra-diatonic scale ("12 + 7")

F-C-G-D-A-E-B-F♯-C♯-G♯-D♯-A♯-E♯-B♯- F♯♯-C♯♯-G♯♯-D♯♯-A♯♯

| Section which forms the twelve regular degrees | Section which forms the seven auxiliary degrees |

The quantitative interrelation of all the degrees belonging to the three scales herein discussed may be simply expressed by a specifically progressive mathematical series which will convey a clearer idea of the principle applied for the formation of the new scale:

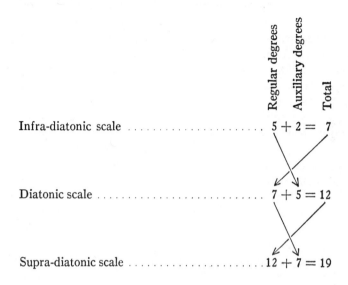

Infra-diatonic scale .... $5 + 2 = 7$

Diatonic scale .... $7 + 5 = 12$

Supra-diatonic scale .... $12 + 7 = 19$

However, neither this "quantitative" Table nor even the demonstrated series of natural Fifths of the supra-diatonic scale conveys to us an equally clear idea of the *qualitative* acoustic structure of the latter.

First and foremost it should be pointed out that the very possibility of extending the number of the twelve natural Fifths is somewhat foreign to the average musical mind accustomed at present to think of all tonal relations in their equally tempered form. For instance, the section of the above series which forms the seven auxiliary degrees (E♯-B♯-F♯♯-C♯♯-G♯♯-D♯♯-A♯♯) of the supra-diatonic scale will impress the practical musician as being no more than an exact duplication of some regular degrees (F-C-G-D-A-E-B) of the same scale, which, of course, is not actually the case where *natural* Fifths are concerned.

Furthermore, somewhat confusing may appear the exclusive application of the literal and other designations of the degrees of the *diatonic scale* ("7 + 5") in *all* three series of natural Fifths given above. As a result the group of regular degrees of the supra-diatonic scale contains a few chromatically altered notes (F♯-C♯-G♯-D♯-A♯); this, as we know, conflicting with the very notion of a *regular* degree. Again, the group of auxiliary degrees of the infra-diatonic scale is represented by independent notes (E-B) instead of their previously established and obviously more correct infra-chromatically altered equivalents (F♭-C♭). However, all the designations of various scale-degrees that will be used in this chapter are only provisional and, in spite of their inadequacy, more convenient for a general comprehension of the subject. The necessary substitution, in place of the temporarily altered notes, of independent and new letters within the group of regular degrees of the supra-diatonic scale, will be effected later on.*

Finally, it may be added that if one could at once imagine how the whole series of natural Fifths of the supra-diatonic scale will be arranged when comprised within the compass of an octave, even then one would not yet have a *full* conception of the actual structure of this scale. This is because the Pythagorean intonation which results from the construction of the supra-diatonic scale by natural Fifths deviates too perceptibly from the just (i.e. normal) intonation of the same scale, the two having practically nothing in common.

The question of just intonation of the supra-diatonic scale will be discussed at greater length in the following chapter, after the structure of the common consonant chords of this scale (a knowledge of which is indispensable for that purpose) has been disclosed. As regards the Pythagorean intonation, because of the negative property referred to, its rôle will naturally be confined solely to the general determination of the number and relative position (even though not absolutely accurate from the standpoint of just intonation) of the regular and auxiliary degrees of the supra-diatonic scale ("12 + 7"). And since the Pythagorean intonation would be of no practical use whatever, it does not matter in the least how closely, acoustically, the seven auxiliary degrees of this scale (temporarily designated by the notes E♯-B♯-F♯♯-C♯♯-G♯♯-D♯♯-A♯♯) come to its seven near-by regular degrees (F-C-G-D-A-E-B), when the principle of scale-formation by consecutively arranged natural Fifths is applied. For the same reason it also would make no difference whether the ascending or descending Fifths, or even simultaneously both series, leading to similar results, were used for that purpose. In all these instances the Pythagorean intonation will invariably fill the function of some sort of "common denominator" for all three scales, thereby producing—so to speak—a preliminary and rough outline of the supra-diatonic scale which then, and only *then*, may be "retuned," as necessary, either to its just intonation or to its equally tempered intonation.

Of these two intonations the latter (which henceforth will be named with reference to the new scale *supra-tempered intonation*) will be the most suitable for practical purposes by reason of its simplicity. Requiring a certain acoustic compromise, the supra-tempered intonation will yield us, in return, the greatest

---

* See Footnote on page 157 and the corresponding text in the following chapter.

advantages, especially in modulation, preserving at the same time the funda-mental and specific characteristics of the supra-diatonic scale.*

The true nature of the supra-tempered intonation, as well as of the Pythag-orean intonation referring to the same scale, will be properly understood with the aid of parallel calculations and diagrams which will also convey a clear idea of the distinction between them. However, the interrelation between all three scales, already pointed out, obliges us to make a preliminary and analogous dem-onstration of the two different intonations with regard to the diatonic and infra-diatonic scales. Let us, therefore, immediately enter upon this demonstration, starting with the diatonic scale ("7 + 5") as the one most familiar to us.

If we append to the series of twelve natural Fifths on which the Pythagorean intonation of the diatonic scale ("7 + 5") is based, numbers expressing the dimension of every Fifth in centitones (351 ctn.) and gradually add these num-bers as shown below, we shall ultimately obtain a total amount of 4212 ctn., exceeding by 12 ctn. the series of seven Octaves, similarly dealt with, amounting in all to 4200 ctn.:

EXAMPLE 59:

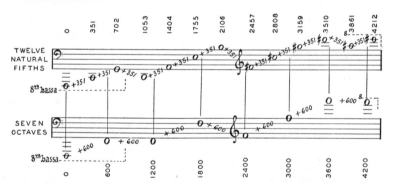

It is opportune to remark here incidentally that the difference of 12 ctn. (called "Pythagorean comma") between these two series of intervals is not always realized by musicians accustomed to the equally tempered intonation in everyday practice, although sometimes this difference is partly and quite audibly revealed during a musical performance, especially in string ensembles.

The very fact that there is a certain discrepancy between the twelve natural Fifths and the seven Octaves does not represent, however, an outstanding or even

* The comparative Table of "acoustic com-promises," i.e. acoustic deviations of infra-tem-pered, tempered and supra-tempered intonations from the just intonations of their respective scales, is given in the following chapter on page 190.

characteristic exception in acoustics, as one may think, perhaps, when hearing for the first time of such a seemingly negligible difference as the Pythagorean comma, which distinguishes these two series of intervals rather close to each other in their general scope. On the contrary, this difference is simply a particular instance of a single acoustic law according to which no one series of natural and, of course, identical intervals can ever exactly embrace any series of other natural intervals, each of which is also identical with the other. Thus, for instance, no number of consecutively arranged natural Fifths can exactly coincide, in general acoustic dimension, with some number of consecutively arranged Octaves as is particularly shown above. In the same way no number of, let us say, natural Thirds will coincide, in general acoustic dimension, with some number of similarly arranged natural Fifths or Octaves, or of any other natural intervals, etc.

The acoustic difference between various series of natural intervals fluctuates to a high degree, depending on their manifold and unlimited combinations but, in all cases, *independently* of any proportion to their increasing or decreasing general acoustic dimension and of the number of intervals they comprise.

Some of the series of natural intervals very closely approximate each other, in general acoustic dimension, sometimes to such a degree that the difference between them represents an interval that is barely perceptible to the human ear. Such, for instance, is the difference (already mentioned in the survey of Chinese scales) between 53 natural Fifths and 31 Octaves, equal to less than 2 ctn. This may be easily verified by multiplying the exact dimension of a natural Fifth (350.9775 ctn., using four decimals) by 53, and the interval of an Octave (600 ctn.) by 31. The subtraction of the smaller of these products from the greater, viz. 18,600 out of 18,601.8075, leaves the difference of 1.8075 ctn. (or 18 mtn. in round numbers.)

How trifling is this quantity may be judged from the fact that even the Pythagorean comma (exact dimension 11.72 ctn.), which exceeds it approximately six and a half times, is deemed a comparatively small difference between the various series of natural Fifths and Octaves. Moreover, the Pythagorean comma may be considered, strictly speaking, as a rare and, from a practical viewpoint, fortunate instance of approximation of these two series of intervals—an instance that predetermined the ease with which the Western world adopted the equally tempered scale ("7 + 5"), which has been such a significant factor in the history of musical progress.

The principle of Equal Temperament in regard to the scale "7 + 5" theoretically appears to be nothing but an artificial levelling of the demonstrated twelve natural Fifths to seven Octaves through the reduction of the former of these series, in its entirety, by the dimension of the Pythagorean comma (12 ctn. in round numbers), this being actually done by means of an equal and scarcely perceptible flattening of every one of these Fifths one-twelfth of this comma, i.e. 1 ctn. Through this operation, a series of twelve *tempered* Fifths exactly covering a series of seven Octaves and thus leading up to acoustic identity of their concluding notes, viz. E♯ and F, respectively, is ultimately obtained:

EXAMPLE 60:

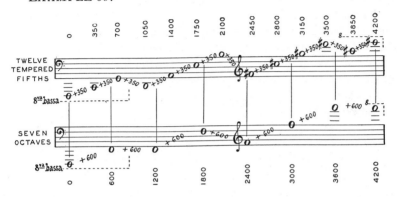

The manner of comprising all twelve tones, forming a series of *natural* Fifths, within the compass of an octave, is already familiar to the reader through the musical practice of the Chinese who, while constructing this series, used to transpose instantly an octave down, each tone exceeding the octave of the fundamental tone (see Ex. 5).

This method, equally applicable to the series of *tempered* Fifths, mathematically consists in subtracting 600 ctn. (the interval of an Octave) from the numbers which exceed this quantity and which are arrived at as the Fifths are added together. But to add the interval of a Fifth to a certain number, already obtained, and then to subtract the interval of an Octave from the total is the same thing as to subtract immediately the interval of a Fourth from that original number before the addition is effected. Thus, instead of adding one natural Fifth to another (351 + 351) and then subtracting the interval of an Octave (600 ctn.) from the total (702 ctn.), which will give us the interval of a Pythagorean major Second (102 ctn.), it is sufficient simply to subtract the interval of a natural Fourth (249 ctn.) from the original natural Fifth (351 ctn.), which will give the very same result (102 ctn.). One must deal in similar fashion, of course, with tempered Fifths and Fourths, which are equal to 350 ctn. and 250 ctn. respectively.

The following pair of drawings (Ex. 61 *ᵃ* and *ᵇ*) illustrates this method of comprising the twelve tones (forming natural Fifths, in one instance, and tempered Fifths in another) within the compass of an octave. This operation in no way alters the fundamental properties of the two series of natural and tempered Fifths demonstrated above (Ex. 59 and 60). Therefore, the Pythagorean comma (12 ctn.), characteristic of the former of these series (Ex. 59), is bound to and, indeed, does appear also in one of the new drawings (Ex. 61ª) and prevents its two terminal points (E♯ and F) from contacting, thereby communicating to it the form of a spiral-like segment. But in the second of these drawings (Ex. 61ᵇ), released from the comma, the two terminal points coincide and thus form a closed circle, familiar to every musician. The outer numbers of both drawings indicate the addition and subtraction of Fifths and Fourths respectively, while the inner numbers give the result of these two arithmetical operations, indicating the exact position of all the degrees of the scale within an octave:

EXAMPLE 61:

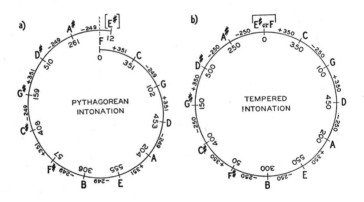

Arranging in parallel fashion the inner numbers of each of these drawings in progressive order and graphically representing the intervals formed by them, we shall obtain a comparative diagram of the Pythagorean and equally tempered intonation of the scale "7 + 5." [See Ex. 62.]

The "flats" which are absent in the Pythagorean intonation of the scale "7 + 5," as represented in Ex. 62, would not acoustically coincide, from all evidence, with the "sharps" close to them and derived, in each instance, from the adjacent regular degrees of the same scale. This practical deficiency, due to the incommensurability of natural whole tones and half tones, is characteristic, as known, of every intonation except the equally tempered one in which perfect coincidence of sharps and flats is a direct result of the absolute equality of all the homogeneous intervals constituting an octave in the scale referred to. It is, of course, not difficult to gather that in the light of the above method of Tempera-

EXAMPLE 62: *

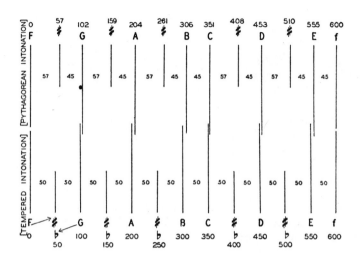

ment, this equality, in turn, automatically results from the artificial levelling of one series of intervals down to another and originally dissimilar series. Thus, twelve Fifths and seven Octaves served as the two "dissimilar" series of intervals, necessary for this purpose in the scale "7 + 5."

However, the result obtained by equalizing these two series again does not represent in any way an individual instance in acoustics, any more than does their natural disparity, as may be recalled. This is because any other number of natural Fifths artificially levelled to a more or less approximate (in general acoustic dimension) number of Octaves will inevitably lead to a similar equality of all musically homogeneous intervals, and, consequently, to the familiar coincidence of sharps and flats derived from the regular degrees of the scale thus constructed.

Starting from this rule we shall avail ourselves of an analogous method of equalizing two different series of Fifths and Octaves (but dimensionally as approximate as possible) for the purpose of obtaining the tempered form of the infra-diatonic scale ("5 + 2"), which comes next in our exposition. The two series of intervals to be equalized in this instance are apparently seven natural Fifths and four Octaves:

---

* It will be remembered that we have already had occasion to deal with the form of the Pythagorean intonation represented in this diagram, when demonstrating the intonation of twelve Chinese "lüs" (see above, Ex. 7) which are based on the same principle of *ascending* natural Fifths or their equivalent descending natural Fourths.

EXAMPLE 63:

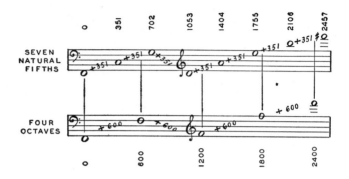

The difference between these series of intervals being equal to 57 ctn. (we shall call it *infra-comma*) represents a quantity so greatly exceeding the Pythagorean comma that one might doubt the practical expediency of Equal Temperament in regard to the infra-diatonic scale, if this Temperament did not have a true precedent in Siamese musical practice, to which reference has already been made more than once. And inasmuch as in problems of art actual facts have to be considered in preference to theoretical premises, we may accept as an indisputable truth that the infra-comma, after it has been gradually absorbed in the process of Temperament, at the cost of acoustic purity of the seven natural Fifths, will produce an artificial flattening, within every one of them, to which the human ear adjusts itself without any particular difficulty.

The degree of this flattening which results from dividing the infra-comma by the number of natural Fifths (viz. 57:7) is expressed by 8.14 ctn., which being then subtracted from the natural Fifth (351—8.14) makes the dimension of an "infra-tempered" Fifth equal to 342.86 ctn. Seven infra-tempered Fifths will now exactly cover, in their general acoustic dimension, four octaves, thereby leading to identity of the concluding notes (F♯ and F) of both these series of intervals. [See Ex. 64.]

When grouping together the tones of the natural as well as of the infra-tempered series of Fifths within the compass of an octave, it is necessary, as heretofore, to transpose every tone, exceeding this compass, an octave down, which again may be replaced by the simple subtraction (before this excess takes place) of the interval of a Fourth, equal to 249 ctn. in the Pythagorean intonation and to 257.14 ctn. in the infra-tempered intonation. This procedure is illustrated by a pair of drawings, resembling those given in Example 61 and merely diminished in tonal scope, one of which represents a spiral-like segment with an infra-comma separating its two terminal points (F♯ and F), while the other

*EXAMPLE 64: **

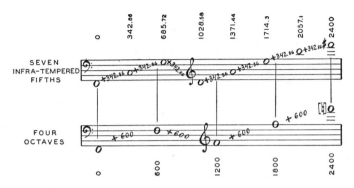

appears as a closed circle with the infra-comma equally distributed among all its component intervals:

*EXAMPLE 65:****

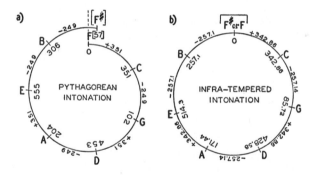

Arranging now the inner numbers of each of these drawings in progressive order and graphically representing the intervals formed by them, we shall obtain a comparative diagram of Pythagorean and infra-tempered intonation of the scale "5 + 2," or, in other words, a comparative diagram of the present Chinese and Siamese scales as demonstrated above (Ex. 14), although in a different infra-mode ("F-f" instead of "C-c"):

* The minute errors which occur in this series of figures, as well as in some other examples, are negligible, as they result merely from the gradual accumulation of decimals that are not quite exactly expressed.

** The drawing on the right of this Example (b) with its proper "infra-diatonic" notation is given in the Footnote on page 158 of the following chapter.

EXAMPLE 66:

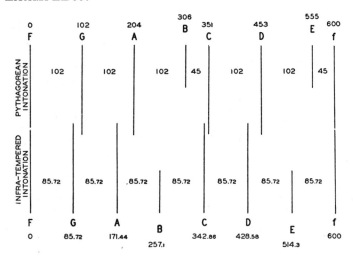

From the numerical data of this example (as well as of Ex. 62) one may reasonably draw the conclusion that Equal Temperament can be theoretically effected in regard to the two scales referred to simply by dividing an octave by the general number of tones constituting a given scale, but provided that, together with this number, the relative position of its regular and auxiliary degrees in some non-tempered intonation be already known. Such an arithmetical division of an octave determines the dimension of a minimum interval (half step) of any scale in its tempered intonation, and this dimension serves as a standard, in accordance with which all the rest of the minimum intervals (half steps) of the non-tempered scales are remoulded.

Consequently, two different methods of Equal Temperament could be applied to the diatonic as well as to the infra-diatonic scale, leading in each instance to identical results. The successive steps of these two methods may be summed up as follows:

First Method:

a.   Formation of two parallel series of consecutively arranged natural Fifths and Octaves disclosing the acoustical difference between them (Ex. 59 and 63).

b.   Determination of the dimension of the tempered or infra-tempered Fifth (depending on the scale dealt with) by dividing the above acoustical difference (Pythagorean comma or infra-comma, respectively) by the general number of tones constituting a given scale and subtracting from the dimension of a natural

Fifth the quotient so obtained. This operation for the tempered Fifth may be expressed by the formula:

$$351—(12:12) = 350 \text{ ctn.}$$

and for the infra-tempered Fifth by the formula:

$$351—(57:7) = 342.86 \text{ ctn.}$$

c.   Construction of a closed circle of tempered or infra-tempered Fifths and Fourths (the dimension of a Fourth is found by subtracting the tempered or infra-tempered Fifth from the Octave, i.e. from 600 ctn.) which determines the dimensions of intervals between the fundamental tone and every one of the other scale-degrees, thus establishing their position within the compass of an octave (Examples 61^b and 65^b.)

Second Method:

a.   Construction of a spiral-like segment of natural Fifths and Fourths determining the dimensions of intervals between the fundamental tone and every one of the remaining scale-degrees, and, consequently, establishing their "Pythagorean" position within an octave (Examples 61^a and 65^a).

b.   Equal division of an octave into the general number of scale-degrees that determines the standard dimension for every minimum interval (half step) in the tempered and infra-tempered intonation. For the diatonic scale, this operation may be simply expressed by the formula:

$$600 : 12 = 50 \text{ ctn.}$$

and for the infra-diatonic scale by the formula:

$$600 : 7 = 85.72 \text{ ctn.}$$

c.   Consecutive addition of the number expressing the minimum interval to the fundamental tone (represented by zero), thereby retuning all the regular and auxiliary scale-degrees, whose relative position has been disclosed through the initial operation, from Pythagorean to tempered intonation (Ex. 62 and 66).

The first of the two methods described serves as a mathematical background for the practical tuning of musical instruments with fixed intonation, while the second and simpler method is applicable only to theoretical constructions.

I have purposely dwelt upon the nature and the different methods of Equal Temperament more than may seem necessary, because in connection with it we shall subsequently come across a somewhat unexpected peculiarity, of which a few words may be said beforehand.

This peculiarity, which in no way alters the matter at hand in any essential, lies in the fact that the two different methods of Equal Temperament, when applied to the supra-diatonic scale, will lead not to one but to two different supra-

modes,—a result which, as we know, has no analogous precedent in either the
diatonic or the infra-diatonic scale. Both these supra-modes will be equally
correct, of course, for the distinction between them, as is readily understood,
does not presuppose an actual change in structure of the supra-diatonic scale
on which they rest. In other words, they will represent no more than different
"phases" of the same supra-diatonic scale, just as different "phases" of the two
foregoing scales are represented by their modes and infra-modes respectively.

I shall explain later the reasons for this, in any case, unusual result and
in the meantime shall turn to the actual formation of the supra-diatonic scale
in its Pythagorean and supra-tempered intonations, similarly to the formation
of the two preceding scales.

Nineteen natural Fifths, on which the Pythagorean intonation of this new
scale is based, approximately cover eleven Octaves, as will be seen from the
following example. For the convenient notation of tones within so many octaves
we have availed ourselves of some additional designations, namely, a Bass Clef
and Treble Clef respectively marked with a Roman numeral below and above,
which indicates that the actual pitch of all the notes that follow is *three* octaves
lower than written, in the former case, and *three* octaves higher than written
in the latter case:

EXAMPLE 67:

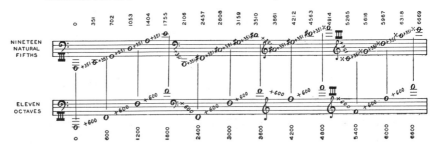

The difference of 69 ctn. between these two series of intervals, which will
be henceforth called *supra-comma,* exceeds by 57 ctn. the Pythagorean comma,
and by 12 ctn. the infra-comma. The supra-comma, after it has been gradually
absorbed in the process of Temperament, at the cost of acoustic purity of the
nineteen natural Fifths, will flatten every one of them 3.6 ctn., which will bring
the dimension of a "supra-tempered" Fifth to 347.4 ctn. The two arithmetical
operations connected with the determination of this interval, viz. dividing of
the supra-comma by the general number of scale-degrees and subtraction of
the quotient so obtained from the natural Fifth, may be formulated together in
the following manner:

$$351—(69 : 19) = 347.4 \text{ ctn.}$$

Nineteen supra-tempered Fifths will now exactly cover eleven Octaves and will lead to the identity of the two concluding notes (E♯♯ and F) of both these series of intervals:

EXAMPLE 68:

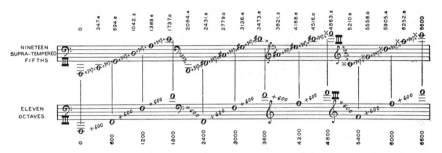

When grouping together all the tones of these two series within an octave, we shall apply, as heretofore, the method of alternating addition and subtraction of Fifths and Fourths pictorially represented below by a spiral-like segment with a supra-comma separating its terminal points, where the natural intervals are concerned, and by a closed circle, where supra-tempered intervals are involved. It will be noted incidentally that the dimension of a supra-tempered Fourth equals 252.6 ctn. (i.e. 600—347.4):

EXAMPLE 69:*

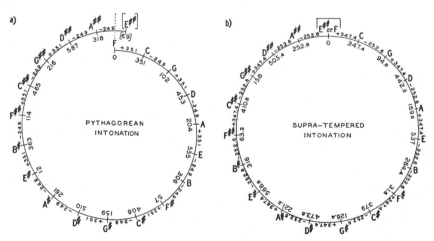

* The drawing on the right of this Example (b) with its proper supra-diatonic notation is given in the Footnote on page 158 of the following chapter.

Should we arrange the inner numbers of each of these drawings in progressive order and graphically represent the intervals they form, we shall obtain a comparative diagram of the Pythagorean and supra-tempered intonations of the scale "12 + 7," as is respectively demonstrated by the middle set of dotted lines and upper set of solid lines in the following example. The lower set of solid lines represents the same scale in the supra-tempered intonation obtained through the second method of Temperament, i.e. by simple division of an octave into nineteen equal parts (conformably to the general number of tones of the scale "12 + 7") and by borrowing the formula of the relative position of the regular and auxiliary degrees of this scale from its Pythagorean intonation:

EXAMPLE 70:

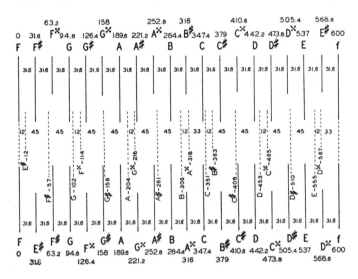

The supra-mode of the lower set of lines of this diagram being, by virtue of its origin, identical with the supra-mode of the middle set of lines (despite the difference in intonation) does not coincide, as already observed, with the supra-mode of the upper set of lines (despite the identity in intonation), obtained through a different method of Equal Temperament. The reason is that every auxiliary degree of the scale "12 + 7," when the latter is supra-tempered by the "flattening-the-Fifths" method (Ex. 68), is pitched down a much larger interval than the one which separates it (in Pythagorean intonation) from the lower of the two regular degrees encompassing it, and therefore ultimately turns out to occupy a position between a different pair of regular degrees than before

Temperament was effected. Meanwhile we know that the "dividing-the-octave" method of Temperament, when applied to the same scale, does not involve such a leap of its auxiliary degrees. This is because the latter method, mechanically equalizing all the nineteen "minimum" intervals (half steps) of the supra-diatonic scale, pitches down only those of its degrees that are *above* the norm standardized by Equal Temperament, and, on the other hand, pitches up all the rest of the degrees which are *below* this norm.

Thus, in the first method of Temperament, the auxiliary degree E♯, being pitched down 3.6 ctn. simultaneously with *every* Fifth that precedes it, forms as a final result an interval of 43.4 ctn. counting from its original position in the Pythagorean intonation (see Examples 67 and 68), a small "cumulative" error being taken into consideration. And since this note (E♯) lies 12 ctn. above its adjacent regular degree F, in the Pythagorean intonation, one will readily understand that, being pitched down 43.4 ctn. in the supra-tempered intonation, it will ultimately be found 31.4 ctn. (i.e. 43.4—12) below the same note F; consequently, between the regular degrees E and F and not between F and F♯, as heretofore.

But in the second method of Temperament the same auxiliary degree E♯, placed originally (i.e. in the Pythagorean intonation) 19.6 ctn. below the standard (31.6 ctn.) determined by dividing the octave into nineteen equal parts (see Ex. 70), will be pitched *up* to the extent of the difference indicated (19.6 ctn.) and *not* still further *down* as in the former instance. Hence, it will remain between the same pair of notes as before Equal Temperament was effected, being merely changed in intonation.

All that has been said here regarding the auxiliary degree E♯, also applies to the rest of the auxiliary degrees of the supra-diatonic scale which, being similarly shifted to a different "vicinage" of regular degrees by the first method of Temperament, preserve their original environment (notwithstanding the change in intonation) when the second method of Temperament is used. These two different positions of the auxiliary degrees in relation to their adjacent regular degrees—the result of two different methods of Temperament—are precisely what leads up to the two different supra-modes of the new scale.

It follows naturally that the supra-mode which preserves the original arrangement of its regular and auxiliary degrees, i.e. the one that is represented by the lower set of lines in the foregoing example, should be considered as the fundamental one, and, consequently, the supra-mode represented by the upper set of lines will appear merely as one of the derivative "phases" of the supra-diatonic scale.

The Pythagorean and the equally tempered intonation of all three scales within the compass of an octave being now definitely established, it will be interesting to observe the form acquired by the two aspects of interrelation of their different groups of degrees which are familiar to us through the various series of natural Fifths, demonstrated at the beginning of this chapter (pp. 113 and 114) and which gave us a clue to the construction of the supra-diatonic scale.

The initial section of the first of these series, consisting of five tones, F-C-G-D-A, is correlated, as we then pointed out, with the closing section of the second series, consisting of five tones F♯-C♯-G♯-D♯-A♯, apparently tuned a Pythagorean semitone (57 ctn.) above the former. When comprised within an octave, they are certainly bound to preserve the correlation of their component tones originally arranged, in both instances, by natural Fifths. This preservation may be readily observed in that both these sections of natural Fifths, when transformed into two scale-like progressions, will coincide in acoustic structure, although they will differ in absolute pitch. In other words the two new series, F-G-A-C-D and F♯-G♯-A♯-C♯-D♯, obtained by comprising the above sections within an octave, will represent the very same infra-diatonic scale but in two different keys. And since the latter series is the one which represents the group of auxiliary degrees of the scale "7 + 5," its correlation with the former series, which represents the group of regular degrees of the scale "5 + 2," may be demonstrated, within an octave, by the following diagram showing both these scales:

EXAMPLE 71:

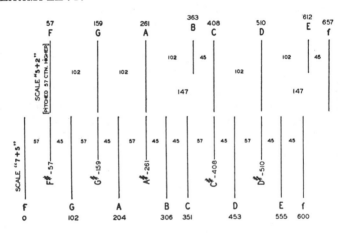

The similarity in acoustic structure manifested by these groups of degrees belonging to two different scales is the reason for the universally known fact that any typically infra-diatonic melody (such as Chinese, Scotch, etc.) may be easily performed on the five black keys of our piano. True, the tempered intonation of the latter gives some acoustic deviations as compared with the Pythagorean intonation of the infra-diatonic scale which, incidentally, happens to serve also as the just intonation in the case of this particular scale, as will be seen later. But these deviations are much slighter than even those that exist between the Pythagorean and the infra-tempered intonation used, at present, by the Siamese (see Ex. 14 and 66); therefore they are obviously unable to alter essentially the basic character of melodies of this sort.*

Hence it is not difficult to foresee that any typically diatonic melody could be similarly performed—although with somewhat greater discrepancies in intonation—on the seven "black" keys that will be comprised in every octave of the future supra-tempered piano.** But under the condition of Pythagorean intonation the group of regular degrees of the diatonic scale will, of course, coincide absolutely, in acoustic structure, with the group of auxiliary degrees of the supra-diatonic scale; in this instance, therefore, there would be no discrepancies of any sort. The diagram on the following page (Ex. 72) demonstrates this interrelation of degrees of the two scales referred to.

The structural identity of different groups of degrees of the three scales in Pythagorean intonation, shown in Examples 71 and 72, represents but one of the two aspects of their interrelation as described earlier (page 114). The other aspect is much more obvious, for it is virtually manifested by the simple absorption, each time, of all the degrees of every scale by the group of regular degrees of the next and more complicated scale. This aspect of their interrelation is demonstrated by a general diagram (Ex. 73) in which the entire series of degrees of the scale "5 + 2" absolutely coincides, in acoustic structure, with the group of regular degrees of the scale "7 + 5," and the entire series of degrees

<table>
<tr><td>

* The following diagram discloses the acoustic deviations between the justly intoned regular degrees of the infra-diatonic scale and the five "black keys" of our present tempered piano. The deviations which occur when these regular degrees are retuned according to the Siamese Equal Temperament may be gathered from Ex. 75 of the text.

</td><td>

** The following diagram shows the acoustic deviations between the justly intoned regular degrees of the diatonic scale and the seven "black keys" of the future supra-tempered piano. The deviations which will occur when these regular degrees are retuned according to our familiar Equal Temperament may be gathered from Ex. 75 of the text.

</td></tr>
</table>

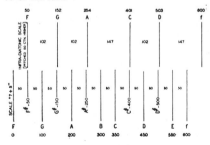

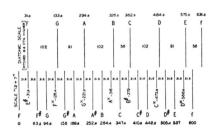

EXAMPLE 72:

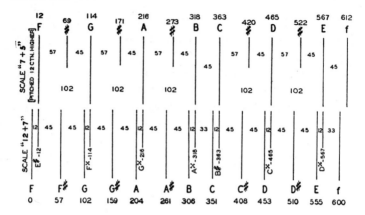

of the latter similarly coincides with the group of regular degrees of the scale "12 + 7":

EXAMPLE 73:

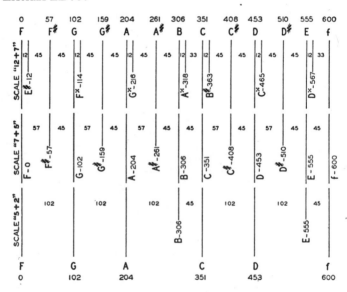

This diagram already gives us a fairly clear conception of the laws to which the structural development of scales is subject in the process of musical evolution. Thus, for instance, the equalization of functions of the regular and auxiliary degrees of the scale "7 + 5," so striking a characteristic in modern musical art, is merely, from the above point of view, the forerunner of their complete absorption by the group of regular degrees of the scale "12 + 7." Which is similar to the gradual equalization of functions of the regular and auxiliary degrees of the scale "5 + 2" that once occurred in Celtic music and subsequently led to their absorption by the group of regular degrees of the scale "7 + 5."

The transition to the practical use of the scale "12 + 7" in place of the scale "7 + 5" would probably occur in modern music as gradually and, at any rate, with comparatively as much ease, as the former transition from the scale "5 + 2" to the scale "7 + 5," were not the latter, at present, encased within the armor of equally tempered intonation. Both the regular and auxiliary degrees of the scale "7 + 5," when tempered, produce a rather perceptible acoustic difference, compared with any intonation of the scale "12 + 7," this preventing them from being actually absorbed in a natural way by the latter's group of regular degrees, in spite of the fact that, from a historical point of view, the time for such an "absorption" is undoubtedly already at hand. Thus, the equally tempered intonation which was of such signal service to musical art during the past few centuries (i.e. during the period of exclusive use of the scale "7 + 5") has now turned from a positive into a negative factor, retarding the natural course of musical development.

The same hampering situation that now confronts modern composers (who, subconsciously sensing the basic structure of the scale "12 + 7," are compelled to use the tonal material of the scale "7 + 5") will some day probably be faced by Siamese composers who so far have but entered the path of infra-tempered intonation. Their transition from the infra-tempered scale "5 + 2" to any intonation of the scale "7 +5" will encounter in the future most serious obstacles and, in any case, will be immeasurably more difficult than the natural transition from the scale "5 + 2" to the scale "7 + 5," which took place in the music of the Celts who were unfamiliar (at least to any extent) with the principle of Temperament.

The various attempts of modern composers to break their way through to the tonal plane of the scale "12 + 7," as well as the obstacles which lie in wait for the Siamese composers of the future, will be discussed at greater length in subsequent chapters of this book. For the present, therefore, we shall confine ourselves to the demonstration of acoustic deviations that occur in the correlated groups of degrees of all three scales which have been subjected to Equal Temperament. Beginning with the demonstration of the groups that are shown in the foregoing diagram (Ex. 73) we shall retain their Pythagorean intonation for comparison, in the form of dotted lines, and shall designate the equally tempered intonation of these groups by solid lines. The numbers given in the following example refer solely to the latter intonation:

EXAMPLE 74:

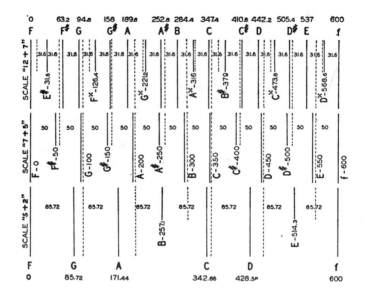

There is scarcely any necessity to explain in detail the reasons for the above acoustic deviations which result entirely from the application of Equal Temperament to quantitatively *different* series of natural Fifths underlying the three scales in question. In contradistinction to natural Fifths always equal to 351 ctn. and identical therefore in the Pythagorean intonation of every scale, the infra-tempered, tempered and supra-tempered Fifths are dissimilar in acoustic dimension, being equal to 342.86 ctn. in the first instance, to 350 ctn. in the second and to 347.4 in the third. This dissimilarity manifests itself in the guise of acoustic deviations, demonstrated above, when the different groups of degrees of all three scales are compared to each other within the compass of an octave.

Now, as regards the acoustic deviations existing, under the condition of the infra-tempered, tempered and supra-tempered intonations, between the other groups of degrees belonging to our three different scales (whose structural identity in the Pythagorean intonation was demonstrated by two separate examples, 71 and 72) one may judge of them from Ex. 75, on the opposite page, in which all the correlated groups of degrees are represented by one unified diagram.

Similar interrelations between the respective groups of degrees of different scales, as demonstrated by the aid of various diagrams, would certainly exist should still more complicated scales (to which theoretically there is no limit) be constructed in conformity with our basically established principle. Their correla-

*EXAMPLE 75:**

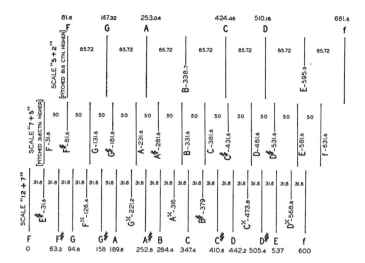

ted groups of degrees would coincide, in the Pythagorean intonation, as regards acoustic structure, and would show inevitable deviations when equally tempered.

From this angle the infra-diatonic, diatonic and supra-diatonic scales may be regarded as three consecutive links in one common and theoretically infinite chain of "organic" scales, which gradually become more complex in tonal constitution and proportionately more subtle from the point of view of their minimum intervals. The concatenation of these links is due to the simple fact that every one of their corresponding series of natural Fifths actually represents a mere portion of the subsequent series which, in turn, comprises all the preceding series and may be considered as their natural extension (see Ex. 63, 59 and 67). This mutual linking of quantitatively different series of natural Fifths is certainly preserved when comprised within an octave, and in the latter case may be demonstrated in the form of a common and continuous spiral which combines their three corresponding representations (Ex. 65^a, 61^a, 69^a), as shown in the following illustration:

* The diagrams of Ex. 74 and 75 are represented in illustrative keyboard form in Addendum II of this volume (Plates I and II respectively).

EXAMPLE 76:

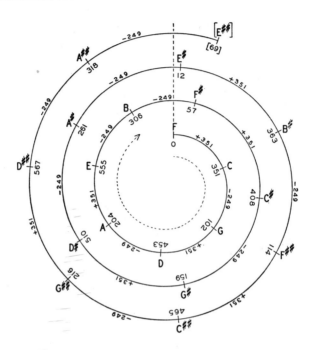

Hence it follows that the formation of these as well as of all subsequent "organic" scales in the Pythagorean intonation only calls for a continuation, in each case, of their uniting spiral with the preservation, of course, of their common principle of division of all scale-tones into regular and auxiliary degrees.* This spiral, although gradually more complex, nevertheless leaves the acoustic relations within its component spiral-like segments (Ex. 65ᵃ, 61ᵃ, 69ᵃ) totally undisturbed. Meanwhile the successive formation of the same scales in incompatible infra-tempered, tempered, supra-tempered, etc. intonations, requires each time

* In that way all the subsequent turns of the spiral would serve as a basis for scales in which the combination of their regular and auxiliary degrees would be expressed, according to the principle disclosed, first, by the formula "19+12," then by the formula "31+19" and so on, until the still unknown physiological limit (for there is no *theoretical* limit) is reached in the *ultra-diatonic scale,* as it could be called in a *practical* sense. These scales of the very distant future are not dwelt upon in this book, as they are of no interest whatever for our immediate purpose, not to mention the fact that, while becoming more complex, they do not exclude the possibility of acquiring new structural features which cannot be foreseen at present. Much more deserving of attention, on the other hand, is that primitive scale which, in historical evolution, *precedes* the three scales examined, and which, considering its position in the general chain of "organic" scales and, consequently, its still less complicated structure as compared to the infra-diatonic scale, should be named *sub-infra-diatonic scale.* A full account of the structure of this scale as well as of the musical system based on it, is given at the end of this chapter (Supplement).

the construction of separate and closed circles (Ex. 65^b, 61^b, 69^b), every one of which acoustically excludes all the rest, as may be visually illustrated, for comparison, by the following representation:

EXAMPLE 77:

Thus, if Equal Temperament brings dissimilar acoustic results when applied to different scales, and if, consequently, a formation of every scale in this artificial form predetermines a break with the preceding scale, then it is evident that by *attempting to remain on the acoustic plane of one of the above "circles" of Fifths and Fourths* while intending to build up a new and more complex scale (i.e. attempting to avoid the necessary break), one can never succeed in producing a true "organic" formation of the latter. Any efforts to increase, under this limiting condition, the tonal material of the circles in question, i.e. practically the scales they represent, would inevitably result in a purely mechanical insertion therein of some number of new tones having no organic connection with the initial series and, on the strength of this, producing no more than an impression of the old tones of this series, but as if repeated "out of tune."

It is hardly necessary, I think, to give proofs to the effect that such a mechanical complication (should it ever be adopted) would turn out to be, from the point of view of musical evolution, totally unjustified and, in practical application, nonsensical. Musical art would gain nothing, or at best, almost nothing, from this sort of tonal complexity, for no scale can ever be creatively used in music without marked and mutual coherence of its component elements.

And yet this mechanical complexity is the very direction to which turn the efforts of those modern theorists who, starting from the inviolability of the equally tempered intonation of the scale "7 + 5," propose to supply it with quarter tones or sixth tones, etc. as if the whole problem merely consisted in determining the acuteness of the musical ear in regard to various "microtonic" subdivisions. These theorists chiefly lose sight of the fact that the equally tempered intonation of the scale "7 + 5" can in no way be regarded as an infallible acoustic principle by which we must be guided for all possible future complications in our tonal language. This artificial intonation represents no more than one specific instance of adjustment of one of the scales to practical use and therefore only fits the scale for which it is introduced. To adopt this intonation as a starting point for all subsequent tonal complications is to convert a particular instance into a general rule, i.e. deliberately to accept an error which, in practice, will inevitably crop out, resulting before long in a great dearth of promising creative work.

Later we shall have yet another occasion to touch upon this particular subject and in a somewhat different way. Temporarily confining ourselves, therefore, to the above considerations, let us now revert to the spiral of Fifths and Fourths (Ex. 76) in order to complete the examination of its characteristics with one additional observation that will conclude the main body of this chapter.

This observation refers to the one-sided structure of our spiral, already briefly noted, which, in accordance with all the formations preceding it, is exclusively based on the principle of *ascending* Fifths or, what comes to the same thing, of descending Fourths. That is why all the chromatic designations found in it consist exclusively of *sharps* (or double sharps) which, as we know, do not acoustically coincide with *flats* (or double flats) in the Pythagorean intonation.

But just as one-sided would be a spiral constructed in the opposite direction, i.e. by *descending* Fifths or, what is the same, by ascending Fourths. The sole difference between these two spirals would be that the chromatic designations of the latter would consist exclusively of *flats* (or double flats) instead of sharps (or double sharps) as may be seen from the following representation. [To facilitate comparison, the centitone numbers of the seven regular degrees of the diatonic scale found in the preceding spiral have been preserved for the same degrees here].

EXAMPLE 78:

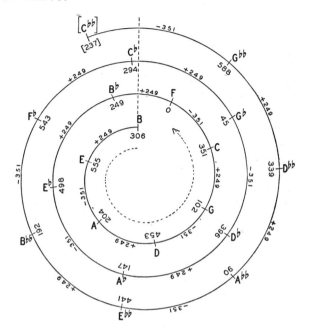

Hence it is clear that should one intend to avail himself of the principle of natural Fifths and Fourths for *practical* musical purposes, i.e. to use it as a basis of intonation of one scale or another, he would have simultaneously to apply both the above spirals (Ex. 76 and 78) mutually completing each other in tonal constitution. The following diagram will convey an idea of the acoustic construction which would be acquired, for instance, by our diatonic scale ("7 + 5") as a consequence of such an application:

EXAMPLE 79:

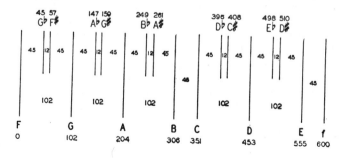

In the same way we could form a diagram of any other scale that enters in each of the above spirals and, consequently, also the diagram of the supra-diatonic scale.

However, we have already had occasion to mention that the Pythagorean intonation, resulting from the application of this principle, is only acceptable to a slight degree for practical musical purposes—especially, we may now add, as the tonal complexity of the scales increases—and that we utilized it exclusively as a constructive schema revealing (rather loosely, as far as acoustic accuracy is concerned) the relative arrangement of the regular and auxiliary degrees of the supra-diatonic scale. After this arrangement is found and the Pythagorean intonation replaced by the supra-tempered intonation (in which "sharps" and "flats" are acoustically equivalent) there is apparently no further need for an additional schema, i.e. for a series of descending natural Fifths showing only the position of "flats" of the new scale. It follows as a matter of course that there would be equally no need for a spiral containing the "sharps," should we from the very beginning avail ourselves of the spiral containing the "flats," ultimately leading to identical results.

SUPPLEMENT TO CHAPTER X

THE SUB-INFRA-DIATONIC SYSTEM

Before proceeding with the principal subject of our discussion it is necessary, for further reference, to describe in detail, at this point, the sub-infra-diatonic system and its underlying scale, incidental mention of which was made in the foregoing Footnote.

It is quite a simple matter, of course, to determine the tonal constitution of this scale since the general constructive principle of all the "organic" scales is already known. According to this principle, the sub-infra-diatonic scale should evidently be composed of two regular degrees (i.e. quantitatively equalling the auxiliary degrees of the infra-diatonic scale) and three auxiliary degrees (i.e. quantitatively equalling, jointly with the former, the regular degrees of the infra-diatonic scale) and expressed therefore in its entirety by the formula "2 + 3." The greater number of auxiliary degrees as compared to that of regular degrees represents one of the peculiarities of this primitive scale which, however, is not thereby deprived of the fundamental features characteristic of other scales constructed upon the general spiral of Fourths and Fifths, as we shall see later. And in order to make clear its structural interconnection with these scales we shall demonstrate, in the first place, how its combination of regular and auxiliary degrees, indicated above, fits into the earlier given evolutionary progression of other combinations which, now preceded by the formula "2 + 3," will appear as follows:

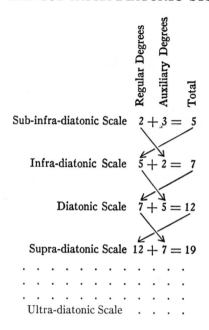

	Regular Degrees	Auxiliary Degrees	Total

Sub-infra-diatonic Scale $2 + 3 = 5$

Infra-diatonic Scale $5 + 2 = 7$

Diatonic Scale $7 + 5 = 12$

Supra-diatonic Scale $12 + 7 = 19$

. . . .

. . . .

Ultra-diatonic Scale   . . . .

It is not difficult to infer from this progression that no scale can be actually constructed according to the same principle that will precede the one expressed by the formula "2 + 3," since to continue the above series further in the *reverse* direction would take us out of the domain of positive mathematical quantities—the only ones practically applicable to a concrete tonal material.

The sub-infra-diatonic scale ("2 + 3") must, then, be considered as the one which, in point of fact, forms the initial link of the common spiral of scales represented incompletely (for simplification) in Ex. 76 of the text. And should this "initial link" be included in the common spiral, the latter would accordingly acquire the following and somewhat altered form:

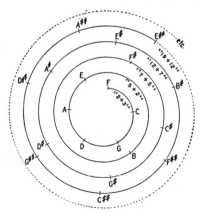

As to the structure of the "initial link" itself, which serves as the basis of the sub-infra-diatonic scale ("2 + 3"), it originates in the same way as the spiral-like segments of all other scales. We shall, therefore, similarly demonstrate the entire process of its construction, which, as may be readily understood, will automatically lead to the formation of the sub-infra-diatonic scale in the Pythagorean intonation. This, as in the instances already dealt with, will go hand-in-hand with the formation of the same scale in the equally tempered (sub-infra-tempered) intonation. Following which we shall corroborate our thesis regarding the theoretical and practical possibility of such a scale by evolving a complete sub-infra-diatonic system similar to the rest of the systems, and by pointing to a few commonly known facts which dimly suggest its use, even if in a somewhat unconscious and, consequently, quite imperfect way.

A series of five tones arranged by natural Fifths serves as the fundamental acoustic basis of the sub-infra-diatonic scale ("2 + 3") and, as was the case in other scales, generates, first, the group of its regular degrees, and after that the group of its auxiliary degrees:

Series of natural Fifths which forms the sub-infra-diatonic scale ("2 + 3")

F-C-G-D-A

Section which forms the   Section which forms the
two regular degrees   three auxiliary degrees

This series of natural Fifths, when brought within the compass of an Octave, produces the Pythagorean intonation of the sub-infra-diatonic scale, as will be shown later. But in order to obtain the equally tempered (sub-infra-tempered) intonation of the same scale, a few more operations are necessary.

As before, the first thing to be done in this process of Temperament is to find out the acoustic difference between the above series of natural Fifths and the series of Octaves (three in number, in this instance) which approaches it most closely in general acoustic dimension. This difference (which will be called *sub-infra-comma*) is disclosed by the aid of the following comparison, which shows that it equals 45 ctn.:

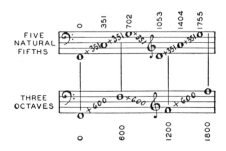

This happens to be the only instance where the series of natural Fifths is *exceeded* by the series of Octaves, and not *vice versa*, as in other scales. Therefore, in order to equalize the former series with the latter, every natural Fifth has to be *raised* (and not lowered, as before) one-fifth of the sub-infra-comma, i.e. 9 ctn., which will bring the dimension of every sub-infra-tempered Fifth to 360 ctn.

The series of five sub-infra-tempered Fifths will now exactly cover the series of three Octaves and will, consequently, lead to identity of pitch of their concluding notes, E and F respectively:

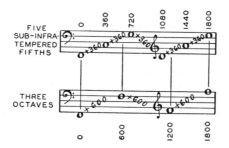

The construction of a spiral-like segment of Fifths and Fourths will show the exact position of all the degrees of the scale "2 + 3" in Pythagorean intonation and within the compass of an Octave, while the construction of a circle of sub-infra-tempered Fifths and Fourths will show the position of the same degrees in the equally tempered (sub-infra-tempered) intonation of this scale:

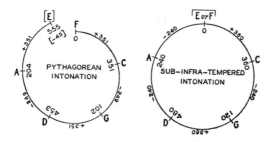

Arranging now the inner numbers of each of these drawings in progressive order and graphically representing the intervals formed by them, we shall obtain a comparative diagram of Pythagorean and sub-infra-tempered intonation (upper and lower solid lines respectively) of the scale "2 + 3." The dotted lines indicating the equally tempered intonation of the diatonic scale are given here merely for the sake of comparison:

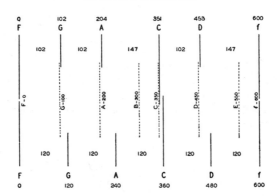

Other particulars of the sub-infra-diatonic system will be better understood with the aid of a keyboard illustration, in which the scale "2 + 3" is represented (similarly to the rest of the scales) a Fifth above the original "sub-infra-mode" shown in the preceding diagram:

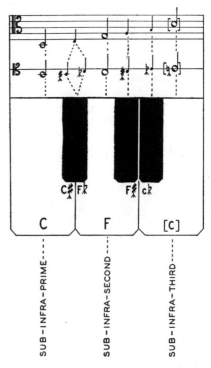

The two white and three black keys in this illustration correspond to the regular and auxiliary degrees of the sub-infra-diatonic scale respectively. The three auxiliary degrees, designated up to this point by the notes D, G and A, will, of course, now lose these independent appellations and will obtain new ones in the conventional way by borrowing them from the regular degrees which are merely supplemented, for this purpose, by a "sub-infra-sharp" or "sub-infra-flat," as the case may be. Incidentally, the graphic notation of these two signs of alteration has been slightly changed for differentiation.

As to the musical notation of the entire sub-infra-diatonic scale, it does not require more than one stave line, by the aid of which two complete Octaves, including the regular degrees as well as their sub-infra-chromatic alterations, are conveniently arranged, as will be seen from the following representation, accompanied for elucidation (as in the preceding illustration) by a five line stave. [Clef *C* will be used in all examples relating to this scale because the absence of the note G among its regular degrees precludes the use of the Treble Clef for its notation]:

Owing to the unusual number of auxiliary degrees of the scale "2 + 3," quantitatively exceeding its regular degrees, the latter do not form any half steps between themselves but a whole step in one instance (C-F) and a sesqui-step in the other (F-C). Half steps (minimum intervals) can be found in this scale only between degrees one of which at least is sub-infra-chromatically altered. However, the fact that the intervals between the regular degrees, although deprived of half steps, are not equal to each other, makes it possible to form two different "sub-infra-modes" of the scale "2 + 3," one of which will have the note F and the other the note C as its Tonic: *

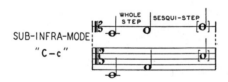

SUB-INFRA-MODE
"C-c"

---

*Besides these two *principal* sub-infra-modes, a few of their variations, or *altered* sub-infra-modes, may be formed in this scale through the familiar substitution of certain auxiliary degrees for the original regular degrees. Thus, by lowering note *C* in the sub-infra-mode "F-f," we obtain a variation of the latter composed of two notes, *F-C sub-infra-flat*, which are equivalent to the notes *F-A*, in our diatonic notation. Similarly, we may obtain other altered sub-infra-modes composed of notes C-D, or D-F, for instance, all of which will cover several very primitive two-tone scales known to be actually used by certain tribes in different parts of the world. It is needless to add that the practical use of such scales does not presuppose, by any means, a knowledge of their theoretical derivation on the part of these tribes. Neither does it imply that these altered sub-infra-modes necessarily came into use *after* the principal sub-infra-modes were already known.

SUB-INFRA-MODE
"F – f"

Any of these sub-infra-modes may be freely transposed into different keys which, being systematically arranged under the condition of sub-infra-tempered intonation, will form, in each instance, a closed circle of five keys a sub-infra-tempered Fifth (360 ctn.) apart. The letters above the notes indicate their approximate equivalents in the diatonic system:

	KEY "C"	KEY "F♯"	KEY "C♯"	KEY "C♭"	KEY "F"
SUB-INFRA-MODE "C-c"					
SUB-INFRA-MODE "F-f"					

Turning now to the classification of intervals of this scale, it is easy to understand that sub-infra-Primes (C-C and F-F) and their inversions—sub-infra-Thirds (C-c and F-f) which represent nothing else but our familiar Octaves—can be the only consonances in the sub-infra-diatonic system. This is because the rest of the intervals—sub-infra-Seconds C-F and F-C, i.e., virtually, our Fourth and Fifth—are formed by *contiguous* degrees in this system, and therefore must be considered as dissonances, this being the general rule for all scales constructed according to our principle. In the following Table, consonances will be designated by the term *perfect*, and dissonances by the terms *minor* and *major*, depending on the smaller or greater number of half steps they respectively contain:

	I	II
SUB-INFRA-PRIMES	perfect 0	perfect 0
SUB-INFRA-SECONDS	minor 1	major $1\frac{1}{2}$
SUB-INFRA-THIRDS (Octaves)	perfect $2\frac{1}{2}$	perfect $2\frac{1}{2}$

The general principle of chord-formation ("by Thirds" and "by infra-Thirds" in their respective scales), when applied to the sub-infra-diatonic scale ("by sub-infra-Thirds"), will evidently produce in each instance an interval of an Octave. But this interval, as already mentioned, itself represents the inversion of a Prime (Unison) or, speaking in terms of Harmony, of a *Monad,* which, therefore, is to be regarded as a *complete* common (consonant) "chord" of the sub-infra-diatonic scale.

Hence it is not difficult to build up a miniature system of sub-infra-diatonic Harmony, similar in its main characteristics to infra-diatonic and diatonic Harmony.

Two-part harmony, resulting from the duplication of a chordal Root, must be considered "normal" in this system, just as three-part harmony, for the same reason, is normal in the infra-diatonic system, and four-part harmony in the diatonic system.

One of the two regular degrees of the sub-infra-diatonic scale being assumed as the Tonic (I), the second automatically becomes the Dominant (II). Accordingly, the two common chords in each of the sub-infra-modes will be designated as a tonic Monad and dominant Monad. It will be noticed, incidentally, that the extended position of a Monad and the single inversion of the latter become identical in sub-infra-diatonic Harmony; also that the Dominant of this scale invariably plays the part of leading note in it.

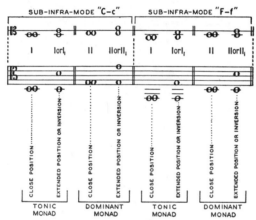

The rudimentary rule of Harmony proscribing the similar motion of parts will limit the progressions of Monads to the following instances:

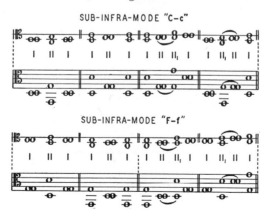

Parallel Octaves must not be too rigidly prohibited in this system, however, since they are *sub-infra-Thirds* in it and as such have about the same right to progress in a "parallel" way as have infra-Thirds and Thirds in their respective harmonic systems.

The only more complicated (dissonant) chord in the sub-infra-diatonic system (not speaking of sub-infra-chromatically altered chords) will evidently be represented by one containing both regular degrees (C and F) but taken in different Octaves (when dealing with strict Harmony), and therefore borrowing its name from the interval of a sub-infra-Fourth formed by these notes. The chord of a sub-infra-Fourth built on the Dominant (II) of the sub-infra-diatonic scale permits the following fundamental progressions:

a. without preparation; b. with preparation of the sub-infra-Fourth; c. with an intermediate resolution into the dominant Monad (II).

SUB-INFRA-MODE "C-c"

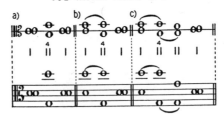

SUB-INFRA-MODE "F-f"

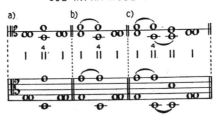

Suspension and Anticipation are likewise possible in sub-infra-diatonic Harmony:

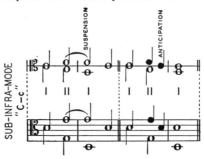

Even modulation can be effected in the sub-infra-diatonic system according to the principle of community of chords applied in other systems. The following example represents a modulation from the key of C to that of F sub-infra-sharp, the "chord" C-C simultaneously serving therein as a tonic Monad (I) of the former and as a dominant Monad (II) of the latter:

Such is the theoretical background of the sub-infra-diatonic system which, of course, was never used in musical practice in the elaborated form represented above, but which, no doubt, was unconsciously "felt out" and applied in a rudimentary way (probably just as a plain two-tone scale with occasional "passing notes" and, isolatedly used, Octave duplications for accompaniment) at the very dawn of the history of music of all nations. In fact, this was the first intuitive attempt to express a rather limited range of emotions with the aid of a most primitive but indubitably self-contained tonal scheme (sub-infra-Tonality), whose certain innate completeness together with the obviously inherent tonal gravitation can be sensed by everybody, it seems, even now, without any particular aural strain. Incidentally, these inherent qualities of the sub-infra-diatonic scale ("2 + 3"), which are also characteristic, as we know, of the infra-diatonic and diatonic scales ("5 + 2" and "7 + 5") yield us additional assurance that they hold good for all scales constructed (in the manner already familiar) upon the spiral of Fifths and Fourths and, consequently, for the supra-diatonic scale ("12 + 7"), of the utmost importance to us.

Regarding now the genuine musical material and historical data which are supposed to prove the actual existence of the sub-infra-diatonic scale ("2 + 3") among various nations, anything more than mere suggestions in this respect can hardly be expected.

Even the practical use of the comparatively more complicated infra-diatonic scale ("5 + 2") has not been as yet thoroughly investigated by musical science. And the vast musical material, long collected among primitive peoples by casual travellers or various expeditions for whom musical exploration was only a side issue, is, with a few exceptions, unreliable, as it has not been recorded from all angles in the majority of cases, and therefore may often lead to confusion rather than to the definite solution of the problem in question. The same is partly true of a great portion of the historical information relating to the early stages of the musical development of mankind in general.

Yet there are a few fundamental facts whose authenticity seems to raise no doubts, and which it is worth while to mention in connection with the subject under discussion. Thus, it is generally agreed that in a good number of the most primitive tunes, usually two definite notes, which stand out among the rest in musical significance and sheer steadiness of pitch, can be distinguished without any particular effort. These two "obvious notes" or points of rest, as A. H. Fox Strangways calls them (*Music and Letters,* October, 1926), are invariably placed at an interval of a perfect Fourth or a perfect Fifth —there is, of course, only one such note if the compass of a tune does not reach the extent of a Fourth—one or the other of these intervals forming a sort of pivot about which a group of less conspicuous notes is (sometimes rather strangely) distributed. The fact that the pitch and number of notes of the latter group vary with different tribes and thus seemingly preclude the establishment of a single and all-embracing principle in this respect, ceases to be a puzzle if one bears in mind that some of these notes are of purely "declamatory" origin, so to speak, and as such cannot be regarded as scale-notes in the strictly *musical* sense. These "declamatory" notes are often simply omitted in various performances of the same tune and, if present, greatly fluctuate in pitch, this being easily detected even without the aid of acoustical instruments.

Although the author has not the slightest intention, at this point, to try to decide the old, and probably, insoluble controversy between Darwinians and Spencerites as to the priority of pure song or "excited speech," yet he is inclined to believe that some at least of the "fluctuating" notes which are waveringly touched in a song as well as in "excited speech," are of a much earlier origin than the two "obvious notes" referred to above, and, in all likelihood, preceded even the very capacity of primitive man to produce any long-continued sound of definite and steady pitch at all. Moreover, it can hardly be doubted that, in certain instances, these fluctuating notes resulted from tentative attempts to *find* the "obvious notes" which were first *subconsciously* sensed by primitive peoples and, after being discovered, were fixed on their crudely musical instruments, while the old fluctuating notes continued to exist side by side in their songs as the result of long acquired habit, usually very strong in matters of this sort. If, therefore, each and every shade of "excited speech" as reflected in the fluctuating notes is to be reckoned with, one may expect sometimes to come across a much greater number of gradations in pitch (and, indeed, very subtle ones) among primitive peoples—i.e. actually a greater number of notes, in the broad sense—than among the more advanced races who usually strive to "purge" their musical language of these non-musical (declamatory) elements and thus gradually elaborate a purely *tonal* system with a strictly limited number of component notes, acoustically interconnected and logically subordinated to one organic whole.

The sub-infra-diatonic scale ("2 + 3") is the most elementary system to which the term *tonal* can be applied in the fullest sense of the word. Its two regular degrees correspond absolutely to the two "obvious notes" found in primitive tunes, and to them are most simply related (in an acoustical sense) the three auxiliary degrees which, in practice, gradually become definitely established after the purging process mentioned above is completed.

The musical history of ancient Greece gives us a certain clue to the theoretical and practical existence of such a scale, although reference is definitely made only to the two *regular* degrees. This clue is the well-known *Dichord*—a scale of two tones a perfect Fourth apart—which derived its name from a musical instrument (of the Lyre family) with two strings tuned in accordance with this interval. It is said that the Greek Rhapsodists—wandering reciters or chanters, especially of Homer's poetry, whose period is approximately given as the ninth century B. C.—availed themselves of this scale and, while declaiming their epic stories (apparently in a sort of *modo recitativo*), they used to pluck the two strings of their Lyre for the purpose of "keeping their voice in pitch." If we assume, as was probably the case, that the regular degrees (C and F) of the sub-infra-diatonic scale served the Rhapsodists as two sustaining props for the "obvious notes" of their semi-chanted recitations, then it is very likely that, while their narrative ran between and about these notes, the auxiliary degrees of the same scale were also occasionally "touched" by their voice.* This is partly proved by the fact that eventually one more note (G, equivalent to F sub-infra-sharp) was "felt out" by them and added to the Dichord which was thereby transformed into a *Trichord* (C, F, G). The conscious application of the rest of the auxiliary degrees (D and A, equivalent to C sub-infra-sharp and C sub-infra-flat respectively) of the scale "2 + 3," in other words, the complete use of the latter, evidently took place soon afterwards, although we possess but indirect information in this respect. Besides a certain five-stringed *Cithara* said to be in existence at that time and supposedly tuned to a series of notes equivalent, in intervals, to F, G, A, C, D (Helmholtz, p. 257), there is a statement by Plutarch that a scale of five notes was already in use as early as the eighth century B. C. True, Plutarch offers an entirely different and rather far-fetched explanation in regard to the origin of this scale which, in his opinion, was evolved as a result of the intentional avoidance of some notes from a more complicated seven-tone scale already known to the Greeks. But, as Riemann thinks, there is not much ground for believing Plutarch too implicitly in this particular explanation (*Handbuch der Musikgeschichte*, Vol. I, part 1, page 162), because, according to other writers—among them Nicomachus, Plutarch's contemporary and the oldest authority on the Pythagorean theory of music—even the classic period of the history of Greece (c. 6th and 5th century B. C.) did not witness the existence of

---

* It will be worth while to note in this connection that the ancient Greek theorists distinguished two principal movements of the voice: (1) the *continuous,* characteristic of speaking, in which the voice glides by imperceptible degrees from higher to lower or the reverse, and (2) the *discrete,* characteristic of singing, in which the voice proceeds by intervals, remaining for a certain time on one note and then passing on to another. Besides these principal movements, however, the Greeks also recognized a third or *inter-* *mediate* movement of the voice, which was employed in the recitation of poetry and which apparently combined (and simultaneously softened) the distinct features of the two former, the speaking passages of a recitation probably acquiring a semi-gliding character and the singing portions merely touching (and not necessarily remaining on) the musical tones. Compare with *The modes of ancient Greek music* by D. B. Monro (Oxford, 1894), pp. 115, 116.

the seven-tone scale, all the melodies in the Temple worship of that and, naturally, of earlier time, being exclusively based on the scale of five tones (comprising no semitones).

Without actually hearing an adequate performance of these melodies (even if all of them were at hand in a written form) nobody, of course, could ever decide which of them belong to the *complete* sub-infra-diatonic scale ("2 + 3") and which are based on the five regular degrees of the infra-diatonic scale, historically following the former, since the same five notes—F, G, A, C, D—are involved in both cases. The distinction could be made (in principle) more or less accurately by token of the harmony applied to these melodies, inasmuch as Unisons and Octaves, as we know, are characteristic consonant combinations of the sub-infra-diatonic scale ("2 + 3"), while perfect Fourths and Fifths are characteristic, in the same sense, of the infra-diatonic scale ("5 + 2"). But, unfortunately, only very vague and general information concerning the use of Unisons and "magadized" Octaves in ancient Greece is actually at our disposal so far, the simultaneous combinations of perfect Fourths and Fifths in the music of that time remaining a confused riddle yet to be solved by historians.

There is one more, though artificial indication by which the melodies based on the same (or, in this instance, approximately the same) series of tones can be properly attributed to their respective tonal systems. It is the principle of Equal Temperament which, if known to be actually applied at a given period, immediately tells us which of the two historically "neighboring" scales we are dealing with, not to mention the fact that it also furnishes us direct proof of one or the other scale being regarded as a *self-contained tonal system*. Thus, we can never attribute a Siamese melody comprising seven different tones, to a diatonic scale, because Siamese music is known to be based on the infra-tempered scale ("5 + 2") which lacks the inherent characteristics of the former and, which, subsequently, leads to the disclosure that only five notes of that melody constitute its body, the two others serving merely as embellishments; and the fact that the infra-diatonic scale ("5 + 2") *is* tempered in Siamese musical practice tells us at least that this scale *may* be considered as a closed and self-contained tonal system. No such frank indication ever existed in European music and that is why frequent attribution of various old melodies to wrong scales is bound to be a common matter there.

Reverting now to the sub-infra-diatonic scale ("2 + 3") we must say that according to present-day knowledge, never in the history of European music, pre-Christian or post-Christian alike, has the principle of Equal Temperament been applied to it, just as it has never been completely applied to the infra-diatonic scale ("5 + 2"). No one, therefore, could ever draw a sharp line between the two historical periods that have availed themselves of the former and the latter scale respectively, and no melodies, even if their component notes are correctly deciphered, could be properly classified with regard to their underlying scales. Furthermore, no considerations other than those set forth above can be advanced in favor of the fact that the sub-infra-diatonic scale ("2 + 3") was sensed by the ancient Greeks of the Homeric period as a self-contained tonal scheme.

But if such is the state of affairs in European music, then one is certainly astounded to find that the principle of Equal Temperament is being applied in Oriental countries not only to the infra-diatonic scale ("5 + 2") but, apparently, to the sub-infra-diatonic scale ("2 + 3") as well. The division of an Octave into seven equal intervals results from the application of this principle to the former of these two scales ("5 + 2") and, as we already know, serves as the basis of the Siamese infra-tempered system. The division of an Octave into five equal intervals results from the application of this principle to the latter scale ("2 + 3"), as demonstrated above (page 144), and serves as the basis of the so-called *Salendro* scale, used at present by the Javanese .

The reservation must be made at this point, however, that while the distinction between the regular and auxiliary degrees of the infra-tempered scale ("5 + 2") has been preserved, from all evidence, in the musical practice of the Siamese, no distinction of this kind has been observed so far in Javanese music based on the *Salendro* scale, which we identify with the sub-infra-tempered scale ("2 + 3"). Two different explanations for the absence of such recorded observations in the latter instance, may be offered on more or less equal grounds. One is that the Javanese *do* make a certain distinction between the two regular and three auxiliary degrees of the sub-infra-tempered scale, but an Occidental musician, not being aware of the possibility of such an interpretation of the *Salendro* scale, very naturally fails to realize the distinction that may manifest itself in a genuine performance of Javanese music in too subtle a way to attract particular attention. The other explanation is that the Javanese have already long passed the stage when the above distinction had a place in their music and, like our own modern composers, they now use the regular and auxiliary degrees on an equal footing, thereby automatically precluding any observation on the part of the Western explorer that would suggest to him the original structure of the *Salendro* scale. We shall have more than one occasion to mention that the equalization of functions of the regular and auxiliary degrees is typical for a musical consciousness which, upon reaching the final stage of development within a given tonal system, anticipates a scale of a relatively "higher order" and exerts every possible effort to utilize the latter—incidentally, an almost impossible task when the former scale is used in its equally tempered form. The supposition that such may be the case with the Javanese, who perhaps have already reached the final stage within the limits of the sub-infra-diatonic scale ("2 + 3") and are thereby brought much closer to the infra-diatonic scale ("5 + 2"), is rather strongly supported by the fact that, side by side with the *Salendro* scale, they also avail themselves of a group of pentatonic scales resembling the infra-diatonic scale and based on the so-called *Pelog* system (untempered) which even allows them to make use, if desired, of the two auxiliary degrees besides the five regular degrees principally dealt with.

It need scarcely be added that all the above considerations in regard to the historical facts and present practice of the sub-infra-diatonic scale are to a great extent hypothetical, the entire subject requiring much more thorough scientific investigation. And if the author has thought it worth while to point out some of these considerations, it is not only because of their plausibility but also for the sake of suggesting the direction in which, along other lines, this particular kind of scientific research ought to be conducted in the future. Hypotheses have always been of great service to science, provided, of course, that their limitations were properly taken into account in each instance. But out of many different hypotheses, the one that rationally embraces the greater number of isolated facts must be provisionally accepted until it is superseded by a final and repeatedly verified conclusion or by a still broader hypothesis.

CHAPTER XI

THE SUPRA-DIATONIC SYSTEM

Having explained the formation of the supra-diatonic scale ("12 + 7"), let us now carefully analyze all its specific characteristics and, finally, inquire to what extent we believe it may be considered in musical art, because of these characteristics, as the historically legitimate successor of the diatonic scale ("7 + 5").

For the sake of clarity I shall precede the examination of the supra-diatonic scale ("12 + 7") by a keyboard illustration (as was done for all the foregoing scales), representing its twelve regular and seven auxiliary degrees by the same number of white and black keys respectively.

EXAMPLE 80:

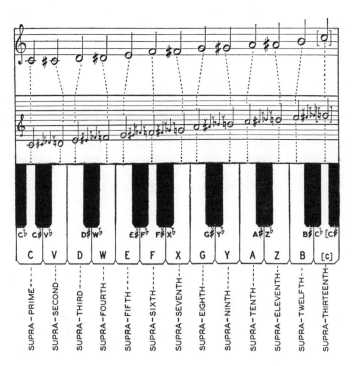

In the first place it should be noted that this new scale is shown here, not in its fundamental supra-mode "F-f," but (similarly to the two preceding scales now used) in the supra-mode "C-c" which is found a Fifth above the former and which is therefore originally constructed by a series of ascending natural Fifths

C-G-D-A-E-B-F♯-C♯-G♯-D♯-A♯-E♯-B♯-F♯♯-C♯♯-G♯♯-D♯♯-A♯♯

plus one descending Fifth

$$C - F.*$$

This change, immaterial as far as the basic structure of the supra-diatonic scale is concerned, will greatly facilitate our discussion.

One more substitution made in the above illustration concerns the letters designating the five newly introduced (in comparison with the diatonic scale) regular degrees which up to this point have been invariably represented by the chromatically altered notes (C♯, D♯, F♯, G♯, A♯) of the scale "7 + 5." In the new scale they are no longer "derivative" or auxiliary degrees, as in the diatonic scale, and therefore should be represented on a par with the seven other regular degrees of the supra-diatonic scale by means of independent designations. The last five letters of the alphabet are used here for that purpose, namely: V (instead of C♯), W (instead of D♯), X (instead of F♯), Y (instead of G♯) and Z (instead of A♯).

In connection with this re-designation of notes, it should be also observed here that for the purpose of facilitating orientation in the unaccustomed musical system, we digress from the formally more accurate *consecutive* order of the literal designations of degrees and preserve the seven "diatonic" designations (C, D, E, F, G, A, B) for those seven regular degrees (out of twelve) of the supra-diatonic scale which acoustically coincide with them in Pythagorean intonation, although they somewhat differ in supra-tempered intonation, according to which (solely for simplification) the above keyboard illustration was made. Because of the latter circumstance the notation of the scale "7 + 5," at the top of this illustration, ought to be considered, acoustically, as being only approximate for the regular degrees of the scale "12 + 7."

The designation of the seven auxiliary degrees of the supra-diatonic scale, for which other chromatically altered notes (B♯, C♯♯, D♯♯, E♯, F♯♯, G♯♯, A♯♯) of the scale "7 + 5" have been used up to this point, should now be replaced by new supra-chromatically altered notes derived from their respective regular degrees. The new signs of alteration will be called here *supra-sharps* and *supra-*

---

* Compare with this series of Fifths those formed for the contemporary diatonic and infra-diatonic scales (page 51).

flats and, to distinguish them from their allied signs applied in the two preceding scales, they will be graphically represented as follows.

$$\text{SUPRA-SHARP} = \breve{\sharp} \qquad\qquad \text{SUPRA-FLAT} = \breve{\flat}$$

These two signs respectively raise and lower the pitch of the regular degrees of the supra-diatonic scale a half step, this interval being of course considerably smaller than a half step in any of the two preceding scales. Inasmuch as the new scale is considered in its supra-tempered intonation, the supra-sharps and supra-flats derived from the contiguous regular degrees will coincide, as indicated above in front of every black key which serves for both these supra-chromatic alterations.*

A more lucid idea of all the changes effected here in regard to the supra-diatonic scale ("12 + 7") will be conveyed by the following diagram which represents the lower set of lines from Ex. 70 of the previous chapter, but with its note C assumed as the Tonic instead of F, conformably to the new supra-mode "C-c," which has replaced the original supra-mode "F-f." The new literal designations of notes as well as their derivative supra-chromatic alterations are placed above the lines, while all the old designations are left, for the sake of comparison, below the lines:

EXAMPLE 81: **

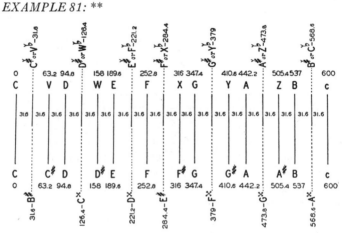

---

  * We may add a remark at this point, similar to the one made above in reference to the signs of alteration of the infra-diatonic scale (Footnote on page 44), viz., that the indicated change of the graphic notation of these signs in the supra-diatonic scale, indispensable in a theoretical exposition, would be superfluous in actual practice, since their presence alone in the ten-line system is sufficient to distinguish them from the same signs in the three-line or five-line systems.

  ** After all the changes regarding the literal designation of the notes and signs of alteration of the supra-diatonic scale are effected, it will be practical, for the purpose of elucidation, to redemonstrate here, in their proper notation, the three series of Fifths, to which the three gradually evolving scales have been provisionally reduced in the foregoing chapter (pp. 113 and 114):

With regard now to the general method of notation of the supra-diatonic scale, it is apparent that our customary five-line system is formally inappropriate for this purpose, as the tonally increased scale requires a greater number

1. Series of natural Fifths which forms the infra-diatonic scale ("5 + 2")

$$\text{F-C-G-D-A-F}\flat\text{-C}\flat$$

Section which forms the   Section which forms the
five regular degrees   two auxiliary degrees

2. Series of natural Fifths which forms the diatonic scale ("7 + 5")

$$\text{F-C-G-D-A-E-B-F}\sharp\text{-C}\sharp\text{-G}\sharp\text{-D}\sharp\text{-A}\sharp$$

Section which forms the   Section which forms the
seven regular degrees   five auxiliary degrees

3. Series of natural Fifths which forms the supra-diatonic scale ("12 + 7")

$$\text{F-C-G-D-A-E-B-X-V-Y-W-Z-F}\sharp\text{-C}\sharp\text{-G}\sharp\text{-D}\sharp\text{-A}\sharp\text{-E}\sharp\text{-B}\sharp$$

Section which forms the   Section which forms the
twelve regular degrees   seven auxiliary degrees

This corrected notation will do away with the confusion which might arise from the presence of some chromatically altered notes within the group of regular degrees of the supra-diatonic scale, on the one hand, and from the absence of any altered notes within the group of auxiliary degrees of the infra-diatonic scale, on the other hand, as was the case in the previous notation of the two respective series of Fifths. A reservation has to be made at this point, however, with regard to the series of Fifths of the supra-diatonic scale to the effect that, in contradistinction to the two other series, the order of its component notes becomes somewhat different after the tonal material of this scale has been subjected to the process of Temperament. And owing to the peculiarities of this process in connection with the supra-diatonic scale, as explained in the foregoing chapter, there will be further dissimilarity in the above order, depending on which of the two methods of Temperament described is applied to this particular scale. Thus, in the case of the "dividing-the-Octave" method, the result of which is plotted down in the lower set of solid lines in Ex. 70 and later represented (with an immaterial change of the supra-mode) in the illustrative form of a keyboard in Ex. 80, the series of supra-tempered Fifths will acquire the following order:

Series of supra-tempered Fifths which forms the supra-diatonic scale ("12 + 7")

$$\text{X-V-Y-W-Z-F-C-G-D-A-E-B-X}\flat\text{-V}\flat\text{-Y}\flat\text{-W}\flat\text{-Z}\flat\text{-F}\flat\text{-C}\flat$$

Section which forms the   Section which forms the
twelve regular degrees   seven auxiliary degrees

Again, in the case of the "flattening-the-Fifths" method the result of which is plotted down in the upper set of solid lines in Ex. 70, the series of supra-tempered Fifths will be expressed as follows:

Series of supra-tempered Fifths which forms the supra-diatonic scale ("12 + 7")

$$\text{F-C-G-D-A-E-B-X-V-Y-W-Z-F}\flat\text{-C}\flat\text{-G}\flat\text{-D}\flat\text{-A}\flat\text{-E}\flat\text{-B}\flat$$

Section which forms the   Section which forms the
twelve regular degrees   seven auxiliary degrees

of stave lines on and between which its twelve regular degrees, with their derivative supra-chromatic alterations, may be easily placed. Should we desire to
create a new stave containing—similarly to the two preceding scales—two com-

An additional keyboard illustration of the
supra-diatonic scale obtained through the "flattening-the-Fifths" method of Temperament (with
a similar change of the supra-mode) will disclose
the grounds for the notation and its order given
in the latter series. It will be noticed, incidentally,
that the entire nomenclature of notes is merely
"shifted" one degree to the right in this keyboard
illustration as compared with the one represented
in Ex. 80 of the text. Thus, note C of the
following illustration is placed on the white key
formerly occupied by note V, and so on:

For the same purpose of elucidation, we shall
re-demonstrate, in this new and proper notation
but without the numbers indicating the dimension
of intervals, the three circles of Fifths and Fourths
referring to the tempered, infra-tempered and
supra-tempered intonations of their respective
scales. These properly modified representations
will now permit a better understanding of all the
terminal points of these series which in the previous notation seemingly manifested a certain
inconsistency, while they were designated by two
different notes in each instance. We all understand
very well why and in what sense the notes E♯
and F are equivalent in the tempered intonation
of the scale "7 + 5," but the equivalence of F♯
and F in the infra-tempered intonation and of
E♯♯ and F in the supra-tempered intonation,
as indicated in the previous representations of
their respective "circles" (see Examples 65b and
69b in the text), probably does not carry similar
conviction at first sight. The inconsistency, however, is purely one of form, since we then availed
ourselves everywhere of the conventional notation of the scale "7 + 5," applying it to all three
scales merely because this notation possessed the
advantage of being familiar to us. By substituting now the new notation for the old one, in so
far as the infra-diatonic and supra-diatonic
scales are concerned, and consequently correcting
the "formal" error, we automatically dispel the
imaginary inconsistency, as pointed above, for the
two different notes by which one and the same
tone is designated in the two scales in question,
are really G♭ and F (not F♯ and F) in the former instance, and X♭ and F (not E♯♯ and F)
in the latter instance:

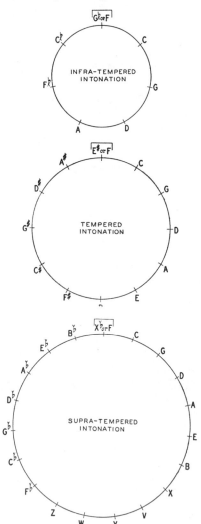

A glance at the keyboard illustrations of the
infra-diatonic scale (Ex. 13 of the text) and of
the supra-diatonic scale (shown in this Footnote) is sufficient to convince one that the two
pairs of notes referred to represent, in each case,
one and the same musical tone in infra-tempered
and supra-tempered intonations, respectively.

plete octaves for each Clef and at the same time retain the notation of two terminal notes (C and c' in the Bass Clef and c' and c''' in the Treble Clef), we
would have to increase the original number of lines to ten, as will be seen from
the following example in which all three staves (relating to three different
scales) are represented side by side:

EXAMPLE 82:

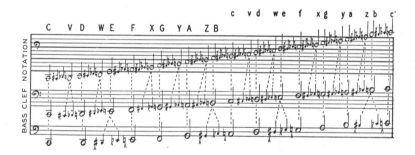

In this example, the white notes refer to the regular degrees of each scale
and the small black notes to their auxiliary degrees. The latter are placed,
within every stave, on or between the same lines as the regular degrees that
generate them. The use of heavier lines in the new stave is *solely* for the sake
of facilitating visual perception of the unaccustomed number of lines and has
no other meaning.

On account of the four heavier lines the new stave looks as if it were divided into
three sections. Any pair of notes separated from each other by two such sections will
invariably express the interval of an Octave (supra-Thirteenth) which, no doubt, will
also be of considerable help in the matter of reading the music according to the new
system. Thus, the note d' is placed on the first (lowest) heavy line (in the Treble

TREBLE CLEF
NOTATION

BASS CLEF
NOTATION

Clef) ; hence the same note an Octave higher (d'') will at once be found on the third heavy line. The note y' is placed on the second heavy line, and its octave (y'') will therefore be found on the fourth heavy line. The notes placed on the ordinary light lines— as well as between the lines—of the corresponding sections of the stave will of course bear the same relationship. All these characteristics of the new stave will be better grasped from the two accompanying enlarged representations, with the literal designations of the notes.

Attention may also be called to the fact that the notes c'' and c are placed—in the Treble and Bass Clefs respectively—on the light lines of the *middle* section of the stave, which in conjunction with the identity (already pointed out) of the notation of the remaining c's on the three different staves used for the different scales, will again serve to facilitate matters. The ten-line stave placed immediately above the keyboard illustration of the scale "12 + 7" in Ex. 80, besides its representation in Ex. 82, will undoubtedly be of additional assistance for a better understanding of this system of notation, much less complicated than at first appears.

The chain of whole steps and half steps, formed by the supra-diatonic scale, as well as their characteristic arrangement, establishes a close connection between it and the two preceding and organically evolved scales, and, on the other hand, radically opposes it to the twelve-tone chromatic (tempered) scale in so far as the latter is adopted by certain modern composers as an independent basis for their musical and theoretical constructions, and it is sometimes named, in such case, duodecuple or semitonal scale. Taking into consideration, however, the fact that the duodecuple scale (when quite unambiguously applied as such) totally lacks those "organic" characteristics expressed by Mode and Tonality, I shall henceforth call it *atonal scale,* and shall, at times, designate the series of its twelve independent and equidistant degrees by the figure "12." *

The specific succession of whole steps and half steps is what imparts to the supra-diatonic scale that live and individual character by which, no doubt, it will be just as easily "recognized" in all musical compositions in which it is used as are diatonic and infra-diatonic scales in music that is based on them. But this character is certainly lacking in the anemic and neutralized atonal scale ("12") since its component intervals are rigorously levelled in comparison to

---

* A. Eaglefield Hull in his book entitled *Modern Harmony, its explanation and application* (London) rather illogically, in our judgment, considers the duodecuple scale under two different aspects: (a) as preserving the "tonal" center and (b) as abolishing it. It seems that the preservation of this center deprives the duodecuple scale of its most distinctive, though negative, characteristic—atonality in its strictest form —without which it continues to remain, in essence, nothing but a diatonic scale replete with chromatic alterations, very freely used.

the series of supra-diatonic whole steps and half steps. It is this characteristic order of intervals of the supra-diatonic scale that enables us to form upon it twelve supra-modes, differentiated from one another simply by the formula of arrangement or distribution of the unchangeable number of whole steps and half steps (i.e. in the same way as modes and infra-modes are distinguished in each of the preceding scales) namely:

*EXAMPLE 83: ***

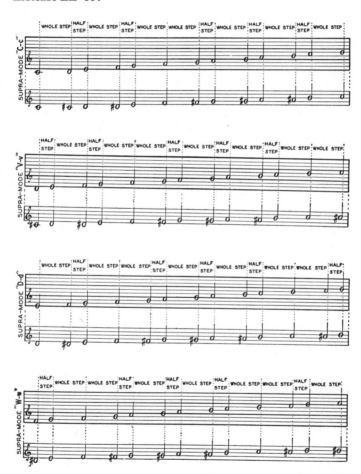

---

* In addition to these twelve principal supra-modes, a number of altered supra-modes could be, of course, formed here, similarly to the altered infra-modes given in Chapter VII of this volume, and to the altered diatonic modes, too well-known to be mentioned. These additional supra-modes, which the reader may easily form for himself, are entirely omitted in this work, however, as they are scarcely necessary for further reference in the course of our discussion.

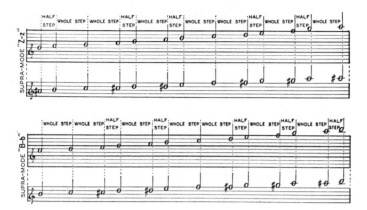

To facilitate the reading of the unfamiliar ten-line system, I have attached to this example (and to many others) the acoustically inadequate and merely approximate notation of the chromatic or, in the above sense, atonal scale ("12"). The latter precludes, of course, the formation upon it of any sort of "modes" as, in contradistinction to the supra-diatonic scale, the formula of arrangement of its component intervals, by reason of their equality, remains unaltered through all their possible permutations.

Conformably to the common number of degrees of the scale "12 + 7," every one of its twelve supra-modes may be freely transposed—under the condition of Equal Temperament—into nineteen different keys consecutively arranged a Fifth apart, similarly to the seven modes of the scale "7 + 5," every one of which may be transposed into twelve different keys, and to the five infra-modes of the scale "5 + 2," every one of which may be transposed into seven different keys.

The similarity of these three scales in the matter of transposition will also manifest itself in the gradual and systematic increase of the signs of alteration of the scale "12 + 7" as it departs from the key of "C," and in their decrease as it returns to the latter. In this way the supra-chromatic (auxiliary) degrees varying, through their participation, the tonal material of every key (which, under all circumstances, preserves the number and the formula of arrangement of the whole steps and half steps of the new scale), they not only fulfill the function of "embellishing" tones but like the chromatic and infra-chromatic degrees in their respective scales, also serve as a medium of transposition and modulation.

There is no necessity, of course, to dilate upon the fact that the atonal scale ("12") which, in contradistinction to the supra-diatonic scale, does not allow the formation of different "modes," does not permit, either, the formation of different "keys" i.e. *different* in the same sense as, for instance, the tonal material of the C-major key of the diatonic scale differs from the tonal material of the G-major or D-major keys, etc., or—which comes to the same thing—as the tonal material of some key of the infra-diatonic scale differs from any other of its keys.

The maximum number of signs of alteration in the supra-diatonic scale will be contained in its keys with twelve supra-flats and twelve supra-sharps (i.e. equalling the number of regular degrees of this scale) similarly to the diatonic and the infra-diatonic scale in which the maximum number of signs of alteration falls on keys with seven sharps or flats and with five infra-sharps or infra-flats respectively. But since there are only nineteen keys in the new scale (conformably to its general number of tones), differing in *actual* tonal material, it is evident that some of the twelve keys with the "supra-flat" signature will be enharmonically equivalent to some of the twelve keys with the "supra-sharp" signature, as it is also the case with certain keys in the two preceding scales.

The following example comprises all the keys of the new scale pertaining to its supra-mode "C-c," the arrows showing which of them are enharmonically equivalent to each other. [The supra-chromatically altered degrees of the new scale in this representation naturally prevent the use of the guiding five-line notation].

EXAMPLE 84:

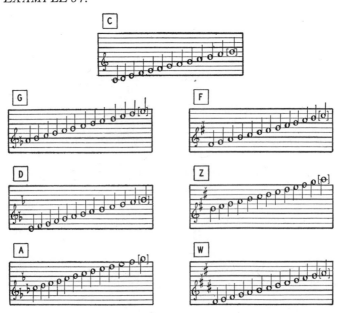

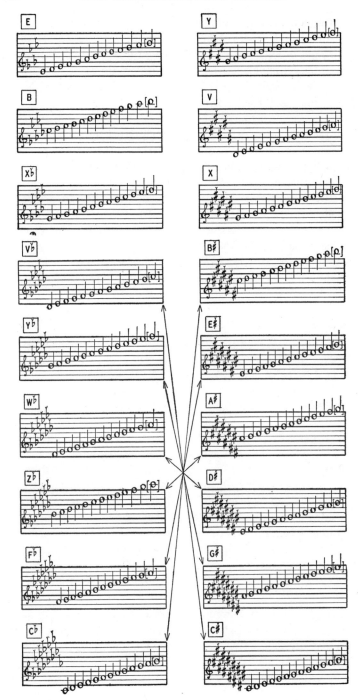

It goes without saying that similar cycles of keys may be formed in regard to all the remaining supra-modes of this scale. On the opposite page (Example 85) the complete set of such cycles is represented in the form of a general and condensed Table containing nineteen different keys for every one of the twelve supra-modes of the scale "12 + 7." The enharmonically equivalent keys are omitted this time for the sake of brevity.

Turning now to the definition of the intervals of the supra-diatonic scale, we face one of the most complex problems of the present research. To make up a Table of these intervals with the exact indication of the number of whole steps or half steps they contain, would, of course, present no difficulty at all. For this would merely require a simple reckoning, familiar to every musician, of the distance between every possible pair of white keys by which the regular degrees of the new scale are represented above (Ex. 80).

This, however, would only solve one—and the easiest—part of our immediate problem, since, besides the quantitative dimension of intervals, we have also to determine—already far less simple a matter—the *quality* of every one of them in the sense of its satisfactoriness or unsatisfactoriness for *an ear which will organically adjust itself, in the future, to the structure of the supra-diatonic scale.*

The mere intent to solve such a problem will doubtless strike one, at first sight, as rather unusual, not to say absurd. How is it possible, indeed, to speak of satisfactoriness or unsatisfactoriness of intervals which nobody has yet had a chance to hear actually (at least outwardly), let alone the fact that the very principle of dividing all the intervals into consonances and dissonances in general is nowadays subjected to the severest criticism and is considered by many musicians to be decidedly obsolete.

I shall temporarily postpone discussing the principle itself, as I shall have occasion to dwell later upon this subject at greater length. As for the objection that the intervals of the supra-diatonic scale have not been heard by anybody yet, I shall make it stronger still (instead of trying to remove it) by saying that were these intervals to be heard for the first time by any one, they could not be easily distinguished from each other (for lack of practice), so far as satisfactoriness or unsatisfactoriness is concerned. Moreover, I venture to say that not only these intervals, but the supra-diatonic scale itself when heard for the first time, even in its just intonation, will impress every musician, including the most extreme modernist, as sounding somewhat "false" because of its disparity with our present intonation.

The human ear is such, however,—at least in its present stage of development—that it regards as "false" every intonation that is different from the one to which it is accustomed. It is a well-known fact that even the just intonation

	KEY "C"	KEY "G"	KEY "D"	KEY "A"	KEY "E"	KEY "B"	KEY "X♭"	KEY "V♭"	KEY "Y♭"	KEY "W♭"	KEY "A♯"	KEY "E♯"	KEY "B♯"	KEY "X"	KEY "V"	KEY "Y"	KEY "W"	KEY "Z"	KEY "F"
SUPRA-MODE "c – c"																			
SUPRA-MODE "v – v"																			
SUPRA-MODE "D – d"																			
SUPRA-MODE "W – w"																			
SUPRA-MODE "E – e"																			
SUPRA-MODE "F – f"																			
SUPRA-MODE "X – x"																			
SUPRA-MODE "G – g"																			
SUPRA-MODE "Y – y"																			
SUPRA-MODE "A – a"																			
SUPRA-MODE "Z – z"																			
SUPRA-MODE "B – b"																			

of the diatonic scale sounds partly "false" to an ear long accustomed to the tempered intonation and that special conditions are necessary for the ear to regain its natural ability to recognize the purity of just intonation and the acoustic inaccuracy of tempered intonation.

This physiologically unexplained flexibility of the musical ear to adjust itself to certain acoustic inaccuracies, however, seems to be a most valuable auditory faculty, if only for the reason that it permits the highly significant practice of Equal Temperament.* The latter, as we know, found its application not only in Occidental music with reference to the diatonic scale ("7 + 5") but also in Far-Eastern music in relation to the infra-diatonic scale ("5 + 2"). And there are, besides, some grounds for believing that it will be possible in the future to apply to the same extent the principle of Equal Temperament as regards the supra-diatonic scale ("12 + 7").

But, on the other hand, this very auditory faculty, so useful in musical prac-

---

* The opinion is voiced from time to time that Equal Temperament spoils the musical ear, which becomes disaccustomed to acoustically pure intervals, so that its receptivity weakens. Others go still further and assert that the artificial deviations of Equal Temperament hinder the normal development of the human ear and, in a certain sense, even clog the wheels of normal development of the musical art. The author however, is inclined to take quite the opposite view in these matters and believes that the practice of Equal Temperament not only does not spoil but refines the musical ear which is compelled to develop its adaptability and thus increases its range of physiologically detectable tones and sonorities in general. Equal Temperament serves the ear as a useful stumbling block, which broadens and enriches its experience, just as in ordinary life obstacles (and not their absence) add to our experience, thereby teaching us how to live. As for Equal Temperament being a "hindrance to normal development of musical art," the upholders of just intonation would be right, in this sense, on one condition only: were a musical composition *directly* based on the acoustically pure series of tones as they are represented by the natural Harmonics (overtones). But between a musical composition and pure acoustic relations there exists an *intermediate agent* in the form of a *scale* which, even when acoustically pure, possesses its own and most essential structural characteristics. The latter, as already stated, allow certain limited deviations from pure acoustic relations, provided these characteristics themselves are not thereby affected. The principle of specific distribution of whole steps and half steps within an octave, with which we are already acquainted, is the most distinctive feature of every "organic" scale constructed upon the spiral of Fifths and Fourths. And it is on this very principle (not on pure acoustic relations) that actual music is based. As long as this characteristic is preserved, any familiar music will be instantly "recognized" in one scale or another, even if its acoustic deviations are very noticeable (for instance on a badly tuned piano). But should this characteristic (i.e. the specific arrangement of whole steps and half steps) be changed ever so slightly, and the very same music will hardly be recognized in certain cases (for instance, should some of the church modes be substituted for our major mode) and in other cases it will not be recognized at all. The existence of this intermediate agent between music and pure acoustics is precisely what explains the possibility of practical use of Equal Temperament, or rather, the possibility and harmlessness of an acoustical compromise for the "normal" development of musical art—a compromise which is unavoidable but at the same time justified by the long history of music. Should we exclude this peculiar agency of the scale as an indispensable condition in music, then the slightest deviation from acoustical accuracy, inevitable in every performance, would have to be considered as a perversion of a musical composition because the ear would not know in relation to what norm (scale serving as such) the psychological correction of this or that acoustical error has to be effected. The place of this norm certainly cannot always be filled by such factors as the maximum simplicity of acoustic relations, or the absence of beats, etc., because it is quite possible that the composer may have precisely in view, in certain instances, *complicated* acoustic relations and the *presence* of beats. In the latter connection I would refer to a highly interesting and thoroughly scientific article entitled *Beats and their significance in modern music* by Ivan E. Orloff, published in a collection of researches on musical acoustics by the State Institute of Musical Science (First Issue, Moscow, 1925).

tice, makes our ear quite unreliable in matters and definitions connected with our present problem. It is impossible, even from the standpoint of plain logic alone, to determine the degree of satisfactoriness or unsatisfactoriness of intervals with the aid of an ear which itself has first to be adjusted to the results of these determinations.

Hence, it is evident that it will be absolutely immaterial, for the solution of our problem, whether one has or has not actually heard the intervals of the supra-diatonic scale. This is because the experimental (inductive) method could not in any case be applied for the *qualitative* determination of intervals, just as the same method cannot be applied in chemistry, for instance, for the determination of the properties of those elements which are but theoretically predicted and not yet actually found in nature. However, as in chemistry it was possible to apply for this purpose some other (deductive) method, starting from a certain observed conformity to a hitherto unknown law—from a certain "Gesetzmässigkeit" as the Germans most appropriately call it—manifested by the various properties of elements that have been *actually found,* so one may avail himself of a similar method for the qualitative determination of the intervals of the supra-diatonic scale, starting from an undeniable conformity to some presumptive law, as manifested in a specific opposition of consonances and dissonances in each of the two preceding scales. And as in chemistry it was afterwards necessary to make an experimental verification of elements which, after first being hypothetical, in the course of time were gradually discovered, so it would be quite proper to make an extensive experimental verification of consonances and dissonances of the supra-diatonic scale after they are theoretically established,—a verification which, of course, presupposes a preliminary adjustment of the ear to new tonal combinations.

It should be added, furthermore, that an unquestionable "Gesetzmässigkeit" (in the above sense) governs not only the intervals of the infra-diatonic and diatonic scales but also their chords, which are specifically opposed, in each case, as concords and discords, depending on the kind and combination of intervals they respectively contain. This circumstance greatly facilitates the solution of our problem, for it is quite clear that to find, for instance, the complete consonant chord of the supra-diatonic scale (i.e. the chord not "requiring" resolution in it) also means automatically to find all the latter's consonant intervals which, as in the preceding scales, should be all contained in this chord and its inversions. Accordingly, every other interval which is *not* included in this consonant chord would have to be considered, generally speaking, as a dissonance. And any chord containing even one of these dissonant intervals would have to be classed as a dissonant chord of the supra-diatonic scale.

The most characteristic constructive feature of all infra-diatonic and diatonic chords in general, is, as already mentioned, their formation by intervals, covering in every instance the space occupied by *three* contiguous regular degrees of their respective scales. So, in the former instance those formative functions are filled by infra-Thirds, while in the latter case they are filled by Thirds. Hence, it will be plausible to conjecture that the functions of intervals forming the chords of the new scale will be filled by supra-Thirds.

Admitting provisionally this principle of chord-construction in the supra-diatonic scale—a principle thus formally identical in all three scales—it is now necessary to determine the *number* of tones which, being successively arranged by supra-Thirds, will form the new consonant chords. It will be recalled that the number of tones constituting the consonant chords of the two preceding scales is not the same and increases simultaneously with the acoustical contraction of their formative intervals. So the consonant chord of the infra-diatonic scale represents a *Dyad* (C-F, for instance), i.e. a harmonic combination of two notes a perfect infra-Third apart. In the diatonic scale we already have, as a consonant chord, the *Triad* (C-E-G, let us say), i.e. a harmonic combination of three notes arranged by Thirds, every one of which, of course, is acoustically smaller than the former infra-Third. Hence it will be logical to infer that the new consonant chord formed by supra-Thirds, i.e. by intervals still smaller than Thirds, would have to contain a greater number of tones. But how shall we find this number?

It was comparatively easy—in the foregoing chapter—to discover the rule which governs the quantitative increase of the scales themselves (diatonic and infra-diatonic), thanks to the very obvious interrelation existing between the different groups of their component degrees. But such "obvious" indications are not in evidence in the consonant chords of these scales (*Dyads* and *Triads*), since the numbers 2 and 3 expressing their quantitative constitution may have various interrelations and therefore alone do not definitely predetermine the only possible quantitative constitution of the consonant chord of the supra-diatonic scale.

Thus, these two figures may express a simple arithmetical progression and then the consonant chord of the supra-diatonic scale will be a *Tetrad*, i.e. a chord consisting of four notes. But no less plausible would be the hypothesis that the number of tones constituting the consonant chord of the new scale equals the sum of the figures 2 and 3 (as is approximately true with reference to the tonal constitution of the scales) and in such a case this chord will be a *Pentad*, i.e. it will consist of five notes. Finally it is just as possible that the number we are looking for equals the product of the figures 2 and 3, which would apparently oblige us to adopt a *Hexad*, i.e. a six-tone harmonic combination, for the consonant chord of the supra-diatonic scale. A Hexad represents the limit of chord-formation by supra-Thirds in this scale, since their further addition to this chord would only repeat the cycle it already contains. Which, then, of these harmonic combinations—Tetrad, Pentad or Hexad—is the consonant chord of the supra-diatonic scale?

To answer this question let us first examine, for greater "safety," the simplest of these three chords, i.e. the Tetrad, assuming it to be the chord sought for. This chord, formed by supra-Thirds, will apparently be expressed by the notes C-D-E-X (See Ex. 80.) Inasmuch as it is assumed to be a *consonant* chord, all the intervals it comprises, as well as their inversions (according to the generally known rule), must be considered as consonances, namely:

POSITIONS		INVERSIONS	
Supra-Thirds	C-D (1½ steps) D-E (1½ steps) E-X (2 steps)	Supra-Elevenths	D-c (8 steps) E-d (8 steps) X-e (7½ steps)
Supra-Fifths	C-E (3 steps) D-X (3½ steps)	Supra-Ninths	E-c (6½ steps) X-d (6 steps)
Supra-Seventh	C-X (5 steps)	Supra-Seventh	X-c (4½ steps)

Temporarily leaving aside the question of all other intervals of the supra-diatonic scale, let us now see what intervals would be introduced into the above tables by two other chords designated as Pentad and Hexad. These chords, formed by supra-Thirds, similarly to the Tetrad, will be respectively expressed by the following notes: C-D-E-X-Y and C-D-E-X-Y-Z.

The new note Y of the first of these chords, i.e. the Pentad, will add to the above table the following intervals:

POSITIONS		INVERSIONS	
Supra-Ninth C-Y	(6½ steps)	Supra-Fifth Y-c	(3 steps)
Supra-Seventh D-Y	(5 steps)	Supra-Seventh Y-d	(4½ steps)
Supra-Fifth E-Y	(3½ steps)	Supra-Ninth Y-e	(6 steps)
Supra-Third X-Y	(1½ steps)	Supra-Eleventh Y-x	(8 steps)

The concluding note Z of the latter chord, i.e. the Hexad, will add a few more intervals namely:

POSITIONS		INVERSIONS	
Supra-Eleventh C-Z	(8 steps)	Supra-Third Z-c	(1½ steps)
Supra-Ninth D-Z	(6½ steps)	Supra-Fifth Z-d	(3 steps)
Supra-Seventh E-Z	(5 steps)	Supra-Seventh Z-e	(4½ steps)
Supra-Fifth X-Z	(3 steps)	Supra-Ninth Z-x	(6½ steps)
Supra-Third Y-Z	(1½ steps)	Supra-Eleventh Z-y	(8 steps)

Carefully examining these two supplementary tables, obtained by the addition of two more supra-Thirds to the Tetrad, we shall literally not find a single interval that is not already represented (although on different degrees) in the first table of consonances given, and that consequently could not be considered, to the same extent, as a consonance.

In this way neither the Pentad nor the Hexad contains any other intervals aside from those we have assumed as consonances, and they may therefore be considered as consonant chords of the supra-diatonic scale, with as much justification as the Tetrad. But at the same time, inasmuch as these three chords are distinguished from one another merely by their quantitative tonal constitution, and not by their quality, they cannot be regarded as *different* chords, in the musical sense of the word. We know, for instance, that the chord C-E-c of the diatonic scale is never considered as an independent chord, different from the Triad C-E-G-c, but only as an abbreviated or incomplete form of the latter. Similarly, neither the Tetrad nor the Pentad can be regarded otherwise as abbreviated forms of the Hexad which includes them both and which therefore represents the sought-for *consonant chord of the supra-diatonic scale in its complete form.*

Knowing the structure of this chord, which by its very nature comprises—as a rule—all the consonances, and absolutely excludes all the dissonances of the supra-diatonic scale, it is not difficult now to make a full classification of intervals pertaining to this scale with the indication not only of their dimension but also of their quality. In the following Table which contains these intervals (for simplification, the supra-chromatic intervals, as previously the chromatic and infra-chromatic intervals, are entirely eliminated from it and from our further discussion), the Roman numerals show the (regular) degrees of the new scale and the Arabic numerals the number of whole steps and half steps each interval contains; the literal designations of notes (with reference to the key of "C") are added for the sake of clarity:

TABLE OF INTERVALS OF THE SUPRA-DIATONIC SCALE

(SUPRA-MODE "C-c")

	I	II	III	IV	V	VI	VII	VIII	IX	X	XI	XII
Supra-Primes (P. C.)	perf. 0 C-C	perf. 0 V-V	perf. 0 D-D	perf. 0 W-W	perf. 0 E-E	perf. 0 F-F	perf. 0 X-X	perf. 0 G-G	perf. 0 Y-Y	perf. 0 A-A	perf. 0 Z-Z	perf. 0 B-B
Supra-Seconds (I.D.)	major 1 C-V	minor ½ V-D	major 1 D-W	minor ½ W-E	major 1 E-F	major 1 F-X	minor ½ X-G	major 1 G-Y	minor ½ Y-A	major 1 A-Z	minor ½ Z-B	major 1 B-c
Supra-Thirds (I.C.)	minor 1½ C-D	minor 1½ V-W	minor 1½ D-E	minor 1½ W-F	major 2 E-X	minor 1½ F-G	minor 1½ X-Y	minor 1½ G-A	minor 1½ Y-Z	minor 1½ A-B	minor 1½ Z-c	major 2 B-v
Supra-Fourths (P.D.)	perf. 2½ C-W	dim. 2 V-E	perf. 2½ D-F	perf. 2½ W-X	perf. 2½ E-G	perf. 2½ F-Y	dim. 2 X-A	perf. 2½ G-Z	dim. 2 Y-B	perf. 2½ A-c	perf. 2½ Z-v	perf. 2½ B-d
Supra-Fifths (I.C.)	minor 3 C-E	minor 3 V-F	major 3½ D-X	minor 3 W-G	major 3½ E-Y	minor 3 F-A	minor 3 X-Z	minor 3 G-B	minor 3 Y-c	major 3½ A-v	minor 3 Z-d	major 3½ B-w
Supra-Sixths (P.D.)	perf. 4 C-F	perf. 4 V-X	perf. 4 D-G	perf. 4 W-Y	perf. 4 E-A	perf. 4 F-Z	dim. 3½ X-B	perf. 4 G-c	perf. 4 Y-v	perf. 4 A-d	perf. 4 Z-w	perf. 4 B-e
Supra-Sevenths (I.C.)	major 5 C-X	minor 4½ V-G	major 5 D-Y	minor 4½ W-A	major 5 E-Z	minor 4½ F-B	minor 4½ X-c	major 5 G-v	minor 4½ Y-d	major 5 A-w	minor 4½ Z-e	major 5 B-f
Supra-Eighths (P.D.)	perf. 5½ C-G	perf. 5½ V-Y	perf. 5½ D-A	perf. 5½ W-Z	perf. 5½ E-B	perf. 5½ F-c	perf. 5½ X-v	perf. 5½ G-d	perf. 5½ Y-w	perf. 5½ A-e	perf. 5½ Z-f	augm. 6 B-x
Supra-Ninths (I.C.)	major 6½ C-Y	minor 6 V-A	major 6½ D-Z	minor 6 W-B	major 6½ E-c	major 6½ F-v	minor 6 X-d	major 6½ G-w	minor 6 Y-e	major 6½ A-f	major 6½ Z-x	major 6½ B-g
Supra-Tenths (P.D.)	perf. 7 C-A	perf. 7 V-Z	perf. 7 D-B	perf. 7 W-c	augm. 7½ E-v	perf. 7 F-d	perf. 7 X-w	perf. 7 G-e	perf. 7 Y-f	augm. 7½ A-x	perf. 7 Z-g	augm. 7½ B-y
Supra-Elevenths (I.C.)	major 8 C-Z	minor 7½ V-B	major 8 D-c	major 8 W-v	major 8 E-d	major 8 F-w	minor 7½ X-e	major 8 G-f	major 8 Y-x	major 8 A-g	major 8 Z-y	major 8 B-a
Supra-Twelfths (I.D.)	minor 8½ C-B	minor 8½ V-c	major 9 D-v	minor 8½ W-d	major 9 E-w	major 9 F-e	minor 8½ X-f	minor 8½ G-x	major 9 Y-g	minor 8½ A-y	minor 8½ Z-a	major 9 B-z
Supra-Thirteenths (P.C.)	perf. 9½ C-c	perf. 9½ V-v	perf. 9½ D-d	perf. 9½ W-w	perf. 9½ E-e	perf. 9½ F-f	perf. 9½ X-x	perf. 9½ G-g	perf. 9½ Y-y	perf. 9½ A-a	perf. 9½ Z-z.	perf. 9½ B-b

Half the number of the above intervals of course simply represent the inversions of the other half, being governed in this respect by the well-known rule according to which consonances are inverted into consonances, dissonances into dissonances, major intervals into minor, augmented intervals into diminished, and *vice versa*. It is also easy to *find* the inversions of all these intervals since any given interval added up with its inversion will always equal 9½ steps of the supra-diatonic scale, i.e. the dimension of an Octave (supra-Thirteenth) as is the case in the preceding scales.

Should we now compare this Table with the two previous Tables of intervals relating to the diatonic and infra-diatonic scales (see pages 61 and 109) we shall find, in addition to their common characteristics, certain specific peculiarities which it will be necessary later to take into account.

The very division of intervals into two principal and contradistinctive classes, consonances and dissonances, is a common characteristic of all scales. But the manner of division, of course, is quite different in each particular scale (whence the notions of consonance and dissonance acquire a relative meaning) and also shows, above all, a certain dissimilarity in regard to further subdivision within these two principal classes. Thus, we find one undivided class of consonances (perfect) as well as one undivided class of dissonances (known under its double "major and minor" aspect) among the different groups of intervals (infra-Seconds, infra-Thirds, etc.) of the infra-diatonic scale. And while there still remains one undivided class of dissonances in the next diatonic scale (the additional augmented and diminished intervals found within its regular degrees do not create, of course, a new "class"), its consonant intervals are already subdivided into two different kinds known as perfect and imperfect.

The term *perfect* is familiarly applied to those consonances of the diatonic scale which are characterized within the groups that contain them, by one constant dimension (like the Fourths or the Fifths)—their deviations, augmented and diminished intervals, encountered on some degrees of these groups but absent among the component intervals of the consonant chord of this scale thus becoming automatically qualified as dissonances—while the term *imperfect* is applied to those consonances which are characterized within their groups by two different dimensions (like the two kinds of Thirds, for instance) designated as major and minor.

In the supra-diatonic scale, for the first time we encounter a very similar subdivision among the *dissonances*, resulting from the natural existence of a few intervals within some of their groups, equal in dimension to the previously established consonances of this scale *without being supra-chromatically altered*. These few intervals representing "deviations" from dissonances in the direction of consonances are accordingly designated by the terms "augmented" and "diminished," both of them for the first time being applied in the new scale also to non-dissonant intervals. Such are, for instance, the three diminished supra-Fourths (found on the second, seventh and ninth degrees), each of which contains two whole steps, i.e. as many as the consonant major supra-Third; also the diminished supra-Sixth (on the seventh degree) which containing three and a half steps equals the consonant major supra-Fifth, etc. The rest of the intervals of the groups in which these deviations occur, are thus characterized by one constant dimension and therefore are named *perfect dissonances* (P.D.). Contrarily to the latter, the qualification of *imperfect dissonances* (I. D.) is assigned to those intervals that are characterized, within their corresponding groups, by two different dimensions and further designated by the terms "major" and "minor." Such are the supra-Seconds and their inversions, the supra-Twelfths.*

As regards the consonant intervals of the supra-diatonic scale in general, their subdivision into *perfect* and *imperfect* (P. C. and I. C.), which we encountered for the first time in the diatonic scale, is also preserved here, but indirectly gives rise to a rather unexpected and puzzling phenomenon which we shall inquire into at once.

That some dissonances of the diatonic scale became (imperfect) consonances in the supra-diatonic scale is, of course, quite natural, since a similar transformation has already taken place in regard to the dissonances of the infra-diatonic scale which became (imperfect) consonances in the diatonic scale. Such is, for instance, the diminished infra-Third (F-A) which became a major Third, and such is also the case with the diminished Fifth (B-F) which becomes a major supra-Seventh in the new scale. At the same time, however, two groups of intervals of the diatonic scale—perfect Fourths and Fifths—are not only excluded from the field of perfect consonances of the supra-diatonic scale but are classed among its perfect dissonances, being labeled under the names of perfect supra-Sixths and supra-Eighths respectively. As a result of this "exclusion" of Fourths and Fifths, (supra-Sixths and supra-Eighths) from the field of perfect consonances, the latter are confined to the Primes and Octaves (supra-Primes and supra-Thirteenths) in the supra-diatonic scale.

In this way the principle of gradual absorption of the dissonances of a certain scale by the consonances of the more complicated scale which follows it, proves to be less direct than might be expected, and apparently admits of some sort of "reversion," i.e. in certain instances, a transference of consonances from one scale to the category of dissonances of another and more complex scale.**

---

* The terms "major" and "minor" are thus applied to imperfect dissonances as well as to imperfect consonances of the supra-diatonic scale.

** One instance of a somewhat similar "reversion"—although not too obvious to every one— is, strictly speaking, already encountered in the diatonic scale in which the interval of a Fourth defined as a *perfect* consonance sounds less consonant to the ear accustomed to this scale than, let us say, the interval of a major Third repre-senting an *imperfect* consonance. A major Third is *psychologically* more consonant to such an ear than a perfect Fourth, in spite of the fact that from a purely *acoustical* point of view the relation between these two intervals is just the reverse. (Compare Helmholtz, p. 197). To a musician who thinks "diatonically" a perfect Fourth, taken alone on a piano, definitely tends to resolve into a major Third (a perfect Fourth is invariably considered a dissonance in strict two-part Harmony). But to a musician who thinks "infra-

This paradoxical but inevitable inference requires, however, a detailed and adequate explanation, for how is it possible indeed, that an interval which used to be a consonance in a less complicated scale should become a dissonance in a more complicated one? Or, concretely speaking, how can one admit, for instance, that an acoustically pure Fifth, C-G ($\frac{3}{2}$ or 351 ctn.), which is a consonance even for the most primitive ear, should be perceived as a dissonance by an immeasurably more developed ear, broken in to all the complexities of the supra-diatonic scale?

The explanation of this imaginary paradox—for *imaginary* it is—lies in the fact that apart from purely psychological reasons which we shall discuss later, acoustically pure Fifths (and, with them, acoustically pure Fourths expressed by $\frac{4}{3}$ or 249 ctn.) simply do not exist in the supra-diatonic scale, its supra-Eighth C-G, for instance, merely approximating and not coinciding with the acoustically pure Fifth C-G. And, what is of most importance, this discrepancy occurs not only in the supra-tempered intonation of this scale (which is to be expected) but also in its just intonation. Such an explanation will doubtless appear, at first sight, rather unsatisfactory and may even seem to intensify our paradox. For, first of all—one may ask—how is it possible that the interval C-G is not acoustically pure in just (i.e. in acoustically pure) intonation of the supra-diatonic scale, and secondly, even should this thesis be proved, why cannot a highly developed ear adjust itself, in the familiar manner, to the inaccuracy of this interval and perceive it as an acoustically pure Fifth, i.e. as a long accepted consonance?

In order to unravel this knot of imaginary paradoxes and inconsistencies and to answer adequately the question asked, we shall have to start some distance back and give a clear and accurate account of those acoustical and musical notions on which we base our constructions and proofs.

Let us first define as precisely as possible what is really meant by so-called *Just Intonation* in general. This term usually implies an intonation subject

---

diatonically" a major Third tends, on the contrary, to resolve into a perfect Fourth. And since this latter type of musician historically precedes the former it is easy to understand why the subdivision of consonances into *perfect* and *imperfect*, in European music, resulted in the familiar grouping which is nominally preserved to this day through the force of inertia.

In connection with these two intrinsically different types of musicians, the author may add that, judging from his own experience, the barrier that separates them does not seem to be too solid and that, from all evidences, it is not very difficult for either of them to inwardly comprehend the turn of the other's musical mind. Thus, during his long work on the construction of the infra-diatonic harmonic system, the author, unex-

pectedly to himself, became accustomed fairly soon to the perception of the major Third (diminished infra-Third) as a dissonance "requiring" resolution into a perfect Fourth, i.e. he got used to what is diametrically opposed to the "diatonic" way of thinking. This ability to fathom a musical psychology foreign to one (which, by the way, any one may easily verify for himself if he will take the trouble for a few weeks to deal exclusively with infra-diatonic harmony, barring all other musical perceptions for this time) is a highly valuable property of our inward ear and again inspires a certain conviction that a similar penetration, in the future, into "supra-diatonic" psychology, alien so far to the vast majority of musicians, will not prove to be as difficult in practice as might be expected.

to those elementary acoustic laws which are manifested in the Natural Harmonic Series (overtones) known to every musician. Before proceeding, let us pictorially represent this series:

EXAMPLE 86:

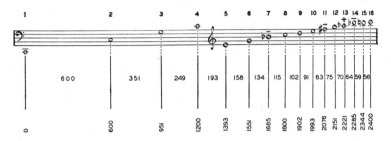

The series of overtones theoretically extends *ad infinitum* but for our purpose its four initial octaves will suffice. They are supplemented here by a diagram showing (in centitones and in round numbers) the dimensions of intervals formed by contiguous overtones (figures between the lines) and also the dimensions of intervals formed by every overtone and the common fundamental note C (figures below the lines). Figures above the notes indicate the ratios of overtones to the fundamental tone, which is assumed to be *one,* and also serve as their ordinal designations. Signs (+) and (—) above some notes indicate the approximation of their pitch in regard to any intonation of the diatonic scale (the latter's musical notation will be invariably used to designate overtones) and, consequently, require certain mental corrections when this particular scale is concerned. The exact degree of these corrections will become evident in the course of the following discussion.

Having now before us the series of overtones and knowing that it is the basis of just intonation of any scale, we are still far from having an adequate idea of this intonation. This is because our definition only says that just intonation is subject to the acoustic laws of the Natural Harmonic Series but does not specify in *what form,* whilst this form of subjection itself is apt to vary and to lead, in each case, to quite different results. For instance, a musician looking at this Series for the first time may think (and it happens fairly often) that a certain number of its constituent notes, when comprised within an octave, produce what is known as just intonation of the diatonic scale. In reality, however, such a *direct* subjection to acoustic laws does not take place at all, since the just intonation of the seven regular degrees of the diatonic scale but partly coincides with the intonation of the seven consecutive overtones (disregarding their octave duplications) brought within the compass of an octave, as may be learned from the following diagram in which both these intonations are represented and to which is added, for the sake of comparison (in dotted lines and without figures) the equally tempered intonation of the same scale. [The numbers enclosed in boxes show the *original* ratios of overtones, i.e. *before* they have been comprised within an octave].

EXAMPLE 87:

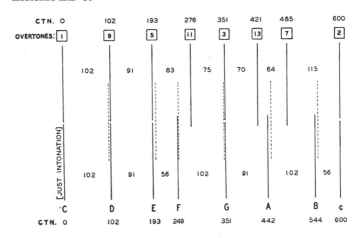

The discrepancy between three notes (F, A, B) of the justly intoned diatonic scale and three overtones (*11, 13, 7*) of the Harmonic Series, as shown in this diagram, would be by no means eliminated, but merely somewhat reduced, should some other modes of this scale be substituted for the familiar major mode, of which we have availed ourselves in our comparison. Thus, in the instance of the Lydian mode (F-f″) which has an augmented instead of a perfect Fourth on its first degree, the note F♯ (assuming C as the Tonic) would reach the mark of 295 ctn. (since the Tritone F-B equals 544—249), a number exceeding that of the overtone *11* (276 ctn.) by 19 ctn. Consequently, the discrepancy between the fourth degree of the scale and the overtone *11* would be reduced by 8 ctn. in comparison with that occurring in the major mode (276 — 249 = 27 ctn.), the position of the other "non-coinciding" degrees (A and B) remaining unchanged. Again, should we substitute the Mixolydian mode ("G-g") for the major mode, its leading note B♭ (assuming C as the Tonic) would go down to 498 ctn. (600—102, in order to obtain 351 ctn. for the purely tuned Fifth B♭—F), making a difference of 13 ctn. with the overtone *7*. The discrepancy between the seventh degree of the scale and the overtone *7* would therefore be reduced by 46 ctn. in this instance, as compared with that occurring in the major mode (544 — 485 = 59 ctn.), the position of the other "non-coinciding" degrees (F and A) likewise remaining unchanged. Finally, should we use, in our diagram, the so-called harmonic major mode with the sixth degree flatted (A♭ instead of A), the difference between the overtone *13* and the note A♭ would be 14 ctn., since the pure minor Sixth ($\frac{8}{5}$) equals 407 ctn. and the interval formed by the overtone referred to and the Tonic equals 421 ctn. within the compass of an Octave. Consequently, the discrepancy between the sixth degree of the scale and the overtone *13* would be reduced here by 7 ctn. in comparison to that occurring in the major mode (442 — 421 = 21 ctn.), while the rest of the "non-coinciding" degrees (F and B) would similarly remain unchanged, as heretofore.

But suppose we decide to overlook, in the above diagram, the principle of bringing the overtones within one octave in *consecutive* order, and to look for the notes corresponding to the just intonation of the diatonic scale beyond the limits of the seven consecutive overtones, even then one may add but one more overtone (*15*) to those which coincide with the just intonation of the diatonic scale. No overtones corresponding to the rest of the notes (F and A) of this scale will be found even in the subsequent octaves of the Natural Harmonic Series.

It is evident, then, that the form of subjection of just intonation of the diatonic scale to acoustic laws of this Series is of a somewhat particular nature. As a matter of fact it consists in tuning every one of the three principal common (consonant) chords of this scale in accordance with the intervals formed by three consecutive overtones which are designated in the Harmonic Series by the notes and figures C-E-G. The dimensions of these intervals being indicated in centitones, the three chords mentioned will have the following appearance:

TONIC TRIAD:	C	193	E	158	G
DOMINANT TRIAD:	G	193	B	158	D
SUBDOMINANT TRIAD:	F	193	A	158	C

This sort of "tuning" of three consonant chords—though different in their absolute pitch—in accordance with one and the same group of overtones is easily attained, owing to the fact that these chords are interconnected by common notes and thereby permit the construction of one continuous chain exclusively composed of natural major and minor Thirds, i.e. of the very intervals which are formed by the overtones C-E-G, namely:

subdominant Triad   dominant Triad

F   193   A   158   C   193   E   158   G   193   B   158   D

tonic Triad

This chain of natural Thirds apparently covers all seven (regular) degrees of the diatonic scale and is the very one which produces the latter's just intonation, when comprised within an octave. (See lower set of lines of the foregoing diagram, Ex. 87.)

In this way, even though the just intonation of the diatonic scale has, after all, the Natural Harmonic Series as its foundation, yet it is based on it not directly but through the *medium* of the consonant chords, this factor leading to entirely different results, as demonstrated above (Ex. 87).*

This same principle of "mediumship" should guide us in the establishment of just intonation for the infra-diatonic as well as for the supra-diatonic scale.

The structure of the perfect Dyad, which is the consonant chord of the infra-diatonic scale, corresponds to the position of two overtones $\overset{3\ 4}{\text{G-C}}$ (See Ex. 86). The consonant chords of the other degrees of this scale must therefore also be tuned in accordance with them. This is again easily attained owing to the fact that the Dyads of the infra-diatonic scale are interconnected by common notes, thereby allowing the construction of one continuous chain exclusively composed of natural infra-Thirds, i.e. of intervals of the same dimension as those formed by the overtones $\overset{3\ 4}{\text{G-C}}$, namely:

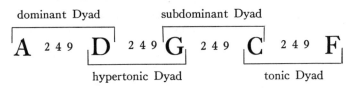

This chain of natural infra-Thirds covers all five regular degrees of the infra-diatonic scale (similarly to the chain of Thirds covering all seven regular degrees of the diatonic scale) and being comprised within an octave will lead up to its just intonation, as shown in the following line of notes:

C   102   D   147   F   102   G   102   A

Should we now compare this just intonation of the infra-diatonic scale with its Pythagorean intonation represented in one of the previous chapters of this book (Ex. 14, upper set of long lines) we shall observe, perhaps unexpectedly,

---

* In explaining the just intonation of all three scales, the author purposely confines himself to their regular degrees. This is done merely for simplification since the auxiliary degrees of the scales cannot be fixed, in each instance, by a single note, inasmuch as they change in absolute pitch, depending on whether they are considered as "sharps" or "flats." In spite of this duality, however, they psychologically represent, in both instances, the very same auxiliary degrees, inasmuch as the latter divide every whole step into two half steps (and no more) even if not quite equal to each other. It is evident that should we assume the "sharp" and the "flat" as two separate auxiliary degrees, every whole step would be thereby divided into three parts, two of which would still have to be regarded as half steps, an absurdity.

that these two intonations are absolutely identical. The reason for this identity, however, is easily explained in this instance, since the chain of natural infra-Thirds A-D-G-C-F, on which the just intonation of the infra-diatonic scale is based, represents nothing else but the acoustically most exact inversion of the chain of natural infra-Fourths F-C-G-D-A which underlies the Pythagorean intonation of this scale. It follows as a matter of course that both these chains are bound to lead to perfectly identical results, when comprised within an octave, just as it is well understood that such a coincidence of the just and Pythagorean intonations cannot occur in any scale more complicated than the infra-diatonic scale.

Hence we draw the direct conclusion that not only the overtones $\overset{3}{G}$-$\overset{4}{C}$ may serve as the nucleus of the just intonation of the infra-diatonic scale, but also the overtones $\overset{2}{C}$-$\overset{3}{G}$, their combination evidently representing an inversion of the former. This conclusion is of the utmost importance to us, as it permits us to formulate a single acoustic principle embracing, with a certain regularity, the application of isolated groups of overtones as "nuclei" for the just intonations of different scales arranged, in consecutive order, upon the spiral of Fifths and Fourths, thereby giving us an additional clue in our search for just intonation of the supra-diatonic scale. The regularity in question consists in that every one of these isolated and gradually increasing groups of overtones always has its beginning in a new octave of their common Natural Series (Ex. 86), and therefore the initial overtone of every group will always coincide with the fundamental tone of the entire series but in a different octave.

The first of these octaves has no overtones beyond the fundamental tone ($\overset{1}{C}$) which generates them all and which itself may be considered as the nucleus of the just intonation of the most primitive scale whose sole consonance is represented by a unison, in other words, a *Monad*.* The second octave of the same series contains two overtones ($\overset{2}{C}$-$\overset{3}{G}$) which serve as the nucleus of the just intonation of the infra-diatonic scale, inasmuch as they represent the tonal material which forms its consonant chord, i.e. a *Dyad*. Similarly the nucleus of the just intonation of the diatonic scale is represented by those three overtones ($\overset{4}{C}$-$\overset{5}{E}$-$\overset{6}{G}$) of the third octave, which form its consonant chord, i.e. a *Triad*. Hence it will be logical to assume that the nucleus of the just intonation of the supra-diatonic scale will turn out to be the group of overtones which starts from the fourth octave of their common Natural Series.

There are altogether eight overtones within the span of this fourth octave

---

* The nature of this primitive (sub-infra-diatonic) scale as well as its inherent harmony was fully described in the supplement to the foregoing chapter.

(namely, $\overset{8\ \ 9\ \ 10\ \ 11\ \ 12\ \ 13\ \ 14\ \ \ 15}{\text{C-D-E-F}\sharp\text{-G-A}\flat\text{-B}\flat\text{-B}\natural}$), among which we have to find *six* for the purpose of "tuning" the consonant chord of the supra-diatonic scale which, as we know, is found to be an *Hexad*. The instance of the diatonic scale has shown us that the establishment of its just intonation does not exhaust all the overtones of the third octave of the Natural Harmonic Series on which this intonation is based, one of its overtones ($\overset{7}{\text{B}}\flat$), which forms with the initial tone of this octave ($\overset{4}{\text{C}}$) an interval (C-$\bar{\text{B}}\flat$) that is missing in the consonant chord of this scale, being definitely excluded therefrom. Starting from this precedent we shall exclude from the next fourth octave, on which the just intonation of the supra-diatonic scale is to be based, those overtones ($\overset{12}{\text{G}}$ and $\overset{15}{\text{B}}$) which form, with the initial tone of this octave ($\overset{8}{\text{C}}$), two intervals that are likewise definitely missing in the consonant chord (Hexad C-D-E-X-Y-Z) of this scale, i.e. the intervals C-G (supra-Eighth) and C-B (supra-Twelfth).

As a result of this exclusion there will remain six overtones ($\overset{8\ \ 9\ \ 10\ \ 11\ \ \ \ 13}{\text{C-D-E-F}\sharp\text{-A}\flat\text{-}}$ $\overset{14}{\text{B}}\flat$) of the group constituting the fourth octave of the Natural Harmonic Series, according to which the supposedly *principal* Hexads of the supra-diatonic scale will now be "tuned."* These Hexads must be selected, *first,* so that the arrangement of their major and minor supra-Thirds shall approximately correspond to the arrangement of intervals formed by the above six overtones, and, *secondly,* in such number that they (the Hexads) shall jointly cover all twelve regular degrees of our new scale.

In order to facilitate this operation, let us as a preliminary, compose a Table of all the Hexads of the supra-diatonic scale taken from every one of its twelve (regular) degrees, with an indication of the dimension of their component intervals in terms of whole steps and half steps, using for this purpose number 2 to designate a major supra-Third and number $1\frac{1}{2}$ to designate a minor supra-Third:

---

* The presence, in this group, of the overtone 14, which is no more than an octave-duplication of the overtone 7, shows that the exclusion of the latter from the previous (third) octave does not create a gap in the general Harmonic Series, while its different sections are being used as respective "nuclei" for tuning the gradually evolving scales. As a matter of fact, it would be just as correct to designate the six overtones (to whose ratios the supra-diatonic scale is supposed to be tuned) as 7:8:9:10:11:13, the overtone 7 being substituted for 14. This substitution, moreover, would even spare us the necessity of dealing with the overtone 15, the exclusion of which becomes inevitable only when the different sections of the Harmonic Series, in the capacity of "nuclei" referred to, are considered as representatives of its separate octaves. And if we have preferred the latter attitude towards these "sections," and have designated the overtones as shown in the text, it is merely with the object of finding a ground for a certain regularity to which their arrangement could be reduced in the general Series. It will be remembered that for the same reason and also without detriment, we redesignated the "nucleus" for tuning the infra-diatonic scale (overtones 2:3 instead of 3:4).

TABLE OF HEXADS OF THE SUPRA-DIATONIC SCALE

DEGREES

I.   C   1½   D   1½   E   2   X   1½   Y   1½   Z   1½   c

II.   V   1½   W   1½   F   1½   G   1½   A   1½   B   2   v

III.   D   1½   E   2   X   1½   Y   1½   Z   1½   C   1½   d

IV.   W   1½   F   1½   G   1½   A   1½   B   2   V   1½   w

V.   E   2   X   1½   Y   1½   Z   1½   C   1½   D   1½   e

VI.   F   1½   G   1½   A   1½   B   2   V   1½   W   1½   f

VII.   X   1½   Y   1½   Z   1½   C   1½   D   1½   E   2   x

VIII.   G   1½   A   1½   B   2   V   1½   W   1½   F   1½   g

IX.   Y   1½   Z   1½   C   1½   D   1½   E   2   X   1½   y

X.   A   1½   B   2   V   1½   W   1½   F   1½   G   1½   a

XI.   Z   1½   C   1½   D   1½   E   2   X   1½   Y   1½   z

XII.   B   2   V   1½   W   1½   F   1½   G   1½   A   1½   b

Starting now to select the Hexads sought for from their general set represented in this Table and comparing, for this purpose, their component supra-Thirds with the intervals formed by the above six overtones, we are faced by a new difficulty, for every one of the twelve Hexads of the supra-diatonic scale includes in its structure only two kinds of qualitatively different supra-Thirds (major and minor), whereas the six overtones, according to which these Hexads are supposed to be tuned, form six dimensionally different intervals, as shown in the following representation:

OVERTONES: 8   9   10   11   13   14   [16]

$$\text{C } _{102} \text{ D } _{91} \text{ E } _{83} \text{ F}\sharp _{145} \text{ A}\flat _{64} \text{ B}\flat _{115} \left[\text{c} \right]$$

[The figures above the notes are numeral designations of overtones; the figures between the notes indicate, in centitones, the dimension of the intervals formed by them].

We have already had occasion to mention, however, that the quality of intervals is not gauged by their absolute dimension (which is somewhat flexible) but by the number of whole steps and half steps they contain. This is proved not only by long practice of various tempered intonations, in which the intervals preserve their musical qualities in spite of a certain disparity with just intonation, but also by the very nature of just intonation itself, in which qualitatively homogeneous intervals do not necessarily coincide (in absolute dimension) on different degrees of the same scale. Thus, the major Second C-D of the diatonic and justly intoned scale does not dimensionally coincide with the major Second D-E of the same scale, there being a difference of 11 ctn., as may be seen from Ex. 87. At the same time the musico-psychological meaning of these two intervals, or what is known as their quality in the theory of music, is absolutely identical, being expressed by the same number of component whole steps (each one of these intervals comprises one whole step).

Starting from this, we may utilize, without any risk, the dimensionally different intervals formed by the above group of overtones for "tuning" the qualitatively homogeneous supra-Thirds found in the Hexads of the supra-diatonic scale.

Judging from the general Table of these Hexads every one of them contains five minor (consequently homogeneous in quality) supra-Thirds and one major. The latter evidently has to be tuned in accordance with the widest interval found between the overtones referred to, i.e. with the interval F$\sharp$ $_{145}$ A$\flat$, which automatically predetermines a consecutive tuning of all the minor supra-Thirds in accordance with the natural intervals formed by the rest of these overtones.

Of the twelve Hexads of the supra-diatonic scale there could be selected but two in which the position of the major supra-Third among the minor supra-Thirds corresponds to the position of the widest interval among the rest of the natural intervals formed by the overtones, and, which, furthermore, jointly cover all twelve degrees of the supra-diatonic scale. The two Hexads in question (F-G-A-B-V-W and Z-C-D-E-X-Y) are found on the sixth and eleventh degrees of this scale, and placed side by side with the six overtones C-D-E-F$\sharp$-A$\flat$-B$\flat$ they will represent two identical instances of maximum approximation to the latter, possible under the given conditions. This is demonstrated by the following diagram in which the upper set of lines corresponds to the intonation of this group of overtones and the lower set of lines corresponds to the supra-tempered intonation of each of the two Hexads selected. The numbers in brackets indicate the dimension of intervals in terms of whole steps and half steps, the rest of the numbers (not counting, of course, the numeral designations of the overtones) indicating the dimension of the same intervals in terms of centitones:

EXAMPLE 88:

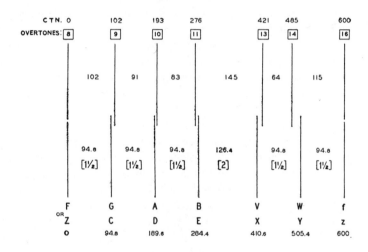

The fact that neither of the two selected chords is a tonic Hexad in the supra-mode "C-c" has no importance at this point since each of them *could* be a tonic Hexad in their respective supra-modes, and it is immaterial, for our purpose, in relation to what supra-mode the just intonation of the new scale will be found.

But before the final step revealing this intonation is taken, i.e. before the two Hexads have to be brought within the compass of an Octave, one more unexpected obstacle lies in wait for us. This is the impossibility of forming one continuous chain of the supra-Thirds constituting these Hexads, because of the absence of any interconnecting common note between the latter. Therefore, having tuned one of these Hexads, let us say, F-G-A-B-V-W, in accordance with the six overtones, as shown in the above diagram, we are at once confronted by a new problem and a rather difficult one, consisting in the exact determination of the interval at which the other Hexad, i.e. Z-C-D-E-X-Y, has to be placed.

What we know so far is only the dimension of this interval in terms of whole steps or half steps, i.e. we know that the Tonics of both Hexads are separated from each other by the interval of a perfect supra-Sixth comprising four whole steps. But we do not yet know the dimension of these same whole steps in just intonation, and it is obvious, therefore, that we can have no idea of the acoustic dimension of their resultant interval (perfect supra-Sixth) in the same intonation. Added to this it must be said that the absence of a common note between these two Hexads is not an exception but a rule equally applicable to any other pair of Hexads jointly covering the twelve regular degrees of the supra-diatonic scale. It is not difficult to guess that this rule, as well as the impossibility of covering the twelve regular degrees in any other way but by two Hexads *not* connected by common notes, results from the specific structure of this scale, namely from the *even* number of its regular degrees.

However, the very nature of the supra-diatonic scale, as if in compensation for its specificalness, shows us the way out of this seemingly inextricable position. We already know that the structure of this scale gave rise to the new subdivision of dissonances into two different kinds—perfect and imperfect—resulting from the existence of a few "deviated" intervals among the former, equal to certain consonant intervals, as far as the number of their whole steps and half steps is concerned, and therefore qualified as consonances. We also know that the diminished supra-Fourths, in particular, belong to this sort of intervals, inasmuch as they are dimensionally equivalent to the major supra-Thirds, comprising two whole steps each. Judging from the table of intervals of the supra-diatonic scale (page 173) none of these diminished supra-Fourths could be found within the limits of *either* of our two selected Hexads (F-G-A-B-V-W or Z-C-D-E-X-Y). But since the latter jointly cover the twelve regular degrees of the supra-diatonic scale without exception, which naturally include the component notes of every diminished supra-Fourth, it is evident that these notes will be found, in every instance, in two *different* Hexads. Thus, of the two notes constituting the diminished supra-Fourth V-E, one (V) belongs to the former of the two Hexads and the other (E) belongs to the latter. The same is true of the rest of the diminished supra-Fourths X-A and Y-B.

Hence it is apparent that should we avail ourselves of the already known dimension of the natural major supra-Third (145 ctn.) for the diminished supra-Fourth, with which it fully coincides in the number of whole steps contained, we shall thereby create a sort of connecting bridge between the two Hexads which will determine their respective position in relation to each other as shown in the following representation, preserving (besides the newly added "bridge" of 145 ctn. for the diminished supra-Fourth Y-B) the dimensions of all intervals in accordance with Example 88:

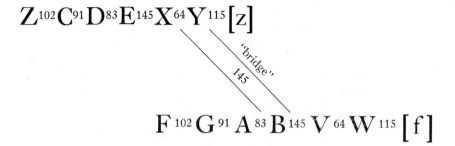

Taking this formula as our starting point, it is now easy to construct (similarly to the preceding scales) one continuous chain of both Hexads connected, in this instance, by a "bridge" whose acoustic dimension, however, is in no wise alien to the supra-Thirds constituting these chords.

$$Z^{102}C^{91}\ D^{83}\ E^{145}\ X^{64}\ Y^{145}\ B^{145}\ V^{64}\ W^{115}\ F^{102}G^{91}\ A$$

with "bridge" bracket over $Y^{145}B$

Although the supra-diatonic scale contains altogether three diminished supra-Fourths, each of which, strictly speaking, could serve as a "bridge" between the two Hexads, yet it is only the supra-Fourth Y-B (i.e. the one used in the above formula) whose place in the supra-diatonic scale is such as to allow one of the two Hexads to be constructed in its complete form *before* the connection between them has occurred. It seems probable therefore that this very formula is one of those that will serve, in the future, as a basis for the formation (by means of the familiar "imposition" of supra-Thirds) not only of consonant but of dissonant chords of the supra-diatonic scale as well (i.e. chords containing over six notes), similarly to the chains of Thirds and infra-Thirds serving, in each instance, as a basis of chord-formation in the two preceding scales. From this point of view it would be correct to consider the chord Z-C-D-E-X-Y, constituting the first half of our formula, as a *dominant Hexad* in relation to the chord F-G-A-B-V-W which in this (fundamental) position can only be a *tonic Hexad*. This is because the latter, in contradistinction to the former, does not permit any subsequent imposition of supra-Thirds (as having no intermediate diminished supra-Fourth on its concluding note W), and therefore it precludes the formation of any dissonant chords which, as a rule, are based on *dominant* harmony or, at least, can always be reduced to it.

The principal consonant chords of the supra-diatonic scale are confined to the dominant and tonic Hexads and in this limitation one may again observe a certain law to which they comply jointly with the respective chords of the two preceding scales, and which may be simply formulated as follows: the principal consonant chords of all these different scales, while gradually increasing in tonal constitution, simultaneously decrease in number. For instance, we have four consonant chords in the infra-diatonic scale (tonic, dominant, subdominant and hypertonic Dyads), three principal consonant chords in the diatonic scale (tonic, dominant and subdominant Triads), and finally two principal consonant chords in the supra-diatonic scale (tonic and dominant Hexads). But proportionately to the decrease in number of the principal consonant chords in every scale, gradually becoming more complicated, the number of its subsidiary (secondary) consonant chords naturally increases. Thus, we know that the infra-diatonic scale has no subsidiary consonant chords at all, while the diatonic scale contains three such chords (for instance, minor Triads in its major mode or major Triads in its minor mode) and the supra-diatonic scale has as many as ten subsidiary Hexads for every one of its supra-modes.

There are two specific characteristics of the supra-diatonic scale which it is opportune to mention here. *First*, unlike the infra-diatonic and diatonic scales in which respectively one diminished (dissonant) Dyad and one diminished (dissonant) Triad may be found, the supra-diatonic scale contains no dissonant Hexads whatever (within the boundaries of its regular degrees) and, *Second*, any of its Hexads may be regarded, if desired, as one of the inversions of some other Hexad taken from a different degree of this scale, and vice versa. Both these facts, however, result directly from another characteristic quality of the supra-diatonic scale, already mentioned, viz. from the *even* number of its regular degrees.

Reverting now to our foregoing construction, i.e. the chain of natural supra-Thirds connected by the intermediate link of a diminished supra-Fourth, we have merely to comprise all its component tones within an octave and thereby conclusively establish the just intonation of the supra-diatonic scale.

In order to obtain this intonation for the supra-mode "F-f," whose principal consonant chords are two Hexads F-G-A-B-V-W and Z-C-D-E-X-Y, it is sufficient to adopt, as a starting point, the note F which ought to be considered as a fundamental tone (Tonic) in relation to the intervals on its right side, and as an octave of the fundamental tone in relation to the intervals on its left side. In the former instance this note (F) is designated by a zero, and in the latter by the number 600, which indicates the dimension of an octave in centitones. Gradually adding to the zero the dimensions of all intervals on the right side of the note F, and subtracting from the number 600 the dimensions of all intervals on the left side of this note (upon exhaustion, even incomplete, of the number 600, preventing further subtraction, another quantity of 600 ctn. has to be added to the remainder), we shall obtain a series of figures indicating the position of every tone within the limit of an octave. In the following representation of the chain of natural supra-Thirds these figures are placed below the notes:

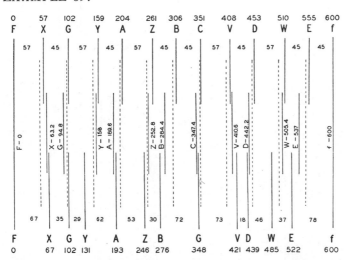

"bridge"

Tonic

$$Z^{102}C^{91}D^{83}E^{145}X^{64}Y^{145}B^{145}V^{64}W^{115}F^{102}G^{91}A$$

(add) →

246   348   439   522   67   131   276   421   485   **0**   102   193

$$[667]$$ ← (subtract) $$[600]$$

Arranging now the lower figures of this chain in their progressive order, we obtain the desired just intonation of the supra-mode "F-f".* In the following diagram this just intonation (indicated by lower solid lines) is represented parallel to the Pythagorean intonation (upper solid lines) and to the supra-tempered intonation (middle solid lines). The dotted lines (without their corresponding figures) represent, for comparison, the twelve equidistant degrees of the atonal scale ("12"):

EXAMPLE 89:

0	57	102	159	204	261	306	351	408	453	510	555	600
F	X	G	Y	A	Z	B	C	V	D	W	E	f

57   45   57   45   57   45   45   57   45   57   45   45

F – 0   X – 63.2   G – 94.8   Y – 156   A – 189.6   Z – 252.8   B – 284.4   C –347.4   V – 410.6   D – 442.2   W – 505.4   E – 537   f –600

67   35   29   62   53   30   72   73   18   46   37   78

F	X	G	Y	A	Z	B	G	V	D	W	E	f
0	67	102	131	193	246	276	348	421	439	485	522	600

* The very same method has to be applied, of course, to the previously constructed "chains" of natural Thirds and infra-Thirds when comprising them within the compass of an octave. That is to say, the note assumed as the Tonic has to be designated by zero and by the number 600, all the intervals, according to their position, being either added to the former or subtracted from the latter.

This diagram is at present of threefold importance. *First*: it discloses the impracticability of the Pythagorean intonation when applied to the supra-diatonic scale, whose characteristic and musically indispensable succession of whole steps and half steps is too perceptibly distorted in this case, as compared with the just (i.e. normal) intonation.

Secondly: it enables us to lay out, for comparison, three Tables showing the amount and degree of corrections which have to be made by our inner ear when Equal Temperament is applied to the three principal scales discussed in this book.

INFRA-DIATONIC SCALE (infra-mode "F-f")

	JUST INTONATION	INFRA-TEMPERED INTONATION	DIFFERENCE (correction required)
F	0	0	**0**
G	102	85.7	**+16.3**
A	204	171.4	**+32.6**
C	351	342.8	**+ 8.2**
D	453	428.5	**+24.5**
f	600	600	**0**

maximum correction required: 32.6 ctn.

DIATONIC SCALE (mode "F-f")

	JUST INTONATION	TEMPERED INTONATION	DIFFERENCE (correction required)
F	0	0	**0**
G	102	100	**+2**
A	193	200	**−7**
B	295	300	**−5**
C	351	350	**+1**
D	453	450	**+3**
E	544	550	**−6**
f	600	600	**0**

maximum correction required: 7 ctn.

SUPRA-DIATONIC SCALE (supra-mode "F-f")

	JUST INTONATION	SUPRA-TEMPERED INTONATION	DIFFERENCE (correction required)
F	0	0	**0**
X	67	63.2	**+ 3.8**
G	102	94.8	**+ 7.2**
Y	131	158	**−27.0**
A	193	189.6	**+ 3.4**
Z	246	252.8	**− 6.8**
B	276	284.4	**− 8.4**
C	348	347.4	**+ 0.6**
V	421	410.6	**+10.4**
D	439	442.2	**− 3.2**
W	485	505.4	**−20.4**
E	522	537	**−15.0**
f	600	600	**0**

maximum correction required: 27 ctn.

These Tables bear witness to the fact that the corrections required by supra-tempered intonation, though greater than those with which we have to deal in every-day practice when using the diatonic scale, are smaller than those required by infra-tempered intonation actually and successfully applied nowadays by the Siamese. It is true that the minimum interval of the infra-tempered scale (half step 85.7 ctn.) far exceeds, in dimension, the minimum interval of the supra-tempered scale (half step 31.6 ctn.) and thus renders even the greatest correction (32.6 ctn.) in the former instance comparatively less difficult for the ear than the greatest correction (27 ctn.) in the latter instance. In spite of this, however, the practical use, in the future, of supra-tempered intonation (as far as can be predicted in theory) leaves very little room for doubt, especially if we take into consideration the possibility of utilizing the supra-chromatic alterations when the correction required approximates (as in the above instance where it equals 27 ctn.) the dimension of a half step (31.6 ctn.) of the new scale. Thus, it may probably be wise, and, perhaps, even compulsory, to use the note Y♭̌ instead of Y, and the note W♭̌ instead of W in consonant harmonic combinations, thereby reducing the required correction of 27 ctn. to 4.6 ctn., in the former instance, and that of 20.4 ctn. to 11.2 ctn., in the latter.

The *third* and last important point of the above diagram (Ex. 89) is that with its aid we are now able to solve the previously mentioned "paradox" (p. 176) regarding the transformation of a consonance of one scale into a dissonance of another and more complicated scale. We may now be convinced of the fact that the interval of a Fifth, in its acoustically pure form ($\frac{3}{2}$ or 351 ctn.) is indeed absent in the just intonation of the supra-diatonic scale and that the interval designated therein by the notes C-G, as well as all the other "supra-Eights" comprising the same number of whole steps or half steps, simply more or less approaches but never coincides with the former.* The following complete Table of supra-Eighths (perfect dissonances with the exception of one augmented supra-Eighth), showing their various dimensions in just intonation with regard to the supra-made "F-f," will confirm the above assertion:

DEGREES

I.	F-C (perfect Supra-Eighth, 5½ steps)	348 ctn.
II.	X-V (perfect Supra-Eighth, 5½ steps)	354 ctn.
III.	G-D (perfect Supra-Eighth, 5½ steps)	337 ctn.
IV.	Y-W (perfect Supra-Eighth, 5½ steps)	354 ctn.

* What has been found in regard to supra-Eighths (and, automatically, to supra-Sixths—their inversions) will also be true in regard to supra-Fourths and their inversions (supra-Tenths), namely, that they will merely approach the nearest pure intervals (minor Third, $\frac{6}{5}$ or 158 ctn. and its inversion, $\frac{5}{3}$ or 442 ctn.) in just intonation of the supra-diatonic scale, but will never coincide with it.

DEGREES

V.	A-E	(perfect Supra-Eighth, 5½ steps)	329 ctn.
VI.	Z-F	(perfect Supra-Eighth, 5½ steps)	354 ctn.
VII.	B-X	(augmented Supra-Eighth, 6 steps)	391 ctn.
VIII.	C-G	(perfect Supra-Eighth, 5½ steps)	354 ctn.
IX.	V-Y	(perfect Supra-Eighth, 5½ steps)	310 ctn.
X.	D-A	(perfect Supra-Eighth, 5½ steps)	354 ctn.
XI.	W-Z	(perfect Supra-Eighth 5½ steps)	361 ctn.
XII.	E-B	(perfect Supra-Eighth, 5½ steps)	354 ctn.

This Table, however, solves but the first part of our "paradox," viz. that the mere existence of a Fifth, in its acoustically pure form ($\frac{3}{2}$ or 351 ctn.), in certain scales (diatonic, infra-diatonic and sub-infra-diatonic), does not necessarily predetermine its existence in the just intonation of more complicated scales, particularly that of the supra-diatonic scale. The latter, as we see, distorts on every degree the acoustic purity of this interval (which is *not* a consonance in the supra-diatonic scale) and in this respect does not even appear to produce an exceptional case, since in a similar way the acoustic purity of some "non-consonant" intervals is distorted by the two preceding and justly intoned scales. Thus, the interval F-A, being a dissonance (diminished infra-Third or diminished Dyad) in the infra-diatonic scale, does not coincide, in the latter's just intonation, with the acoustically pure major Third (expressed by the ratio $\frac{5}{4}$ or 193 ctn.), but exceeds it by 11 ctn., as will be seen from Ex. 109 in the following chapter. In the same way none of the minor Sevenths of the diatonic scale coincides, in the latter's just intonation, with the acoustically pure minor Seventh ($\frac{7}{4}$ or 485 ctn.). Depending on their position in this scale, the various minor Sevenths, representing no more than exact inversions of major Seconds (this being also musically justified), will exceed the acoustically pure minor Seventh by 13 ctn. in three instances (D-C, G-F and B-A, equalling 498 ctn. each) and by 24 ctn. in two instances (E-D and A-G, equalling 509 ctn. each), as may be learned from the acoustic diagram of the diatonic scale given earlier. (See Chapter IX).

As for the second half of our "paradox," viz. that the musical ear, while possessing the ability to adjust itself to various acoustic discrepancies, will *not* make the corresponding psychological correction with reference to the interval of a Fifth "distorted" by the just intonation of the supra-diatonic scale, it is explained as follows. The interval of a Fifth which becomes a supra-Eighth in the new scale does not occur in the latter's *consonant* chords. But in musical practice the consonant chords, generally speaking, are the only ones for which a highly developed ear is inclined to make the psychological correction referred to. With regard to the dissonant chords of the new scale in which the interval of a supra-Eighth (formerly a Fifth) may be encountered, this sort of correction would be positively out of place as it would only weaken that esthetically desirable tension so characteristic of dissonances and which we look upon as a "requirement" of their resolution into consonances.*

In this way, the nature of the just intonation establishing absolute acoustic purity for the consonances of a given scale, on the one hand,** increases as if of

* In defense of the inappropriateness of any corrections in regard to dissonances in general, one may point to the results of experiments conducted by E. H. Pierce, whose work has already been quoted and who does not go, of course, beyond the limits of the diatonic system. This circumstance, however, does not essentially alter the matter. According to this writer, the chord of the dominant Seventh, for instance, in which (besides both Thirds and the Fifth) the *minor Seventh* is acoustically just (i.e. equals 485 ctn. or $\frac{7}{4}$), sounds rather "flavorless and seems to demand no resolution,"—an opinion which, by the way, one often hears expressed by a number of acousticians nowadays. Hence we may rightly infer that should any real facts appear which show the tendency of the human ear to psychological correction not only of the inaccuracy of consonances (which is perfectly normal) but also of the inaccuracy of dissonances, it would only prove "so much the worse for the facts." This is because such a tendency in regard to dissonances would by no means speak in favor of the esthetic taste of those who, by the correction referred to, diminish the fundamental contrast between consonances and dissonances. There is no sign of equation between acoustic and esthetic truth, as some theorists believe. One may be acoustically right and at the same time esthetically wrong. The use or perception of the "natural" minor Seventh ($\frac{7}{4}$) *on the plane of the diatonic system* errs against esthetic truth, as is confirmed by the age-long practice of composers who, when unambiguously using this system invariably *resolved* the minor Seventh, even in cases of constant dealing with music *a cappella*, as in the Russian Church, for instance, where the "bad influence" of instrumental intonation, to which acousticians sometimes like to point, has manifestly to be ruled out. It is then immediately evident that these composers, inasmuch as they did resolve the minor Seventh, *never* had this interval in view in its acoustically pure form which demands no resolution. Such are the *facts* of musical creation which have to be taken into consideration besides those of musical acoustics in order to remain on a strictly scientific basis. And that is why, start-

ing from these facts, we may say that the interval of a natural minor Seventh ($\frac{7}{4}$) being absolutely true from the acoustical point of view, nevertheless is musically false in the diatonic system and, therefore, inadmissible in music which does not go beyond the limits of this system. This paradoxical distinction between facts of musical and acoustical order (which, incidentally, we shall again have occasion to discuss from a different angle in the following chapter) would not exist, however, were musical art an exclusively physical and physiological and not, principally, an esthetico-psychological phenomenon. It is fairly safe to admit that whatever has been said in regard to the correction of consonances and dissonances of the diatonic scale also holds good for the consonances and dissonances of all the rest of the "organic" scales, and, consequently, for those of the supra-diatonic scale.

** The objection could be advanced here that just intonation establishes absolute acoustic exactitude only in regard to the *principal* consonant chords of a given scale and not in regard to all its secondary consonant chords. Thus, taking as an example the just intonation of the major mode of the diatonic scale, one will at once observe that, besides its three major Triads, only two minor Triads (A 158 C 193 E and E 158 G 193 B) turn out to be acoustically correct, while its third minor Triad (D 147 F 193 A) gives rise to an error of 11 ctn. with respect to its initial minor Third (D 147 F) as compared with the just minor Third (158 ctn.) and the same error with respect to its perfect Fifth (D 340 A) as compared with the acoustically just Fifth (351 ctn.). These errors, however, may serve as an indirect indication of the fact that, as far as the *major* mode of the diatonic scale is concerned, only major Triads represent consonant chords in the full sense of the word, while the minor Triads, although they are not discords, can hardly be considered, strictly speaking, as consonant chords on a par with the former. True, they do not require "resolution" as discords do, but, as we know, they require "restoration" (in a musical work) to the principal consonant chords and from this point of view they are psychologically subject to the latter.

set purpose the harshness of its dissonances on the other hand, and thereby intensifies between these two polar elements that eternal psychological antagonism which, varying in form in the process of historical evolution, will forever remain an irrevocable factor of musical art, based on the same organic laws as Life itself.

But in the *minor* mode of the diatonic scale the principal consonant chords are minor Triads to which major Triads ("secondary" in this instance) are subject in the above sense and require their "restoration" in a musical work based on this mode. Therefore, in the just intonation of the minor mode all three minor Triads should be most accurately tuned, which automatically leads to an acoustical inaccuracy in one of the major Triads (G-B-D), as will be seen from the following chains of Thirds underlying the natural A minor mode:

subdominant Triad   dominant Triad

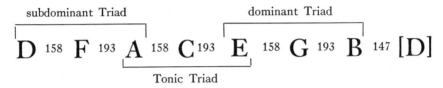

Tonic Triad

There are two modes, however, in musical practice, whose just intonation establishes acoustic accuracy for all their consonant chords without exception, the "errors" falling only on their dissonant chords, this being, of course, a most desirable state of affairs. These two modes are: (1) the *harmonic major mode* with the sixth degree flatted (A♭ in C Major, for instance) and therefore containing a minor subdominant Triad instead of a major, and (2) the familiar *harmonic minor mode* containing a major dominant Triad instead of a minor. Consequently the former comprises altogether two major Triads (C-E-G and G-B-D), two minor Triads (F-A♭-C and E-G-B), two diminished Triads (B-D-F and D-F-A♭) and one augmented Triad (A♭-C-E), all of which may be found in the following general chain of Thirds:

subdominant Triad   dominant Triad

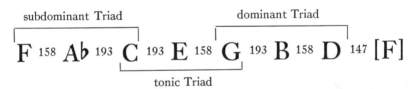

tonic Triad

The latter of these two modes comprises two minor Triads (A-C-E and D-F-A), two major Triads (E-G♯-B and F-A-C), two diminished Triads (G♯-B-D and B-D-F) and one augmented Triad (C-E-G♯), all of which may, in turn, be found in the following general chain of Thirds:

subdominant Triad   dominant Triad

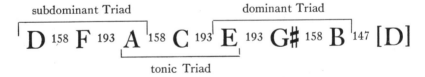

tonic Triad

As one may judge from the numbers given in both of these series, the acoustic inaccuracies (147 ctn. instead of 158 ctn. for the minor Thirds) fall exclusively on the diminished (i.e. dissonant) Triads of both modes. Further details regarding acoustical inaccuracies which occur in Just Intonation will be found in the supplement to this chapter immediately following.

NORMS AND ODDITIES OF JUST INTONATION

The foregoing chapter would be incomplete without certain additional considerations which, however, will be of interest to an acoustician rather than to a musician, and may therefore be omitted in a general reading.

These considerations mainly concern the just intonation of the supra-diatonic scale (represented by the lower set of solid lines in the diagram of Ex. 89) which probably will not satisfy, or at least will not seem sufficiently convincing to some, on account of the complexity of certain acoustic relations involved. The acoustical values represented, in the diagram referred to, in terms of centitones, do not explicitly disclose, of course, the *character* of these relations, in the sense of their simplicity or complexity, this character becoming evident only when the values in question are expressed in terms of vibration-ratios, as was generally explained on an earlier occasion (Chapter V). Before actual discussion of the subject itself, therefore, we shall demonstrate these ratios as well as the simple way of obtaining them in this instance.

In order to effect the entire operation, it is necessary first to revert to the chain of natural supra-Thirds (immediately preceding Ex. 89), and to replace all the figures comprised between its notes by their respective vibration-ratios, which may be ascertained from the overtone numbers given in Ex. 88. This being done, the note F has to be designated by the number 1, when it is assumed as the Tonic in relation to the intervals on its right side, and by the number 2, when it is considered as an Octave of the Tonic in relation to the intervals on its left side. The operations of addition and subtraction which have been used in this "chain" are, then, replaced by those of multiplication and division which will give, as the result, a series of vibration-fractions (below the notes) expressing all the intervals between each note of the supra-diatonic scale and its Tonic in just intonation. [In the following series, the fraction $\frac{121}{112}$ under the note X is multiplied by 2 for the purpose of keeping the entire set of notes within the compass of an Octave, i.e. just as number 67 under this note was formerly increased by 600].

$$\text{"bridge"}$$

$$Z\tfrac{9}{8}\,C\tfrac{10}{9}\,D\tfrac{11}{10}\,E\tfrac{13}{11}\,X\tfrac{14}{13}\,Y\tfrac{13}{11}\,B\tfrac{13}{11}\,V\tfrac{14}{13}\,W\tfrac{8}{7}\,F\,\overset{\text{Tonic}}{}\,G\tfrac{9}{8}\,A\tfrac{10}{9}$$

$$\xrightarrow{\text{(multiply)}}$$

| $\frac{121}{91}$ | $\frac{1089}{728}$ | $\frac{605}{364}$ | $\frac{1331}{728}$ | $\frac{121}{112}$ | $\frac{121}{104}$ | $\frac{11}{8}$ | $\frac{13}{8}$ | $\frac{7}{4}$ | 1 | $\frac{9}{8}$ | $\frac{5}{4}$ |

$$\left[\frac{121}{56}\right] \qquad\qquad \xleftarrow{\text{(divide)}} \quad [2]$$

Arranging now all these notes in successive "scale-like" order, we shall also obtain fractions expressing the intervals *between* the contiguous degrees of this scale:

$$F\tfrac{121}{112}\,X\tfrac{126}{121}\,G\tfrac{121}{117}\,Y\tfrac{130}{121}\,A\tfrac{484}{455}\,Z\tfrac{91}{88}\,B\tfrac{99}{91}\,C\tfrac{1183}{1089}\,V\tfrac{1210}{1183}\,D\tfrac{637}{605}\,W\tfrac{1331}{1274}\,E\tfrac{1456}{1331}\,f$$

| 1 | $\frac{121}{112}$ | $\frac{9}{8}$ | $\frac{121}{104}$ | $\frac{5}{4}$ | $\frac{121}{91}$ | $\frac{11}{8}$ | $\frac{1089}{728}$ | $\frac{13}{8}$ | $\frac{605}{364}$ | $\frac{7}{4}$ | $\frac{1331}{728}$ | 2 |

Some of the fractions given in this series certainly appear rather complicated and, at first sight, they are unquestionably apt to inspire a serious doubt as to the soundness of the fundamental principle applied for the just intonation of the supra-diatonic scale. This doubt will probably increase after one learns that another form of just intonation with much simpler acoustic relations, is easily attainable in regard to this scale, if a somewhat different principle is applied for this purpose. Before explaining the reasons for which the above complicated intonation is nevertheless preferred by the author in spite of the temptation offered by the simpler intonation, it is necessary to demonstrate the acoustic relations of the latter as well as the way they are arrived at.

It will be recollected, in passing, that just intonation of the supra-diatonic scale was originally obtained through the two principal Hexads (Z-C-D-E-X-Y and F-G-A-B-V-W) being tuned to the intervals of a certain group of overtones (8:9:10:11:13:14) and both of them connected by a "bridge" (between their notes Y and B) equalling the dimension of a major supra-Third ($\frac{13}{11}$ or 145 ctn.). This form of just intonation of the supra-diatonic scale (represented above in terms of vibration-fractions) will be hereafter known as its *first version,* in contradistinction to its other (and simpler) form, which will be known as its *second version* and which we shall presently describe.

The principle of tuning of the tonic and dominant Hexads to the intervals formed by the group of overtones referred to holds good for the first as well as for the second version, but the acoustic interrelation *between* these two principal Hexads is established and, accordingly, the final figures, are obtained differently in both instances. While a "bridge" connecting only two preselected notes (Y-B) of these Hexads and thus automatically determining the relative position of the rest of their component notes, is what brings us to the *first version,* one definite and the simplest possible acoustic relation between their two *entire* sets of notes is arbitrarily adopted as a substitute for that "bridge" in the *second version.* This particular relation being established, it becomes an easy matter to determine the position of all the component notes of both Hexads and, consequently, of the supra-diatonic scale itself, within an octave. The following mathematical operations will show how these results for the second version are obtained.

Let us assume the dominant Hexad of the supra-mode "F-f" to be tuned in conformity to the group of six overtones which, according to our theory, serves as the "nucleus" for either form of just intonation of the supra-diatonic scale:

$$\overset{8}{Z}—\overset{9}{C}—\overset{10}{D}—\overset{11}{E}—\overset{13}{X}—\overset{14}{Y}$$

The figures of this "nucleus," as we know, indicate not only the ordinal overtone numbers but (in their succession) also the acoustic ratios between the notes of the Hexad over which they appear. Now, in order to deduce, from these ratio numbers, those for the tonic Hexad which, being composed of intervals of the very same dimension, is supposed, at the same time, to bear the simplest relation to the dominant Hexad, it is sufficient to multiply each of these numbers by the smallest possible figure, which merely should *not* be one of those that lead to the repetition of the same notes (Z-C-D-E-X-Y) when this operation is effected. And since the multiplication of these numbers by 1 or by 2 *will* lead to a repetition of these notes in unison and in Octave respectively, it is evident that the figure 3, precluding any repetition of the *same* notes, is the smallest possible multiplicator which meets our requirements. This figure will obviously establish the relation 3:1 between the dominant Hexad and the tonic Hexad, the latter being expressed, therefore, by the following ratio numbers:

$$\overset{24}{F}-\overset{27}{G}-\overset{30}{A}-\overset{33}{B}-\overset{39}{V}-\overset{42}{W}$$

When comprising all the twelve notes of both series within the compass of an octave —the next step in our construction—the ratio numbers of the tonic Hexad remain unchanged, while those of the dominant Hexad are either doubled or quadrupled (i.e. transposed one or two octaves up), this being dependent on the condition that none of them should be exceeded by the ratio number of the fundamental tone F, i.e. by 24, or should exceed the ratio number of its Octave, which is twice as great and, consequently, equals 48. As a result of this operation, the ratio numbers of the dominant Hexad will acquire the following designations in the order of their progression:

$$\overset{26}{X}-\overset{28}{Y}-\overset{32}{Z}-\overset{36}{C}-\overset{40}{D}-\overset{44}{E}$$

By inserting this series of notes into the preceding one, in progressive order, we shall obtain a complete set of ratio numbers for the *second version* of just intonation of the supra-diatonic scale:

$$\overset{24}{F}-\overset{26}{X}-\overset{27}{G}-\overset{28}{Y}-\overset{30}{A}-\overset{32}{Z}-\overset{33}{B}-\overset{36}{C}-\overset{39}{V}-\overset{40}{D}-\overset{42}{W}-\overset{44}{E}-\overset{48}{F}$$

For the sake of comparison with the *first version* represented earlier, it only remains to convert all these ratio numbers into vibration-fractions, showing the dimension of the intervals between each degree of the scale and the Tonic (F), as well as between all the contiguous degrees. This, as one readily gathers, is done by dividing each of the above ratio numbers by 24 (the result is placed below the notes), and by dividing each ratio number by the one which precedes it (the result is placed between the notes):

$$F\tfrac{13}{12}X\tfrac{27}{26}G\tfrac{28}{27}Y\tfrac{15}{14}A\tfrac{16}{15}Z\tfrac{33}{32}B\tfrac{12}{11}C\tfrac{13}{12}V\tfrac{40}{39}D\tfrac{21}{20}W\tfrac{22}{21}E\tfrac{12}{11}f$$

$$1 \quad \tfrac{13}{12} \quad \tfrac{9}{8} \quad \tfrac{7}{6} \quad \tfrac{5}{4} \quad \tfrac{4}{3} \quad \tfrac{11}{8} \quad \tfrac{3}{2} \quad \tfrac{13}{8} \quad \tfrac{5}{3} \quad \tfrac{7}{4} \quad \tfrac{11}{6} \quad 2$$

The acoustic relations of this second version, no doubt, appeal more to the "naked eye," so to speak, than those of the first version, on account of their comparative simplicity. But a careful analysis of both versions soon discloses that this very simplicity, otherwise greatly desirable, is what disturbs the proper interbalance of consonances and dissonances, in the second version, and what, therefore, makes it inferior to the first version, in which this interbalance is well preserved.

In order fully to understand all subsequent argumentation in regard to this particular point, it must be well borne in mind that, according to the basic principles of our theory, the specific division of consonances and dissonances within a given system is a constant characteristic of the latter and cannot be changed, unless the system itself is replaced by another one with its own division of consonances and dissonances. It is due to the inner structural logic of each musical system dealt with in this book, that the interval between the first and the third scale-degree, let us say, is unfailingly a consonance. Therefore, no arbitrary tuning of any sort will ever transform it into a dissonance, although it may easily put it "off pitch,"—an entirely different matter from a musical standpoint, as will be explained later. Likewise no arbitrary tuning of a dissonance, however "pure," will transform it into a consonance, although it may somehow weaken its property of resolution, which is but another way of putting an interval "off pitch," inasmuch as the acutest possible form of this property is highly desirable in regard to dissonances. This rule, be it remembered, applies to all musical systems (consequently, also to the supra-diatonic system), in spite of the fact that the proper tuning for each of them is different, and just as specific as is the division of all their intervals into consonances and dissonances.

Hence it is evident that before deciding which of the two versions of just intonation is correct, we have to take into consideration the division of consonances and dissonances, as it is predetermined by the structural logic of the supra-diatonic scale. This division, which has been laid down as the basis for the classification of intervals in the foregoing chapter (page 173), will serve as a criterion to determine the fitness or unfitness of one or the other intonation in regard to isolated intervals found, in each instance, in the two different versions. It is understood, of course, that the standard Table of intervals which was formed with reference to the supra-mode "C-c," holds good for every other supra-mode, with the single reservation that the designation of degrees with their relative succession has to be changed, depending on which of them is assumed as the Tonic. Thus, in the case of the supra-mode "F-f" (in regard to which our acoustic calculations are given), the Roman numeral VI, in the Table referred to, has to be redesignated by I, the numeral VII by II, etc., all other indications of quality, dimension (in terms of whole steps and half steps) and even of the notes comprising the intervals, remaining unaltered.

The following two series of Roman numerals indicating the position and the succession of (regular) degrees of the supra-modes "C-c" and "F-f" in relation to each other, will demonstrate how the entire redesignation has to be effected, when one of these supra-modes is substituted for another:

Supra-Mode "C-c":	I	II	III	IV	V	VI	VII	VIII	IX	X	XI	XII
	↕	↕	↕	↕	↕	↕	↕	↕	↕	↕	↕	↕
Supra-Mode "F-f":	VIII	IX	X	XI	XII	I	II	III	IV	V	VI	VII

The classification of intervals represented in their standardized Table shows us that supra-Primes, supra-Thirds, supra-Fifths, supra-Sevenths, supra-Ninths, supra-Elevenths and supra-Thirteenths constitute the consonances of the supra-diatonic system, while supra-Seconds, supra-Fourths, supra-Sixths, supra-Eighths, supra-Tenths and supra-Twelfths constitute (with the exception of a few diminished and augmented intervals) its dissonances. With this principal division of intervals definitely established, let us first examine the acoustic relations by which the *consonances* are expressed in the first and the second version of just intonation of the supra-diatonic scale represented above. The following five Tables demonstrate the ratios of consonances taken from each (regular) degree of the scale and accompanied, in each version, by the mathematical operations through which these ratios are obtained. The groups of supra-Primes and supra-Thirteenths (the only *perfect* consonances in the supra-diatonic scale) are omitted here for abbreviation, since they represent no more than Unisons and Octaves, and therefore will give, for each degree, no other ratios but 1:1 or 2:1.

SUPRA-THIRDS

DEGREES	INTERVALS	FIRST VERSION	SECOND VERSION
I	F-G (minor)	$\frac{9}{8} : 1 = \frac{9}{8}$	$\frac{9}{8} : 1 = \frac{9}{8}$
II	X-Y (minor)	$\frac{121}{104} : \frac{121}{112} = \frac{14}{13}$	$\frac{7}{6} : \frac{13}{12} = \frac{14}{13}$
III	G-A (minor)	$\frac{5}{4} : \frac{9}{8} = \frac{10}{9}$	$\frac{5}{4} : \frac{9}{8} = \frac{10}{9}$
IV	Y-Z (minor)	$\frac{121}{91} : \frac{121}{104} = \frac{8}{7}$	$\frac{4}{3} : \frac{7}{6} = \frac{8}{7}$
V	A-B (minor)	$\frac{11}{8} : \frac{5}{4} = \frac{11}{10}$	$\frac{11}{8} : \frac{5}{4} = \frac{11}{10}$
VI	Z-C (minor)	$\frac{1089}{728} : \frac{121}{91} = \frac{9}{8}$	$\frac{3}{2} : \frac{4}{3} = \frac{9}{8}$
VII	B-V (major)	$\frac{13}{8} : \frac{11}{8} = \frac{13}{11}$	$\frac{13}{8} : \frac{11}{8} = \frac{13}{11}$
VIII	C-D (minor)	$\frac{605}{364} : \frac{1089}{728} = \frac{10}{9}$	$\frac{5}{3} : \frac{3}{2} = \frac{10}{9}$
IX	V-W (minor)	$\frac{7}{4} : \frac{13}{8} = \frac{14}{13}$	$\frac{7}{4} : \frac{13}{8} = \frac{14}{13}$
X	D-E (minor)	$\frac{1331}{728} : \frac{605}{364} = \frac{11}{10}$	$\frac{11}{6} : \frac{5}{3} = \frac{11}{10}$
XI	W-f (minor)	$2 : \frac{7}{4} = \frac{8}{7}$	$2 : \frac{7}{4} = \frac{8}{7}$
XII	E-x (major)	$\frac{121 \times 2}{112} : \frac{1331}{728} = \frac{13}{11}$	$\frac{13 \times 2}{12} : \frac{11}{6} = \frac{13}{11}$

SUPRA-FIFTHS

DEGREES	INTERVALS	FIRST VERSION	SECOND VERSION
I	F - A (minor)	$\frac{5}{4} : 1 = \frac{5}{4}$	$\frac{5}{4} : 1 = \frac{5}{4}$
II	X - Z (minor)	$\frac{121}{91} : \frac{121}{112} = \frac{16}{13}$	$\frac{4}{3} : \frac{13}{12} = \frac{16}{13}$
III	G - B (minor)	$\frac{11}{8} : \frac{9}{8} = \frac{11}{9}$	$\frac{11}{8} : \frac{9}{8} = \frac{11}{9}$
IV	Y - C (minor)	$\frac{1089}{728} : \frac{121}{104} = \frac{9}{7}$	$\frac{3}{2} : \frac{7}{6} = \frac{9}{7}$
V	A - V (major)	$\frac{13}{8} : \frac{5}{4} = \frac{13}{10}$	$\frac{13}{8} : \frac{5}{4} = \frac{13}{10}$
VI	Z - D (minor)	$\frac{605}{364} : \frac{121}{91} = \frac{5}{4}$	$\frac{5}{3} : \frac{4}{3} = \frac{5}{4}$
VII	B - W (major)	$\frac{7}{4} : \frac{11}{8} = \frac{14}{11}$	$\frac{7}{4} : \frac{11}{8} = \frac{14}{11}$
VIII	C - E (minor)	$\frac{1331}{728} : \frac{1089}{728} = \frac{11}{9}$	$\frac{11}{6} : \frac{3}{2} = \frac{11}{9}$
IX	V - f (minor)	$2 : \frac{13}{8} = \frac{16}{13}$	$2 : \frac{13}{8} = \frac{16}{13}$
X	D - x (major)	$\frac{121 \times 2}{112} : \frac{605}{364} = \frac{13}{10}$	$\frac{13 \times 2}{12} : \frac{5}{3} = \frac{13}{10}$
XI	W - g (minor)	$\frac{9 \times 2}{8} : \frac{7}{4} = \frac{9}{7}$	$\frac{9 \times 2}{8} : \frac{7}{4} = \frac{9}{7}$
XII	E - y (major)	$\frac{121 \times 2}{104} : \frac{1331}{728} = \frac{14}{11}$	$\frac{7 \times 2}{6} : \frac{11}{6} = \frac{14}{11}$

SUPRA-SEVENTHS

DEGREES	INTERVALS	FIRST VERSION	SECOND VERSION
I	F - B (minor)	$\dfrac{11}{8} : 1 = \dfrac{11}{8}$	$\dfrac{11}{8} : 1 = \dfrac{11}{8}$
II	X - C (minor)	$\dfrac{1089}{728} : \dfrac{121}{112} = \dfrac{18}{13}$	$\dfrac{3}{2} : \dfrac{13}{12} = \dfrac{18}{13}$
III	G - V (major)	$\dfrac{13}{8} : \dfrac{9}{8} = \dfrac{13}{9}$	$\dfrac{13}{8} : \dfrac{9}{8} = \dfrac{13}{9}$
IV	Y - D (minor)	$\dfrac{605}{364} : \dfrac{121}{104} = \dfrac{10}{7}$	$\dfrac{5}{3} : \dfrac{7}{6} = \dfrac{10}{7}$
V	A - W (major)	$\dfrac{7}{4} : \dfrac{5}{4} = \dfrac{7}{5}$	$\dfrac{7}{4} : \dfrac{5}{4} = \dfrac{7}{5}$
VI	Z - E (minor)	$\dfrac{1331}{728} : \dfrac{121}{91} = \dfrac{11}{8}$	$\dfrac{11}{6} : \dfrac{4}{3} = \dfrac{11}{8}$
VII	B - f (major)	$2 : \dfrac{11}{8} = \dfrac{16}{11}$	$2 : \dfrac{11}{8} = \dfrac{16}{11}$
VIII	C - x (major)	$\dfrac{121 \times 2}{112} : \dfrac{1089}{728} = \dfrac{13}{9}$	$\dfrac{13 \times 2}{12} : \dfrac{3}{2} = \dfrac{13}{9}$
IX	V - g (minor)	$\dfrac{9 \times 2}{8} : \dfrac{13}{8} = \dfrac{18}{13}$	$\dfrac{9 \times 2}{8} : \dfrac{13}{8} = \dfrac{18}{13}$
X	D - y (major)	$\dfrac{121 \times 2}{104} : \dfrac{605}{364} = \dfrac{7}{5}$	$\dfrac{7 \times 2}{6} : \dfrac{5}{3} = \dfrac{7}{5}$
XI	W - a (minor)	$\dfrac{5 \times 2}{4} : \dfrac{7}{4} = \dfrac{10}{7}$	$\dfrac{5 \times 2}{4} : \dfrac{7}{4} = \dfrac{10}{7}$
XII	E - z (major)	$\dfrac{121 \times 2}{91} : \dfrac{1331}{728} = \dfrac{16}{11}$	$\dfrac{4 \times 2}{3} : \dfrac{11}{6} = \dfrac{16}{11}$

SUPRA-NINTHS

DEGREES	INTERVALS	FIRST VERSION	SECOND VERSION
I	F - V (major)	$\dfrac{13}{8} : 1 = \dfrac{13}{8}$	$\dfrac{13}{8} : 1 = \dfrac{13}{8}$
II	X - D (minor)	$\dfrac{605}{364} : \dfrac{121}{112} = \dfrac{20}{13}$	$\dfrac{5}{3} : \dfrac{13}{12} = \dfrac{20}{13}$
III	G - W (major)	$\dfrac{7}{4} : \dfrac{9}{8} = \dfrac{14}{9}$	$\dfrac{7}{4} : \dfrac{9}{8} = \dfrac{14}{9}$
IV	Y - E (minor)	$\dfrac{1331}{728} : \dfrac{121}{104} = \dfrac{11}{7}$	$\dfrac{11}{6} : \dfrac{7}{6} = \dfrac{11}{7}$
V	A - f (major)	$2 : \dfrac{5}{4} = \dfrac{8}{5}$	$2 : \dfrac{5}{4} = \dfrac{8}{5}$
VI	Z - x (major)	$\dfrac{121 \times 2}{112} : \dfrac{121}{91} = \dfrac{13}{8}$	$\dfrac{13 \times 2}{12} : \dfrac{4}{3} = \dfrac{13}{8}$
VII	B - g (major)	$\dfrac{9 \times 2}{8} : \dfrac{11}{8} = \dfrac{18}{11}$	$\dfrac{9 \times 2}{8} : \dfrac{11}{8} = \dfrac{18}{11}$
VIII	C - y (major)	$\dfrac{121 \times 2}{104} : \dfrac{1089}{728} = \dfrac{14}{9}$	$\dfrac{7 \times 2}{6} : \dfrac{3}{2} = \dfrac{14}{9}$
IX	V - a (minor)	$\dfrac{5 \times 2}{4} : \dfrac{13}{8} = \dfrac{20}{13}$	$\dfrac{5 \times 2}{4} : \dfrac{13}{8} = \dfrac{20}{13}$
X	D - z (major)	$\dfrac{121 \times 2}{91} : \dfrac{605}{364} = \dfrac{8}{5}$	$\dfrac{4 \times 2}{3} : \dfrac{5}{3} = \dfrac{8}{5}$
XI	W - b (minor)	$\dfrac{11 \times 2}{8} : \dfrac{7}{4} = \dfrac{11}{7}$	$\dfrac{11 \times 2}{8} : \dfrac{7}{4} = \dfrac{11}{7}$
XII	E - c (major)	$\dfrac{1089 \times 2}{728} : \dfrac{1331}{728} = \dfrac{18}{11}$	$\dfrac{3 \times 2}{2} : \dfrac{11}{6} = \dfrac{18}{11}$

SUPRA-ELEVENTHS

DEGREES	INTERVALS	FIRST VERSION	SECOND VERSION
I	F - W (major)	$\dfrac{7}{4} : 1 = \dfrac{7}{4}$	$\dfrac{7}{4} : 1 = \dfrac{7}{4}$
II	X - E (minor)	$\dfrac{1331}{728} : \dfrac{121}{112} = \dfrac{22}{13}$	$\dfrac{11}{6} : \dfrac{13}{12} = \dfrac{22}{13}$
III	G - f (major)	$2 : \dfrac{9}{8} = \dfrac{16}{9}$	$2 : \dfrac{9}{8} = \dfrac{16}{9}$
IV	Y - x (major)	$\dfrac{121 \times 2}{112} : \dfrac{121}{104} = \dfrac{13}{7}$	$\dfrac{13 \times 2}{12} : \dfrac{7}{6} = \dfrac{13}{7}$
V	A - g (major)	$\dfrac{9 \times 2}{8} : \dfrac{5}{4} = \dfrac{9}{5}$	$\dfrac{9 \times 2}{8} : \dfrac{5}{4} = \dfrac{9}{5}$
VI	Z - y (major)	$\dfrac{121 \times 2}{104} : \dfrac{121}{91} = \dfrac{7}{4}$	$\dfrac{7 \times 2}{6} : \dfrac{4}{3} = \dfrac{7}{4}$
VII	B - a (major)	$\dfrac{5 \times 2}{4} : \dfrac{11}{8} = \dfrac{20}{11}$	$\dfrac{5 \times 2}{4} : \dfrac{11}{8} = \dfrac{20}{11}$
VIII	C - z (major)	$\dfrac{121 \times 2}{91} : \dfrac{1089}{728} = \dfrac{16}{9}$	$\dfrac{4 \times 2}{3} : \dfrac{3}{2} = \dfrac{16}{9}$
IX	V - b (minor)	$\dfrac{11 \times 2}{8} : \dfrac{13}{8} = \dfrac{22}{13}$	$\dfrac{11 \times 2}{8} : \dfrac{13}{8} = \dfrac{22}{13}$
X	D - c (major)	$\dfrac{1089 \times 2}{728} : \dfrac{605}{364} = \dfrac{9}{5}$	$\dfrac{3 \times 2}{2} : \dfrac{5}{3} = \dfrac{9}{5}$
XI	W - v (major)	$\dfrac{13 \times 2}{8} : \dfrac{7}{4} = \dfrac{13}{7}$	$\dfrac{13 \times 2}{8} : \dfrac{7}{4} = \dfrac{13}{7}$
XII	E - d (major)	$\dfrac{605 \times 2}{364} : \dfrac{1331}{728} = \dfrac{20}{11}$	$\dfrac{5 \times 2}{3} : \dfrac{11}{6} = \dfrac{20}{11}$

The figures obtained in the above calculations, manifestly—though perhaps sur-prisingly—prove that all the consonances constituting these five groups of intervals are expressed for each degree by absolutely identical ratios in both versions of just intonation; furthermore, that these ratios express no other acoustical magnitudes but those which are formed by various combinations of the overtone-numbers 8, 9, 10, 11, 13, 14, or their inversions. Therefore, inasmuch as these numbers, according to our premise, form the basic "nucleus" for either version of just intonation of the supra-diatonic scale, the ratios obtained ought to be regarded as perfectly correct, and the problem, in so far as the groups of consonances are concerned, as requiring no further investigation.

As regards the dissonances found in the remaining group of intervals, there can be, strictly speaking, only one unquestionable, though *negative* requirement in connection with their proper tuning, which will certainly provoke no dissent whatever even among those who in other respects may have different opinions on this subject. This requirement is that in order to preserve true interbalance between the mutually "opposite forces" within a tonality, no dissonance should be represented by a ratio which is acoustically *simpler* than any of those by which the consonances are expressed. Taking this as a starting point in the matter of proper tuning of dissonances, let us inquire what are the ratios by which the latter are represented in the first and in the second version of just intonation of the supra-diatonic scale. The following six Tables show all the dissonances, as well as their occasional deviations, comprised within their corresponding groups, each interval, similarly to the consonances, being accompanied by the mathematical operation which gives its acoustical ratio. [See pages 205-210.]

Contrary to the consonances found in the former five groups of intervals (pp. 199-203), there is not a single dissonance within the latter six groups (pp. 205-210) that has an identical ratio in both versions of just intonation. True, the difference between each pair of these ratios is very small, and, perhaps, even negligible, so far as the actual dimension of an interval is concerned. It equals everywhere $\frac{364}{363}$ or about 3 ctn., which approximates but a quarter of the Pythagorean comma, a petty magnitude indeed! But this difference, small as it is, may become fairly noticeable, at least in some instances, when the acoustical *character* of an interval (not its dimension) is of primary concern. At any rate, it is quite a sufficient magnitude to change perceptibly the character of an acoustically very *simple* interval, and to impart to it some sort of dissonant "tense-ness," when acoustic simplicity is decidedly out of place in connection with that partic-ular interval. This is precisely the case with some of the dissonances of the supra-diatonic scale, which are expressed by such simple acoustical ratios in the second version of just intonation, as to place them, in degree of "tenseness," much below any or the majority of consonances,—an obvious absurdity from the standpoint of proper inter-balance between consonances and dissonances within a musical system. And it is the above small magnitude of about 3 ctn. that virtually maintains the requisite interbalance in the first version of just intonation.

Thus, seven supra-Eighths, out of twelve, are expressed by the ratio $\frac{3}{2}$ in the *second* version, and the same number of supra-Sixths (which are merely inversions of the supra-Eighths) are expressed therein by the ratio $\frac{4}{3}$. Both these ratios are acoustically simpler than any of those by which the consonances of the supra-diatonic scale (given in the initial five Tables) are expressed. But in the *first* version the same intervals are repre-

SUPRA-SECONDS

DEGREES	INTERVALS	FIRST VERSION	SECOND VERSION
I	F - X (major)	$\dfrac{121}{112} : \mathbf{1} = \dfrac{121}{112}$	$\dfrac{13}{12} : \mathbf{1} = \dfrac{13}{12}$
II	X - G (minor)	$\dfrac{9}{8} : \dfrac{121}{112} = \dfrac{126}{121}$	$\dfrac{9}{8} : \dfrac{13}{12} = \dfrac{27}{26}$
III	G - Y (major)	$\dfrac{121}{104} : \dfrac{9}{8} = \dfrac{121}{117}$	$\dfrac{7}{6} : \dfrac{9}{8} = \dfrac{28}{27}$
IV	Y - A (minor)	$\dfrac{5}{4} : \dfrac{121}{104} = \dfrac{130}{121}$	$\dfrac{5}{4} : \dfrac{7}{6} = \dfrac{15}{14}$
V	A - Z (major)	$\dfrac{121}{91} : \dfrac{5}{4} = \dfrac{484}{455}$	$\dfrac{4}{3} : \dfrac{5}{4} = \dfrac{16}{15}$
VI	Z - B (minor)	$\dfrac{11}{8} : \dfrac{121}{91} = \dfrac{91}{88}$	$\dfrac{11}{8} : \dfrac{4}{3} = \dfrac{33}{32}$
VII	B - C (major)	$\dfrac{1089}{728} : \dfrac{11}{8} = \dfrac{99}{91}$	$\dfrac{3}{2} : \dfrac{11}{8} = \dfrac{12}{11}$
VIII	C - V (major)	$\dfrac{13}{8} : \dfrac{1089}{728} = \dfrac{1183}{1089}$	$\dfrac{13}{8} : \dfrac{3}{2} = \dfrac{13}{12}$
IX	V - D (minor)	$\dfrac{605}{364} : \dfrac{13}{8} = \dfrac{1210}{1183}$	$\dfrac{5}{3} : \dfrac{13}{8} = \dfrac{40}{39}$
X	D - W (major)	$\dfrac{7}{4} : \dfrac{605}{364} = \dfrac{637}{605}$	$\dfrac{7}{4} : \dfrac{5}{3} = \dfrac{21}{20}$
XI	W - E (minor)	$\dfrac{1331}{728} : \dfrac{7}{4} = \dfrac{1331}{1274}$	$\dfrac{11}{6} : \dfrac{7}{4} = \dfrac{22}{21}$
XII	E - f (major)	$\mathbf{2} : \dfrac{1331}{728} = \dfrac{1456}{1331}$	$\mathbf{2} : \dfrac{11}{6} = \dfrac{12}{11}$

SUPRA-FOURTHS

DEGREES	INTERVALS	FIRST VERSION	SECOND VERSION
I	F - Y (perfect)	$\dfrac{121}{104} : \mathbf{1} = \dfrac{121}{104}$	$\dfrac{7}{6} : \mathbf{1} = \dfrac{7}{6}$
II	X - A (diminished)	$\dfrac{5}{4} : \dfrac{121}{112} = \dfrac{140}{121}$	$\dfrac{5}{4} : \dfrac{13}{12} = \dfrac{15}{13}$
III	G - Z (perfect)	$\dfrac{121}{91} : \dfrac{9}{8} = \dfrac{968}{819}$	$\dfrac{4}{3} : \dfrac{9}{8} = \dfrac{32}{27}$
IV	Y - B (diminished)	$\dfrac{11}{8} : \dfrac{121}{104} = \dfrac{13}{11}$	$\dfrac{11}{8} : \dfrac{7}{6} = \dfrac{33}{28}$
V	A - C (perfect)	$\dfrac{1089}{728} : \dfrac{5}{4} = \dfrac{1089}{910}$	$\dfrac{3}{2} : \dfrac{5}{4} = \dfrac{6}{5}$
VI	Z - V (perfect)	$\dfrac{13}{8} : \dfrac{121}{91} = \dfrac{1183}{968}$	$\dfrac{13}{8} : \dfrac{4}{3} = \dfrac{39}{32}$
VII	B - D (perfect)	$\dfrac{605}{364} : \dfrac{11}{8} = \dfrac{110}{91}$	$\dfrac{5}{3} : \dfrac{11}{8} = \dfrac{40}{33}$
VIII	C - W (perfect)	$\dfrac{7}{4} : \dfrac{1089}{728} = \dfrac{1274}{1089}$	$\dfrac{7}{4} : \dfrac{3}{2} = \dfrac{7}{6}$
IX	V - E (diminished)	$\dfrac{1331}{728} : \dfrac{13}{8} = \dfrac{1331}{1183}$	$\dfrac{11}{6} : \dfrac{13}{8} = \dfrac{44}{39}$
X	D - f (perfect)	$\mathbf{2} : \dfrac{605}{364} = \dfrac{728}{605}$	$\mathbf{2} : \dfrac{5}{3} = \dfrac{6}{5}$
XI	W - x (perfect)	$\dfrac{121 \times 2}{112} : \dfrac{7}{4} = \dfrac{121}{98}$	$\dfrac{13 \times 2}{12} : \dfrac{7}{4} = \dfrac{26}{21}$
XII	E - g (perfect)	$\dfrac{9 \times 2}{8} : \dfrac{1331}{728} = \dfrac{1638}{1331}$	$\dfrac{9 \times 2}{8} : \dfrac{11}{6} = \dfrac{27}{22}$

SUPRA-SIXTHS

DEGREES	INTERVALS	FIRST VERSION	SECOND VERSION
I	F - Z (perfect)	$\dfrac{121}{91} : 1 = \dfrac{121}{91}$	$\dfrac{4}{3} : 1 = \dfrac{4}{3}$
II	X - B (diminished)	$\dfrac{11}{8} : \dfrac{121}{112} = \dfrac{14}{11}$	$\dfrac{11}{8} : \dfrac{13}{12} = \dfrac{33}{26}$
III	G - C (perfect)	$\dfrac{1089}{728} : \dfrac{9}{8} = \dfrac{121}{91}$	$\dfrac{3}{2} : \dfrac{9}{8} = \dfrac{4}{3}$
IV	Y - V (perfect)	$\dfrac{13}{8} : \dfrac{121}{104} = \dfrac{169}{121}$	$\dfrac{13}{8} : \dfrac{7}{6} = \dfrac{39}{28}$
V	A - D (perfect)	$\dfrac{605}{364} : \dfrac{5}{4} = \dfrac{121}{91}$	$\dfrac{5}{3} : \dfrac{5}{4} = \dfrac{4}{3}$
VI	Z - W (perfect)	$\dfrac{7}{4} : \dfrac{121}{91} = \dfrac{637}{484}$	$\dfrac{7}{4} : \dfrac{4}{3} = \dfrac{21}{16}$
VII	B - E (perfect)	$\dfrac{1331}{728} : \dfrac{11}{8} = \dfrac{121}{91}$	$\dfrac{11}{6} : \dfrac{11}{8} = \dfrac{4}{3}$
VIII	C - f (perfect)	$2 : \dfrac{1089}{728} = \dfrac{1456}{1089}$	$2 : \dfrac{3}{2} = \dfrac{4}{3}$
IX	V - x (perfect)	$\dfrac{121 \times 2}{112} : \dfrac{13}{8} = \dfrac{121}{91}$	$\dfrac{13 \times 2}{12} : \dfrac{13}{8} = \dfrac{4}{3}$
X	D - g (perfect)	$\dfrac{9 \times 2}{8} : \dfrac{605}{364} = \dfrac{819}{605}$	$\dfrac{9 \times 2}{8} : \dfrac{5}{3} = \dfrac{27}{20}$
XI	W - y (perfect)	$\dfrac{121 \times 2}{104} : \dfrac{7}{4} = \dfrac{121}{91}$	$\dfrac{7 \times 2}{6} : \dfrac{7}{4} = \dfrac{4}{3}$
XII	E - a (perfect)	$\dfrac{5 \times 2}{4} : \dfrac{1331}{728} = \dfrac{1820}{1331}$	$\dfrac{5 \times 2}{4} : \dfrac{11}{6} = \dfrac{15}{11}$

SUPRA-EIGHTHS

DEGREES	INTERVALS	FIRST VERSION	SECOND VERSION
I	F - C (perfect)	$\dfrac{1089}{728} : \mathbf{1} = \dfrac{1089}{728}$	$\dfrac{3}{2} : \mathbf{1} = \dfrac{3}{2}$
II	X - V (perfect)	$\dfrac{13}{8} : \dfrac{121}{112} = \dfrac{182}{121}$	$\dfrac{13}{8} : \dfrac{13}{12} = \dfrac{3}{2}$
III	G - D (perfect)	$\dfrac{605}{364} : \dfrac{9}{8} = \dfrac{1210}{819}$	$\dfrac{5}{3} : \dfrac{9}{8} = \dfrac{40}{27}$
IV	Y - W (perfect)	$\dfrac{7}{4} : \dfrac{121}{104} = \dfrac{182}{121}$	$\dfrac{7}{4} : \dfrac{7}{6} = \dfrac{3}{2}$
V	A - E (perfect)	$\dfrac{1331}{728} : \dfrac{5}{4} = \dfrac{1331}{910}$	$\dfrac{11}{6} : \dfrac{5}{4} = \dfrac{22}{15}$
VI	Z - f (perfect)	$\mathbf{2} : \dfrac{121}{91} = \dfrac{182}{121}$	$\mathbf{2} : \dfrac{4}{3} = \dfrac{3}{2}$
VII	B - x (augmented)	$\dfrac{121 \times 2}{112} : \dfrac{11}{8} = \dfrac{11}{7}$	$\dfrac{13 \times 2}{12} : \dfrac{11}{8} = \dfrac{52}{33}$
VIII	C - g (perfect)	$\dfrac{9 \times 2}{8} : \dfrac{1089}{728} = \dfrac{182}{121}$	$\dfrac{9 \times 2}{8} : \dfrac{3}{2} = \dfrac{3}{2}$
IX	V - y (perfect)	$\dfrac{121 \times 2}{104} : \dfrac{13}{8} = \dfrac{242}{169}$	$\dfrac{7 \times 2}{6} : \dfrac{13}{8} = \dfrac{56}{39}$
X	D - a (perfect)	$\dfrac{5 \times 2}{4} : \dfrac{605}{364} = \dfrac{182}{121}$	$\dfrac{5 \times 2}{4} : \dfrac{5}{3} = \dfrac{3}{2}$
XI	W - z (perfect)	$\dfrac{121 \times 2}{91} : \dfrac{7}{4} = \dfrac{968}{637}$	$\dfrac{4 \times 2}{3} : \dfrac{7}{4} = \dfrac{32}{21}$
XII	E - b (perfect)	$\dfrac{11 \times 2}{8} : \dfrac{1331}{728} = \dfrac{182}{121}$	$\dfrac{11 \times 2}{8} : \dfrac{11}{6} = \dfrac{3}{2}$

SUPRA-TENTHS

DEGREES	INTERVALS	FIRST VERSION	SECOND VERSION
I	F - D (perfect)	$\dfrac{605}{364} : 1 = \dfrac{605}{364}$	$\dfrac{5}{3} : 1 = \dfrac{5}{3}$
II	X - W (perfect)	$\dfrac{7}{4} : \dfrac{121}{112} = \dfrac{196}{121}$	$\dfrac{7}{4} : \dfrac{13}{12} = \dfrac{21}{13}$
III	G - E (perfect)	$\dfrac{1331}{728} : \dfrac{9}{8} = \dfrac{1331}{819}$	$\dfrac{11}{6} : \dfrac{9}{8} = \dfrac{44}{27}$
IV	Y - f (perfect)	$2 : \dfrac{121}{104} = \dfrac{208}{121}$	$2 : \dfrac{7}{6} = \dfrac{12}{7}$
V	A - x (augmented)	$\dfrac{121 \times 2}{112} : \dfrac{5}{4} = \dfrac{121}{70}$	$\dfrac{13 \times 2}{12} : \dfrac{5}{4} = \dfrac{26}{15}$
VI	Z - g (perfect)	$\dfrac{9 \times 2}{8} : \dfrac{121}{91} = \dfrac{819}{484}$	$\dfrac{9 \times 2}{8} : \dfrac{4}{3} = \dfrac{27}{16}$
VII	B - y (augmented)	$\dfrac{121 \times 2}{104} : \dfrac{11}{8} = \dfrac{22}{13}$	$\dfrac{7 \times 2}{6} : \dfrac{11}{8} = \dfrac{56}{33}$
VIII	C - a (perfect)	$\dfrac{5 \times 2}{4} : \dfrac{1089}{728} = \dfrac{1820}{1089}$	$\dfrac{5 \times 2}{4} : \dfrac{3}{2} = \dfrac{5}{3}$
IX	V - z (perfect)	$\dfrac{121 \times 2}{91} : \dfrac{13}{8} = \dfrac{1936}{1183}$	$\dfrac{4 \times 2}{3} : \dfrac{13}{8} = \dfrac{64}{39}$
X	D - b (perfect)	$\dfrac{11 \times 2}{8} : \dfrac{605}{364} = \dfrac{91}{55}$	$\dfrac{11 \times 2}{8} : \dfrac{5}{3} = \dfrac{33}{20}$
XI	W - c (perfect)	$\dfrac{1089 \times 2}{364} : \dfrac{7}{4} = \dfrac{1089}{637}$	$\dfrac{3 \times 2}{2} : \dfrac{7}{4} = \dfrac{12}{7}$
XII	E - v (augmented)	$\dfrac{13 \times 2}{8} : \dfrac{1331}{728} = \dfrac{2366}{1331}$	$\dfrac{13 \times 2}{8} : \dfrac{11}{6} = \dfrac{39}{22}$

SUPRA-TWELFTHS

DEGREES	INTERVALS	FIRST VERSION	SECOND VERSION
I	F - E (minor)	$\dfrac{1331}{728} : 1 = \dfrac{1331}{728}$	$\dfrac{11}{6} : 1 = \dfrac{11}{6}$
II	X - f (minor)	$2 : \dfrac{121}{112} = \dfrac{224}{121}$	$2 : \dfrac{13}{12} = \dfrac{24}{13}$
III	G - x (major)	$\dfrac{121 \times 2}{112} : \dfrac{9}{8} = \dfrac{121}{63}$	$\dfrac{13 \times 2}{12} : \dfrac{9}{8} = \dfrac{52}{27}$
IV	Y - g (minor)	$\dfrac{9 \times 2}{8} : \dfrac{121}{104} = \dfrac{234}{121}$	$\dfrac{9 \times 2}{8} : \dfrac{7}{6} = \dfrac{27}{14}$
V	A - y (major)	$\dfrac{121 \times 2}{104} : \dfrac{5}{4} = \dfrac{121}{65}$	$\dfrac{7 \times 2}{6} : \dfrac{5}{4} = \dfrac{28}{15}$
VI	Z - a (minor)	$\dfrac{5 \times 2}{4} : \dfrac{121}{91} = \dfrac{455}{242}$	$\dfrac{5 \times 2}{4} : \dfrac{4}{3} = \dfrac{15}{8}$
VII	B - z (major)	$\dfrac{121 \times 2}{91} : \dfrac{11}{8} = \dfrac{176}{91}$	$\dfrac{4 \times 2}{3} : \dfrac{11}{8} = \dfrac{64}{33}$
VIII	C - b (minor)	$\dfrac{11 \times 2}{8} : \dfrac{1089}{728} = \dfrac{182}{99}$	$\dfrac{11 \times 2}{8} : \dfrac{3}{2} = \dfrac{11}{6}$
IX	V - c (minor)	$\dfrac{1089 \times 2}{728} : \dfrac{13}{8} = \dfrac{2178}{1183}$	$\dfrac{3 \times 2}{2} : \dfrac{13}{8} = \dfrac{24}{13}$
X	D - v (major)	$\dfrac{13 \times 2}{8} : \dfrac{605}{364} = \dfrac{1183}{605}$	$\dfrac{13 \times 2}{8} : \dfrac{5}{3} = \dfrac{39}{20}$
XI	W - d (minor)	$\dfrac{605 \times 2}{364} : \dfrac{7}{4} = \dfrac{1210}{637}$	$\dfrac{5 \times 2}{3} : \dfrac{7}{4} = \dfrac{40}{21}$
XII	E - w (major)	$\dfrac{7 \times 2}{4} : \dfrac{1331}{728} = \dfrac{2548}{1331}$	$\dfrac{7 \times 2}{6} : \dfrac{11}{6} = \dfrac{21}{11}$

sented by the ratios $\frac{182}{121}$ and $\frac{1089}{728}$ in the case of supra-Eighths and by $\frac{121}{91}$ and $\frac{1456}{1089}$ in the case of supra-Sixths—all of them apparently exceeding in complexity the acoustical ratios of the consonances.

Again, two of the supra-Fourths (A-C and D-F) are expressed, in the second version, by the ratio $\frac{6}{5}$, and two others (F-Y and C-W) by $\frac{7}{6}$, both these ratios being simpler than those of the great majority of consonances; the same will be true, naturally, of their inversions found in the group of the supra-Tenths and expressed by the ratios $\frac{5}{3}$ and $\frac{12}{7}$. In the first version, however, all the intervals enumerated exceed in complexity the ratios of the consonances.

There are also a few ratios found in the group of supra-Seconds and supra-Twelfths of the second version, viz. $\frac{12}{11}, \frac{13}{12}, \frac{11}{6}, \frac{24}{13}$, which, on the average, are about of the same acoustical quality as the consonances and, as such, they are hardly fit to function as alleged "counterforces" to the latter, i.e. as dissonances. Proper interbalance in this respect, on the other hand, is well preserved in the first version, where the intervals found on the same scale-degrees are of a much "tenser" quality than the consonances.

It remains, finally, to analyze several intervals within the groups of perfect dissonances which, representing the diminished and augmented forms of the latter (i.e. "deviations" from the normal type of perfect dissonances) and equalling in dimension some intervals of the consonant groups, must likewise be considered as consonances.

As we already know, there are three such (diminished) intervals in the group of supra-Fourths (X-A, Y-B, V-E) comprising two whole steps each, i.e. as many as there are in a major supra-Third, which is classed among imperfect consonances. The comparison of these intervals in just intonation discloses the fact that at least one of them (Y-B) is expressed, in the first version, by the same ratio as a major supra-Third, viz., by $\frac{18}{11}$, while there is no identity of acoustical expression whatever with either of these intervals in the second version. The latter, therefore, precludes the construction of a (musically important) continuous chain of intervals consisting of major and minor supra-Thirds interconnected by a justly intoned interval of a diminished supra-Fourth, which serves therein as a "bridge." What has been found in regard to the diminished supra-Fourths is true also of their inversions, i.e. augmented supra-Tenths, of which there is one (B-Y), expressed in the first version by the same ratio as a minor supra-Eleventh ($\frac{22}{13}$), both these intervals comprising seven and a half steps and qualifying, therefore, as consonances. No such identity exists between any of the ratios of the augmented supra-Tenths and those of the minor supra-Elevenths, in the second version.

Another pair of groups of perfect dissonances, which contain "deviations" in the form of diminished and augmented intervals, are those of supra-Sixths and supra-Eighths. Among the former, we find one diminished supra-Sixth (X-B), comprising three and a half steps, and among the latter, one augmented supra-Eighth (B-X), comprising six whole steps. They are respectively equal, in terms of these measurements, to a major supra-Fifth and a minor supra-Ninth, which belong to imperfect consonances. But an examination of the purely acoustical expressions of these intervals instantly reveals that only in the first version of just intonation is there an identity of ratios between the diminished supra-Sixth (X-B) and two of the major supra-Fifths (B-W and E-Y), on the one hand ($\frac{14}{11}$), and between the augmented supra-Eighth (B-X) and two of the minor supra-Ninths (Y-E and W-B), on the other ($\frac{11}{7}$). The same diminished supra-Sixth and augmented supra-Eighth are expressed, in the second version, by ratios $\frac{3\,3}{2\,6}$ and $\frac{5\,2}{3\,3}$, which, aside from their dissimilarity to those of the major supra-Fifths and minor supra-Ninths, are too complicated to function as consonances.

Looking back on the entire analysis of just intonation of the supra-diatonic scale, hardly any doubt is left, it seems, as to the superiority of its first version, in spite of the greater appeal of the "mathematical" appearance of the second,—probably its sole advantage. The proper interbalance between the two mutually "opposite forces" within the supra-diatonic system, i.e. between its consonances and dissonances, is found in the former of these versions but is positively lacking in the latter. This, at least, is what may be inferred so far, although one can never be absolutely certain in theoretical speculations, until exhaustive experimental data, which may bring to light unexpected factors, are at hand. But whatever the truth may ultimately turn out to be, it can scarcely have a negative effect upon our theory at large, since the actual difference between the intervals in both versions of just intonation is too small for the resultant error (if any) to invalidate, to any extent, the fundamental calculations relating to the entire "supra-diatonic" structure. Moreover, the question of the advantage of one version over the other will probably remain, in the future, a minor matter of purely theoretical interest (about which more or less difference of opinion is inevitable), if only the *supra-tempered* intonation proves to be adaptable in musical practice from the acoustic viewpoint. The comparison of the first version of just intonation with the supra-tempered intonation demonstrated in Ex. 89, as well as the figures shown in the Tables that immediately follow it, gives rather strong support to the belief that such practical adaptability of Equal Temperament in regard to the supra-diatonic scale is more than probable. And our conviction would in no way be shaken should we substitute the second version of just intonation for the first in this comparison. The reason is that such a substitution, leaving all the consonant intervals untouched, would merely extend some of the dissonant intervals by 3 ctn. and contract the rest of them by the same quantity, the average approximation of just intonation to supra-tempered intonation remaining, therefore, about the same. The following diagram, in which both versions of just intonation are placed side by side, will give a fair idea of their difference and of their common approximation to the supra-tempered intonation (dotted lines indicate the position of supra-chromatic alterations under the condition of the latter intonation). The acoustical values in this diagram are given both in centitones and in vibration-fractions, with the exception of the supra-tempered intonation, which is represented only in terms of centitones. [See Ex. 89ᵃ.]

*   *   *

In connection with the above discussion, it will be worth while to bring to light a few more points. They concern the *relative* value of any form of Just Intonation which, contrary to what the term itself is apt to suggest, does not imply, by any means, an idea of absolute acoustic truth. As a matter of fact, the very nature of Just Intonation, strange as this may seem, somehow precludes rigid impeccability in all possible directions. In one or more of them its "justness" is always impaired by certain "flaws" which, however slight and negligible, cannot be rectified otherwise than at the cost of a definite loss in some other direction. And this is exactly what has caused—and still

EXAMPLE 89a:

RATIOS 1	$\frac{121}{112}$	$\frac{9}{8}$	$\frac{121}{104}$	$\frac{5}{4}$	$\frac{121}{91}$	$\frac{11}{8}$	$\frac{1089}{728}$	$\frac{13}{8}$	$\frac{605}{364}$	$\frac{7}{4}$	$\frac{1331}{728}$	2
CTN. 0	67	102	131	193	246	276	348	421	439	485	522	600
	F	X	G	Y	A	Z	B	C	V	D	W	E	f

SUPRA-TEMPERED JUST INTONATION [FIRST VERSION]

	$\frac{121}{112}$	$\frac{126}{121}$	$\frac{121}{117}$	$\frac{130}{121}$	$\frac{484}{455}$	$\frac{91}{88}$	$\frac{99}{91}$	$\frac{1183}{1089}$	$\frac{1210}{1183}$	$\frac{637}{605}$	$\frac{1331}{1274}$	$\frac{1456}{1331}$
	67	35	29	62	53	30	·72	73	18	46	37	78

SUPRA-TEMPERED INTONATION

F-0; X-31.6; G-63.2; ♯ or ♭-94.8; Y-126.4; ♯ or ♭-158.0; A-189.6; ♯ or ♭-221.2; Z-252.8; B-284.4; ♯ or ♭-316.0; C-347.4; ♯ or ♭-379.0; V-410.6; D-442.2; ♯ or ♭-473.8; W-505.4; E-537.0; ♯ or ♭-568.6; f-600

JUST INTONATION [SECOND VERSION]

	70	32	32	59	56	27	75	70	21	43	40	75
	$\frac{13}{12}$	$\frac{27}{26}$	$\frac{28}{27}$	$\frac{15}{14}$	$\frac{16}{15}$	$\frac{33}{32}$	$\frac{12}{11}$	$\frac{13}{12}$	$\frac{40}{39}$	$\frac{21}{20}$	$\frac{22}{21}$	$\frac{12}{11}$

	F	X	G	Y	A	Z	B	C	V	D	W	E	f
CTN. 0	70	102	134	193	249	276	351	421	442	485	525	600
RATIOS 1	$\frac{13}{12}$	$\frac{9}{8}$	$\frac{7}{6}$	$\frac{5}{4}$	$\frac{4}{3}$	$\frac{11}{8}$	$\frac{3}{2}$	$\frac{13}{8}$	$\frac{5}{3}$	$\frac{7}{4}$	$\frac{11}{6}$	2

causes—the appearance of various systems of pure tuning, in an endeavor to find the most advantageous, if not the perfect, solution of the problem.

The relativity of Just Intonation, generally speaking, is a vast and absorbing subject which, if delved into deeply, would easily fill another and rather extensive volume. We shall only touch upon it, therefore, in so far as it has a direct bearing on our final deductions in regard to the pure tuning of the supra-diatonic scale.

We have already discussed this subject at length with reference to three gradually evolving "organic" scales, every one of which, it will be recalled, requires that a different set of pure intervals be employed for its just intonation, according to our theory. Therefore, each of these intonations is only *relatively* just, holding good for no more than one given scale and, consequently, of no value for another. This is the first point of the relativity in question, and there are two more.

It is not often realized by musicians that any scheme of pure tuning is worked out for a given scale mainly with regard to its *harmonic* intonation, provided, of course, that the number of tones used for this purpose does not exceed the number of degrees naturally comprised in that scale. In regular cases, therefore, the problem of *melodic* intonation is not completely and automatically solved together with the harmonic intonation of one and the same scale, as is sometimes supposed, since the former, though coinciding in certain parts with the latter, is not fully equivalent to it. In other words, the tuning of a scale which is well adjusted for harmonic combinations does not necessarily serve the purpose for melodic progressions. This, then, is the second point of the relativity of Just Intonation: adapted for the harmonic relations of a scale, it does not hold good for strictly melodic relations, and, if rectified in the latter direction, will inevitably and proportionately produce detrimental effects in the former, as will be presently seen.

It must be noted, in the first place, that, in contradistinction to harmonic intonation which, as a rule, may always be acoustically determined by exact mathematical ratios, melodic intonation is largely of a "variable" nature, its manifold shadings differing in pitch, depending on the musical context in which they appear. And if broad generalizations were to be ventured upon in this respect, with the intention to represent the "fluid" melodic intonation in more or less definitely fixed acoustical terms—which, with due reservations, are admissible in limited scientific inquiries—then many discrepancies between the harmonic and melodic intonation would certainly crop out in a quite obvious manner.

Thus, it has often been observed that the leading note of the major diatonic scale, let us say, has a natural tendency, in melodic progressions, to rise considerably in pitch before falling into the Tonic. The same is partly true of the major Third which, to some extent, may likewise be regarded as a "leading note," but in the lower Tetrachord of the scale, while the major Seventh performs this very function in the upper. Similar tendencies have been observed with reference to chromatically altered notes, of which the "sharps," when considered melodically, are usually higher than their respective "flats" (C$\sharp$, for instance, is higher than D$\flat$, etc.). This is particularly evident with players on bow instruments, and especially in compositions written in unaccompanied style, the exceptions being frequently made only for passages of a decidedly harmonic nature (various arpeggios and the like), or for occasional progressions, in the melodic line, that suggest harmonic patterns.

The widely known scientific experiments conducted by CORNU and MERCADIER (quoted and commented by A. J. Ellis in his translation of Helmholtz's work, *Sensations of Tone*, p. 486-488), led them to the belief that the melodic intonation of violinists and cellists—in passages containing no modulations and double notes—agrees with that of the Pythagorean tuning. And needless to say, this is precisely the tuning which the natural tendencies of melodic intonation, described above, most closely approximate, as may be learned from the diagram of Ex. 79 of this volume. One has merely to compare the intonation given in this diagram with the one represented in Ex. 110 (upper set of lines) to realize the difference between them which immediately catches the eye. Particularly with regard to the chromatically altered notes, it will at once be noticed that the relation between the "sharps" and "flats" found in Ex. 110 is just the reverse, as compared to Pythagorean intonation (Ex. 79), i.e. the "sharps" are lower (and not higher, as in the latter) than their respective "flats." Also, the leading notes, E and B, in both the lower and upper Tetrachords (viz. C-D-E-F and G-A-B-C, if we deal with the major and not the Lydian mode represented in the Examples referred to) are differently tuned in these two intonations, all these incongruities being due to the two distinct principles involved: a series of just Fifths ($\frac{3}{2}$) in the first instance, and a series of just Thirds—major ($\frac{5}{4}$) and minor ($\frac{6}{5}$) alternatingly—in the second.

From the purely melodic point of view, the intonation represented in Ex. 79 shows a structure of exquisite proportions which, however, is unfit for the harmonic formations of the diatonic scale. On the contrary, the intonation represented in Ex. 110 answers fairly well the harmonic purpose of that scale and, in fact, is even actually based on purely tuned diatonic Triads variously interconnected, depending on the mode desired, but the consecutive position of the tones thus obtained scarcely meets the specific requirements of melodic intonation. Without dwelling any longer on certain natural tendencies of genuinely melodic progressions which are practically disregarded in harmonic intonation, and even leaving aside the matter of occasional inequality of *chromatic* semitones (like F-F♯ and G-G♯ etc. in Ex. 110), melodically unjustified under ordinary conditions, let us confine ourselves to the seven *regular* intervals of the diatonic scale in our analysis of their position, including their possible permutations for melodic purposes, as well as of the resulting effect of these permutations upon the standard form of harmonic intonation.

This analysis brings us in close touch with the third point of relativity of Just Intonation, about which a few words have to be said before proceeding. This concerns the unavoidable acoustic "flaws" which usually exist within the harmonic sphere itself of one and the same scale. As we have already demonstrated in the concluding Footnote to Chapter XI, out of the six Triads, which are supposed to be consonant according to the structural logic of the diatonic scale, one always remains acoustically incorrect in the latter's Just Intonation. It is the minor Triad D-F-A in the major mode, and the major Triad G-B-D in the natural minor mode. Both these Triads contain the Pythagorean minor Third ($\frac{32}{27}$ or 147 ctn.) instead of the pure minor Third ($\frac{6}{5}$ or 158 ctn.) and the so-called grave Fifth ($\frac{40}{27}$ or 340 ctn.) instead of the pure Fifth ($\frac{3}{2}$ or 351 ctn.). Of these two intervals, faulty in the diatonic scale, the grave Fifth produces clearly sensible beats (Helmholtz, p. 335) and is particularly unfit for a consonant chord of the diatonic scale. In conjunction with the somewhat less inharmonious minor Third, it is naturally bound to make the still worse impression of a "defective" minor or major Triad, decidedly off pitch. The same characteristics will also be found, of course, in the inversions of the intervals and chords enumerated. Thus, Just Intonation, even in regard to the group of supposedly consonant formations of the diatonic system, is only *relatively* "just," and because of the intrinsic nature of acoustic laws cannot be otherwise. [This, however, does not always apply to altered modes of this system, in which we may easily shift the "error" in intonation to a diminished Triad—especially formed for this purpose by means of chromatic alterations—availing ourselves of the fact that acoustical inaccuracies in dissonant chords are disregarded in Just Intonation.]

The position of scale-tones of the justly intoned major diatonic mode, to be now analyzed, has been given at the beginning of Chapter IX, and is based on the principle originated by PTOLEMY, confirmed and upheld much later by a galaxy of scientists and theorists including Zarlino, Kepler, Descartes, Mersenne and many others. This long accepted form of Just Intonation, nevertheless, cannot conceal a certain inconsistency from a strictly *melodic* point of view, inasmuch as the intervals comprised within each of the two musically identical Tetrachords C-D-E-F and G-A-B-C manifest an acoustically different arrangement in their succession, as will be instantly seen in the following comparison:

LOWER TETRACHORD: C 102 D 91 E 56 F

UPPER TETRACHORD: G 91 A 102 B 56 C

In spite of the inconsistency, however, this is the most advantageous arrangement from the *harmonic* point of view, since the error in intonation, in this instance, viz. $\frac{81}{80}$ or 11 ctn., falls on the chord D-F-A which is, musically, of secondary importance in the harmonic scheme of the major diatonic mode, and therefore can be limited in application without any particular harm, being viewed and actually used as a component part of dissonant harmonic combinations (like D-F-A-C, for instance), and not as a minor Triad.* But should we venture to improve, for melodic purposes, the arrangement of the above intervals by making their succession identical in both Tetrachords, the harmonic aspect of the scale, according to the infallible law previously mentioned, will immediately suffer in one form or another, as we shall now demonstrate.

There are, obviously, two possible ways of obtaining the melodically desirable identity of these Tetrachords, i.e. either by reversing the position of the major and minor whole tones (102 ctn. and 91 ctn.) in the lower Tetrachord, or by a similar operation (with the opposite result) in the upper. The former method would bring us back to the fundamental principle of DIDYMUS, predecessor of PTOLEMY, who invariably placed the minor whole tone ($\frac{10}{9}$ or 91 ctn.) below the major ($\frac{9}{8}$ or 102 ctn.) in diatonic Tetrachords and never knew any other arrangement.** Our major diatonic mode, therefore, would have the following appearance, when formed according to this principle:

$$\text{C} \quad 91 \quad \text{D} \quad 102 \quad \text{E} \quad 56 \quad \text{F} \mid 102 \quad \text{G} \quad 91 \quad \text{A} \quad 102 \quad \text{B} \quad 56 \quad \text{C}$$

upper Tetrachord (bracket over G A B C)

lower Tetrachord (bracket under C D E F)

In order to investigate the changes which would be created in the harmonic intonation of our scale by the above reversal of intervals, it is best to represent all its component notes in the form of a chordal chain with the three principal Triads consecutively interconnected, similarly to previous demonstrations, namely:

subdominant Triad (bracket over F A C)   dominant Triad (bracket over G B D)

$$\text{F} \quad 193 \quad \text{A} \quad 158 \quad \text{C} \quad 193 \quad \text{E} \quad 158 \quad \text{G} \quad 193 \quad \text{B} \quad 147 \quad \text{D} \quad 158 \quad [\text{F}]$$

tonic Triad (bracket under C E G)

It is immediately evident from this representation that the error of 11 ctn. (*comma of Didymus*) is shifted from the interval D-F (of the Ptolemaic intonation) to B-D, the former consequently becoming pure ($\frac{6}{5}$) and the latter acoustically inaccurate ($\frac{32}{27}$). This shifting automatically removes the very same error from the interval D-A, trans-

---

* Compare Charles Koechlin's *Some Questions concerning musical acoustics* in *Pro Musica Quarterly* (New York), October 1926, p. 8. Incidentally, it is interesting to note in this connection, how Ebenezer Prout stresses the musically subordinate role of another minor Triad in the harmonic scheme of the major mode (*Harmony*, page 186). It is the Triad on the third degree which, in its inverted form (G-B-E), is regarded

by him as an incomplete chord of the dominant Thirteenth with the Fifth, Seventh, Ninth and Eleventh omitted, which resolves into the tonic Triad.

** See the article under the heading of *Zarlino*, by William S. Rockstro in Grove's Dictionary of Music, Vol. 5, page 776 (1928); also the *Allgemeine Geschichte der Musik* by Johann N. Forkel, Band I, p. 362-363 (Leipzig, 1788).

ferring it to G-D, and therefore transforms, in a similar manner, the former into a pure Fifth ($\frac{3}{2}$) and the latter into the acoustically inaccurate grave Fifth ($\frac{40}{27}$). As a result, the minor Triad D-F-A acquires acoustic purity at the expense of the dominant Triad G-B-D, which most definitely loses it, and which accordingly would have to be avoided, as such, in harmonic progressions of the justly intoned scale.

Anyone who fully realizes the part played by the dominant Triad in the harmonic scheme of the diatonic scale, which ranks in importance next only to the tonic Triad (particularly in cadences—the bone and marrow of strict harmonizations), will readily understand the failure of the Didymus principle from the harmonic point of view, so that obviously no further commentaries in this connection are necessary. To sum up: the gain in the melodic direction, in which structural symmetry of Tetrachords was achieved, was promptly counterbalanced, in this instance, by a marked loss in the direction of harmonic relations.

The other way of arranging intervals which would lead to a scale comprising structurally symmetrical Tetrachords, calls for the reversed position of the two whole tones in each of them, ultimately producing the following modified formula of Just Intonation: *

upper Tetrachord

C 102 D 91 E 56 F 102 G 102 A 91 B 56 C

lower Tetrachord

This arrangement of intervals, from a *melodic* point of view, is, no doubt, still better than the one built on the principle of Didymus and far better than that of Ptolemy, whose asymmetrical Tetrachords are the least advantageous in melodic intonation. Thus, the succession of two whole tones with the major (102 ctn.) followed by the minor (91 ctn.), is in general more natural than the opposite, as proved by their consecutive position in the series of overtones in which the former precedes the latter, both of them being respectively found between the overtones 8:9:10 which determine their acoustic ratios. Furthermore, this arrangement permits the leading notes of both Tetrachords, viz. E and B, to be considerably raised in pitch, whenever the natural tendency of the melodic line requires it, without any particular detriment to the interval (91 ctn.) which precedes them in each instance, inasmuch as this interval will remain essentially a whole tone so long as it does not exceed the limit of 102 ctn. in its expansion caused by the raising of the notes referred to. This possibility, however, is totally precluded in the Didymus arrangement, since the major whole tone immediately preceding the notes E and B is *originally* equal to 102 ctn. and with its smallest expansion, therefore, a still greater acoustical disparity between the major and minor whole tones would proportionately begin to manifest itself—an obvious disadvantage in melodic progressions. Finally, even such a detail as the slight tendency to raise the pitch of a

---

* This formula is adopted by ARIEL (*pseudonym*) in his treatise *Das Relativitätsprincip der musikalischen Harmonie*, Bd. I, (Leipzig, 1925); see Table I (pure seven-tone division of an Octave). This writer also gives a few other pure divisions, based on a single principle (entirely different from ours), which include scales of 2, 4, 12, 19 and 59 tones. He is one of the protagonists of the nineteen-tone tempered system, and will be mentioned in this connection later on.

major Sixth in certain melodic constructions, which has been frequently observed (and proved by scientific records) finds its justification in the above (last) version of Just Intonation of the diatonic scale, this interval being of a larger dimension in it (453 ctn.) than in the two other versions (442 ctn.).

But if this last version, according to our argumentation, ought to be regarded as the most advantageous for melodic intonation, then inferentially one may safely predict that it will prove to be the worst of all from the standpoint of harmonic intonation. To be convinced of this, it is sufficient to represent this version of Just Intonation —like the two others—in the form of a consecutively interconnected chain of three principal Triads, namely:

subdominant Triad   dominant Triad

F 204 A 147 C 193 E 158 G 193 B 158 D 147 [F]

tonic Triad

A close examination of this chordal chain soon discloses the fact that out of six (supposedly) consonant Triads, *three* are acoustically inaccurate—an enormous percentage, as compared to the two other versions of Just Intonation in which only *one* of the Triads is impaired. The error of 11 ctn. falls, in this instance, on one major Third, F-A (204 ctn. instead of 193 ctn.), on two minor Thirds, A-C and D-F (147 ctn. instead of 158 ctn.), and on one Fifth, A-E (340 ctn. instead of 351 ctn.). This, naturally, has a proportionately negative effect upon the Triads that contain these intervals, the subdominant and the supertonic Triads, F-A-C and D-F-A, acquiring the Pythagorean intonation (whose *harmonic* inferiority is too well known to elicit comment), and the submediant Triad A-C-E becoming faulty, similarly to the chord D-F-A of the Ptolemaic intonation. In other words, neither Triad of the subdominant group retains a place among the justly intoned chords and, consequently, no purely tuned plagal cadences of any sort would be any longer possible in strict harmonizations, when the above version of Just Intonation is used. Similarly, with the submediant Triad acoustically impaired, the use of the interrupted cadence which comprises the latter chord is also precluded by this version of Just Intonation.

Weighing now the results of our inquiry, scarcely any further proof will be needed as to the validity of the general law stated, according to which the qualities of the harmonic and melodic aspects of any given form of Just Intonation are in inverse ratio to each other. The better an intonation serves for harmonic constructions, the worse does it answer melodic purposes and *vice versa*.

As for the two pre-diatonic scales (i.e. sub-infra-diatonic and infra-diatonic), whose harmonic intonation coincides with the Pythagorean, this law holds good only when their auxiliary degrees (subject to the same natural tendencies as those of the diatonic scale) are taken into consideration. Briefly speaking, the altered tones of these scales (two for each auxiliary degree, when *not* tempered) have to be designated in exactly the opposite way, depending on whether harmonic or melodic intonation is implied (see, for instance, Ex. 109 with its Footnote relating to both intonations of the infra-diatonic scale).

Turning, finally, to the two versions of Just Intonation for the supra-diatonic scale (Ex. 89^d) one may fairly well estimate their *melodic* value long before the actual analysis is made in this respect, if only one recalls the results of our investigation in regard to their *harmonic* value given earlier. We have, then, arrived at the conclusion that *all* the intervals constituting the five groups of consonances of the supra-diatonic scale express (in both versions) no other acoustical magnitudes but those which are formed by various combinations of the overtone-numbers 8, 9, 10, 11, 13, 14, or their inversions, i.e. the numbers which form the basic "nucleus" of Just Intonation of this scale (page 204). In other words, no interval comprised in either the principal or subsidiary Hexads is in the least impaired from the standpoint of acoustical purity.

Such perfect results in regard to *all* consonant chords of the supra-diatonic scale, without exception, could be achieved only for the simple reason that, owing to the *even* number of the regular degrees of this scale, any of its subsidiary Hexads may be regarded as an inversion of one of its two principal Hexads. And since the latter are *originally* tuned according to the pure intervals comprised in the above series of overtones, it is evident that their intonation, which is naturally retained by their inversions, will also be that of all the subsidiary Hexads. The acoustic "flaws" which any form of Just Intonation (beginning with the diatonic scale) is bound to contain, according to our deductions, will be found, in the case of the supra-diatonic scale, in its "indirect" consonances, as they may be called, i.e. those which derive from diminution or augmentation of perfect dissonances. Such are the intervals of diminished supra-Fourths and augmented supra-Tenths, the latter being mere inversions of the former. The mathematical Tables which precede Ex. 89^d show that—in the first version of Just Intonation—only one diminished supra-Fourth out of three (the one which serves as a "bridge" between our two principal Hexads) is acoustically pure and equals, as it should, the dimension of a major supra-Third ($\frac{13}{11}$), the rest of the diminished supra-Fourths being quite inaccurate in this respect ($\frac{140}{121}$ and $\frac{1331}{1183}$). This is also true, naturally, of their inversions, one of which is acoustically pure and equals the dimension of a minor supra-Eleventh ($\frac{22}{13}$), while the two others are inaccurate ($\frac{121}{70}$ and $\frac{2366}{1331}$). As for the second version of Just Intonation, none of these intervals manifests any acoustical purity, according to the same mathematical Tables.

The important point, however, is that none but the "indirect" consonances are impaired, to a greater or lesser degree, in the justly intoned supra-diatonic scale, and that the entire mass of *fundamentally* consonant intervals remains acoustically pure in both versions of Just Intonation. This fact being borne in mind, little effort will be required to reach the conclusion we are seeking. The acoustical conditions mentioned are, from all evidence, almost ideal in regard to the *harmonic* justness of this scale. Therefore, by virtue of the law of inverse relation referred to above, the very same conditions are bound to be proportionately unfavorable in so far as the *melodic* fitness of either of the two versions of the supra-diatonic Just Intonation is concerned.

Even a cursory glance at the graphic representation of this Just Intonation (Ex. 89^d) supports our conclusion. Neither of its two versions possesses the kind of structural proportions that could be considered fully satisfactory from the melodic point of view. Some of the basic intervals that constitute the scale (whole steps and half steps) show, at times, a wide disparity in dimension and, in both instances, are very seldom equal to each other. The interval G-Y, particularly, is contracted to such a degree as to suggest an altered supra-mode with the note Y flatted, which is not the case, however, from the harmonic point of view, etc.

It is easy to prove, on the other hand, that a different form of Just Intonation having structural proportions which are more satisfactory for melodic progressions will instantly impair the acoustical purity of certain fundamentally consonant intervals of the supra-diatonic scale and, consequently, disqualify, to the same extent, its validity for harmonic purposes. We have availed ourselves, for this demonstration, of the acoustically pure twelve-tone division of an Octave calculated by Ariel (found in the work quoted), and have adjusted it to the twelve regular degrees of the supra-diatonic scale (supra-mode "F-f"). To the original figures showing the vibration-ratios of intervals comprised in this division, we have added the expression of the same intervals in terms of centitones (two lower series of figures).

$$1 \quad \frac{16}{15} \quad \frac{10}{9} \quad \frac{32}{27} \quad \frac{100}{81} \quad \frac{4}{3} \quad \frac{25}{18} \quad \frac{3}{2} \quad \frac{8}{5} \quad \frac{5}{3} \quad \frac{16}{9} \quad \frac{50}{27} \quad 2$$

$$F \overset{\frac{16}{15}}{\underset{56}{}} X \overset{\frac{25}{24}}{\underset{35}{}} G \overset{\frac{16}{15}}{\underset{56}{}} Y \overset{\frac{25}{24}}{\underset{35}{}} A \overset{\frac{27}{25}}{\underset{67}{}} Z \overset{\frac{25}{24}}{\underset{35}{}} B \overset{\frac{27}{25}}{\underset{67}{}} C \overset{\frac{16}{15}}{\underset{56}{}} V \overset{\frac{25}{24}}{\underset{35}{}} D \overset{\frac{16}{15}}{\underset{56}{}} W \overset{\frac{25}{24}}{\underset{35}{}} E \overset{\frac{27}{25}}{\underset{67}{}} F$$

| 0 | 56 | 91 | 147 | 182 | 249 | 284 | 351 | 407 | 442 | 498 | 533 | 600 |

The symmetrical arrangement of intervals so desirable for melodic purposes is immediately evident in this representation. All the "minimum" intervals (half steps) of the supra-diatonic scale are acoustically alike, according to this construction, and invariably equal 35 ctn. The whole steps have no more than two different variations, viz. 67 ctn. and 56 ctn., which is another advantage, compared with the number of variations manifested in this respect in Example 89ᵈ. No evidence here of the exaggerated contractions or expansions of intervals which are found in the two former versions of Just Intonation. This fact, incidentally, causes the new form of intonation to approach closer to supra-tempered intonation—practically the ideal of intervallic symmetry—than is the case with the two other forms.

To investigate the effect which this new form of intonation has upon the harmonic aspect of the supra-diatonic scale, it is sufficient to "isolate," from the above formula, the two principal Hexads of this scale which are supposed to comprise all its (originally) consonant intervals. It is a simple matter to figure out that these two isolated Hexads will have the following acoustic relations:

TONIC HEXAD

$$1 \quad \frac{10}{9} \quad \frac{100}{81} \quad \frac{25}{18} \quad \frac{8}{5} \quad \frac{16}{9} \quad 2$$

$$F \overset{\frac{10}{9}}{\underset{91}{}} G \overset{\frac{10}{9}}{\underset{91}{}} A \overset{\frac{9}{8}}{\underset{102}{}} B \overset{\frac{144}{125}}{\underset{123}{}} V \overset{\frac{10}{9}}{\underset{91}{}} W \overset{\frac{9}{8}}{\underset{102}{}} F$$

| 0 | 91 | 182 | 284 | 407 | 498 | 600 |

DOMINANT HEXAD

$$1 \qquad \frac{9}{8} \qquad \frac{5}{4} \qquad \frac{25}{18} \qquad \frac{8}{5} \qquad \frac{16}{9} \qquad 2$$

$$\underset{102}{Z} \overset{\frac{9}{8}}{} \underset{91}{C} \overset{\frac{10}{9}}{} \underset{91}{D} \overset{\frac{10}{9}}{} \underset{123}{E} \overset{\frac{144}{125}}{} \underset{91}{X} \overset{\frac{10}{9}}{} \underset{102}{Y} \overset{\frac{9}{8}}{} Z$$

$$0 \qquad 102 \qquad 193 \qquad 284 \qquad 407 \qquad 498 \qquad 600$$

It is readily seen from these two formulae that while the minor supra-Thirds are represented therein by two different and simple ratios ($\frac{9}{8}$ and $\frac{10}{9}$), the major supra-Third—the most characteristic interval—is quite markedly impaired. Its ratio ($\frac{144}{125}$) is far too complicated, compared with the original ratio ($\frac{13}{11}$) assigned to this interval, and naturally has a detrimental effect upon the entire chord as a consonant unit. This will be still more evident if the acoustical interrelation of all the notes constituting each of the two Hexads is expressed by whole numbers and compared to the original interrelation. In the latter case, it will be remembered, either of the two Hexads could be expressed by the following single series:

TONIC AND DOMINANT HEXADS

$$\overset{8}{F}—\overset{9}{G}—\overset{10}{A}—\overset{11}{B}—\overset{13}{V}—\overset{14}{W}$$

or

$$\overset{8}{Z}—\overset{9}{C}—\overset{10}{D}—\overset{11}{E}—\overset{13}{X}—\overset{14}{Y}$$

The same two Hexads formed according to their respective formulae given above cannot be represented by a series of smaller numbers than those that follow:

TONIC HEXAD

$$\overset{810}{F}—\overset{900}{G}—\overset{1000}{A}—\overset{1125}{B}—\overset{1296}{V}—\overset{1440}{W}$$

DOMINANT HEXAD

$$\overset{360}{Z}—\overset{405}{C}—\overset{450}{D}—\overset{500}{E}—\overset{576}{X}—\overset{640}{Y}$$

Thus, it is clear that the law of inverse relation between harmonic and melodic fitness of any (non-tempered) intonation holds good not only for the diatonic but for the supra-diatonic scale as well.

This conclusion, however, must not be erroneously taken as implying that the new twelve-tone division of an Octave, which we have just demonstrated merely for comparison, is the actual basis of melodic intonation for the supra-diatonic scale, or, more accurately, that it is the theoretical norm to which all the variations of melodic intonation will gravitate when this scale is introduced in musical practice. We must frankly admit, in the first place, that the problem of melodic intonation for any given scale can only be solved experimentally and not speculatively. This, of course, is due to the simple fact that the variability and "fluidity" of any melodic intonation allow the establishment of a theoretical norm of only a very *conventional* nature which, being deduced from a great number of actual performances, represents no more than a sort of average index of the most typical tendencies of intonation manifested in melodic progressions. In other words, the theoretical norm of melodic intonation is not one which is based on its *own* definite and objective laws of tonal organization, but one which *we* subjectively liken, for practical convenience, to some of the known forms of organized intonation, as is the case, for instance, with the Pythagorean tuning conventionally assumed as the theoretical norm of melodic intonation for the diatonic scale.

It is, therefore, the artist and not the scientist who will intuitively solve the problem of the new melodic intonation *first*. Only after a sufficient number of musical data are accumulated in this connection, will it become the scientist's task to classify them and eventually to draw final conclusions from them. This statement readily explains why the author has refrained from suggesting any theoretical construction that might later serve as a conventional "norm" for the melodic intonation of the supra-diatonic scale, and confined himself solely to the problem of its harmonic intonation, which it was necessary to work out in order to demonstrate the basic acoustical relations of the new Tonality.

It must be remembered, however, that Tonality is not just another name for the harmonic intonation of the scale it represents. Tonality is more than that, in spite of the fact that it is acoustically based on this intonation. Psychologically speaking, Tonality (which to a great extent, *is* a psychological phenomenon) unites harmonic and melodic intonation—its rational and non-rational aspects—in one organized whole. Harmonic intonation is, as it were, the more or less rigid skeleton of Tonality, while melodic intonation may be compared to its living and pulsating flesh and blood. Though dependent on the general scheme of the former, the latter does not cover it, so to speak, in an even and unchangeable manner. On the contrary, the very nature of melodic intonation, as we know, is such that it always manifests itself in a multiplicity of subtly diversified forms which, furthermore, are reducible to their own, even if purely conventional "norm." When handled by great artists, these variable forms of melodic intonation become of great esthetic value, and seem to have, in this capacity, but a very remote connection with the narrow harmonic scheme to which they are fundamentally subordinated.

The impossibility of predicting at present the probable theoretical norm of melodic intonation in regard to the supra-diatonic scale, even in the most general way, is one of the strong reasons why the author is inclined to adopt, for practical purposes, the supra-tempered intonation at the very start. The advantage of any tempered intonation is not only that it reduces the number of tones necessary for modulation and transposition, but also that it conveniently adjusts the differences of harmonic and melodic intonation, this being especially important when the salient characteristics of the latter are not yet known. There can hardly be any doubt that supra-tempered intonation will be of great help to the artists of the future in this particular respect; moreover, it may even suggest the right direction in which to search for the theoretical norm of melodic intonation for the supra-diatonic scale.

*   *   *

It will be opportune, in conclusion of this supplement and in addition to the diagram represented in Ex. 89^a, to append a separate Table of ratios of the supra-tempered intonation (all nineteen scale-degrees) jointly with the vibration-numbers calculated for the middle Octave (c'-c'') on the basis of international pitch ($a' = 435$ vib.).

In computing the acoustical values of the supra-tempered intonation in terms of centitones, it was sufficient to divide the value of an Octave (600 ctn.) by the general number of scale-degrees (19) and to multiply the minimum interval thus obtained (31.6 ctn.) by 2, 3, 4, etc., for each subsequent degree. But in order to obtain the same values in terms of vibration-ratios, the operations of division and multiplication have to be replaced by those of evolution and involution. In other words, a root with an index equalling the general number of scale-degrees ($\sqrt[19]{}$) has to be extracted from the ratio of an Octave (2:1 or, simply, 2), and the acoustical value of the minimum interval thus obtained ($\sqrt[19]{2} = 1.0372$) is then raised to the 2nd, 3rd, 4th, etc. power for each subsequent degree, as shown below. [See Table on the following page.]

INTERVALS (to C′)	RATIOS (to 1)	vibrations	centitones
c′	1	261.02	0
c♯ or v♭	$\sqrt[19]{2} = 1.0372$	270.72	31.6
v′	$\sqrt[19]{2^2} = 1.0757$	280.78	63.2
d′	$\sqrt[19]{2^3} = 1.1157$	291.21	94.8
d♯ or w♭	$\sqrt[19]{2^4} = 1.1571$	302.03	126.4
w′	$\sqrt[19]{2^5} = 1.2001$	313.25	158.0
e′	$\sqrt[19]{2^6} = 1.2447$	324.89	189.6
e♯ or f♭	$\sqrt[19]{2^7} = 1.2909$	336.96	221.2
f′	$\sqrt[19]{2^8} = 1.3389$	349.48	252.8
f♯ or x♭	$\sqrt[19]{2^9} = 1.3887$	362.47	284.4
x′	$\sqrt[19]{2^{10}} = 1.4402$	375.94	316.0
g′	$\sqrt[19]{2^{11}} = 1.4938$	389.90	347.4
g♯ or y♭	$\sqrt[19]{2^{12}} = 1.5493$	404.39	379.0
y′	$\sqrt[19]{2^{13}} = 1.6068$	419.45	410.6
a′	$\sqrt[19]{2^{14}} = 1.6665$	**435.0**	442.2
a♯ or z♭	$\sqrt[19]{2^{15}} = 1.7284$	451.16	473.8
z′	$\sqrt[19]{2^{16}} = 1.7927$	467.93	505.4
b′	$\sqrt[19]{2^{17}} = 1.8593$	485.31	537.0
b♯ or c♭	$\sqrt[19]{2^{18}} = 1.9284$	503.34	568.6
c″	$\sqrt[19]{2^{19}} = 2$	522.04	600

CHAPTER XII

SUPRA-TONALITY VERSUS ATONALITY

The few essential points regarding the *chordal formations* of the supra-diatonic scale that have been brought out in the foregoing chapter represent almost the limit of what may be theoretically deduced from the nature of this scale with any degree of plausibility. The application of the same (deductive) method in order to disclose the *tonal functions* of the chords and, consequently, to find the rules of harmonization of future supra-diatonic melodies (similarly to what has been done above with the comparatively simple infra-diatonic scale and the melodies based on it) would be most uncertain, in this instance, because of the fairly complex nature of the supra-diatonic scale, which is apt to manifest in practice quite unforeseen properties. Moreover, should we assume that with the help of comparisons and remote analogies some of the most rudimentary functions of the chords of this new scale may be theoretically guessed at, even then the results (presumably correct) thus obtained would reveal nothing to the musical ear in its present state. This is because the ear, accustomed to the existing musical intonation, would inevitably apprehend those chordal functions on the externally approximate plane of the twelve-tone tempered scale, the only one largely used at present, whose inherent inadequacy, in relation to the supra-diatonic scale, has already been sufficiently shown.

Indeed, even the very structure of the simplest supra-diatonic Hexad, not to speak of its functions, we would apprehend quite incorrectly should we attempt actually to produce this chord through the medium of the twelve-tone tempered scale which, as we know, is structurally identical with the atonal scale ("12"). The reason is that the whole-step chord * which is included in this scale and which externally approximates the supra-diatonic Hexad, consists exclusively of equal intervals, whereas this Hexad, irrespective of its intonation, contains two different kinds of supra-Thirds (see both chords on the following page).

It is difficult fully to realize the musical importance of this distinction without having at hand the true tonal embodiment of the supra-diatonic scale and an ear adjusted to it. But at the same time it will not be far-fetched to surmise that these two chords differ, in actual sound, no less, for instance, than the characteristic major or minor Triad of the diatonic scale differs from an artificially

---

* The whole-step succession C-D-E-F♯-G♯-A♯ is usually, though quite erroneously, called whole-step or whole-tone *scale*. This succession is not a scale but a *chord* and, inasmuch as it is considered in tempered intonation, an artificial chord bred in the depths of the equally artificial atonal scale.

WHOLE-STEP CHORD

| C | whole step | D | whole step | E | whole step | F♯ | whole step | ♯ | whole step | A♯ | whole step | c |

SUPRA-DIATONIC HEXAD

| C | minor supra-Third | D | minor supra-Third | E | MAJOR supra-Third | X | minor supra-Third | Y | minor supra-Third | Z | minor supra-Third | c |

decolored "neutral" Triad, which becomes such as the result of an equalization of the former's two component and dimensionally different Thirds within the span of the same interval of a perfect Fifth. And just as it is no easy matter to form even an approximately correct idea of the highly characteristic major or minor Triad from the neutral Triad, decolorized through the process of equalization referred to, likewise the equalized whole-step chord can give us no adequate conception of the supra-diatonic Hexad despite the seemingly negligible but in practice most essential structural difference between them. It is fairly safe to believe that the presence of one major supra-Third among the series of minor supra-Thirds in this Hexad is already sufficient to communicate to it that "live" and characteristic essence which distinguishes it from the decolorized whole-step chord probably to no lesser degree than a real object is distinguished from its shadow.

Notwithstanding the inadequacy of these two outwardly similar chords, however, the mere fact that the first flashes of modern music (in the sense used before) manifested themselves in the use of the whole-step harmonic combination as an independent chord not necessarily requiring resolution—usually ascribed to Debussy—is most significant. There is scarcely any doubt that this use resulted from an intuitive, though not perfectly clear perception of the fundamental harmony of the supra-diatonic scale unknown at that time.

This point of view is particularly corroborated by the revealing fact that subsequent evolution of the whole-step chord (which on account of the equality of its component intervals fairly soon betrayed its musical paucity) turned in the direction of "approximate rectification" of its disclosed inadequacy as compared to the structure of the supra-diatonic Hexad. It must, of course, be pretty well understood that under the conditions of our present twelve-tone system this could be effected only in a very crude manner. For instance, the slightest expansion of the interval E-F♯ in the above whole-step chord (for the purpose of likening it to the major supra-Third E-X of the respective Hexad) would obviously result either in lowering the note E or in raising the note F♯ a half step which, being thus added to this interval equalling a whole step, would constitute a sesqui-step, i.e. either E♭-F♯ or E-G. But, owing to the conditions mentioned, this expansion of a whole step can only be done at the cost of a proportionate contraction of one of its adjacent intervals, that is, of the interval D-E or F♯-G♯, in our instance. By losing, because of such a contraction, half a step, one of these two intervals would therefore be automatically transformed from a whole step into a half step, i.e. into D-E♭ or G-G♯ (G-A♭).

As a result of this operation, the former unbroken series of whole steps would then be interrupted, in the "rectified" chord, by two new intervals, viz. by a sesqui-step (150 ctn., an interval rather close to the natural supra-Third equalling 145 ctn.) and by a half step (50 ctn., an interval considerably smaller than its corresponding minor supra-Third equal to 83 ctn. in one instance and to 64 ctn. in the other). The following comparison of the two possible versions of this "rectified" chord with the tonic Hexad of the supra-mode "C-c" will convey a general idea of what approximation could be attained between them under the conditions of our present equally tempered scale:

"RECTIFIED" CHORD
(first version)

SUPRA-DIATONIC
HEXAD

"RECTIFIED" CHORD
(second version)

This comparison shows that out of six consecutive intervals of the whole-step chord it is the third one, counting from the Tonic, which undergoes the expansion, according to the position of the major supra-Third (E-X) in the tonic Hexad of the supra-diatonic scale. But since the position of the major supra-Third is not the same in different Hexads, each of which may serve as a tonic Hexad in its respective supra-mode, it is apparent that according to the permutations of this interval, the expanded interval (sesqui-step) of the "rectified" chord must also be correspondingly shifted. Supposing, for instance, that a composer inwardly hears the tonic Hexad of the supra-mode "D-d," it is easy to figure out that should he desire to express this intuitive sensation by means of the tonal resources of our modern piano, he will have to expand the second interval (counting from any assumed Tonic) of the whole-step chord and, of course, to contract accordingly one of its neighboring intervals, like this:

"RECTIFIED" CHORD
(first version)

| C | half step | D♭ | sesqui-step | E | whole step | F♯ | whole step | G♯ | whole step | A♯ | whole step | c |

SUPRA-DIATONIC
HEXAD

| D | minor supra-Third | E | MAJOR supra-Third | X | minor supra-Third | Y | minor supra-Third | Z | minor supra-Third | C | minor supra-Third | d |

"RECTIFIED" CHORD
(second version)

| C | whole step | D | sesqui-step | E♯ | half step | F♯ | whole step | G♯ | whole step | A♯ | whole step | c |

Similarly, if the composer hears the tonic Hexad of the supra-mode "E-e" he will expand the first interval of the whole-step chord (the contraction of one of the neighboring intervals goes on everywhere automatically):

"RECTIFIED" CHORD
(first version)

| C♭ | sesqui-step | D | whole step | E | whole step | F♯ | whole step | G♯ | whole step | A♯ | half step | c♭ |

SUPRA-DIATONIC
HEXAD

| E | MAJOR supra-Third | X | minor supra-Third | Y | minor supra-Third | Z | minor supra-Third | C | minor supra-Third | D | minor supra-Third | e |

"RECTIFIED" CHORD
(second version)

| C | sesqui-step | D♯ | half step | E | whole step | F♯ | whole step | G♯ | whole step | A♯ | whole step | c |

In the case of the tonic Hexad of the supra-mode "X-x," the sixth interval of the whole-step chord will evidently have to be expanded:

"RECTIFIED" CHORD
(first version)

| C | whole step | D | whole step | E | whole step | F♯ | whole step | G♯ | half step | A | sesqui-step | c |

SUPRA-DIATONIC
HEXAD

| X | minor supra-Third | Y | minor supra-Third | Z | minor supra-Third | C | minor supra-Third | D | minor supra-Third | E | MAJOR supra-Third | X |

"RECTIFIED" CHORD
(second version)

| C♯ | half step | D | whole step | E | whole step | F♯ | whole step | G♯ | whole step | A♯ | sesqui-step | c♯ |

The tonic Hexad of the supra-mode "Y-y" will require an expansion of the fifth interval of the whole-step chord:

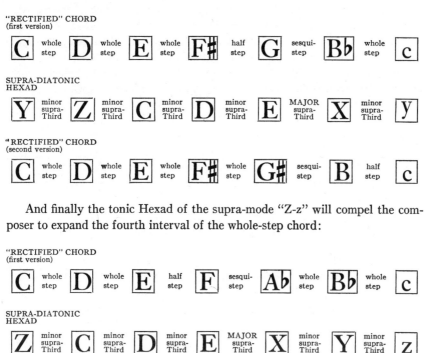

"RECTIFIED" CHORD
(first version)

| C | whole step | D | whole step | E | whole step | F♯ | half step | G | sesqui-step | B♭ | whole step | c |

SUPRA-DIATONIC
HEXAD

| Y | minor supra-Third | Z | minor supra-Third | C | minor supra-Third | D | minor supra-Third | E | MAJOR supra-Third | X | minor supra-Third | y |

"RECTIFIED" CHORD
(second version)

| C | whole step | D | whole step | E | whole step | F♯ | whole step | G♯ | sesqui-step | B | half step | c |

And finally the tonic Hexad of the supra-mode "Z-z" will compel the composer to expand the fourth interval of the whole-step chord:

"RECTIFIED" CHORD
(first version)

| C | whole step | D | whole step | E | half step | F | sesqui-step | A♭ | whole step | B♭ | whole step | c |

SUPRA-DIATONIC
HEXAD

| Z | minor supra-Third | C | minor supra-Third | D | minor supra-Third | E | MAJOR supra-Third | X | minor supra-Third | Y | minor supra-Third | z |

"RECTIFIED" CHORD
(second version)

| C | whole step | D | whole step | E | whole step | F♯ | sesqui-step | A | half step | B♭ | whole step | c |

The tonic Hexads of the six remaining supra-modes require no special demonstration in this connection, as being identical in construction with the six Hexads already dealt with, they will merely repeat the entire set of "rectifications" represented above.

Now, it is one of these very forms of "rectification" or of expansion of a whole step into a sesqui-step with the proportionate and inevitable contraction of another whole step into a half step that is actually encountered for the first time in the so-called "synthetic" chord which was intuitively found by Scriabin and which, by the way, was considered and emphatically maintained by him as an indubitable consonant chord. Judging from the position of the newly-formed sesqui-step in this chord, Scriabin inwardly perceived the Hexad of the supra-diatonic scale (assuming that it was a tonic chord) either in the supra-mode "Z-z" or in the supra-mode "F-f." But, from the considerations set forth in the previous chapter, the tonic Hexad of the supra-mode "Z-z" may also be regarded as a dominant Hexad of the supra-mode "F-f," and this fact inclines us to the belief that Scriabin was dimly aware of the fundamental structure of the supra-mode "F-f," tentatively availing himself of its two most characteristic and homogeneous principal Hexads. A comparison of these two Hexads (which jointly cover the twelve regular degrees of the supra-diatonic scale) with Scriabin's "synthetic" chord will convey a better idea of our theory.

SCRIABIN'S CHORD
(close position*)

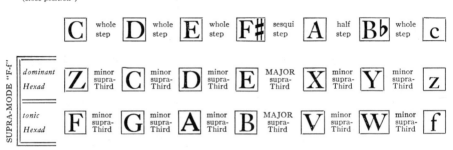

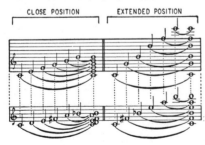

* Scriabin considered this series of six notes as a scale, when comprised within an octave (C-D-E-F♯-A-B♭), and as a chord, when arranged "by Fourths" (C-F♯-B♭-E-A-D). Thus, he repeated practically the same error that has been admitted with regard to the whole-step chord, as described in the preceding footnote. As a matter of fact these two Scriabin arrangements of the six notes in question merely represent the very same chord (approximatively intoned supra-diatonic Hexad) in its close and in one of its extended positions, respectively, as will be better comprehended from the following illustration in which this chord is properly notated:

CLOSE POSITION　　　EXTENDED POSITION

The true reason for Scriabin's arrangement of

his chord "by Fourths" seems to be that its still more extended position, obtained through the simple inversion of the original close position—[C]-B♭-A-F♯-E-D-C—would be rather inconvenient, so far as technical handling is concerned, and one could therefore naturally expect all the Sevenths (which mostly constitute the latter version) to be "halved" and thus transformed into a succession of Fourths. It is quite probable that many other modern composers were also (subconsciously) guided, in the matter of chord-formation, by the same technical considerations. Striving to avoid the too awkward, though characteristic (from the supra-diatonic viewpoint) constructions "by Sevenths," on the one hand, and the too characteristic (from the diatonic viewpoint) and therefore undesirable constructions "by Thirds" on the other hand, they acquired the habit of building up their chords "by Fourths." It is also not impossible that the constant use of chords built in this manner, which to a smaller extent, as we know, is characteristic of infra-diatonic and not of supra-diatonic harmony, was the intrinsic cause of the frequent creation of pentatonic melodies by some modern composers (like Debussy and Stravinsky) who unknowingly "attuned" their mind to infra-diatonic Tonality and thus sometimes fell into a "primitivism" not at all foreign to their otherwise dissimilar musical styles.

In addition to this, I shall also give a diagram which will clearly show the degree of approximation of Scriabin's chord as well as of the whole-step chord to the tonic or dominant Hexad of the supra-mode "F-f" in just and supra-tempered intonations (the latter is represented by dotted lines):

EXAMPLE 90:

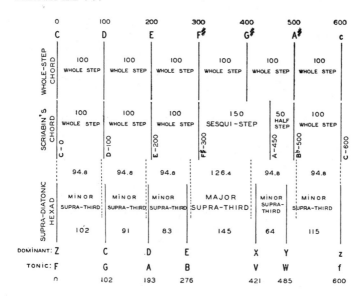

As is known, Scriabin himself felt, though perhaps not quite distinctly, a certain discrepancy between the "synthetic" chord as he established it by the tonal means of the existing tempered system, on the one hand, and the same chord as he inwardly heard it, on the other. It seemed to him that this was the result of the disparity between the just and tempered intonation of the existing tonal system ("7 + 5") while in reality this was the result of disparity between the fundamental structure of chords belonging to two radically different scales (atonal and supra-diatonic).

It will be well to note here that Scriabin did not always confine himself to the practical application of the "synthetic" chord exclusively in the supra-mode "F-f," although this form represents its original and, at one time, most recurrent version. Thus, judging from the position of the "expanded" interval (sesquistep) of this chord as it appears in the opening measures of Scriabin's "Prometheus," it corresponds there to the tonic Hexad either of the supra-mode "W-w" or of the supra-mode "Y-y."

EXAMPLE 91:

THE OPENING CHORD OF THE POEM "PROMETHEUS" BY SCRIABIN

a) extended position   *b) close position*

[theoretical reduction]

This statement will be quite evident if one actually compares the close position of this chord with the two Hexads referred to, in which the major and minor supra-Thirds are identically distributed:

SCRIABIN'S
"PROMETHEUS"

 whole step whole step whole step whole step sesqui-step half step

G	whole step	A	whole step	B	whole step	C♯	whole step	D♯	sesqui-step	F♯	half step	g

tonic Hexad
"W-w"

W	minor supra-Third	F	minor supra-Third	G	minor supra-Third	A	minor supra-Third	B	MAJOR supra-Third	V	minor supra-Third	W

tonic Hexad
"Y-y"

Y	minor supra-Third	Z	minor supra-Third	C	minor supra-Third	D	minor supra-Third	E	MAJOR supra-Third	X	minor supra-Third	y

The poem "Prometheus" represents one of the most striking examples of Scriabin's application of his "synthetic" chord in other supra-modes of the scale "12 + 7" besides its original supra-mode "F-f." And the fact that this chord continuously sounds from the very beginning of this composition, through 12 measures, and serves, above all, as a harmonic basis for the exposition of the opening theme, compels us to look upon it as the *tonic* Hexad of another supra-mode and not as one of the inversions of its original form, as might be thought at first sight.

As regards the well-known theory of Scriabin's chord in general (hardly evolved by Scriabin himself), which directly deduces it from the series of overtones *without* the intervention of the supra-diatonic scale (or, in fact, of any scale), it has little validity for the following reasons. This theory (which, incidentally, was at one time applied to the origin of the whole-step chord) considers the Scriabin chord as a concord (this, as we know, was also the view of the composer himself) which becomes such as the result of the natural adjustment of the musical ear to different intervals consecutively arranged in the series of overtones and gradually converted from dissonances into consonances in the process of musical evolution. Thus, for a long period, the only consonance recognized by the primitive ear was the interval of an Octave C-C (fundamental tone 1 and overtone 2) to which later on was added the Fifth G (overtone 3). Then, with the development of musical intuition and with the gradual refining of the human ear, the number of consonant intervals was increased by the Third E (overtone 5) which, as is known, was considered a dissonance for many centuries. After adjusting itself to all the above intervals, our ear—says this theory —also transfers into the field of consonances other (heretofore dissonant) intervals, thus adding to the former combination of tones the Seventh $\overline{B}\flat$ (overtone 7), the Ninth D (overtone 9), the Eleventh $\overline{F}\sharp$ (overtone 11) and finally the Thirteenth $\overline{A}$ (overtone 13).*

It is, then, the resulting harmonic combination C-G-E-B♭-D-F♯-A which is supposed to justify the legitimacy of Scriabin's synthetic chord C-F♯-B♭-E-A-D, although, contrary to one's expectation, these two constructions differ, first of all, in their intervallic arrangements, the former being virtually built up "by Thirds" and the latter "by Fourths." Aside from this the theory furnishes no explanation whatever as to why comparatively so many dissonances (viz. overtones 7, 9, 11 and 13), or, at any rate, why this particular number of dissonances (no more and no less) was introduced in the capacity of consonances in such a relatively short time. Furthermore, this theory entirely ignores the seemingly immaterial but in fact most significant omission of the note G (overtone 3) from Scriabin's chord (as well as from the whole-step chord), this note being one of the first to be adopted in the historic process of gradual complication of harmonic formations and, therefore, from the purely acoustical point of view, producing one of the most ideal consonances. Besides its failure to explain this omission (intelligible only under the structural conditions of the supra-diatonic scale and through the single principle of chord-formation for all "organic" scales), the theory in question also betrays its inconsistency in connection with the oft-debated problem of consonances and dissonances in general.

While it explains the historical evolution of harmonic formations by the

---

* The last named overtone (13) is notated as A♭ if this theory has in view the whole-step chord. As a matter of fact, this overtone falls between the note A♭ of the whole-step chord and the note A of Scriabin's chord. It is, however, closer to the former, lying at the interval of 21 ctn. from the note A♭ and at the interval of 29 ctn. from the note A (see diagrams of Ex. 87 and 90).

series of overtones (without the intervention of scales which, as we know, leads to different results), this theory is compelled to consider as temporary and provisional not only every dissonance but also the very principle of division of intervals and chords into consonances and dissonances, whatever their particular grouping may be. This is because in proportion to the increase in musical art of the number of consonances which, according to this theory, are no longer subject to further transformations, the number of dissonances is bound to decrease gradually within the limit of harmonic constructions our ear can perceive. Such— if one wishes to be consistent—is the logic of this popular theory which, in reality, goes still further (at least in its latest version) and without waiting for the *gradual* exhaustion of the field of dissonances, claims that the time has long since arrived for abolishing the very principle of division of all harmonic combinations into consonances and dissonances and therefore automatically disposes of the entire problem without appeal.

Such a suspiciously hastened "historic" process which, as will be seen, has its own causes, only undermines the—in any case—uncertain foundations of the theory of "harmonic monism" (as I call it in distinction to the "harmonic dualism" upheld in the present book) and apart from that contains another and purely psychological inconsistency.

Inasmuch as musical art, in its innermost depths, feeds exclusively on human emotions (the recently advanced "anti-emotional" theory will be touched upon further on), it can exist, strictly speaking, only under the conditions of a tonal system whose inner laws correspond, in a certain way, to the most rudimentary laws of these emotions. And since the latter, irrespective of their subtlety and complexity, may in the last analysis be reduced to two fundamental and distinctive groups: *satisfying* and *unsatisfying* emotions whose interaction in the most diverse combinations creates our entire and many-colored inner world (in its emotional aspect), it is apparent that to this rudimentary distinction there must correspond, in every "organic" tonal system (also irrespective of its complexity), a division into two classes of *satisfying* and *unsatisfying* harmonic combinations, i.e. a division into consonances and dissonances whose interaction in various ways is supposed to weave into musical tissue the emotions referred to.*

* It should be explained here that satisfying and unsatisfying harmonic combinations (i.e. consonances and dissonances) are by no means psychologically equivalent to pleasant and unpleasant harmonic combinations, just as satisfying and unsatisfying sensations, in general, are not equivalent to pleasant and unpleasant sensations. For instance, appetite is essentially an unsatisfying sensation (since it requires satisfaction), yet it may certainly be classed as a pleasant sensation, at least as long as it does not develop into definite hunger. On the other hand satiety is a satisfying sensation but it also is pleasant only as long as it does not grow to surfeit which, of course, does not "require" further satisfaction and therefore cannot be classed among unsatisfying sensations, yet it is decidedly unpleasant. In this way, pleasantness and unpleasantness do not represent constant quantities in relation to satiety and appetite, and are wholly dependent on the admitted intensity of these sensations which, however, always retain their intrinsic characteristics of satisfaction and non-satisfaction.

The very same considerations apply to consonances and dissonances which, representing

The appurtenance of our emotions to one or the other of two fundamental and opposite groups has, of course, no absolute significance and is subject to evolutionary changes and permutations, but *the fact itself of this division,* the very existence of these two polarities cannot be shaken until our *psyche,* from the strength of its nature, reacts in a radically different manner to what we understand as "opposite" sensations, even if the objective stimuli of these sensations differ only in degree and not in essence (for instance, like the different degrees of room temperature arousing the "opposite" sensations of warmth and cold). Similarly, the division of consonances and dissonances in music is not absolute; we have seen that it is subject to evolutionary changes and admits various permutations and intergroupings, but the fact of this division, the very principle of polarity of consonances and dissonances, found at different epochs, cannot be shaken and without any doubt represents—to periphrase Kant—a certain "categorical imperative" of the musical consciousness.

(within a given system) constant entities in the sense of satisfying and unsatisfying harmonic combinations (i.e. requiring resolution in the latter instance and not requiring it in the former), change their characteristics of pleasantness and unpleasantness according to their admitted intensity, duration, fitness, etc. i.e. briefly speaking, according to the skillful or unskillful use the composer makes of them. The etymological construction of these two musical terms does not give any direct indication as to which pair of the above characteristics (pleasantness and unpleasantness or satisfaction and non-satisfaction) is implied by them. True, when a *practical* classification of the different harmonic combinations was made for the first time by the medieval theoreticians, consonances were defined as those combinations which meet the requirements of a musical ear, while dissonances were defined as those combinations which fail to do so. But such a definition which rather leans to the adoption of pleasantness and unpleasantness as respective characteristics of consonances and dissonances was, of course, quite natural at a historical period when the secret of a skillful use of qualitatively different harmonic combinations was not perfectly known yet. As a result, the combination of a tense or "unsatisfying" character (for that time) when inappropriately used or taken isolatedly (which must be regarded as an unfavorable condition for such a combination) could certainly produce the impression of "not meeting the demands of a musical ear." By the same token, however, one could assert that appetite does not meet the demands of a stomach, for the sole reason that under certain "unfavorable" conditions it may grow into hunger.

The fact itself of opposition of consonances and dissonances is, of course, largely a psychological phenomenon, since such opposition does not exist objectively. Acoustics gives us one *continu-* *ous* series of harmonic combinations gradually increasing in harshness but it cannot point to a perfectly objective and convincing indication according to which certain combinations are to be considered as consonances and the others as dissonances. The so-called *beats,* which cause this harshness, are found in consonances (except the Prime and its inversion) as well as in dissonances, differing merely in number and volume; and the reaction of a musical ear to this or that number and volume of beats and, consequently, to the harshness they produce, changes with the development of musical art, as was admitted even by Helmholtz (*Sensations of Tone,* page 234), who thoroughly investigated this acoustical phenomenon. Moreover, this sharp-sighted scientist definitely stated (*ibid.* pages 227 and 229) that objectively no sharp line can be drawn between consonances and dissonances because the boundary that separates them changes its place as *tonal systems* change in the course of evolution. From this he drew the further and well-founded conclusion that the reason for assigning such a boundary does not depend on the individual effect of this or that harmonic combination but exclusively on the entire construction of the tonal system used at a given period. But the construction of a tonal system is largely a matter of psychology, not only of acoustics. Or, as Helmholtz brilliantly puts it (*ibid.* page 235): . . . "The system of Scales, Modes and Harmonic Tissues does not rest solely upon unalterable natural laws, but is also, at least partly, the result of esthetic principles, which have already changed, and will still further change, with the progressive development of humanity." It is at once evident, therefore, that the opposition of consonances to dissonances, which is inseparably connected with one tonal system or another, represents at least an acoustico-psychological if not a purely psychological phenomenon.

It is, then, the subconscious considerations of this polarity by which musical intuition is guided—or at least that it has to reckon with—at different epochs, while evolving various tonal systems. And that is why musical intuition adopts the natural series of overtones (which is deprived of this polarity) not as a *direct* acoustic foundation for musical art but as a source of acoustic laws *potentially* comprising a chain of tonal systems, structurally similar and becoming gradually more complicated, through each of which only a limited and specific range of emotions can be expressed.

Were musical art of rational and not of emotional origin, the division into consonances and dissonances would be unnatural. Music, then, would be monistic instead of dualistic, from the viewpoint of harmony. It is highly probable that it would be *directly* based, in that case, on the series of overtones, because the "categorical imperative" of rational musical thinking can only be an absolute acoustic exactitude (peculiar to this series), without the slightest deviation, and nothing else. But since musical art is dualistically emotional and not monistically rational, it tends already in the intuitive evolution of tonal systems to avoid harmonic monism by means of specific inclusion, into one or the other system, of some tones which do not belong to a given series of overtones (like, for instance, the tones F and A in the diatonic system, already mentioned). Such an inclusion gives rise to that amount of "conflict" necessary between the degrees of every scale, which results in a different power of gravitation of these degrees to each other and of all of them towards a single and firm tonal center.

In the previously described and rather popular theory connected with the name of Scriabin, only one point is certain, namely, that musical art, while progressing forward, gradually expands the range of consonances. But this does not justify the inference that through such an expansion every subsequent historic period contracts the range of dissonances and, therefore, gradually erases the boundary between consonances and dissonances, thus annihilating their very polarity. History teaches us, on the contrary, that this boundary is by no means erased, but that it is merely transferred with the change of tonal system, and that the enlargement and complication of the field of consonances is accompanied by the growth and complication of the field of dissonances. Such an interpretation of the musico-historical process is, of course, possible only if the dissonances imply not all the imaginable non-consonant intervals but only those which, not being consonances in relation *to a given tonal system*, can be found, nevertheless, within its limits.

But dissonances can only be viewed in this way because, similarly to consonances, they represent phenomena not of a purely acoustical, but of an acoustico-psychological nature, being perceived as such merely in an organic connection with some consciously or subconsciously sensed tonal system, in which both these kinds of intervals are governed, in their opposition, by the laws of some inner logic. Intervals which are not found in a given tonal system can be considered, in relation to it, neither as consonances nor as dissonances. Such intervals, irrespective of their degree of acoustic purity, will be out of place or, simply speaking, *false* in relation to this system; therefore, to distinguish them from consonances and dissonances, I shall henceforth designate them as *falsonances,* which of course will possess a relative meaning, like the other two notions.

Thus, the interval of an acoustically pure subminor Seventh $(\frac{7}{4}$ or 485 ctn.$)$, as it is technically called, will be a falsonance in relation to the diatonic scale because, as already explained on a former occasion, it is excluded by the just intonation of this scale. But the very same interval $(\frac{7}{4})$ will not be a falsonance in relation to the *supra-diatonic scale* because it is not only found in the just intonation of this scale but furthermore fills therein the place of a consonance under the name of major supra-Eleventh (F-W, for instance). Similarly, the acoustically pure major Third $(\frac{5}{4}$ or 193 ctn.$)$ which is a consonance in the diatonic scale, turns out to be a falsonance in relation to the infra-diatonic scale because the only major Third (diminished infra-Third F-A) which is found in the just intonation of this scale and which is a dissonance in it, does not coincide with the former $(\frac{5}{4})$, being expressed by the fraction $\frac{81}{64}$ or 204 ctn. For the same reasons, the acoustically pure minor Second $(\frac{16}{15}$ or 56 ctn.$)$, being a falsonance in relation to the infra-diatonic scale and holding the place of a dissonance in the diatonic scale, again becomes a falsonance in relation to the supra-diatonic scale; the acoustically pure Fifth $(\frac{8}{2}$ or 351 ctn.$)$ which is a dissonance in the sub-infra-diatonic scale and a consonance in the infra-diatonic as well as in the diatonic scale, becomes a falsonance in relation to the supra-diatonic scale, etc.* The last two instances, especially the second one, refute the existence of any directness in the matter of transition of intervals from one group to another in the process of historical evolution, and they particularly uncover the error of the above so-called "Scriabin theory," with respect to the supposed infallibility

* While discussing the nature of these "pure" intervals in relation to this or that scale, I have paid no attention to intervals resulting from its tempered intonation, because the latter represents merely a conventional substitute for just intonation.

Another important remark which it is necessary to add in connection with the theory of falsonances for the first time advanced in this work, is that, similarly to consonances and dissonances, this newly determined class of intervals should be further subdivided into two fairly distinct groups, termed *perfect* and *imperfect.* It will be proper to attach the name of *perfect falsonances* to those intervals which, being totally foreign to a given tonal system, are positively excluded by its Just Intonation, as has been ex-emplified in the text. The designation *imperfect falsonances* should be given to intervals which, strictly speaking, are also foreign to a given tonal system but which, nevertheless, are found in it, owing to certain acoustic oddities of Just Intonation, explained earlier. (See Supplement to Chapter XI of this volume.) Imperfect falsonances, therefore, are simply acoustically impaired consonances, such as the "grave" Fifth D-A, for instance, which is found in the justly intoned major diatonic scale, being expressed therein by the ratio $\frac{40}{27}$ (340 ctn.) instead of $\frac{3}{2}$ (351 ctn.), or a diminished supra-Fourth, X-A, let us say, which is found in the justly intoned supra-diatonic scale and is expressed therein by the ratio $\frac{140}{121}$ (126 ctn.) instead of $\frac{13}{11}$ (145 ctn.), etc.

of regeneration of dissonances into consonances—an infallibility which really does not exist and which is refuted by Scriabin's own harmony (omission of the Fifth).

The above discussion convinces us, first that the inward perception, by a composer, of some falsonance as an "acceptable" or, even more, as a consonant interval, already reveals his anticipation (even though a subconscious one) of some new tonal system. Thus, a Chinese composer who inwardly feels the pure major Third ($\frac{5}{4}$) as a consonance, has already stopped thinking in terms of the infra-diatonic scale and anticipates more or less the tonal structure of the diatonic scale. Likewise, the inward perception, by a Western composer, of the pure minor Seventh (subminor Seventh $\frac{7}{4}$) as an interval "not requiring resolution," i.e. practically as a consonance, already indicates his departure from the "diatonic" way of thinking as well as his groping anticipation of certain outlines of the supra-diatonic scale. A similar perception of the three subsequent intervals in the series of overtones ($\frac{9}{8}, \frac{11}{8}, \frac{13}{8}$), which we find in the case of Debussy and especially of Scriabin, already denotes a more distinct perception of the outlines of this scale and, at any rate, a much more definite feeling for its fundamental (consonant) harmony.

The present twelve-tone tempered system precluded the possibility of Scriabin's complete awareness of the structure of the supra-diatonic scale, but his foreseeing its basic harmony, particularly the latter's most characteristic interval (the major supra-Third) which he approximately expressed by the notes F♯—A, strikes one as simply prophetic. Scriabin considered this "expanded" interval so essential in the chord found by him that he sacrificed for it a somewhat more accurate notation of the overtone 13, designating it by the note A instead of A♭ (see Footnote on page 233). Such a seemingly insignificant transformation of a whole step into a sesqui-step lies at the very root of Scriabin's intuitive discovery. Not to speak of a certain purely practical harmonic variety (as compared to the whole-step chords) which Scriabin obtained thanks to this "insignificant" transformation, the importance of the latter is further enhanced by the fact that it may serve as indirect proof of the correctness of our basic theoretic constructions. This is because only the specific distribution of regular and auxiliary degrees, as found in the supra-diatonic scale, permits of rather closely forming within it the Scriabin chord according to the principle outwardly similar to that of chord-construction in the diatonic and in the infra-diatonic scales (superimposition of Thirds and of infra-Thirds respectively).

The question now naturally arises: since he had found the basic Hexad of the supra-diatonic scale, why did not Scriabin take the next logical step along the path discovered by him, i.e. why did not he endeavor to evolve even a most elementary system of harmonic functions of this chord and its interrelations with other Hexads formed on different degrees, which would have allowed him to use much more exhaustively their latent musical resources?   And if Scriabin could not achieve this during his comparatively short life, why did not musical art wend its way in this direction after Scriabin?   Why—one may ask—have not modern composers availed themselves of Scriabin's discovery up to this day in order to work out certain rudimentary rules of the new musical grammar, and why have they preferred, instead, to grope in the chaotic world of atonality, with bare intuition as a guide, like half-trained *dilettanti* who usually disregard the necessity of any "rules" in art, or at best, like the alchemists of old who sought to solve the most complicated scientific problems without any knowledge of the elementary laws of matter?

There is only one answer to all these questions and it has already been partly given at the beginning of this chapter. The possibility of evolving even the most rudimentary rules of the new musical grammar is barred at present by the limitedness and inadequacy (in comparison to the structure of the supra-diatonic scale) of the tonal means of our present-day instruments with fixed intonation (such as the piano and organ) as well as by the great difficulty and uncertainty of corresponding experiments upon instruments with variable intonation (such as the strings) in view of the complexity and subtility of the new scale.

Let us illustrate this statement as regards instruments with fixed intonation. Suppose we imagine Scriabin's chord in the capacity of a tonic Hexad of the supra-diatonic scale, in which it appears as such in the supra-mode "F-f" (see page 230). This Hexad will be expressed in the latter instance by the notes F-G-A-B-V-W. Adapting this chord, in Scriabin's manner, to the keys of our piano, we would have to express it by the notes F-G-A-B-D-E♭, of which the notes B-D would evidently represent the major supra-Third B-V. Let us next adapt in a similar manner the chord Z-C-D-E-X-Y which, we have assumed, plays the part of a dominant supra-diatonic Hexad in relation to the former. This chord will be apparently expressed by the notes B♭-C-D-E-G-A♭ of our piano in which the interval E-G would supposedly correspond to the major supra-Third E-X. Comparing now both these Hexads, in the supra-diatonic notation, on the one hand, and in Scriabin's notation, on the other, we immediately discover the inadequacy of the tonal means of our piano in relation to the supra-diatonic scale. This inadequacy will manifest itself by the fact that while the above two Hexads of the supra-diatonic scale (viz. F-G-A-B-V-W and Z-C-D-E-X-Y) have no common note at all, two such notes (G and D) will appear in the adaptation of these chords to our piano according to the method of Scriabin (F-G-A-B-D-E♭ and B♭-C-D-E-G-A♭). Therefore, when these two chords are played consecutively on the piano, each of their common notes, i.e. G and D, will have to fill, quite illogically, two musically opposite functions of two different degrees of the supra-diatonic scale, in conformity with the two opposite functions of the tonic and dominant Hexad, each of which illegitimately contains one of these notes in Scriabin's representation. Concretely speaking, the note G, in this case, would fill the functions of the degrees G and X, while the note D would fill those of the degrees D and V (which are a supra-diatonic half step apart, just as the notes G and X).

This inconsistency will be more readily grasped from the following example, in which a progression of the tonic and the dominant Hexads* of the supra-diatonic scale is demonstrated in the proper notation (upper stave) as well as according to Scriabin's notation (lower stave). In the latter case, the "illegitimate" common notes are indicated by arrows. Both chords are represented in seven-part harmony (which of course will be normal in the new scale with the conventional duplication of the root) and, for the sake of clarity, in an extended position which, it seems, will be preferable in future musical practice to the close postion:

EXAMPLE 92:

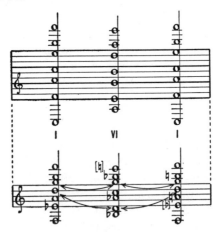

The filling of such a twofold function by one and the same note (viz. G in one instance and D in the other) would perhaps be admissible to a certain extent, were each of these two chords to be considered singly, i.e. without any interconnection. But this compromise would scarcely be tolerable when these chords are connected according to the rules of strict progression of parts, as shown in our example. This is because their common notes, in no way resulting from the

* For the reasons explained in the preceding chapter, the dominant Hexad is built on the sixth degree of the supra-mode "F-f" (see page 187).

structure of the new scale, would inevitably slacken the inner gravitation of one chord to another—that gravitation whose organic laws are at the very core of supra-tonality. A similar weakening of intertonal gravitation would naturally take place when certain Hexads formed on other degrees of the supra-diatonic scale are connected in various combinations.

Should we now attempt to represent more complicated (dissonant) chords of this scale according to Scriabin's method, i.e. expressing each major supra-Third by a sesqui-step interval of our piano, we would find a similar inconsistency within the structure of these chords themselves, besides that manifested in their progressions. This additional sign of inadequacy of the tonal means of our piano for the supra-diatonic scale will be clearly observed if we compare both notations of its dissonant chords, availing ourselves, for their formation, of the general formula worked out in the preceding chapter (viz. Z-C-D-E-X-Y-B-V-W-F-G-A). In the following example, in which every chord is represented in an extended position, the tones that fill the twofold function unlawfully are indicated by arrows:

EXAMPLE 93:

| DOMINANT SUPRA-14TH | DOMINANT SUPRA-16TH | DOMINANT SUPRA-18TH | DOMINANT SUPRA-20TH | DOMINANT SUPRA-22ND | DOMINANT SUPRA-24TH |

This example shows that some of the chords, differing in actual structure, will be absolutely identical when played on a piano. Thus, the chords of the supra-Sixteenth will be precisely the same as the chord of the supra-Fourteenth, being distinguished from the latter merely by the duplication of one of its notes—which certainly does not change its structure essentially and tells only of the impossibility of forming this chord according to Scriabin's method. Similarly, the chord of the supra-Twenty-Second will be the same as the chord of the supra-Twentieth; which again discloses the impossibility of constructing the former according to Scriabin. Furthermore, the most complicated of the above chords will have (for the same reason of fictitious duplications) only ten different notes and not twelve, as might be expected by analogy with the diatonic, infra-diatonic and sub-infra-diatonic tonal systems in which the most complicated chords (disregarding the "altered" chords) cover all the regular degrees of their respective scales. It remains to be said that the above example contains dissonant chords formed only upon the dominant Hexad of the supra-diatonic scale and that, consequently, they do not exhaust all the fictitious harmonic duplications which would certainly be encountered in the formation of discords on other degrees of this scale (wherever such formation is feasible).*

Is it now possible, under these conditions, to speak of even the most elementary harmonic system of the supra-diatonic scale to be constructed upon the principle of Scriabin and with the tonal means of our present-day musical instruments? Certainly not.

Still less could one speak of an elaboration of such a system based on the whole-step chord instead of the one applied by Scriabin. True, the twofold functions of the very same notes, as demonstrated in Ex. 92, are absent when whole-step chords are connected together:

---

* It is not impossible, incidentally, that some later alterations made by Scriabin in his chord resulted from his intuitive perception of *dissonant* chords of the supra-diatonic scale which are represented in Ex. 93. However, the limitation of six tones for his various harmonic combinations, imposed by Scriabin on himself, inevitably led him to the use of these new chords in their *incomplete* form. Thus, the chord in which he flatted the note D (when C was assumed as the root) and which he used chiefly in the Seventh Sonata, could be regarded as a chord of the supra-Fourteenth with the supra-Third (D) omitted, namely: C-E-F♯-A-B♭-D♭. The chord in which he flatted the note E and which he used chiefly in the Eighth Sonata could be regarded as a chord of the supra-Sixteenth with the supra-Fifth (E) and the supra-Fourteenth (D♭) omitted, namely: C-D-F♯-A-B♭-E♭. In order to compare these two chords with those represented in Ex. 93 it is necessary to transpose them a whole step down and to assume B♭ as their root.

EXAMPLE 94:

It is equally true that the fictitious harmonic duplications within one and the same discord evolved from Scriabin's chord, as well as all their consequences already mentioned, likewise do not take place when the whole-step chord is adopted as the nucleus for more complicated (dissonant) constructions:

EXAMPLE 95:

However, all these external advantages of the whole-step chord over Scriabin's chord are more than obliterated by the anemic neutrality of the former (bound to eliminate every vestige of tonal gravitation) as well as by the limitations of its musical resources, resulting from the equalization of its component intervals. In this manner, by trying to apply either of these two chords instead of the other in order to avoid what makes each of them inadequate (in its own way) as compared to a genuine supra-diatonic Hexad, we would find ourselves, so to speak, in the position of those mythical Greek navigators who, when seeking to avoid Charybdis, invariably ran against Scylla.

The resources of Scriabin's chord, as already stated, are somewhat greater than those of the whole-step chord, but this superiority cannot manifest itself any too prominently under the conditions of twelve equidistant tones within an octave, which constitute the atonal scale ("12"). Indeed, because this scale lacks any "auxiliary" degrees which would at least be remotely reminiscent of the distribution of seven supra-chromatic degrees and would, incidentally, change the "equidistant" distribution of its own and exclusively regular degrees, it precludes (as regards both the whole-step chord and that of Scriabin) the simplest modulation or even deviation to another key; moreover, it limits, in a certain sense, the plain transposition of these chords. One has to realize, of course, the whole significance of transposition and modulation in musical creative art in order to understand the narrow limitations we are facing here.

Considering all this, one can hardly be surprised at the hypertrophic and, of necessity, purely "quantitative" harmonic complexity towards which modern music turned after Scriabin. With the limited means for exploiting musical resources contained within the above fundamental chords, such a "quantitative" complexity remained almost the only way out for composers who presumably anticipated the structure of the supra-diatonic scale.

The impossibility of constructing, under the conditions mentioned, a system of harmony deriving from the nature of this scale, also explains the impetuousness with which the path of this mainly external harmonic complexity—the way "from Scriabin to Schönberg," as I schematically designate it—has been trod. It is easy to understand that without a strictly evolved system of harmony determining at least the simplest tonal functions of the new chords, the intrinsic resources of the "approximative" supra-diatonic Hexads (as formed by Scriabin), as well as of the subsequently more complicated chords, could not even be remotely exploited. Without such a system modern composers could not do more than superficially skim all these chords as they were hastily formed. Continuing headlong in the same direction, they, naturally, very soon (not to say ridiculously soon) came to a "free" use of a quasi-consonant twelve-tone chord, seemingly demanding no resolution,—a use for which probably scores of years would be required under normal conditions, i.e. were the adequate tonal material of the supra-diatonic scale actually accessible. It may be added here with a great degree of probability that the tendency of certain modern composers towards the preferential (if not exclusive) use of the most complicated chords, is suggested to them by an instinctive desire to avoid the inadequacy, previously explained, of the atonal scale ("12"). For the perceptibility of this inadequacy to the ear most surely diminishes in proportion to harmonic complication (and *vice versa*), just as, for instance, the inaccuracy of intonation within the diatonic system is less perceptible and, by the way, less essential in the chord of the Thirteenth than in a plain Triad.

But this is not all. The hypertrophy and impetuous tempo of harmonic complication (and, incidentally, rhythmic complication, now so much favored, though musically less important) are also due in great measure to the exceptional limitations, within the conditions of the atonal scale ("12"), of a melodic creation, at the cost of which, no doubt, this complication was effected to a considerable degree. If, with all the inadequacy of the atonal scale, it was still possible to speak of a resemblance between some of its chords and the chords of the supra-diatonic scale, i.e. of a resemblance on the harmonic plane of both these scales, then their melodic plane leaves room, at best, only for a very remote and strained illusion of such a resemblance. The reason is that the harmonic plane of the supra-diatonic scale (like that of any other scale) is based on simultaneous combinations of different notes separated, as a rule, by intervals larger than those found between the adjacent scale-degrees, i.e. on combinations which, even if inadequately, could somehow be constructed within the atonal scale ("12"), especially if we take in consideration the ability of our ear to "correct" acoustical errors in larger intervals. But the melodic plane of the supra-diatonic scale is chiefly based on a characteristic and inwardly logical progression of the whole steps and half steps which is totally absent in the atonal scale and can in no way be "imitated" in it. This characteristic quality of the supra-diatonic scale is neutralized in the atonal scale by the perfectly equal semitones between all its twelve degrees, which on account of this levelling are deprived of any fundamental fulcrum and have neither beginning nor end in their succession. Such a neutralization of the most essential characteristics of an organic scale, strictly speaking, bars the possibility of embodiment, through the medium of the atonal scale, of any genuine "supra-diatonic" musical thought (supra-diatonic melody) which, like every thought, must have at least a certain logical beginning, a middle and an end.

It is interesting, nevertheless, to trace certain intuitive attempts of modern composers to force their way through to the melodic plane of the supra-diatonic scale and to get hold of some approximative or even illusive outline of it while remaining within the physical limits of the atonal scale.

The use by Scriabin of his chord as a "scale," in other words his creation of the entire thematic material exclusively (or almost exclusively) with notes constituting this chord, which to a certain extent approximates the basic Hexad of the supra-diatonic scale, may be regarded as one of the first attempts of this kind. Similarly, of course, whole-step *melodic* formations used long before him could be regarded in the same way. However, the field of application of Scriabin's method in the matter of construction of "supra-diatonic" melodies is again greatly and unavoidably limited, because to avail oneself, for this purpose, of the tonal means of the supra-diatonic Hexad (not quite adequate, besides, in Scriabin's version) is the same as using the tonal means of a Triad for the purpose of constructing diatonic melodies.

In the melodic design of Schönberg we come across an entirely different but no doubt equally intuitive attempt at emancipation from bondage to the levelled intervals of the atonal scale. In contradistinction to Scriabin, Schönberg does not limit himself to the number of harmonic notes, when constructing his melodies. He strives to make use of all the twelve tones at his command. But what is to be done with the equalized intervals (semitones) of the atonal scale in no way corresponding to the whole steps and half steps of the supra-diatonic scale?

That the ear should be able to make some psychological correction in regard to these equalized intervals, especially in the case of the natural "stepwise" progression of the melody, is out of the question. Schönberg's musical instinct, however, quite correctly told him that if one cannot expect of the ear this sort of correction in regard to such a small interval as a semitone (for instance e' - f'), it will be incomparably easier to effect this correction if this interval is augmented by a whole octave (e' - f'') or, what is almost the same, if its upper note is transposed a major Seventh down (e' - f). In this way every semitone in which one of the component notes leaps to the neighbouring octave—and especially, we may suggestively add, when the general intonation of the melody is very much veiled by the "Sprechstimme" production—may already create, depending on its harmonic environment, the illusion either of a whole step or a half step of the supra-diatonic scale.

This will be explained better by the following illustration. Let us imagine a piano properly tuned, with the exception of one note—F, for instance—which in *every* octave is purposely tuned somewhat off pitch. Let us suppose further that the following seven progressions, consisting of two notes each, are played separately and slowly on such a piano:

EXAMPLE 96:

No one will doubt that it will be easiest to detect the falseness of intonation of the note F in the first progression (a) and most difficult in the last one (g), all the rest (b, c, d, e, f) according to their position in the above example, representing intermediate categories in this respect. As a matter of fact many musicians having an unquestionably good ear, the author has observed, find themselves embarrassed in distinguishing an error even as glaring as a semitone when one of the notes of a certain interval is played in the lowest octave of a piano and the other note in the highest.* At any rate we may take it for granted that the larger the interval the easier it is for the ear to "adjust" itself to the error in intonation through a psychological correction of it, i.e. while actually hearing a false intonation to perceive it (sometimes consciously, sometimes not) as if it were correct.

Proceeding with our explanation let us now suppose that all the white keys

* The following simple experiment (which can easily be repeated by any one) was made by the author with a number of professional musicians in regard to the above statement. Two chromatic passages, one in Octaves and the other in minor Ninths were first played on a well-tuned piano, like this:

Naturally, every one could immediately tell by ear which passage was played in Octaves and which in minor Ninths. Thereupon the author announced that he would repeat the same two passages with the mere difference that the left hand part would be played in one of the lower octaves of the piano (in which pitch can still be accurately recognized) and the right hand part in one of the higher octaves, while the listener would be asked to tell by ear which of the above

passages was played first and which second. Following this announcement the author intentionally changed one of the passages and first played it in *major* Ninths and then in *minor* Ninths, like this:

In spite of the fact that the passage in Octaves was not played at all, the great majority of musicians were not even remotely aware of the trick, and answered that the first passage (a) was played in minor Ninths and the second (b) in Octaves, while a very small minority gave the same answer, remarking merely that the piano seemed to be slightly out of tune.

of our piano are tuned to the infra-tempered intonation—as used at present by
the Siamese—which would equalize all the intervals between these keys and thus
destroy the distinction between whole steps and half steps of the diatonic scale
(making, for instance, the interval B-C equal to C-D, etc.). Anyone intending
to play a diatonic melody on such a piano would certainly find the latter greatly
out of tune, this being especially evident when the melody progresses "stepwise,"
practically representing a scale-like passage, as shown in the upper stave (*a*) of
the following example:

EXAMPLE 97:

But the falseness of this intonation (from the standpoint of the regular intonation of a piano) would undoubtedly seem far less perceptible to the ear should
the notes of the same passage, while preserving their succession and rhythm, be
distributed among three octaves instead of one, as shown in the lower stave (*b*)
of our example. This is because the large intervals of Ninths and Sevenths
would give the ear a chance to make the necessary psychological correction and
thus adjust itself to the "wrong" intonation in the manner referred to above. If
therefore, we imagine, for instance, a highly advanced Siamese composer who has
begun to "feel out" the diatonic idiom but still has at his command musical instruments with seven equidistant tones within every octave, we may be sure that not
being consciously aware (by force of long habit) of the inadequacy of these
instruments for his new creative aims, he will intuitively strive, nevertheless, to
avoid "stepwise" progressions while creating his melodies, and move largely in
leaps of wide intervals, particularly of those exceeding an octave.

It is, then, little wonder if a modern Western composer, who has begun to
"feel out" the supra-diatonic idiom but still has at his command musical instruments with twelve equidistant tones within every octave, strives to avoid "stepwise" progressions in similar fashion. The intonation of the twelve fixed tones of
our present musical instruments is virtually false as compared to any intonation

(just or tempered) of the twelve "regular" degrees of the supra-diatonic scale. And although not every modern composer, who feels the latter scale but has long been accustomed to the existing intonation, is consciously aware of this fact, yet some are bound to realize subconsciously that a supra-diatonic melody sounds more adequate on our present musical instruments when it moves in leaps of large intervals and not when it progresses "stepwise." Concretely speaking, they are sure to feel, at least, that if a certain supra-diatonic passage which has come to their mind, contains, for instance, all the twelve "regular" scale-degrees in succession, it is more advantageous, under existing conditions, to perform this passage not in its original version (as shown in the upper stave of the following example) but to distribute its component notes among several octaves (as shown in the lower stave of the same example) and thus give the ear a chance to adjust itself to the inadequacy of intonation of our musical instruments and to make the necessary psychological correction:

EXAMPLE 98:

Something much akin to the passage in the lower stave of this example may be frequently found in Schönberg's compositions and it is quite probable that the above reasons which are behind it may explain, at least in certain cases, that specific curve of the melodic line, characteristic of this composer, which is largely the result of the leaps of its component notes from one octave to another. This method (undoubtedly dominating also the line of Schönberg's harmonic progressions) greatly helps him to avoid—as he carefully does—any continued "stepwise" moves which, however, would be quite natural in the supra-diatonic scale, as they are in every "organic" scale. But Schönberg rightly seems to find them disagreeable within the atonal scale and its respective harmony to which he is held, and with which he can do no more, under the present conditions, than to create merely the illusion of music based on the supra-diatonic scale.

Schönberg also attempts to enhance this illusion by means of rather frequent leaps by intervals of an augmented Fourth (major and minor supra-Sevenths) in regard to which, as a very characteristic consonance of the supra-diatonic scale, the ear can easily make the necessary psychological correction within the same octave—and, in general, by following the laws of so-called dissonant counterpoint which, as a rule, treats the dissonant intervals of the diatonic scale as if they were consonances, this being quite natural since the majority of diatonic dissonant intervals really are consonances in the supra-diatonic scale. It goes, of course, without saying that this hidden system of "psychological correction" known only to the composer himself (and then, but subconsciously, to all appearances) and having no objective representation in musical notation, places an almost unsurmountable barrier between him and the listener, for whom such an inadequate notation—consequently the actual music too—is likely to seem (much against his will sometimes) an insoluble riddle.*

Still another attempt to break through to the melodic plane of the supra-diatonic scale may be observed in the principle of polytonality, so noticeable among modern composers. Polytonality, as the construction of the term suggests, signifies the simultaneous combination in a musical composition of two or more tonalities (in the sense of keys) of the diatonic scale. In spite of such an apparently clear definition, however, quite a serious question arises: is polytonality—and can it be, indeed—logically and practically considered as a *real* musical principle or is it simply a *fiction* having certain purely external indications of the simultaneous use of several tonalities?

For polytonality to have actual existence at all, one indispensable condition, at least, is definitely required, namely, the possibility for any tonality of a given melodic line in general, to retain its specific characteristics when it is contrapuntally interwoven with a *different* tonality or tonalities. If this is impossible, then polytonality is nothing but a fiction, because the disappearance of those characteristics automatically deprives it of the feature of *plurality* of independ-

---

* It is worthy of note that Schönberg himself does not seem to consider his music as "atonal." In an article entitled *Arnold Schönberg in Italy* by Renzo Massarini (*The Sackbut*, July, 1924) we find the following statement made by the composer in an interview during which, according to that writer, he took great pains to be most emphatic lest he should be misunderstood, and weighed his answer very carefully before speaking:

"My music [said Schönberg] is not Atonal. So far tonality has consisted in using the seven notes of the scale in all their combinations. I could not set aside this principle but my tonality uses twelve notes instead of seven. That is the whole difference, and all the new aspects of my music derive from this only."

This statement is utterly characteristic of a composer who anticipates the new "supra-diatonic" plane. He is quite convinced that the music which he creates and *inwardly* hears is not atonal, and at this point he is profoundly right. But he is not aware of the fact that this very music instantly becomes atonal when *outwardly* materialized through the twelve equidistant tones of our present tempered system, instead of the twelve "regular" tones (by no means equidistant in any intonation) of the supra-diatonic scale. On another occasion, Schönberg makes a reservation, however, saying—and this is no less characteristic—that his theory is not quite clear to himself as yet. At any rate, the absence of specific "atonal" feeling (or at least some hesitancy about it) on the part of the most extreme of the atonalists, is highly significant.

ently existing tonalities which, when thus combined, form some new and *single* whole with new characteristics, just as the chemical combination of oxygen and hydrogen produces water, whose properties have nothing in common with those of its component elements. Let us, therefore, first of all investigate whether two or more tonalities produce an effect on each other, when simultaneously combined and, if so, in what way.

It will be expedient for the sake of simplicity and clarity to begin our inquiry with the infra-diatonic and not with the diatonic scale.

I have already had occasion to demonstrate (Ex. 57[a]) how a certain melody, which comprises none but the five regular degrees of the infra-diatonic scale, is nevertheless perceived as a diatonic and not as an infra-diatonic melody for the reason that the two missing notes, which would make it *obviously* diatonic, are suggested by the accompanying harmony. One may therefore readily expect that if two or more infra-diatonic melodies are simultaneously played in different keys (naturally containing different notes), they are bound to suggestively complete each other with the "missing notes," thus making the entire combination sound "diatonic" to the ear. The following will illustrate this statement.

Let us imagine two melodies, the first of which contains no other notes but those constituting the five regular degrees of the infra-tonality "C," while the second contains no other notes but those constituting the five regular degrees of the infra-tonality "G," the latter having one infra-flat, in its key signature, which, as we know, is equivalent to the diatonic note E:

EXAMPLE 99:

These two melodies, when separately harmonized according to the "infra-diatonic" rules, will appear as follows:

EXAMPLE 100:

What would happen now should we combine these two (unaccompanied) melodies, preserving their original keys?

First of all they would form certain harmonic combinations between themselves which could not in any way be considered as typically infra-diatonic. It will be readily observed from the following example, in which these two melodies are combined, that practically not a single Dyad—the basis of infra-diatonic harmony—is found in the course of their progression. On the other hand, intervals characteristic of diatonic harmony like Thirds, Sixths and even perfect Fifths, unquestionably suggestive of incomplete diatonic Triads at the opening and at the close of this fragment, form the real backbone of this contrapuntal combination:

EXAMPLE 101:

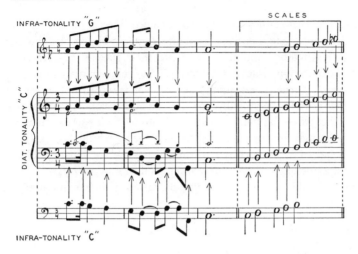

The polyphonic principle of this combination could perhaps be regarded, to some extent, as dissonant infra-diatonic counterpoint (since our Thirds and Sixths are dissonances in infra-diatonic harmony), which would be the only way of preserving the idea of infra-polytonality, as it may be called in this instance. Yet it seems infinitely more logical to accept this principle as a consonant diatonic counterpoint which becomes especially evident through the small notes inserted between the two principal parts of the above example, and thus naturally "filling in" the implied harmony. It is noteworthy, however, that these two melodies, after being played separately a number of times, may continue to give the impression of *two* infra-tonalities, when suddenly combined together. In fact, it is sometimes necessary to play this combination a few times and even finally to support it with the implied harmony (small notes) in order that the ear still retaining the two individual infra-tonalities, may perceive the result as a *single* diatonic tonality.

The diatonic nature of this fragment is revealed also in that the two keys of the infra-diatonic scale, in which our two melodies are written, complete each other somewhat, in the sense mentioned earlier, and jointly producing a scale with more than five notes they deprive these melodies of a "favorable" environment, thereby destroying their infra-diatonic characteristics which, as we know, depend strongly on such environment. Thus, infra-tonality "C-D-F-G-A" supplies infra-tonality "G-A-C-D-E" (when used simultaneously) with the note F, missing in the latter which, in turn, supplies the former with the note E (F infra-flat). With one more infra-tonality "D-E-G-A-B" supplying the two former with the still missing note "B" (C infra-flat), the *complete* impression of a diatonic tonality would be produced.

The conclusion to be drawn is that two or more different infra-tonalities, when combined, do not produce infra-polytonality, as might be expected, but mutually completing each other and thereby losing their specific characteristics (on account of a new environment) they blend in *one* common diatonic tonality.

Now what is true of infra-polytonality, which turned out to be a fiction, will also hold good for polytonality, because different diatonic tonalities completing each other when combined, and thereby losing their specific characteristics (although this may not appear as obvious as in the former instance, on account of the long-acquired habit of clearly distinguishing the familiar diatonic progressions), will automatically blend in one common supra-tonality.

To illustrate this, let us take two diatonic melodies written in C major and B♭ major respectively:

EXAMPLE 102:

Harmonized separately, according to plain "diatonic" rules, they will appear as follows:

EXAMPLE 103:

If we now combine these two (unaccompanied) melodies, preserving their original keys, none of the intervals, formed by them, could be regarded as characteristic of the basic diatonic harmony. With the abundance of Seconds, Sevenths, Ninths and diminished Fifths, they would produce a sort of dissonant counterpoint, when viewed from the diatonic classification of intervals, but a perfectly consonant counterpoint from the angle of supra-diatonic classification. No diatonic Triads could reasonably be placed within these two contrapuntal lines, whereas the supra-diatonic Hexads most naturally "fill in" the implied harmony, as shown in the following example which represents the two melodies in question, simultaneously combined:

EXAMPLE 104:

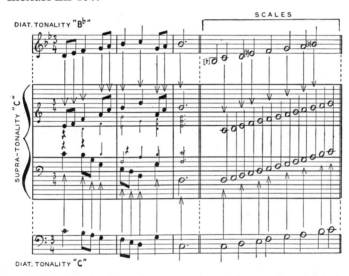

It goes without saying that the supra-diatonic harmonies of this fragment, when played on a "tempered" piano, would be immediately distorted, for the reason already explained, producing merely a set of whole-step chords, as follows:

EXAMPLE 105:

But a similar distortion would occur with the previous fragment combining the two infra-tonalities (Ex. 101), were it played on any infra-tempered instrument, such as now used by the Siamese, as will be seen further on.

After the true nature of polytonality has been disclosed one may readily understand why the so-called polytonal method of composition ought to be regarded as one of the intuitive attempts of modern composers to break through to the melodic plane of the supra-diatonic scale. Whatever is considered by these composers as a combination of different diatonic tonalities in their music is, as a matter of fact, merely one single supra-tonality, though inadequately represented because of the comparative inadequacy of the present twelve-tone tempered system. Hence there can hardly be any doubt that it is the inward anticipation of supra-tonality, and nothing else, that stimulates this particular method of modern composition which, being by no means intrinsically "polytonal" may, however, create externally this very impression.

If we imagine Siamese composers who are thoroughly educated and very advanced in their own music but who know nothing of Western music and who presumably write contrapuntal combinations similar to the one demonstrated above (Ex. 101), it is certain that these composers would consider such combinations as "infra-polytonal" because the two melodies involved would most obviously remind them of two different and familiar infra-tonalities. But a Western composer descrying such contrapuntal combinations in the compositions of his Oriental brethren would immediately say that their musical mind veered in the direction of diatonic tonality, unknown to them though undoubtedly anticipated by them and that this very anticipation stimulated their "infra-polytonal" creation which, in reality, is simply an attempt to break through to the melodic plane of the diatonic scale. An absolutely analogous relation will exist between those composers of the future who will some day consciously use the supra-diatonic scale, on the one hand, and our contemporary composers who but intuitively anticipate this new musical idiom, on the other. The former will quite correctly explain all the "polytonal" experiments of the latter by the trend of their musical mind towards supra-tonality.

This correlation between composers expressing themselves in three different idioms (infra-diatonic, diatonic and supra-diatonic) is, of course, in no way accidental. It results directly from that organic correlation between the infra-diatonic, diatonic and supra-diatonic systems which has been disclosed in previous chapters of this book, and whose actual manifestations may be observed not only in similar ways of anticipating a more complicated system, in each instance, as illustrated above (Ex. 101 and 104), but also in a number of other "resemblances" involving all the other means through which this anticipation is expressed.

By reason of the state of musical art, still comparatively primitive among the Far-Eastern peoples, we will again be compelled, when illustrating these "resemblances," to deal with *imaginary* Siamese composers thoroughly educated in their own musical fields and having no knowledge whatever of Western music. With such an assumption and starting from the indicated organic correlation between different scales, there will be no difficulty at all in casting a complete "horoscope" of the musical development of Siamese composers and even in guessing unerringly all its consecutive phases, from the moment of introduction of the infra-tempered intonation in their musical practice to the most radical experiments of the future which will unambiguously manifest the intuitive anticipation of the (presumably unknown) diatonic scale by Siamese "modernists."

Intercourse between the Western and Eastern worlds, which steadily increases nowadays and which precludes the possibility of complete ignorance of Western music by the Orientals is likely, of course, to endanger our prognostications when dealing with actual circumstances. No one could guarantee now either that the Far-Eastern nations will follow the line of gradual exploitation of the musical resources of the infra-diatonic scale or that they will unfailingly turn, like the Western nations, to the use of the diatonic scale before the former is fully exploited. If, however, the author deems it worth while at this point to try to cast the "horoscope" of their musical development (assuming as a dogmatic premise their complete ignorance of Western music), it is simply because such a prognosis will have, within the scope of the present research, not an historical but a purely theoretical significance. The inevitable and predetermined similarity (for the reason already given) between the consecutive application of methods of musical composition by composers availing themselves, in one instance, of the infra-diatonic scale and, in the other, of the diatonic scale, will be of great service to us in the matter of understanding those particular creative methods in which we are interested and which are undoubtedly evoked, in each case, by the anticipation of a more complicated musical system. Inasmuch as the "more complicated system," in relation to the Siamese composers, will be the familiar diatonic system, it will be easy for us to comprehend their attempts, delusions and potential possibilities—hence it will not be difficult to comprehend perfectly, on the ground of similarity the (partly disclosed) attempts, delusions and potential possibilities of our contemporary Western composers.

The Siamese musical system, as we know, is at present entirely based on the scale "5 + 2," in its infra-tempered intonation, the diagram of which, parallel to its just intonation and to the tempered intonation of the scale "7 + 5," was represented above in Ex. 14. But for the following exposition we need a diagram of the same infra-tempered intonation of the scale "5 + 2," parallel to the just intonation of the *scale "7 + 5,"* which is therefore represented in Ex. 106 (instead of the just intonation of the scale "5 + 2") by the upper set of solid lines, while the infra-tempered intonation of the scale "5 + 2," is represented, as formerly, by the lower set of solid lines, and the tempered intonation of the scale "7 + 5," is charted (for comparison) in dotted lines:

EXAMPLE 106:

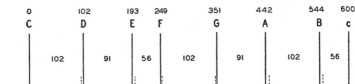

Scanty information on Far-Eastern and, in particular, Siamese music prevents us, unfortunately, from realizing to what extent Siamese musical art has advanced owing to infra-tempered intonation, as compared with music of other Far-Eastern peoples who use the same scale "5 + 2" in its just intonation. However, data on this particular point, unquestionably interesting in themselves, are not of exceptional importance to us at the present moment. For our purpose it is sufficient to know that with the simple and convenient—in every respect— infra-tempered intonation, the Siamese acquired a solid basis for a well-rounded exploitation of the musical resources of the scale "5 + 2," just as an equally simple and solid basis was found at one time by Western composers in the tempered intonation of the scale "7 + 5."

Now, in order not to distract our attention with non-essentials (in this case) regarding the normal and gradual development of the Siamese technique of composition, the probable direction of which may be gathered in a general way from the chapter on infra-diatonic harmony, let us take a long leap into the future of Siamese music. Let us suppose that this music has reached a magnificent stage of development and the highest culture imaginable (within the limits of the infra-diatonic system); that it has passed through its own polyphonic, classic and romantic periods, or whatever they happen to be, and that, finally, it has reached the point where, for the first time, composers have begun to feel, in its depths, an unaccountable weakening of the hitherto quite stable principle of infra-tonality.

This stage of Siamese music will approximately correspond (though on a "lower plane") to the appearance of Debussy in Western music (or to a somewhat earlier period) and, as in the latter case, it will be one of the first signs of anticipation, by Siamese composers, of a musical system of a "higher order," i.e. of the to them entirely novel but to us quite familiar diatonic system. How then will the initial shaking of the foundation of the old infra-tonality and the anticipation of the new diatonic tonality manifest itself in Siamese music?

If we assume that this anticipation will at first be of a harmonic nature, then *new* chords are bound to appear in Siamese music which will be reminiscent, even if remotely, of the common chords (Triads) of the diatonic scale. Let us glance at the above diagram (Ex. 106) and inquire into the matter of these new chords from the standpoint of the normal "infra-diatonic" way of musical thinking.

Suppose a Siamese composer intuitively sensed the structure of the diatonic Triad C-E-G in its just (or tempered) intonation, there can be no doubt that he would endeavor to express these three tones (found among the upper solid lines of our diagram) by the three most approximate tones of the infra-tempered scale "5 + 2" (found among the lower solid lines), namely by C-D♯-G or, what comes to the same, C-F♭-G. From the viewpoint of strict infra-diatonic harmony, the combination of either of these three notes will constitute a discord requiring "resolution" into one of the common chords of the Siamese scale—perhaps into the tonic Dyad C-F, in the first instance, or into the hypertonic Dyad D-G, in the second instance. But those Siamese composers who, according to our assumption, anticipate the diatonic tonality, will feel no pressing necessity for such a resolution, because this new harmonic combination (C-D♯-G) will strike their ear as a self-contained chord tending nowhere.

As the need of using such chords grows with these composers they will probably try to find a certain theoretical justification for their innovation. Observing that the new harmonic combinations discovered by them are arranged by whole steps of the scale "5 + 2," the Siamese composers will most probably consider these combinations as harmonic sections of some new and single whole-step succession C-D♯-G-A♯-D-F-A which, however, from the viewpoint of the diatonic system, unknown to them so far, will simply represent an inadequate reflection (because of the infra-tempered intonation) of a chord formed by Thirds, as may be judged from the following comparison:

EXAMPLE 107:

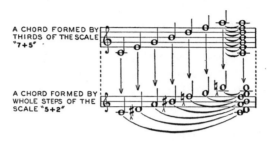

A CHORD FORMED BY THIRDS OF THE SCALE "7 + 5"

A CHORD FORMED BY WHOLE STEPS OF THE SCALE "5 + 2"

This new succession of notes will perhaps be designated by Siamese composers, at first, as a "whole-step scale." But since it will subsequently serve as a direct basis for all the rest of their harmonic formations and could not therefore be simultaneously considered as a scale and a harmony, they (or their successors) will probably reach the conclusion that this new whole-step succession represents a harmonic plane of the infra-chromatic scale which, while absolutely identical, in its tonal constitution, with the scale "5 + 2," differs from it in a purely psychological way, i.e. by the complete independence of all its seven component tones without their conventional division into "regular" and "auxiliary" degrees. [This independence will make it proper to term the infra-chromatic scale *infra-atonal scale* and to designate it by the figure "7"].

In their attempt to justify acoustically the free use of discords (from the viewpoint of the infra-diatonic but not the diatonic scale) the Siamese composers will probably reject the basic difference between consonances and dissonances, and will refer, in this respect, to the Natural Harmonic Series (then known to them by assumption) in which, indeed, no definite or convincing signs of this distinction can be found. The introduction of the interval of a diatonic Third ($\frac{5}{4}$ or 193 ctn.) in the capacity of a consonance, to which a whole step (171.4 ctn.) of the infra-tempered scale would correspond (granted the proper acoustic "compromise"), will be explained by them simply as another and perfectly natural move along the series of overtones, caused by the refinement of their ear as compared with that of their musically less developed predecessors.

The theoretical speculations of the Siamese "Debussyites," quite inevitable within the limited conditions of the infra-diatonic system, will so far fully correspond to similar speculations of Western composers who attempted, at one time, to find theoretical justification for a "free" use of new harmonic combinations based on whole-step successions of the scale "7 + 5." These, however, appeared in reality merely as inadequate reflections (because of the tempered intonation) of chords formed by supra-Thirds of the scale "12 + 7" unknown to modern composers, though anticipated by them, as was explained on an earlier occasion, and as will be still clearer from the following comparison demonstrated in a way similar to the preceding example.* It will be recalled, incidentally, that the two supra-diatonic Hexads, found in our representation, form one continuous chain, being connected by an interval of a diminished supra-Fourth (marked by a bracket) which equals the major supra-Third. This connection, as we know, permits the formation of dissonant chords of the new scale in a fashion similar to the formation of dissonant chords of the two preceding scales:

EXAMPLE 108:

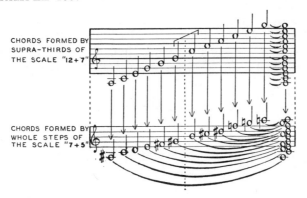

CHORDS FORMED BY SUPRA-THIRDS OF THE SCALE "12 + 7"

CHORDS FORMED BY WHOLE STEPS OF THE SCALE "7 + 5"

Turning now to the practical consequences which would result from the use by the Siamese of the infra-tempered whole-step chords (not to be confused with the tempered whole-step chords of the diatonic scale), this would probably introduce a certain freshness into the well-worn material of their "classic" harmony. It is not difficult, however, to guess that this innovation, applied at first only as a

---

* In this way the whole-step succession of any organic scale represents nothing but a chord, constructed "by Thirds," of a more complicated organic scale which follows the preceding one in the general chain they form. It is evident from Ex. 107 that the whole-step succession of the scale "5 + 2" may be regarded as a chord formed by Thirds, of the scale "7 + 5." It is likewise evident from Ex. 108 that any whole-step succession of the scale "7 + 5" may be regarded as a chord, formed by supra-Thirds, of the scale "12 + 7." In a similar relation will be the respective whole-step successions and chords of the scales "12 + 7" and "19 + 12," then of the scales "19 + 12" and "31 + 19" etc.

As an additional illustration of this statement it will be opportune also to give a parallel demonstration of a chord, formed by infra-Thirds, of the scale "5 + 2," and a whole-step succession of the scale "2 + 3" which, according to the

general rule, represents two identical constructions, but considered from different standpoints:

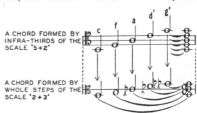

A CHORD FORMED BY INFRA-THIRDS OF THE SCALE "5 + 2"

A CHORD FORMED BY WHOLE STEPS OF THE SCALE "2 + 3"

It goes without saying that the whole-step succession of this as of every other scale will absolutely coincide with the chord formed "by Thirds" of the succeeding scale in Pythagorean intonation only, and will show inevitable acoustic deviations in any other intonation.

supplementary artistic means to the old harmony, would very soon occupy a dominant and eventually an exclusive place in it.

But exactly at this point the Siamese musical innovators would face their first disappointment, for with the exclusive use of whole-step chords, the limitations of their novel resources would soon be felt. Needless to say that these limitations would be solely due to the above-mentioned inadequacy of the infra-tempered whole-step chords, as compared to the chords formed by Thirds of the diatonic scale, tempered or not. Indeed, the whole-step chord C-D♯-G, for the first time found by the Siamese, will be composed of two perfectly equal intervals (C-D♯ contains 171.4 ctn. and so does D♯-G) under the condition of infra-tempered intonation, and therefore will differ essentially—musically speaking—from the externally similar diatonic Triad composed of two dimensionally *unequal* intervals, viz. a major and a minor Third. The following comparison of these two chords will clearly show the radical distinction between them:

INFRA-TEMPERED WHOLE-STEP CHORD | C | WHOLE STEP | D♯ | WHOLE STEP | G |

DIATONIC (MAJOR) TRIAD | C | MAJOR THIRD | E | MINOR THIRD | G |

This dissimilarity between the Siamese (infra-tempered) whole-step chord and the diatonic Triad (just or tempered) is much greater than the usually tolerable discrepancy between the just and tempered intonation of chords belonging to one and the same scale. The equality of intervals in the Siamese whole-step chord deprives it of the most distinctive characteristics of the diatonic Triad expressed in the co-existence of the two dimensionally different Thirds, whose mere interchange of position produces two versions (major and minor Triads) musically as different as day and night. Both these Thirds are neutralized in the chord C-D♯-G which, therefore, not only fails to produce the two different versions of the diatonic Triad but which is also deprived of a more or less clearly expressed character, inasmuch as it closely approximates the so-called "neutral Triad" previously mentioned.* Furthermore, it is deprived of (musically important) harmonic functions because, together with the other Siamese whole-step chords (perfectly identical and, consequently, just as "neutral"), it is based on

---

* The Siamese whole-step chord (C-D♯-G) differs slightly from the neutral Triad in the dimension of the Fifth (equal to 342.8 ctn. in the former instance and 351 ctn. in the latter) and, consequently, also in the dimension of each Third (equal to 171.4 ctn. in the first instance and 175.5 ctn. in the second). But the common and principal characteristic of both these chords is the absolute equality (in each instance) of their component Thirds within the span of approximately the same interval of a Fifth. This characteristic permits us, with a certain reservation, to call the Siamese whole-step chord (C-D♯-G) "neutral Triad"—a term which will be used henceforth, for abbreviation, with regard to this chord.

the infra-atonal scale ("7") which lacks any definite center of tonal gravitation determining those functions.

But without harmonic functions, without mutual gravitation of the "equalized" Triads to each other and jointly towards a common center, without variety in the structure of these chords on different degrees of the scale, without their modulation precluded by the seven equidistant tones of the infra-atonal scale ("7"), Siamese composers will never be able to take advantage, even in a limited way, of the resources afforded by the plain diatonic Triads and their "tonal" environment. It is apparent that the Siamese "neutral" or whole-step Triads will bear about the same relation to "live" diatonic Triads as the Western whole-step chords (representing nothing but "neutral Hexads") bear to supra-diatonic Hexads.

Hence, by analogy, we may foretell with a great degree of probability the future of harmonic evolution in Siamese music. In view of the musical limitations of the neutral Triads, just pointed out, this evolution will inevitably move in the direction of breadth, not of depth. In other words, as in our Western music, it will follow the path of a purely external or, better said, "quantitative" harmonic complication whose progress will be swifter the greater the inadequacy of all the chords (compared to the correspondingly "anticipated" chords of the diatonic scale) subsequently used by Siamese modernists, and the smaller the number of temporary halts on that path. Among such halts I rank, for instance, the one that occurred in Western music as the result of "approximative rectification" of the whole-step chord by Scriabin, a rectification that is scarcely possible, however, in relation to the Siamese "neutral" or whole-step Triad.

As regards now the degree of inadequacy of the gradually more complicated chords of the Siamese modernists, compared to the gradually more complicated chords of the diatonic scale, it may be easily gauged from the diagram of Ex. 106. Let us imagine, for instance, that these modernists intuitively anticipated the structure of the dominant Seventh-chord of the diatonic scale, viz. G-B-D-F. The series of notes approaching it most closely in the Siamese scale will apparently be G-A♯-D-F, again arranged by whole steps absolutely equal to each other. In this way the dominant Seventh-chord of the diatonic scale (just as, we may add, any other of its Seventh-chords) will find, in the Siamese scale, merely a "neutral" reflection, infallibly identical on all its degrees. Hence it is plain why the musical resources of this, the only possible "neutral Seventh-chord" will bear the same relation to those of the different diatonic Seventh-chords as do the resources of the Siamese whole-step Triad to those of the different diatonic Triads.

It is not difficult to foresee that the subsequent chords of the diatonic scale, in order of complexity, viz. the Ninth-chord (G-B-D-F-A), the Eleventh-chord (G-B-D-F-A-C) and the Thirteenth-chord (G-B-D-F-A-C-E), of which the latter covers all the seven regular degrees of this scale, will be respectively reflected in the Siamese scale in the form of a neutral Ninth-chord (G-A♯-D-F-A), neutral Eleventh-chord (G-A♯-D-F-A-C) and, finally, neutral Thirteenth-chord (G-A♯-D-F-A-C-D♯). The latter chord, composed of seven notes, will be the limit of harmonic complication in the music of the Siamese, since it comprises the entire tonal material of the infra-tempered scale.

This limit, i.e. the use of seven-tone harmonic combinations (for which centuries were required in the case of the diatonic scale), will probably be reached by the Siamese "Schönbergites" in a very short time—perhaps within the span of one or two decades. Such impetuous speed in the matter of harmonic complication will be accelerated by two principal factors: *first,* by the limited nature of all the neutral chords as regards both structure and function (which mitigates against the normal use of moderately complicated chords) and *second,* by the still greater limitedness—within the conditions of the infra-atonal scale ("7") used instead of the diatonic one—of a melodic creation, at the expense of which this harmonic complication will be effected to a considerable degree.

There is hardly any necessity for commenting on the fact that in so far as the basis of melodic creation is concerned, the infra-atonal scale ("7") will appear merely as the poorest imaginable surrogate of the diatonic scale. There is equally no need to prove here (in fact we have already touched upon this subject before, although in a somewhat different manner) that the seven "independent" and equidistant tones of the former will preclude the formation even of the simplest diatonic melody, i.e. the melody which, according to our supposition, the Siamese modernists will inwardly hear and create.

It is quite possible that musical intuition will suggest to them (as it did to our Western modernists) one or two artificial methods to create an illusion of whole steps and half steps of the diatonic scale while using the neutral intervals of the infra-atonal scale ("7"). Some results could probably be achieved, in this respect, by means of wide leaps in the melodic line—a possibility already discussed (see Ex. 97 and its context). A simultaneous use of different keys of the infra-diatonic scale (infra-polytonality), which has also been demonstrated (Ex. 101), will undoubtedly be one of the fundamental attempts of Siamese composers to break through to the melodic plane of the diatonic scale. Perhaps, too, there will be found other palliatives which will enable Siamese modernists to avoid in part, in their harmonic and melodic constructions, the boring monotony that will follow them everywhere like a shadow cast by the neutral intervals of the infra-atonal scale ("7"). All these temporary measures, however, would never satisfy their "diatonic" cravings, neither could they conceal the paucity of their basic infra-atonal means, compared to the wealth of means of the diatonic scale supposedly anticipated by them.

The manifold efforts of our imaginary Siamese modernists will have, strictly speaking, as their common objective, the exhaustive use of the musical possibilities latent in the scale of a "higher order" (in their eyes), i.e. the diatonic scale, on which all Western classical music is based. But how far they will be from these possibilities! It is difficult, indeed, to picture anything more paltry and impotent than Western classical music with neutral Triads instead of major and minor ones; neutral Seventh-chords instead of the variety of Seventh-chords found on the different degrees of the diatonic scale; neutral and perfectly equalized intervals constituting the infra-atonal scale ("7") instead of the characteristic diatonic whole steps and half steps; a scale having neither beginning nor end, no chromatic (not to be confused with infra-chromatic) alterations; a scale precluding the formation of different modes and permitting only the use of neutral Seconds, Thirds, Sixths and Sevenths instead of major and minor Seconds, Thirds, Sixths and Sevenths, etc.

Any one possessing sufficient imagination to think of Western classical music under these conditions, will come very near to what the future infra-atonal music of the Siamese (leaving aside the factor of musical style, immaterial in this case) will sound like. Such a tragic destiny for this music is easily understood, since all those characteristic properties of the diatonic scale which went into the making of Western classical music, will *a priori* turn out to be decolorized in the hands of the Siamese modernists.   Having at their command exclusively the "neutral" means of the infra-atonal scale ("7") they will hardly be able, however talented they may be, to create anything except "neutral music."

But our modern Occidental composers are in the very same tragic position when, in practice, they avail themselves of the atonal scale ("12") as a medium of expression for their, as yet, dimly sensed "supra-diatonic" creative ideas. Like our imaginary Siamese modernists, they can only construct "neutral," that is, mechanically levelled, harmonic combinations, instead of organic supra-diatonic chords; they have at their command but twelve neutral semitones instead of characteristic supra-diatonic whole steps and half steps; they possess a lifeless equalized scale having neither beginning nor end, a scale which precludes the formation of different modes and keys; a scale which does not permit any sort of modulation, etc.   Hence it is not difficult to understand why there is so little likelihood that those modern composers who are unambiguously applying the atonal principle in composition will be able to produce, even when highly gifted, anything but the inevitable "neutral music."

Being at present compelled to use this neutralized atonal scale ("12") instead of the "live" supra-diatonic scale ("12 + 7"), modern composers are in the same position as would be, for instance, portrait painters compelled to use a machine-made lay figure instead of a living model. And as a portrait painted from such a wax figure would of course prove to be utterly emotionless, quite natural must be considered the absence of emotional characteristics in music wholly based on the atonal scale ("12"), which *a priori* is entirely deprived of those characteristics.

It was probably the latter factor which led to the comparatively recent appearance of the so-called "anti-emotional" theory in musical art. The esthetical failure of this theory as well as of the musical trend connected with it, goes hand-in-hand with the esthetical failure of the atonal scale ("12") from which it is derived, and which inevitably predetermines, by its inorganicalness, the creatively sterile or, in this sense, transitory stage in modern music. But whatever the absolute value of this theory—advanced, I believe, by Stravinsky—one cannot refuse its originator an indubitable, though subconscious perception of that negative, anti-emotional feature of the atonal scale, the permeation of which in modern music he explains by rather inadequate historic-psychological reasons.*

But let us revert to our prognosis with regard to the Siamese modernists and let us try to guess what will be their next steps in the transitory or "decadent" period of their musical art.

Having soon exhausted the musical resources of the infra-atonal scale ("7") or, perhaps, realizing the limitations of these resources before their complete exhaustion, the Siamese composers, in order to recruit new creative means, will undoubtedly turn their efforts towards extending the field of the tonal material itself, that is, in the direction of a purely quantitative increase of the tonal constitution of their scale within an octave.

It is not improbable that the search for a new group of tones within the seven-tone series of the infra-atonal scale will be partly stimulated in these composers by the general intuitive perception of the chromatic group of degrees of the diatonic scale ("7 + 5"), of which they will not yet be completely conscious. Should the Siamese modernists have at their command the diatonic scale even in its incomplete form, as initially applied in Western music, i.e. without its chromatic group, then the way of filling it up with the latter would soon be suggested to them by the five (large) whole steps alternating, in the familiar manner, with the two (small) half steps. But since, instead of this incomplete diatonic scale with intervals of different dimensions, the Siamese will possess the infra-atonal scale with seven absolutely equal intervals, they will have no reason to fill up only *some* of the intervals with newly introduced tones, or to prefer, in this respect, certain intervals to others. There is no doubt, therefore, that the first step

---

* In so far as may be judged from casual statements by Stravinsky and his advocates (since there are no other sources of information available), the "anti-emotional" theory referred to seems to hold that, in contradistinction and historical counterbalance to the "over-emotional" romantic (and, to some extent, post-romantic) periods in music of the past century, the new and purely "objective" art, reflecting our modern civilization, has come to the point where it need not be stirred by any emotions in its creative aspect, nor does it apparently seek to evoke any emotional reactions on the part of the listeners. Whether these reactions, as well as the creative impulses, are supposed to be of a frankly sensory or intellectual nature, or both, the theory in question does not adequately explain, however.

towards increasing the original constitution of the infra-atonal scale ("7") will consist in filling up every one of its seven equal intervals with one new tone (to take the simplest case) or, in other words, in a direct duplication of its seven component degrees within an octave, a quarter step apart from the original series.

Were we to suppose that the seven new tones, thus obtained, will be introduced in the infra-atonal scale ("7") in the capacity of "regular" degrees, then there could not be the slightest suggestion, in this instance, of any approximation whatever of the new fourteen-tone scale ("14") of the Siamese ultra-modernists to the diatonic scale unconsciously sought by them. But should we assume that the seven new tones will enter the infra-atonal scale as "auxiliary" degrees, even then the absurdity of the new tonal combination ("7 + 7"), from the standpoint of the same diatonic scale ("7 + 5"), will be so apparent that doubts might arise as to the plausibility of our "Siamese prognosis," were not a similar method of tonal increase proposed, from time to time, in our own Western music. In this connection, I again refer to those modern composers who see as the shortest if not the only way out of the atonal blind alley the superseding of our present semitonal system by a quartertonal one, through simple quantitative duplication, within every octave, of the twelve tones now at their command, a quarter step higher or lower. This duplication ("24") can be expressed, if desired, as the combination "12 + 12" which is just as absurd with regard to the supra-diatonic scale ("12 + 7") as the above Siamese combination ("7 + 7") in relation to the diatonic scale ("7 + 5").

Among modern composers there are also some who deem it expedient to introduce into our present musical system still smaller subdivisions of a whole tone for the sole reason that our ear is capable of distinguishing not only quarter tones but also sixth tones, eighth tones and even sixteenth tones, if not lesser fractions still. These composers might be right if the mere physiological ability of our ear to distinguish this or that "microtonic" interval were sufficient reason for using them in musical art. History teaches us, however, that besides this auditory capacity, it is also necessary that the newly introduced intervals, irrespective of their dimension, should be organically connected with one or the other tonal system and not mechanically forced upon it. Mere duplication or triplication, etc. of the tonal constitution of a scale not only brings us no nearer to the solution of this pressing problem of musical progress but most assuredly leads us far afield.

Thus, it is not difficult to understand that the new Siamese tonal combination, be it "14" or "7 + 7," will not modify for the better, in the slightest degree, the creatively sterile "neutrality" of the infra-atonal scale ("7"), just as the Western quarter-tone combination, be it "24" or "12 + 12" or anything else, will not bring life to the creatively sterile "neutrality" of the atonal scale ("12"). Indeed, whether the seven and twelve new tones are introduced in the capacity of regular or auxiliary degrees in the Siamese and Western scales respectively, they will do no more than exactly halve the intervals of both scales; consequently, they will not alter in any way the equality itself of intervals which causes the neutrality of these scales.

As to the advantages which these two scales will acquire as a result of the above duplications, they will be rather insignificant compared with what might be expected from such an increase in the number of tones within every octave. The newly introduced tones, having no connection whatever with the former tonal constitution of the infra-atonal ("7") and the atonal ("12") scales, could be used simply, or at least chiefly, as passing notes between every pair of contiguous degrees. In other words these new tones will fulfill but one and the least essential function of the auxiliary degrees: the embellishment of the basic melodic line. They will be deprived, however, of the other and most vital functions that belong to the auxiliary degrees in harmonic constructions as well as in connection with modulation and transposition which, strictly speaking, will remain unperformable on account of the unchanged conditions of both scales.

This leads us to the conclusion that although, in general, the gradual extension of the tonal field itself appears to be quite normal in musical evolution, yet the very process of this extension does not always take place according to the principle of plain "filling up" of the tonal system used at a given historical moment. This is possible only during the periods when this or that scale is being used in its *incomplete* form, as was the case, for instance, in ancient Chinese music exclusively based on the five regular degrees of the infra-diatonic scale, or in Western music a good many centuries ago, when it was exclusively based on the seven regular degrees of the diatonic scale. It goes without saying that, in these instances, the inclusion of auxiliary degrees in each scale could be effected, at the necessary moment, in accordance with the principle of simple filling-up of the tonal system already in use. But since each of these scales, when already filled up with the group of auxiliary degrees, represents a perfectly *closed* system, it is clear that further extension of the tonal material cannot be effected, in each instance, otherwise than through transition from one system to the other and more complex system.

Such a transition represents (by reason of the incongruity of intonations of different scales) a procedure far more radical than plain inclusion of the group of auxiliary degrees in an unchangeable series of regular degrees of one and the same scale. Only under one condition could the procedure of transition from one scale to another be effected by the simple method of adding new tones, without the former tonal constitution being changed, namely, that of the Pythagorean intonation of all scales involved in this transition. The diagram of Ex. 73 illustrates with sufficient clarity the constancy of tonal relations of different scales (becoming gradually more complicated) in Pythagorean intonation and, consequently, the possibility of transitition from the use of one scale to another by the simple addition, in each case, of missing tones which could be found in the infinite series of natural Fifths. But of the three scales demonstrated in this diagram, as we already know, Pythagorean intonation is applicable in practice only with regard to the infra-diatonic scale (in which it serves as its just intonation), being scarcely acceptable in the diatonic scale and still less so in the supra-diatonic scale.* Generally speaking, therefore, all these scales can be applied for practical purposes either in their just or tempered intonations.

The utter incongruity of infra-tempered, tempered and supra-tempered intonations is perfectly apparent from the diagram of Ex. 74. As for the just intonations of these scales they are identical only in relation to *some* of the degrees constituting the latter. Thus, in the following diagram showing the just intonations of the infra-diatonic and diatonic scales (in the modes "F-f," similarly to previous representations) only four notes (including the Tonic) out of seven, viz. F, G, C and D, coincide respectively in pitch:

EXAMPLE 109: **

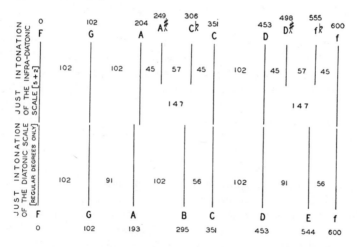

---

* Pythagorean intonation naturally serves as just intonation also in the primitive sub-infra-diatonic scale ("2 + 3"), and this is probably the main reason why the transition of the latter to the infra-diatonic scale ("5 + 2") passed completely unnoticed in the history of European music.

** Either infra-sharps or infra-flats—one of the two in each instance—ought to be regarded, in this Example, as representatives of the two auxiliary degrees of the infra-diatonic scale. The position of the infra-chromatically altered notes obtained through both the ascending and descending series of natural Fifths (Ex. 76 and 78)

is shown here with reference to the *harmonic* intonation of this justly tuned scale which, according to the explanations given in the Supplement to Chapter XI, is the exact reverse (for the altered notes), compared with the *melodic* intonation of the same scale. That is to say, the place assigned in harmonic intonation to infra-sharps is occupied in melodic intonation by infra-flats and *vice versa,* while the position of the regular degrees of the scale remains unchanged in both instances. The distinction will become clear when the harmonic intonation of the scale "5 + 2" (Ex. 109) is compared with its melodic intonation represented by the following diagram:

In this way the transition from the just intonation of the infra-diatonic scale to the just intonation of the diatonic scale requires a definite change in pitch of three noncoinciding degrees—a change whose fundamental principle (retuning the Thirds) was for the first time suggested in medieval European music by Walter Odington (*De speculatione musice*, written about 1275), then gradually developed by various authors, particularly by Bartholomeo Ramis de Pareja (*Musica practica*, 1482) and Lodovico Fogliano (*Musica theorica*, 1529), and finally, established in complete form by Gioseffe Zarlino (*Institutioni armoniche*, 1558). It would not be too speculative, even, to assume that the actual introduction of this change—inadequately explained, of course, by its advocates as a mere retuning of one and the same *diatonic* scale—was the result of insistent pressure on the part of life itself, not *vice versa*, and that the occasional "shifting" in intonation, which eventually caused this change, began to make itself dimly felt in vocal practice before any theories were advanced by medieval authors in this connection, perhaps around the time when the interval of a Third was first proclaimed a consonance (circa 1200). This becomes all the more plausible when it is considered that none of these writers, strictly speaking, could be regarded as the true originator of the new principle of intonation which, as a matter of fact, was already known, in rudimentary form, by Archytas (introduced the major Third, $\frac{5}{4}$ or 193 ctn., about 408 B. C.) and Eratosthenes (introduced the minor Third, $\frac{6}{5}$ or 158 ctn., about 200 B.C.), and was theoretically worked out much later by Didymus (60 A.D.) and somewhat corrected by Ptolemy (130 A.D.), but which, nevertheless, did not come into actual practice in those days.

The comparative ease with which the transition to the just intonation of the diatonic scale was effected towards the close of the Middle Ages was probably due in great part to the simplicity of tonal relations employed in music at the period in question, permitting the use of any of the above intonations without too perceptible a difference, especially in the melodic line.

It would be difficult, however, to expect the same ease in the transition from just intonation of the diatonic scale to just intonation of the supra-diatonic scale in which only three notes (including the Tonic) out of twelve, viz. F, G and A, coincide respectively in pitch as illustrated by the following diagram:

0	102	204	249 C#	306 A#	351	453	498 f#	555 D#	600
f	G	A			C	D			f
	102	102	45	57	45	102	45	57	45
				147				147	

The instability of the infra-chromatically altered notes as regards their position in a scale, which depends on whether they are considered harmonically or melodically and on whether the melody progresses upward or downward, may perhaps explain the long use of the *Semi-sesquitone Temperament* by Scotch bagpipers, to whom we have already referred on an earlier occasion (see Footnote on page 41). It is quite probable that they intuitively felt the above differences in intonation as well as the impossibility of fully rendering them on their instruments, and therefore decided to compromise all these differences by using a single note for each auxiliary degree of the infra-diatonic scale, placing it *exactly midway* between the neighboring regular degrees in each case.

EXAMPLE 110: *

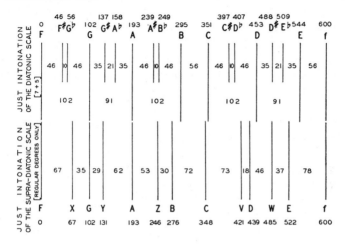

Apart from the small number of coinciding notes in this example, one must admit that were the just intonation of the diatonic scale used to this day in Western music, even then the latter would be sufficiently complicated to make the transition to the use of the unfamiliar just intonation of the supra-diatonic scale anything but easy. One may well imagine, therefore, the incomparably greater obstacles which now stand in the way of Western musical art in its transition from the diatonic to the supra-diatonic scale.

Among these obstacles must be placed, first, the ingrained habit of tonal thought and perception, established for over two centuries through the tempered intonation of the diatonic scale. Inasmuch as this intonation has no notes of common pitch either with the just intonation of the scale "12 + 7" or with its supra-tempered intonation, the overcoming of this habit presupposes a definite change within our ear from a physiological as well as from a psychological standpoint.

---

* Similarly to the foregoing Example, either sharps or flats—one of the two in each instance—ought to be regarded as representatives of the five auxiliary degrees of the diatonic scale. Likewise, the position of the chromatically altered notes is shown here with reference to its *harmonic* intonation, the difference between the latter and the *melodic* intonation of the same scale (Ex. 79) being readily grasped by a simple comparison. The harmonic intonation itself, however, may have different versions, depending on the selection of major and minor Thirds containing chromatically altered notes, that one prefers to preserve acoustically pure. The following two chains of pure Thirds—one for sharps and another for flats—have been used in the above Example:

1. G♯ 158 B 193 D♯ 158 F♯ 193 A♯ 158 C♯
2. G♭ 193 B♭ 158 D♭ 193 F 158 A♭ 193 C 158 E♭

Both these chains are connected with the fundamental series of Thirds (F 193 A 158 C 193 E 158 G193 B 158 D) through common notes, viz. B in the former instance, and F-C in the latter. The advantage of this version over many others is that all its half steps formed by notes with a different literal designation in each instance (familiarly known as diatonic semitones, like F-G♭, F♯-G, A-B♭, B-C, etc.), acquire an equal dimension, viz. 56 ctn. or $\frac{16}{15}$, and thus produce a desirable symmetry in the arrangement of chromatically altered notes.

The difficulty of adapting the abundant and valuable musical literature in existence to any intonation of the supra-diatonic scale appears to be another considerable obstacle to the immediate practical use of this new scale. And it is scarcely to be believed that musical art will ever resolve to evade this difficulty by breaking away sharply from its brilliant past for the sake of the still nebulous future, thus making the transition from the diatonic to the supra-diatonic scale a mere question of accommodation of the ear to one or the other intonation of the latter.

Besides these two main obstacles to the transition referred to there are others, though less important ones, which need not be discussed at this time.

Of course none of the obstacles indicated stands in the way of the now widely used atonal scale ("12")—that illegitimate child of tempered intonation—and here is its indirect advantage over the supra-diatonic scale ("12 + 7") whose rôle it has long but vainly been striving to fill. There can scarcely be any doubt that in view of the serious difficulties that surround transition from the diatonic to the supra-diatonic scale, various attempts to break into the realm of supra-tonality through the inadequate channel of the atonal scale will continue also in the future. But at the same time, considering the limited resources of this scale, pointed out above, one may be certain that modern musical art will not succeed in making a single significant step forward, in the full meaning of the word, so long as the starting-point of its experiments continues to be the inviolability of tempered intonation, which is the structural principle of the atonal scale ("12").

From this, however, it would be hasty to infer that the author is unfaithful to his former defense of the practice of Equal Temperament and that in reality he sides with its adversaries. On the contrary he considers Equal Temperament of great utility to musical art but on the condition that it be accepted merely as an *acoustic compromise* (despite some of its indirect artistic advantages) and not as the basic *structural principle* of this or that scale. Thus, tempered intonation was of invaluable service to Western musical art when, for a slight compromise as regards the absolute acoustic accuracy of the scale "7 + 5," it gave us innumerable benefits without infringing upon that most essential (in every organic scale) inequality between whole steps, on the one hand, and half steps, on the other, or upon their characteristic distribution within an octave. But the same intonation became destructive when the five auxiliary degrees of the scale "7 + 5" acquired the "rights" of regular degrees and, as a result of this change, the former conventional equality between all the twelve degrees, adopted simply as a compromise, became the basic principle of the new atonal scale ("12") thus formed.

The same should be said of infra-tempered intonation which, at the price of a certain acoustic compromise, yielded great advantages to Siamese musical art without affecting the most essential characteristics of the scale "5 + 2." But the same intonation will become a destructive factor if the two auxiliary degrees of this scale acquire some day the "rights" of regular degrees and if, as a result, the former conventional equality between all the seven degrees becomes the basic principle of the subsequent infra-atonal scale ("7").

It is, then, perfectly obvious that the principle of Equal Temperament must be regarded as useful or harmful according to circumstances and not *per se*. When circumstances are unfavorable to the practical application of this principle, i.e. when the auxiliary degrees of any scale transferred to the group of its regular degrees, cease to fill the functions of transposition and modulation to facilitate which Equal Temperament was introduced, the latter is historically doomed and, in this particular form, has to be discarded.

The beginning of the gradual change of functions of the auxiliary degrees of any scale in connection with their gradual transfer to the group of its regular degrees is the first sign of germination of the new and more complicated scale as well as of the decay of Equal Temperament as applied to the former. The lengthy process of practical materialization of the new scale ought to take place, strictly speaking, beyond the artificial conditions of this Temperament in order to avoid still-born formations such as the atonal or infra-atonal scale. And it is only after this process is completed that the new scale, like its predecessor, may be encased in the armor of the new Equal Temperament embracing a greater number of tones but just as convenient and practical.

This process of gradual increase of tonal material in musical art, quite normal from the theoretical point of view, is less happily accomplished in practice, however. For the reasons already given, the tempered intonation which has been used for centuries is not easily to be discarded, and replaced by the new supra-tempered intonation according to the requirements of the moment.

Moreover, should we assume that modern Western composers (as well as our imaginary Siamese modernists) will be wholly aware of the change that is taking place in their musical consciousness, leading to the new and more complicated scale, even then one is inclined to doubt whether they will whole-heartedly part with that habitual intonation so deeply rooted within them. Still less surprising is it that with no such awareness on the part of composers, tempered intonation continues to remain so stable in modern Occidental music (just as infra-tempered intonation will undoubtedly preserve its stability, under similar conditions, in future Siamese music), even after all the causes which gave rise to that intonation have already vanished.

In the meantime the use of tempered intonation on the strength of "inertia" by modern composers who already anticipate the supra-diatonic system does not promise them anything creatively productive and merely diverts them from the channels of actual historic evolution. On the other hand one may readily understand the instinctive adherence of composers to the habitual tempered (or infra-tempered) intonation, *firstly*, as the only reliable prop (from their viewpoint) in our modern creative quicksands which, however, by the strange irony of things, result from the very use of this intonation during the period of its historical doom; and, *secondly,* as the only remaining link between the past and the present of musical art—a link which is able, at least, to preserve all the musical values acquired up to this day.

The necessity of averting any break at all between different periods of musical art in which acoustically incongruous scales are used will hardly be denied by any one. But the possibility of reaching a definitive solution to this problem on the plane of theoretical speculation alone, is very doubtful. A few words about placing this problem on the experimental basis will be said in the concluding chapter of this book, with certain considerations regarding some equally important practical problems.

CONCLUSION

CHAPTER XIII

FROM THEORY TO PRACTICE

The actual transition to a practical use of the supra-diatonic scale in musical art is a much more complicated problem than may appear at first sight. A number of considerations in the preceding chapter unambiguously point to the fact that this scale, long before its official introduction in musical practice (and in adequate form) will have to undergo a most careful and comprehensive test. This will reveal with scientific accuracy whatever is connected with the psychophysiological perception of the new scale, and will also check up experimentally the theories, sometimes of a purely hypothetical nature, contained in this book.

Special experiments will help us, for instance, to find out, among other things, the degree and speed of adjustment of the musical ear to various intonations of different scales in general. All we know is that the transition to the use of a new and more complicated scale in music is caused by some sort of psychological transformation within us. But we cannot theoretically determine the depth of this transformation and we cannot guess, therefore, even approximately, the time required for the adjustment of the average musical ear to the new scale and, particularly, to its necessarily new (natural or artificial) intonation.

The exact determination of this auditory faculty will be of great practical importance to us because *the degree* of adjustment of the ear to various intonations ought to solve a highly essential problem regarding the possibility of application, in the future, of supra-tempered intonation (especially with respect to harmonic formations), while the *speed* of this adjustment ought to solve the no less vital problem concerning the possibility of an effortless return, whenever desired, to the former diatonic scale and its conventional (tempered) intonation. The solution of the latter problem is of especial consequence, not only because the preservation for the future of all creative values heretofore acquired in music depends on it, but also the preservation of permanent contact between the profoundly distinct manifestations of musical art based on tonally incongruous scales.*

---

* Notwithstanding the seemingly radical tendency of the present work, the author is not inclined to accept the opinion, in high favor among modern composers, that the resources of the diatonic scale are nearing complete exhaustion and that, consequently, the use of this scale in musical creation at the present time betrays weakness of the genuine creative gift. Neither are there any grounds, in the author's judgment, for unreservedly recognizing the possession of such a gift by a composer who has given evidence of the utmost sensitiveness in relation to the supra-diatonic scale. A genuine creative gift does not necessarily increase in proportion to this inward and, to a great extent, purely auditory sensitiveness. The appearance, therefore,

Taking into account the well-known flexibility of the ear in respect of its accommodation to different intonations in general, it is logical to suppose that this faculty could be developed through special exercises to such an extent that a musician will eventually be able, when necessary, to switch easily from one scale to another, just as a linguist, for instance, is able to switch without effort from one language to another and to do so smoothly and fluently even in conversation.

As a matter of fact, auditory ability of this kind is well known to exist, for instance, among the natives of Java and, moreover, is actually exercised by them in their music, which is based on two wholly separate systems of scales mutually excluding each other, in so far as their intonation is concerned. As we have already mentioned on an earlier occasion, these two systems are called *Salendro* and *Pelog*, of which the former comprises five equidistant tones within an octave, while the latter comprises seven tones tuned in such a manner that various pentatonic modes, serving as actual bases of Javanese music, and possessing a very dissimilar character from the purely musical standpoint, can be selected therefrom. These two systems are tonally incongruous to such an extent that two entirely different sets of instruments constituting the *Gamelan,* or orchestral ensemble, are separately used by the native musicians, depending on whether the music is composed on the basis of the *Salendro* or of one of the *Pelog* scales. It is readily understood, of course, that with the change to differently intoned instruments, as required by the music to be performed, the ear has accordingly to accommodate itself in each instance, which, however, does not seem to be a source of any confusion or inconvenience in the musical practice of the Javanese.

Another, though somewhat different instance of this faculty of ear-accommodation, one is inclined to see also in the use of the native *Raga* by Hindu musicians. This term designates, musically, a somewhat extended concept of a *mode*, usually consisting of five, six or seven tones, the whole set being differently intoned each time (in part, or entirely) within the range of twenty-two permanent intervals of varying dimensions into which the Octave is divided. It is hardly to be doubted that the use of the various *Raga* presupposes a faculty of ear-accommodation far exceeding in degree, if not in essence, the one required for the use of the various modes in Occidental musical practice.

---

of a highly significant composer availing himself of the diatonic\scale, or even of the tonally still more limited infra-diatonic scale, (although in a manner largely "retrospective") is not precluded either at present or in the future. The complete exhaustion of the musical resources of any scale is hardly possible, generally speaking, just as, for instance, the complete exhaustion of the artistic resources of two-dimensional painting which historically precedes three-dimensional painting, is scarcely conceivable. Genius is an unusually capricious phenomenon and it is not only able to manifest itself with very limited means of expression but sometimes exclusively with such means. Hence it follows that, from the musical viewpoint, no scale excludes the one that historically precedes it (just as three-dimensional painting does not exclude the two-dimensional form of that art) but merely enlarges the methods of expressing that range of emotions which cannot be fully rendered by former tonal means. In this way, the supra-diatonic scale will replace the diatonic scale only in the sense that it will be the *latest* achievement in the matter of utilization of new tonal means which, like the former, are both inevitably limited from the physical aspect, yet musically inexhaustible.

However, if the human ear possesses, in principle, this psycho-physiological faculty of self-adjustment, there is no reason to presume that the latter represents a sort of racial privilege of the Orientals and that it cannot be developed, perhaps even to a greater extent, by the Occidentals who, in their specific musical evolution, have simply never had the opportunity of manifesting this faculty to any degree. True, it is quite probable that the homophonic character of Asiatic music with its mere sporadic sallies in the domain of harmony greatly facilitated the development of this faculty of ear-accommodation in the Orient. And it appears equally probable, therefore, that the tendency to polyphonic forms with the harmonic tissue becoming gradually more complicated, has hindered in the past and, perhaps, will impede still more in the future the development of this particular faculty in Occidental countries. Yet, no one is now in a position to predict, even approximately, how far the development of ear-accommodation among Occidental musicians may go, and, of course, in this respect, no theoretical speculations, however reasonable and plausible, should be relied on too implicitly, if at all. Experiments alone can determine conclusively the likelihood or unlikelihood of our supposition regarding nimble and effortless self-adjustment of the ear to different scales and their various intonations.

The development of such an auditory faculty, if its feasibility is positively established, would of course be the simplest solution of our problem, in so far as the preservation of a permanent contact between the music based on the diatonic and the supra-diatonic scale is concerned. But it is by no means the only possible solution. At least one other though more complicated method could be adopted to preserve this contact, which may even prove to work out more efficiently in the final issue, and which will probably have to be resorted to, in case the experiments conducted for the determination of our faculty of ready ear-accommodation give negative results.

This method is directly connected with a rather old and, during the last decade, strongly sponsored theory, which advocates the introduction of a nineteen-tone equally tempered system for the music based on the *diatonic* scale, this system supposedly being more advantageous from the standpoint of acoustical purity, as compared with the twelve-tone equally tempered system used at the present time.* The fact that a number of theorists—most of them, from all

* The so-called *Clavicymbalum Universale* (once in the possession of Carl Luyton, a sixteenth century Court organist at Prague), which was seen and described by Praetorius (*Syntagmatis Musici; Tomus Secundus de Organographia*, 1619, p. 63-65; the reprinted 1884 edition—pages 74-78) and which comprised seven white and twelve black keys within an octave, is sometimes regarded as an instrument representing the initial attempt to introduce a nineteen-tone system for the music based on the diatonic scale. It must be clearly pointed out, however, that this instrument was tuned according to the *Meantone* Temperament, specifically adjusted, in this instance, to nineteen keys (see A. J. Ellis's note in Helmholtz's *Sensations of Tone*, page 320; also an article entitled *Zur Geschichte des Luytonschen Klavizimbels* by Adolf Koczirz in the *Sammelbände der Internationalen Musikgesellschaft*, Neunter Jahrgang, 1907-1908, Leipzig, page 565, etc.), and, therefore, its principle can be considered as no more

evidence, fully equipped with modern methods of strictly scientific investigation —arrived, in this respect, at the very same conclusions by different roads and quite independently, leaves hardly any doubt as to the correctness of their speculations. And if mere improvement in acoustical purity jointly with some "extra" shadings in intonation and extended possibilities in modulation, with regard to "diatonic" music, do not seem, so far, to be regarded by practical musicians as sufficiently strong arguments in favor of the replacement of the customary twelve-tone Temperament by the new and more cumbersome nineteen-tone Temperament, there is an additional argument in favor of this nineteen-tone Temperament, with probably better chances for its introduction, in the fact that it is the very one which could serve as a basis not only for "diatonic" but for "supra-diatonic" music as well. Thus, our problem of a permanent contact between the music based on the diatonic scale ("7 + 5") and on the supra-diatonic scale ("12 + 7") could be solved through the adoption of an acoustically common and standard tonal system (nineteen equidistant tones within an Octave) which, by merely changing our attitude towards it, could be used for two entirely different purposes.

---

than the historical forerunner of what later developed into the nineteen-tone equally tempered system.

The real initial and unambiguous exposition of this system designed for a more advantageous use of the diatonic scale, as compared to the twelve-tone system, was made by F. W. Opelt in his *Allgemeine Theorie der Musik auf den Rhythmus der Klangwellenpulse gegründet und durch neue Versinnlichungsmittel erläutert* (Leipzig, 1852, pages 36, 52, 53 and 80). This writer for the first time gives the ratios of nineteen equal intervals in ordinary vibration-fractions and in parts of a string, and considers the practical obstacles to the production of these intervals surmountable.

Almost three quarters of a century then elapsed before further pleas—this time in more persistent form—were advanced in favor of the introduction, in musical practice, of the nineteen-tone equally tempered system. We find a concise but quite valuable study by Prof. Dr. Joseph Würschmidt, entitled *Die neunzehn-stufige Scala; eine natürliche Erweiterung unseres Tonsystems*, in the *Neue Musik-Zeitung* (Stuttgart-Leipzig, April 21, 1921; p. 215). Besides a few acoustic calculations this writer demonstrates a complete cycle of *nineteen* (instead of twelve) major keys of the diatonic scale, which become feasible within the new system. He sees no particular difficulties in the correct production of the newly intoned intervals on the generally accepted string instruments.

Next appeared the *Musical Acoustics based on the pure Third-system* by Thorvald Kornerup (Wilhelm Hausen Musik-Verlag, Copenhagen and Leipzig, 1922), a substantial and original

treatise, in which the author discloses through very ingenious calculations that the nineteen-tone Temperament (in regard to the normal intervals alone) is three and a half times more refined than the Temperament of twelve tones. He suggests the introduction of an instrument with nineteen tones to an octave in music schools, academies, etc. for the demonstration of a more exquisite intonation than the piano of twelve tones is able to give.

Das Relativitäts-prinzip der musikalischen Harmonie by Ariel (Leipzig, 1925), of which only the first volume has been published so far (*Die Gesetze der inneren Tonbewegung, das evolutionäre Temperierungsverfahren und das neunzehn-stufige Tonsystem*), represents the most extensive research ever undertaken in connection with the problem of the nineteen-tone tempered system supplanting the twelve-tone system. Exhaustive investigation leads the author to believe that the nineteen-tone Temperament is the closest reduction of the 59 different and natural intervals which, in his opinion, are necessary to produce pure intonation.

Jacques Handschin gives a review of Ariel's book in the *Zeitschrift für Musikwissenschaft* (June-July, 1926, page 579) and brings to light the fact that Prof. Valentin Kowalenkoff, a Russian mathematician and technologist of Leningrad, with whom he collaborated, independently worked out and experimentally verified a theory of a nineteen-tone equally tempered scale representing a convenient reduction of an Enharmonic Series of 21 or 29 pure intervals. The results of his investigation were published in a local scientific bulletin in 1919, and some information regarding his work was given by

We may easily build, for instance, a uniform instrument with a keyboard comprising nineteen keys within an octave, which would only have to be named differently, according to the scale ("7 + 5" or "12 + 7") intended for use at a given moment. The following illustration will show, for instance, how such a keyboard ought to be designated for music based on the scale "7 + 5."

EXAMPLE 111:

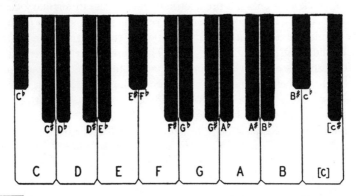

Mr. Handschin in an article *Akustisches aus Russland*, found in the *"Gedenkboek aangeboden aan Dr. D. F. Schreurleer* ('s-Gravenhage, 1925), page 143). Another article, a good portion of which deals with the same subject, was published by Mr. Handschin under the title *Ueber reine Harmonie und temperierte Tonleitern*" in the *Schweizerisches Jahrbuch für Musikwissenschaft* (Zweiter Band, 1927, p. 145-166).

The above list of works pertaining to the problem of nineteen-tone Equal Temperament is not quite complete. Several articles written on the same subject, among them some by Erik Eggen (1911) and Dr. P. S. Wedell (1914), appeared in various periodicals but unfortunately were not available to the author. There is also a harmonium with nineteen tones to the octave said to have been built about the year 1845 by P. S. Munck of Rosensköld, professor at Lund, and now in the Stockholm Museum. Mr. T. Kornerup, who makes mention of this instrument in his treatise quoted above, does not give, however, any data as to its intonation.

In addition to all this information regarding the literature and activities connected with the "nineteen-tone Temperament movement" we shall append a diagram in which the just intonation of the diatonic scale (a single key and regular degrees only) is compared with its equally tempered intonation, the latter being demonstrated in two forms:

(1) on the basis of twelve-tone Temperament and

(2) on the basis of nineteen-tone Temperament.

Even this incomplete representation instantly shows that the chief advantage of the second form is that the consonant intervals which are most characteristic of the diatonic Tonality, viz. Thirds and Sixths, are much nearer to just intonation under the condition of nineteen-tone Temperament than under that of twelve-tone Temperament. But this advantage is somewhat detrimental to the Fourths and the Fifths which, in this form, approach very closely the values of Meantone Temperament (251.7 ctn. and 348.3 ctn., respectively). The dissonant intervals, though of lesser concern, will probably sound better in nineteen-tone Temperament, as a rule.

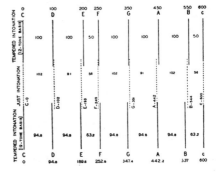

The set of white keys, within each octave, standing for the seven regular degrees of the diatonic scale, in this illustration, is left unchanged in quantity and designation, while the number of black keys is increased to twelve, each of the five auxiliary degrees of the diatonic scale being represented in its double aspect (sharp and flat) by a pair of separate keys, and two other black keys being interpolated between the regular degrees which form the half steps, i.e. between E-F and B-C. It must be borne in mind, however, that the increased number of black keys does not predetermine the increase of auxiliary degrees in the diatonic scale. Their original number remains the same, each of these five degrees acquiring merely an "extra" variation of tuning, the same thing being true of the notes E♯, F♭ and of B♯, C♭. Therefore, in strictly chromatic passages, for instance, either a sharp or a flat ought to be used for each auxiliary degree, both of these alterations never proceeding in succession, except for purposes of a purely coloristic nature, which have nothing to do with the fundamental structure of the scale itself.

Turning now to the question of utilizing the same keyboard for music based on the scale "12 + 7," one has but to recollect that, according to the basic principles of our construction, the seven auxiliary degrees of the supra-diatonic scale are arranged in the same manner within an Octave, as are the seven regular degrees of the diatonic scale (Ex. 72 and 75). And since the differences in intonation of these two series of degrees are no longer of any concern within the common nineteen-tone tempered system, which serves both scales, it is evident that the white keys of the above illustration may quite adequately fulfill the functions of the auxiliary degrees of the supra-diatonic scale. As to the twelve regular degrees of this scale, one readily understands that their arrangement within an Octave wholly depends on the arrangement of the seven auxiliary degrees (see Ex. 80, for instance). Therefore, if the above set of white keys fully meets the requirements of the seven auxiliary degrees of the supra-diatonic scale, then the set of black keys ought automatically to fit the relative position of its twelve regular degrees. In other words, the white keys which are used for the regular degrees of the diatonic scale will also serve for the auxiliary degrees of the supra-diatonic scale and the black keys which are used for the auxiliary degrees of the diatonic scale will also serve for the regular degrees of the supra-diatonic scale. The following illustration (Ex. 112), representing an exact duplication of the keyboard demonstrated above, will show how it ought to be designated for music based on the scale "12 + 7." It is understood, of course, that contrary to the chromatic alterations of the former scale represented, as a rule, by two separate (black) keys for sharps and flats, the supra-chromatic alterations of the latter scale are represented by a single (white) key in each instance.

The possibility of using a uniform and equally tempered instrument (nineteen tones to an Octave) for music based either on the diatonic or the supra-diatonic scale

EXAMPLE 112:

discloses a few additional facts worthy of attention. It will be seen, in the first place, that our familiar twelve-tone chromatic scale, when played on such an instrument, will recover, in a way, one of its most important and *natural* characteristics, which is completely lost on the present instruments with twelve-tone Temperament. We refer here to the specific inequality of intervals which this scale originally possesses (principally, the inequality of its seven diatonic and five chromatic semitones, as may be learned from Ex. 110, upper solid lines), and which inevitably gives it a sort of "modal" character, though of a much more subtle nature in comparison with that of the diatonic scale. The musician of to-day seems to have overlooked the very simple fact that, in their natural forms, *both* the diatonic and chromatic scales possess quite definite though different *modal characteristics*, and that the principle of twelve-tone Equal Temperament, while preserving these characteristics in the former scale, destroys them entirely in the latter. The advantage of the nineteen-tone over the twelve-tone Temperament is that it preserves the modal characteristics of both these scales and thus maintains, so to speak, their original musical balance. Hence, it follows that the present form of the twelve-tone chromatic scale with its artificially equalized intervals offering no variety whatever, regardless of their permutations, will be transmuted on the nineteen-tone equally tempered instruments into a series of different twelve-tone *chromatic modes*, as we may call them, which unquestionably are bound to enrich our musical language, particularly when one takes into account the growing significance of the independent twelve-tone foundation in modern music.

But the most amazing and, probably, unexpected result of this "transmutation" is that, upon careful examination, the twelve-tone chromatic modes thus obtained turn out to be structurally identical with the supra-modes of the scale "12 + 7" represented earlier (Ex. 83), the seven diatonic (larger) semitones and five chromatic (smaller) semitones of each chromatic mode respectively corresponding to the seven whole steps and five half steps of each supra-mode.*

*When comparing the intervallic structure of various chromatic modes with that of the supra-modes given in Ex. 83, one should not be confused by the accompanying notation of the chro- matic scale in which all the five alterations are provisionally designated by *sharps*. This fact, coupled with the visible space between the notes in this Example, may make quite a contrary

It does not require much effort to find that the twelve-tone chromatic scale played on the new instrument from the note *C*, let us say, will produce a "chromatic mode" identical with the supra-mode "Y-y," when progressing upwards, and another one identical with the supra-mode "F-f," when progressing downwards. Thus, a mere change in orthography of the chromatic scale (all sharps, except B♭, in ascending progression, and all flats, except F♯, in descending progression), which is no more than a matter of theoretical correctness in our present twelve-tone equally tempered system, will produce a substantial difference in the new nineteen-tone equally tempered system. Likewise, a change of the starting note of that scale, immaterial in our present system, so far as *structure* is concerned, will result in the transformation of one chromatic mode (and, consequently, of its equivalent supra-mode) into another, when the new system is used.

It is readily seen that this more accurate interpretation of the chromatic scale which becomes possible within the conditions of the new system, brings it in the closest possible contact with the supra-diatonic scale and thus establishes a direct connection between modern chromaticists and future "supra-tonalists" who will follow the former in the natural course of evolution. As a matter of fact, any composer who avails himself, for creative purposes, of the "independent" twelve-tone chromatic scale, as it is represented in the nineteen-tone tempered system, will thereby be automatically using the supra-diatonic scale (twelve regular degrees only), since both are structurally identical in that system. And with all these coincidences one is still further tempted to surmise that the psychological impetus behind the entire modern musical movement, as it drifts away from the seven-tone diatonic modes and their manifold variations, is a subconscious perception of the more subtle twelve-tone chromatic modes and, through them, of the supra-diatonic modes, the two latter formations hardly differing more, broadly speaking, than in the conventional designations of their component tones.

The above illustrations (Ex. 111 and 112), showing merely how two different musical systems may be served by a rigidly tuned instrument with one and the same keyboard, do not predetermine by any means the actual appearance of the latter in future musical practice. It may prove more practical, perhaps, to split the black keys not longitudinally but transversely, similarly to what was done with the keyboard of the sixteenth century *Clavicymbalum Universale*.* Or,

---

(and erroneous) impression as regards the comparative dimension of the diatonic and chromatic semitones referred to in the text, reminding one somewhat of the Pythagorean intonation (see Ex. 79) in which such a dimensionally opposite relation between these semitones does exist. But the five chromatic alterations could just as well be designated by *flats* in Ex. 83, since our chief concern was to facilitate the reading of the unfamiliar ten-line notation with the aid of the approximative designations of our present chromatic scale, when we gave the latter the general representation of the twelve supra-modes. It is important to remember that, in contradistinction to Pythagorean Intonation, diatonic semitones are dimensionally greater than chromatic semitones in Just Intonation, and that it is the latter interrelation of these intervals which is preserved (with certain inevitable acoustic deviations) in

the nineteen-tone Equal Temperament system, when its notation follows that given in Ex. 111.

* According to the description of this instrument by Praetorius, whose work was referred to in the Footnote on page 279, its keyboard must have had the following appearance:

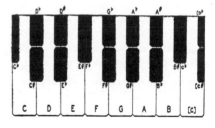

possibly, the type of the keyboard represented in Ex. 80 will better meet the requirements of a standard model for both musical systems. In this case, the functions of the white and black keys, as compared to the keyboards represented in Ex. 111 and 112, would have to be reversed. Thus, the twelve white keys (Ex. 80) used for the regular degrees of the supra-diatonic scale, would also serve for the variously tuned auxiliary degrees of the diatonic scale, and the seven black keys used for the auxiliary degrees of the supra-diatonic scale would also serve for the regular degrees of the diatonic scale. The following illustration will show how that keyboard would have to be designated for music based on the scale "7 + 5." *

EXAMPLE 113:

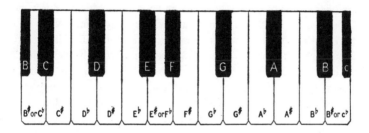

There could be invented, of course, a number of other and, perhaps, still more practical keyboard models, all of which can hardly be preconceived at the present time. And this, after all, constitutes but a part of the general technique of construction of future musical instruments, which represents an entirely separate and rather serious problem, its scope being quite beyond the limits of the present work. We may only note, in passing, that one of the side problems, in this connection, will probably be the necessary elimination from the timbre of the new instrument of the overtone 3 (and its octave duplications) which, as previously explained, becomes a falsonance in the supra-diatonic scale. It seems that this can be solved most satisfactorily only through the lately discovered electrical principle of tone-production, which marks the beginning of a new

---

* Inasmuch as the possibility of constructing a common keyboard for the diatonic and supra-diatonic scales is not accidental but derives from their organic interrelation, there would be a similar possibility if it were necessary to construct a common keyboard for the infra-diatonic and the diatonic scale. This could be effected through the same method as the one used for the former pair of scales, namely, by doubling each of the two black keys of the infra-diatonic scale (Ex. 13) and interpolating three additional black keys between its three half steps. These changes would result in a keyboard with seven black keys and five white keys which, being merely a reversal of our ordinary piano keyboard (seven white and five black keys), could be used not only for the infra-diatonic scale with "varied" intonation of its auxiliary degrees, but for the diatonic scale as well. The following two illustrations (a and b) show how this

era in the field of construction of musical instruments that are probably destined to supersede, in time to come, those now in existence.

I have slightly touched upon only a very few problems directly connected with the practical testing of the supra-diatonic scale. The range of this test is, indeed, immeasurably wider and, above all, not every problem relating to it can now be foreseen in its entirety. Many of them will undoubtedly be suggested as time goes on.

But even after this all-inclusive test is completed and new musical instruments are built subsequently, the hour for creating "supra-diatonic symphonies" will not have struck yet for modern composers. The unusualness of the new tonal order and of the tonal relations of the supra-diatonic scale will require, from the very beginning, a comprehensible text-book containing at least the most elementary principles of the new Harmony and Counterpoint. Such a text-book cannot be prepared, however, in an individual way, as was done and as is still being done for the commonly used diatonic system. We must remember that we shall be dealing with a new musical system differing greatly, in its tonal plane, from the former. Therefore, not only will the new division into consonances and dissonances of all the harmonic combinations feasible in this system, be at first insufficiently clear and convincing to everybody's ear (and such a division generally speaking, is the sole principle on which, as in other scales, all the harmonic and contrapuntal rules and "prescriptions" can be based), but even the very succession of tones in the new scale, no matter in what intonation, will probably produce a somewhat uncomfortable and awkward impression.

---

common keyboard would have to be designated in both instances, and the third illustration (c) explains how our ordinary piano keyboard can be utilized for the infra-diatonic scale with "varied" intonation of its auxiliary degrees. It may also be added that the twelve-tone keyboard improves the purity of intonation of the infra-tempered scale, in much the same way as the nineteen-tone keyboard does in regard to our present tempered scale.

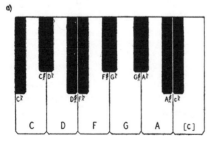

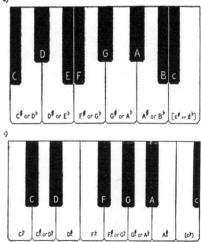

Hence it is evident that in order to avoid blunders, the elaboration of new rules which will at least teach every composer how to approach and to handle in a rudimentary way the unfamiliar tonal material, must be accomplished collectively by a group of specialists who will depend upon their former theoretical knowledge as well as upon all the experimental data obtained, prior to the composition of the new text-book, through practical testing of the supradiatonic scale.

The new theory of music thus worked out, together with the method of its practical application in connection with the scale "12 + 7," will mark the beginning of a *constructive* period in the field of modern musical creation and, simultaneously, the end of that atonal anarchy which is now still going on. Speaking of this anarchy, one has to admit, however, that inevitable historic factors are behind it, this being especially evident if we consider the conditions under which musical art, based on the scale "7 + 5," developed. The chief of these fateful conditions was, as we already know, equally tempered intonation which freeing itself from the subordinate position it occupied as an acoustic compromise or "convenient error" of the diatonic scale, unexpectedly and unjustifiedly usurped the prerogatives of an infallible musical principle in the disguise of an independent atonal scale ("12") hastily erected upon the old and abandoned "diatonic" ruins. This abnormal but at the same time not unusual state of affairs in a revolutionary process, so far feeding exclusively on tempered intonation whose functions have been groundlessly perverted, has swept away all heretofore existing musical laws without creating any new ones.

But the musical mind, influenced by this abnormal state of affairs, on the one hand, and guided by an intuitive perception of the new tonal plane, on the other, cannot think of any new musical laws except as negations of the old ones. Thus, the modern composer is firmly convinced that the scale which he inwardly feels is *not* the familiar diatonic scale ("7 + 5"), and since, for him, the latter, up to the present time, has been the *sole* "carrier" of the principle of Tonality, it is natural that in "ruling out" this old scale as a possible tonal basis for the music of the future, he also relinquishes the very principle of Tonality associated with it. This rejection—practically the essence of Atonality—is further strengthened in his mind by the negative properties of the twelve-tone tempered intonation disclosed above, by which every composer is limited at the present time.

For the same reasons the modern composer also rejects some other principles (for instance, the principle of division of all harmonic combinations into consonances and dissonances) which to his musical mind are exclusive and inalienable properties of the scale "7 + 5." Hence it is easy to understand why this negative mode of thinking gradually brings modern composers to a negation of all, even provisionally established, principles in musical creation, and why it leads to a justification of anarchy, to a legitimation of lawlessness.*

Such an anarchic and, I repeat, inevitable period of tonal revolution as we are witnessing nowadays, is of course highly favorable soil for easily pleased dilettants who sometimes gamble on this alluring freedom and thereby discredit whatever is healthy and valuable in the modern movement. It is difficult, and often plainly disadvantageous, for them to understand that progress in art is characterized not merely by emancipation from the shackles of the past, from antiquated rules, but by the simultaneous appearance of new and more complicated problems, and with them of new restrictions.

Paradoxical as it may seem, these very restrictions (not their absence) open the shortest if not the only road to the most profitable exploitation of the artistic resources embedded in any musical system. The rules and "prescriptions," viewed with such scorn by dilettants because they lack the knowledge to use them to advantage, in the hands of a real master become tools that furnish the greatest possibilities for the methodical and rational elaboration of the tonal mass. Without these rules (which, of course, may be occasionally transgressed *after* they have been thoroughly mastered), even the most gifted of composers are doomed to grope and wander in the darkness of the new tonal medium, and unwittingly to join hands with, and perhaps accomplish but little more than, the veriest tyros.

The more complex the tonal material the more careful handling it requires, and the number of technical restrictions grows in the same proportion as the "freedom" of exploitation of the tonal means. It is not difficult to illustrate this by the following simple example. In the infra-diatonic system, as we know, only Dyads are admitted in the capacity of concords, whereas in the tonally increased diatonic system, Triads are already admitted in the same capacity. But this greater freedom is counterbalanced, in the (strict) diatonic system, by the prohibition of parallel Fifths, which has no place in the infra-diatonic system. So it may be surmised with reasonable certainty that new and more numerous restrictions will appear in the supra-diatonic system on account of the admission of the Hexad as a concord.

Thus it is apparent that in the process of musical evolution, the field of what is "permissible" grows in *direct* ratio (not inverse, as might be thought) to what is "not permissible," and that even in the most revolutionary art a certain boundary line must exist between these two polarities, which merely changes at different historic periods but is never completely erased. Whenever this boundary line is absent and everything becomes "permissible"—art instantly vanishes.

---

* The subject of this, historically, very natural negation of the principle of Tonality with all its inherent laws—a negation which is expressed in Atonality, as diametrically opposed to the former principle, has been developed by the author from the dialectic point of view, in a special article mentioned in the Foreword of this book and reprinted at the end of it (Addendum II).

The rules or methods in any art can be and, in fact, are changed as temporary conditions alter, but the basic laws which underlie them remain unshaken at all times. In architecture (to which music is so often compared) methods of construction are constantly changing with time, but the basic laws of physics, and especially the law of gravitation of the entire structural mass to a common center, can certainly never change. To this basic law corresponds, in music, the unalterable law of gravitation of all the tones of any "organic" scale to the common Tonic, with which is indissolubly connected another law or principle of specific division of all harmonic combinations (pertaining to this or that scale) into consonances and dissonances. And just as the neglect of the laws of physical gravitation would inevitably result in the wreck of an architectural structure, a similar neglect of the laws of intertonal gravitation results in complete looseness and amorphousness of a musical work. In both cases, we shall obtain a mere pile of building material—not the structure itself.

But if without these laws and the rules and methods based on them, neither architectural structure nor genuine "organic" musical composition can be created, then it is possible, by following entirely different methods, to give the illusion of one as well as the other. The result will be theatrical decoration, in the former instance, and "decorative" music, so much favored nowadays, in the latter. True, the distinction between "organic" and "decorative" musical compositions is not as striking as the distinction between an architectural structure and a theatrical decoration, but the nature of this distinction is identical in both cases, inasmuch as any decorative art is guided—as a rule—by principles utterly dissimilar, not to say contradistinctive, to those of an "organic" art.

The most characteristic distinction between "decorative" music (or decorative tone-painting, as it seems more appropriate to term it) and "organic" music appears to be the absence, in the former, of a fundamental and purely musical idea (a clearly expressed theme) out of which, as from a seed, the whole organically unfolds—an idea which gradually develops and, subsequently, spends itself towards the close of a given musical composition. The absence of such a basic idea automatically precludes also what is supposed to be its logical substantiation (in the musical sense), i.e. a coherent harmonic plane subordinated to certain inner and infallible laws of intertonal gravitation. As a poor substitute for thematic development we find, in decorative music, merely a series of inwardly unconnected melo-rhythmic ornaments (often in quasi-polyphonic form) and, as a surrogate for the harmonic plane, we find a series of similarly unrelated cluster-like chordal formations. The predominance of external effectiveness over inner content, quite natural under the above conditions, is another instance of the kinship between decorative music and theatrical decoration, inasmuch as the latter, dealing only with the directly visible aspect of an architectural structure, bars the most profound and essential side of architectural art, which consists in the artistic solution of the problem of space.*

From this point of view theatrical decoration is anti-architectural in the same sense as decorative tone-painting is anti-musical, which does not mean, however, that decorative principles, generally speaking, are anti-artistic and that, in particular, decorative architecture and decorative music cannot be considered as products of art. But, of course, "all fagots are not alike" and the absolute value of "organic" art differs from that of decorative art. After all, to make an appropriate wall-paper design, for instance, is also an art. Such a design may be very curious and interesting; it may be beautiful and quite artistic, in a certain sense. One can hardly feel, however, that the art of wall-paper designs, even granting its producers exceptional gifts, could ever become a *great* art, in the full meaning of the word. Likewise, it is scarcely conceivable that any decorative art, which follows all sorts of extraneous principles, could ever become a great or, what is virtually the same, a *lasting* art, in spite of the fact that it sometimes has a more immediate appeal because of its outward splendor. Decorative art is largely a matter of fashion and, as such, it is always bound to lose its attraction soon and to be constantly superseded by another fashion in the same line. We may, therefore, safely conclude that decorative art is not only ephemeral, but from its very nature and immediate aims it is not supposed and often does not even attempt to be lasting or "great."

For similar considerations, decorative music can never become *great* because following as it does chiefly extra-musical principles (be they the principles of painting or of scenic action or of anything else), it excludes from its sphere what constitutes the bone and marrow of genuine, unadulterated musical composition, viz. the development of an organic theme and its logical substantiation (appropriate harmonic plane, in the broad sense of the word). Nevertheless, by the strange irony of things, these very (negative) characteristics of decorative music readily explain to us why so many modern composers resort to it at the present time. There can hardly be any doubt that they are compelled to this choice by the impossibility of creating a genuinely organic theme and its harmonic plane within the conditions of the atonal scale ("12"). Moreover, it seems that these artificial conditions are able eventually to lead to complete hegemony of decorative tendencies in modern music. The reason is that these conditions erase the sharp distinction between "musical decorators," on the one hand, and composers striving to find—or, rather, to devise in an avowedly artificial way—some new melodic and contrapuntal rules upon the atonal basis, on the other hand, since the latter, creating but an *inadequate* image of an organic musical composition, by this very fact already approach the former, in spite of their creation

---

* The German word "Raumkunst" directly points to this exact and profound definition of architecture as the "art of space."

being stimulated by entirely different motives. It may be added that neither of these two types of modern composers is encountered in its absolutely "pure" form, and just as the musical decorators, sacrificing integrity of style for the sake of variety, quite often use the methods of the neo-contrapuntists, similarly the latter do not always shun the characteristically decorative methods which, by virtue of their frank dynamism, are able to preserve the ultra-amorphous works of these composers from completely falling to pieces.

All these circumstances, of course, are scarcely favorable for the appearance of highly significant and, still less, of really great works in modern music (how-ever sublime their underlying "literary" idea, if any, may sometimes be), although the existence of a *potentially* strong creative gift among modern com-posers is not an impossibility here and there.

Such works are hardly to be expected, even in the future, so long as com-posers have no clear conception of the basic functions of the tonal material they mentally use in the process of creation. But before any idea of these functions is possible, the latter must first have actual existence. In the meantime we know that they are positively missing in the atonal scale ("12"), since it in no way represents what we understand by a "closed" organic system but merely a mechanical aggregation of independent and inwardly isolated units of sound. Unfortunately, however, the atonal scale is so far the only one which, for techni-cal reasons, is *actually* at the disposal of modern composers and thus becomes the involuntary source of all creative evil.

It is, then, perfectly evident that from whatever side modern music is ap-proached, it shows markedly and conspicuously ripe need for a new tonal system which will lead music from the atonal blind alley in which it is floundering and will unite what, to this day, has seemed irreconcilable: tonal complexity satisfy-ing the modern way of musical thinking and firm basic principles derived from the *unchangeable* laws of our musical mind. These conditions are apparently met by the supra-diatonic scale ("12 + 7"), the introduction of which into modern musical art, therefore, becomes a problem that cannot be deferred.

This scale, which represents, practically, nothing more than a sort of propor-tionally magnified diatonic scale, will restore to modern composers those "organic" advantages of the diatonic scale which have been temporarily lost by them through their unconsidered alliance with the atonal scale ("12"). The supra-diatonic scale will give back to them, in the first place, the definitely lost *tension* of the melodic line (i.e. at bottom, the tension of musical thought) which, properly speaking, can find material embodiment only within the conditions of a tonal system which itself has a certain original and intrinsic tension, even though in the form of a plain mutual gravitation of all its component tones to each other and to a common center. This scale will enrich them with entirely new harmonic possibilities and will open to them those ample avenues of exploitation of new chordal formations—all of which is obtained in music not only through greater freedom resulting from the use of new tonal means but through strictly substantiated restrictions as well. Besides having an increased number of tones within an octave, this new scale will reduce the existing minimum interval (semitone) to a magnitude somewhat smaller than a third of a whole tone (31.6 ctn. in supra-tempered intonation), which, consequently, will form the new "semi-step." Thus, despite its seemingly "old-fashioned" principles, the supra-diatonic scale will bring about one of the most radical revolutions which has ever occurred in the realm of music. But, as atonement for such radicalism, it will be the first *constructive* revolution in modern music, placing at the disposal of modern composers a perfectly definite tonal system, logically substantiated and historically justified; a system which will not destroy but merely transform their manner of musical thinking; a system which will ultimately give them a definite conception of the functions of every one of its component tonal units, and which, therefore, will be able to guarantee a rational exploitation of the new tonal material and thereby secure the musical progress (granted, of course, the indispensable creative gift in the composer) which infallibly results from such an exploitation.

The introduction of the supra-diatonic scale will also put an end to that uncertainty which is found at times among modern composers who have become weary of existing musical anarchy and who, in their longing for the lost stability, call their brethren "back to diatonic Tonality." There is no way back, however, for composers who have inwardly sensed the new tonal plane. Psychologically, they have already departed, to a considerable extent, from the old Tonality, and, therefore, could hardly create, within its conditions, anything of real value at the present time. Their hesitations are, no doubt, but temporary ones and are bound to disappear when the new scale is actually introduced in musical art. This event, one is inclined to believe, will inspire them with new assurance and will awaken new forces for vigorous creative flight into the unknown and enticing world of supra-Tonality.

ADDENDA

ADDENDUM I

THE SUPRA-DIATONIC SCALE AS THE ORGANIC BASIS OF THE MUSIC
OF THE FUTURE *

PROBLEM OF THE RESEARCH

Whatever one's attitude toward the radical musical tendencies of to-day, and whatever the absolute artistic value of modern musical compositions may be, yet considering all the manifold historic, theoretic and acoustic data accumulated up to the present time, one can hardly doubt that those radical tendencies are signs or reflections or at least anticipations of some profound and volcanic process in musical art which will ultimately lead to the practical adoption of a new and tonally more complicated and, consequently, more subtle scale.

From the historic viewpoint such an adoption of a new scale in the future should appear in no way unexpected, since we know that our diatonic scale, and later the chromatic scale, were not established in music at one stroke either, but were preceded by less complex scales which, as a rule, have now been abandoned. It was probably due to the slow rate of replacement of various scales in the course of musical evolution that the innate laws which govern this historic process and which could thus give us a clue to the structure of the scale of the future, have not been revealed so far.

And it is ignorance of these laws coupled with scientifically undisciplined speculation that makes some modern composers, who earnestly long for increased tonal material, lean to a "short-cut" solution of this problem, namely, to a purely mechanical division of the equally tempered intervals of our present system into quarter tones or sixth tones or even smaller fractions. However, aside from the fact that such a naïve method is historically unjustified and acoustically absurd, it also proves to be, in spite of the temptation it offers, utterly uncertain and unstable. This is because, starting from the principle of a mechanical and entirely arbitrary splitting of a whole tone, there are no reasons whatever for preferring one of its possible divisions to another. Thus, for instance, quarter tones have no essential advantages over eighth tones, and the latter are in no way better or worse than sixth tones or sixteenth tones, etc.

It is, then, apparent that the problem of increasing our present tonal material within the limit of an octave requires, not a mechanical, but rather a sort of organic and, in any case, more convincing method which, being justified by historic experience, would subsequently lead to only one and not to several solutions.

Through the application of such an "organic" method, the writer's aim is to discover the objective laws to which the structural changes of scales in musico-historical evolution are subject, and with these laws as a basis, to form a new and more complex scale whose properties may explain, at least in rudimentary fashion, the most characteristic

* Reprinted by courtesy of *Pro Musica* (Issue of March-June, 1929).

creative currents and previsions in modern music. It should be remembered, however, that the expression *modern* will here invariably refer only to those musical manifestations which show a perfectly unambiguous tendency to break away from the existing diatonic system. And if a composer displays but a partial tendency of this sort (as is most often observed), then his music will be considered as modern only in that particular portion.

THE DIATONIC, INFRA-DIATONIC AND SUPRA-DIATONIC SCALES

Of all the various scales which in music preceded our present diatonic scale, the particular attention of theorists has always been attracted to the so-called pentatonic scale, whose structure may be approximately expressed by the notes C-D-F-G-A of the generally accepted tempered musical system. Some of these theorists have repeatedly advanced the hypothesis that the pentatonic scale indicated does not seem to be the exclusive musical characteristic of a given nation or group of nations or even of an entire race, but simply represents a certain stage of the musical development of mankind in general. The soundness of this hypothesis is corroborated nowadays, with ever-increasing evidence, by gradually more extensive study of the world's musical folk-lore, which step by step establishes the fact of past or present use of the pentatonic scale in almost every country of the globe.

The above indicated structure of the pentatonic scale, everywhere identical with the exception of the basically immaterial "modal" changes, does not represent, however, its final and complete form, since in some localities where this scale is most firmly established, there has frequently been observed a tendency to extend its tonal material, and consequently its musical resources, by the sporadic application of two additional notes, E and B. But from this it must not be hastily inferred that such a tonal extension inevitably transforms the pentatonic scale into the diatonic scale, for in those recorded instances where the application of the two additional degrees (E and B) takes place, their functions differ profoundly from the functions of the *regular* degrees (C-D-F-G-A) of the pentatonic scale. In contradistinction to these regular degrees, the notes E and B merely play the rôle of *auxiliary* degrees of the pentatonic scale, serving as melodic embellishments, and they can always be omitted at will without detriment to the melody itself.

In other words, the functions of these two auxiliary degrees, interpolated between the five regular degrees of the pentatonic scale, are similar to the functions of the five chromatic (likewise "auxiliary") degrees interpolated between the seven regular degrees of our diatonic scale. And just as the latter is not transformed into an independent twelve-tone scale as long as the functions of its diatonic and chromatic degrees have the familiar demarcations, so the pentatonic scale is not necessarily transformed into an independent seven-tone scale as long as the functions of its regular and auxiliary degrees have similar demarcations.

This characteristic co-existence of two functionally different groups of degrees in the diatonic as well as in the pentatonic scale suggestively disposes one's mind to recognize a certain similarity in the structural plan of these two scales. Such a point of view is further supported by many other conforming features and especially by the little-known fact that in Siamese musical practice the five regular degrees of the pentatonic scale jointly with its two auxiliary degrees, *while strictly retaining their functional distinctions,* are incorporated in one closed equally tempered system, thus forming a set of seven equidistant tones within an octave. Which is similar to our Occidental scale whose seven diatonic and five chromatic degrees are jointly incorporated in a larger but likewise closed equally tempered system forming a set of twelve equidistant tones within an octave.

In this way, considering the similar qualitative characteristics and the dissimilar quantitative constitution of the two scales in question, we may regard the pentatonic scale as a smaller diatonic scale, or rather as a diatonic scale of a "lower order," and we shall therefore term it henceforth the *infra-diatonic scale.* In those instances where it will be desirable to indicate or to emphasize the complete form of this scale, combining its two functionally distinguished, although in some way organically connected groups of degrees, we shall designate it, or supplement its name, by the formula "5 + 2". Accordingly, the diatonic scale will be designated, or its name supplemented, under similar circumstances, by the formula "7 + 5."

The existence in the musical history of mankind of two scales differing quantitatively in their tonal complexity, and at the same time bearing a number of similar structural features, substantiates the forecast advanced above regarding the possible and probable adoption in the future of a new and still more complicated scale, as far as its quantitative constitution is concerned, and yet—we may now add—structurally similar to the former. Such a possibility will subsequently become more plausible, especially when further examination of the diatonic and infra-diatonic scales discloses that besides their many-sided similarity there also exists a quite definite interrelation between the number and arrangement of their regular and auxiliary degrees—an interrelation which contains latently a leading clue to the construction of the new scale with the same characteristic opposition of its two functionally distinguished groups of degrees. This new scale, bearing the same relation to the diatonic scale ("7 + 5") as the latter does to the infra-diatonic scale ("5 + 2") will obviously represent a sort of diatonic scale of a "higher order," and will be, therefore, termed henceforth the *supra-diatonic scale.*

Judging from numerous and significant characteristics of the supra-diatonic scale constructed in this manner, it is the very next one that lies in the path of continuous musical evolution, and which, following infallible historic laws, draws slowly and gradually nearer to us, eventually to replace the diatonic scale.

Moreover, this scale, as we shall see, is the one which, despite its present insufficiently appealing characteristics, is subconsciously anticipated by many modern composers in the course of their creation, although this scale naturally finds but a limited application and very inadequate representation in their compositions.

Two of the most essential and at present least attractive characteristics of the supra-diatonic scale are—by virtue of its structural similarity with the two antecedent scales—the clearly expressed mode and the tonality which, of course, in accordance with the increased complexity of the new scale acquire here a somewhat altered sense and will therefore be termed henceforth *supra-mode* and *supra-tonality,* respectively. These two notions are radically opposed to the now predominant principle of atonality, which signifies no more than a transitory stage in the course of replacement of the old diatonic scale by the new supra-diatonic one. Such an intermediate stage is quite unavoidable and perfectly explainable, not only in this particular instance but in any other similar replacement of some artificially closed musical system (due to equal temperament) by another and more complicated musical system, as will be later shown in the proper place.

RELATIVITY OF SOME STABILIZED MUSICAL NOTIONS

One of the most perplexing points encountered by the writer was the selection and appropriate application of musical terms the meaning of which, hitherto regarded as sufficiently stable, becomes very elastic here because of the unconventional treatment of the subject, and particularly the "relative" views on the notions of diatonicism and chromaticism. Such a flexibility or relativity of musical notions is apt to mislead the reader, especially when they have to be applied in association with some definite acoustic magnitudes (intervals). The latter, as is known, have no independent nomenclature in music and are expressed either by mathematical ratios or—in the few feasible instances—by numerical denotation of the various degrees of the diatonic scale in which some of all the generally conceivable intervals may be found.

To borrow these denotations (e.g. Prime, Second, Third, etc.) for the purpose of terming certain tonal relations is, of course, quite admissible but only as long as they always convey the very same acoustic meaning, i.e. as long as every one of these numerical denotations invariably expresses some definite and constant interval. Here, however, we are dealing for the first time with scales in which, owing to the comparatively increased or decreased number of their "regular" degrees, the numerical denotation of the latter will have, in each case, its own acoustic meaning, incompatible with others. Thus, for instance, the interval formed by the fifth regular degree of the infra-diatonic scale and its Tonic (C-A), i.e. the interval which by etymological determination is a "Fifth" of this scale, will be much wider than the "Fifth" of the diatonic scale (C-G), their difference being exactly a whole tone (G-A).

Hence it is not difficult to foresee that the "relativity" will likewise involve the rest of the numerical denotations of the degrees of all the three scales. Moreover, it will also extend to many other musical notions which, being directly connected with the similar structure of these scales and having in each case a musically similar although acoustically different meaning, should, in consequence, be identically termed. Such are, besides intervals, the notions of mode, tonality, intonation, diatonic succession, chromatic alteration, etc. each of which loses here its absolute stability and acquires a relative meaning.

To avoid inextricable confusion or, to say the least, continual explanations, I have found it expedient to introduce certain additional terminological formations, using exclusively for that purpose the, to the reader, already familiar prefixes "infra" and "supra" as direct indications that a given term refers to one or the other scale. For instance, the usual nomenclature of the regular degrees for which, in the diatonic scale, a consecutive numerical series is accepted, viz. Prime, Second, Third, etc., will become, in the infra-diatonic scale, the following series: infra-Prime, infra-Second, infra-Third, etc., and in the supra-diatonic scale: supra-Prime, supra-Second, supra-Third, etc. Similar transformations, when necessary, will be made in other terms.

This expanded terminology not only will avert the confusion that threatens to overtake musical notions, but will also permit, as heretofore, an unobstructed application of the customary acoustic terms, borrowed from the numerical denotations of the various degrees of the diatonic scale, even in those instances where the argumentation touches upon something having no direct connection with this scale at all.

Before entering into the actual inquiry of the infra-diatonic and supra-diatonic musical systems, I think it necessary to add that all the measurements and calculations regarding the dimensions of various intervals are given here in terms of the new *decimal system* which I have already had an opportunity to submit and to describe in detail (*Pro Musica*, March, 1928). This system assumes an equally tempered tone as a basic measuring unit which is divided, as in the metric system, into tenths, hundredths and thousandths parts, termed *decitones* (dtn.), *centitones* (ctn.) and *millitones* (mtn.), respectively. The calculations in centitones are, as a rule, the most practical and are exclusively used here.

THE INFRA-DIATONIC SYSTEM

The new viewpoint adopted above with reference to the pentatonic scale for the first time regarded here as an infra-diatonic scale (i.e. the diatonic scale of a lower order), is, strictly speaking, the main premise on which rests the solution of the fundamental problem of this work. Its substantiation, therefore, calls for a maximum of thoroughness, and it must be carried through not only as regards theoretic possibility but also as regards the practical viability of an independent infra-diatonic musical system.

Looking for authentic material in order to form a background for this new viewpoint, I naturally came across the music and theoretic speculations of the Far-East, particularly China, as almost the sole source capable of revealing, at least in part, the true nature of the pentatonic scale.

A thorough investigation of this material proved *firstly*, that all the complexity and tremendous intricacy of Chinese musical theory is chiefly the natural result of their numerous and repeated attempts to build up a musical system without the aid of equal temperament (with which, by the way, they have long been familiar) and *secondly*, that all their actual musical creation has never gone beyond the boundaries of the pentatonic scale which at different historical periods was merely either supplemented by the two auxiliary degrees (E and B) or was freed of them for various reasons. It is, however, only the latter point to which the reader's attention is particularly drawn here, namely, that the two auxiliary degrees have *never* been used by the Chinese on a par with the five regular degrees of the pentatonic scale and that, consequently, there has *never* existed in their music (even theoretically) a heptatonic scale in the sense of an independent tonal basis containing seven "regular" scale-degrees.

That the structure of the infra-diatonic scale ("5 + 2") has some profound and subconscious root in the human mind in the comparatively primitive stage of its musical development, can hardly be disputed. This opinion is supported, besides other considerations, by the fact that Far-Eastern music is not the only one in which the functions of the five regular and two auxiliary degrees of the infra-diatonic scale are rigidly distinguished. The very same distinction is found in innumerable ancient songs of the

Celtic nations (especially those of the Irish and Scotch) who also avail themselves of the indicated complete form of the infra-diatonic scale ("5 + 2") established in their music outside of any connection with the distant countries of the Orient.

Properly speaking, however, neither the Celtic nor even the Far-Eastern nations ever possessed a correctly evolved theory of music which would aid them in the exploitation of the intrinsic resources of the infra-diatonic scale. The ancient Celts left no written records in this field, and very remote suggestions of their primitive musical rules are found only in indirect sources. As for the Far Eastern peoples, in spite of all the complexity of their musical theory, one only finds a small amount of semi-embryonic material scattered here and there that bears any reference to the nature of the infra-diatonic scale and its inherent harmony. The logical development of what is potentially involved in this material is the subject of this chapter.

To facilitate an understanding of the following discussion, I shall preface it with a clear keyboard illustration of the infra-diatonic scale, the latter's five regular degrees being therein represented by white keys and its two auxiliary degrees by black keys.

EXAMPLE 1:

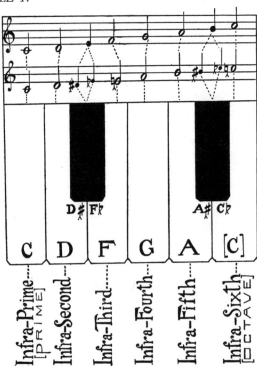

This drawing requires explanation. First of all it must be borne in mind that the infra-diatonic scale is shown here in the Siamese version already mentioned, i.e. in the equally tempered intonation which, of course, does not acoustically coincide with the equally tempered intonation of the diatonic scale (since the octave is divided into seven equal portions in the former case and into twelve equal portions in the latter) and which, therefore, will hereafter be termed, for the sake of distinguishing it, *infra-tempered intonation*. This Siamese version, preserving the essential characteristics of the infra-diatonic scale, will at the same time greatly simplify its description.

Affixing the new numerical terms (infra-Prime, infra-Second, etc.) to the regular degrees of this scale, I have retained, however, for practical reasons, their conventional literal denotations (C-D-F-G-A) borrowed from the diatonic system, this being something of a departure from their more accurate alphabetical order. As to the two auxiliary degrees of the infra-diatonic scale, for which the two letters E and B have been used up to this point, having no independent significance in this scale they should no longer be independently denoted. Similarly to the chromatic degrees of the diatonic scale, these two auxiliary degrees therefore borrow their literal denotations from their adjacent regular degrees, to which one of the two signs of alterations is correspondingly added. For the sake of distinction these two signs will be termed here *infra-sharp* and *infra-flat*, their graphic form being slightly modified as compared with the familiar chromatic accidentals of the scale "7 + 5," as will be easily noticed from the above illustration.

The infra-sharp and infra-flat respectively transpose the regular degrees of the infra-diatonic scale a half step higher or lower. However, since by *half step* is implied here merely a minimum interval in every scale, it is apparent that the actual dimension of a half step is not a constant quantity but is expanded or contracted depending on the general number of the minimum intervals in a given scale. Any pair of adjacent half steps forms one *whole step* which for the same reason will again be accoustically different in scales of dissimilar complexity.

Here is the very point from which the relativity of these two notions ensues. A *half step* and a *whole step* coincide with the notions of half tone and whole tone only in the diatonic scale, but have an entirely different acoustic meaning in the infra-diatonic scale, where they are of a greater dimension than a half tone and a whole tone, as well as in the supra-diatonic scale where, for obvious reasons, they must be of a smaller dimension, as will be seen later.

The infra-tempered intonation equalizes all the half steps as well as all the whole steps of the scale "5 + 2" and therefore also actually identifies, in every instance, an infra-sharp with an infra-flat respectively derived by raising and lowering the two neighboring regular degrees, as indicated in front of every black key which serves for both those chromatic alterations. It is understood that the auxiliary degrees of the scale "5 + 2" which are represented by the two black keys could never fill this twofold function in any other intonation but the infra-tempered one; and in this connection we again find a similarity between them and the auxiliary degrees of the scale "7 + 5" which only in the tempered intonation may likewise be used either as sharps or flats.

The nature of the *infra-tempered intonation* will be visually elucidated by the following diagram in which it is plotted with the lower set of solid lines exactly corresponding to the present-day Siamese scale ("5 + 2"). In this diagram the upper set of solid lines shows the *natural intonation* of the infra-diatonic scale ("5 + 2") as now used in

Chinese musical practice; the dotted lines indicating the equally tempered intonation
of the diatonic scale are given here for the sake of comparison:

EXAMPLE 2:

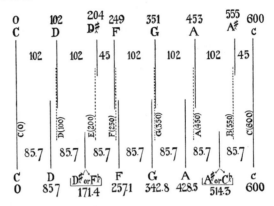

It appears from this diagram that the familiar series of notes of the diatonic scale
placed at the top of the preceding keyboard illustration expresses but approximately
the natural intonation of the scale "5 + 2" and very inaccurately its infra-tempered
intonation. Furthermore it should be noted that the five-line stave is also *formally*
incorrect for the notation of the infra-diatonic scale, since the latter's two auxiliary
degrees are expressed in it by independent notes (E and B), thus conflicting with the
principle of their "derivation" from the regular degrees.

The correct notation of this scale would then obviously call for an abbreviated
stave, eliminating the number of lines which, in the diatonic five-line system, is used
for notes E and B. Their approximate equivalents, (D—infra-sharp—F—infra-flat and
A—infra-sharp—C—infra-flat) indicating but the infra-chromatic alterations of the
regular degrees, should be placed on the same lines (or between the same lines) as the
latter.

It is not difficult to figure out that according to this principle our five-line stave
should be replaced by a three-line stave in which two full octaves are evenly distributed
and, incidentally, the two terminal C's (c′ and c‴) are retained in their notation.

In accordance with these considerations the correct three-line notation of the infra-
diatonic scale is placed just above its keyboard illustration and parallel to the five-line
stave which is added there merely for elucidation.

Proceeding with our examination of the same keyboard illustration we find that the
series of the regular degrees (white keys) of the infra-diatonic scale forms a chain of
definitely arranged whole steps and half steps, reminding one of a more complex and, of
course, differently arranged chain of whole steps and half steps of the diatonic scale.
And inasmuch as the principle of this characteristic arrangement of intervals bears the
name of *mode* in the diatonic scale, it would be appropriate to attach to this principle
the name of *infra-mode* in reference to the infra-diatonic scale.

In Far Eastern as well as in Celtic music one can easily find most obvious proofs of application of various infra-modes (in the appellative sense of the word). The latter, in common with the diatonic modes, are formed on the various regular degrees of their corresponding infra-diatonic scale and consequently differ from each other merely by the formula of arrangement of the very same number of whole steps and half steps. Hence, assuming in turn each of the five regular degrees of the infra-diatonic scale as the Tonic, we shall obtain five infra-modes differing in construction as follows (the various infra-modes will be named after the two terminal notes that occur when the former are constructed exclusively upon the "white keys"):

EXAMPLE 3:

Every one of these infra-modes may be freely transposed into different keys of the infra-diatonic scale, and here is where the advantage of the Siamese equal temperament system over the natural but cumbersome system of the Chinese is particularly evident. Contrarily to the latter all the seven degrees of the Siamese infra-tempered scale ("5 + 2") permit its unobstructed transposition into seven different keys absolutely identical in structure, just as all the twelve degrees of the Western tempered scale ("7 + 5") easily permit its transposition into twelve different keys. And as these twelve keys of the diatonic scale, being consecutively arranged by Fifths, form a complete and closed system, likewise the seven keys of the infra-diatonic scale (without counting, of course, the enharmonically coinciding keys) form a complete and closed system, being consecutively arranged by Fifths in the following order:

EXAMPLE 4:

I have purposely left out in this example the elucidating five-line notation, as with the latter the above series of infra-tempered keys would be given an utterly inadequate acoustic representation.

The definition of intervals of the infra-diatonic scale—to which our discussion now turns—is somewhat facilitated by the commonly established and repeatedly verified fact that perfect Fourths (infra-Thirds) and their inversions (infra-Fourths) are, aside from the Primes and the Octaves, the only consonances recognized as such by an ear well accustomed to the structure of this scale. And inasmuch as besides the intervals enumerated there are left but two more groups—infra-Seconds and infra-Fifths—each of which is the inversion of the other, it is evident that these very groups represent the dissonant intervals of the infra-diatonic scale.

In addition, one diminished and one augmented interval, found in the above mentioned consonant groups and respectively termed diminished infra-Third and augmented infra-Fourth, must likewise be considered as dissonances, their musical significance being relatively similar to those dissonances of the diatonic scale which are found in it under the names of augmented Fourth and diminished Fifth.

No subdivision of perfect and imperfect consonances exists in the intervals of the infra-diatonic scale; therefore the denomination "perfect" will be attached to all of the consonances without exception. There are found, however, two kinds of dissonant intervals, differing in dimension, within every group which contains them. These intervals will be termed "major" and "minor," similarly to the dissonances of the diatonic scale.

The following table in which all the intervals of the infra-diatonic scale are systematically represented will convey a clear idea of their nature:

EXAMPLE 5:

Some of the consonant intervals of the diatonic scale (major and minor Thirds and their inversions) being considered as dissonances by nations who avail themselves of the infra-diatonic scale in their musical practice, the earlier noted principle of "relativity" must be made to extend also to the notions of consonance and dissonance. As a matter of fact there is nothing new in such an attitude towards these notions as far as their general and well-known unstableness is concerned. But this attitude often leads to the grave misconception that the transformation of dissonances into consonances, in the course of musical development, gradually annihilates the very principle of their opposition. Needless to say, a mere comparison of the above table of infra-diatonic intervals with the familiar table of diatonic intervals refutes this, as with the transformation mentioned it may be observed that a quantitative increase of the consonances in no way causes a decrease of the dissonances which, similarly to the former, are subjected to their own structural evolution. Thus, it would be plausible to conjecture that the line between consonances and dissonances is *never erased,* even as the complexity of the tonal systems grows, but is only *transferred* in conformity with the specific grouping of intervals in every system applied.

As regards the harmony of the infra-diatonic scale—our next and, by the way, totally unexplored subject to be touched upon—I shall confine myself here to two statements, the final result of my investigation:

1. The musical practice of the nations availing themselves of the infra-diatonic scale as well as the very structure of the latter lead us to the conviction that the common (consonant) chord of this scale is not a *Triad,* as in the diatonic scale, but a *Dyad,* this term being applied here to a harmonic combination of two notes an infra-Third apart. Hence it evidently follows that a series of Dyads constructed on all the regular degrees of the infra-diatonic scale will absolutely coincide with the series of infra-Thirds represented above (Example 5) in their proper group. Of these intervals the four perfect infra-Thirds are identical in structure with the consonant Dyads, and one diminished infra-Third is identical with the diminished (dissonant) Dyad which relatively corresponds, in its musical significance, to the diminished Triad of the diatonic scale.

2. Conformably to these common chords are also formed, by infra-Thirds, the more complicated dissonant chords of the infra-diatonic scale, some suggestive traces of which, again, are found in the Chinese sources referred to above. So in the field of chord formations we come across an additional sign of similarity between the diatonic and infra-diatonic musical systems. Indeed, as the Third fills the function of a formative unit with reference to the chords of the former of these systems, likewise the infra-Third fills an analogous function with reference to the chords of the latter. And although these two intervals are acoustically incongruent, yet in both instances they invariably cover the space occupied by *three* contiguous regular degrees of their respective scales. Hence, it may easily be conjectured that the chords of these scales having no affinity in their tonal constitution, but being constructed by Thirds in one instance and by infra-Thirds in the other, are similar in their *formal* structure.

Starting from these two statements I have built up a system of entirely independent infra-diatonic harmony which permits Chinese, Celtic and other "pentatonic" tunes to be harmonized within the tonal possibilities of their underlying infra-diatonic scale. This preserves the psychological unity between Harmony and Melody which is absent in all existing harmonizations of the kind of tunes referred to.

As an instance of the advantage of the new "unigenous" method of harmonization over the "mixed" method which adapts diatonic harmony to infra-diatonic (pentatonic) tunes, I offer for judgment a ready-made practical result of the new principle as applied to one of the most popular Chinese tunes:

EXAMPLE 6:

The unity between harmony and melody will be particularly evident in this example when actually compared with some "diatonic" harmonizations of the same tune which will be easily found in various collections of Oriental folk songs.

FORMATION OF THE SUPRA-DIATONIC SCALE

FORMATION OF THE SUPRA-DIATONIC SCALE

The many-sided similarity between the infra-diatonic and diatonic scales, as disclosed above, already inspires a certain preliminary conviction that the supra-diatonic scale being proportionately complicated in conformity with an analogous principle of construction, will display those common characteristics which will permit us to consider it as an "organic" scale to the same extent as the two former.

The common constructive schema to which the formation of the infra-diatonic and the diatonic scales may be reduced is a series of consecutively arranged natural Fifths. The very nature of these scales is such that in the course of their formation, according to this schema, first the group of their regular degrees is generated in every instance— and only after that the group of their respective auxiliary degrees, as shown by these two rows of notes:

1. Series of natural Fifths which forms the Infra-diatonic scale ("5 + 2")

F-C-G-D-A-E-B

Section which forms the   Section which forms the
five regular degrees   two auxiliary degrees

2. Series of natural Fifths which forms the diatonic scale ("7 + 5")

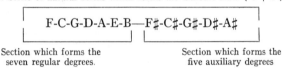

F-C-G-D-A-E-B—F♯-C♯-G♯-D♯-A♯

Section which forms the   Section which forms the
seven regular degrees.   five auxiliary degrees

It was not difficult, of course, to find these two series of natural Fifths in regard to the infra-diatonic and diatonic scales, since we knew *beforehand* the number and arrangement of their component regular and auxiliary degrees within an octave. But obviously the same cannot be said with regard to the supra-diatonic scale, the determination of its tonal constitution being our very next problem.

This problem would be automatically solved, however, should we succeed in finding the series of natural Fifths which corresponds to the supra-diatonic scale, by some other way. Of this new series of Fifths now sought we know nothing, save the fact that by virtue of its predetermined similarity with the two preceding series it has to produce in analogous sequence, first all the regular degrees of the new scale and then all its auxiliary degrees. But how find the *number* of degrees in every one of these groups?

The answer to this pivotal question of our problem is given by the quite definite interrelation between the sections of the two above series of natural Fifths which form different groups of degrees of the infra-diatonic and diatonic scales. This interrelation is twofold and may be expressed as follows:

1. The number and arrangement of tones (by Fifths) comprised in the section which forms the group of regular degrees of the infra-diatonic scale is identical with the number and arrangement of tones comprised in the section which forms the group of auxiliary degrees of the diatonic scale (the difference in the absolute pitch of these two sets of tones is at present immaterial).

2. The general number and arrangement of tones of the entire series of natural Fifths which forms the infra-diatonic scale ("5 + 2") is identical with the number and arrangement of tones comprised in the section which forms but one group of regular degrees of the diatonic scale.

Inasmuch as it is at the core of this very interrelation that lies the root of all those characteristics of both scales that make so many of their aspects similar, notwithstanding their different tonal constitution, it is apparent that the principle of analogous interrelation used for the formation of the new scale will solve the above problem. In order to apply this principle to such a formation it would be necessary to adopt the complete series of natural Fifths which forms the scale "7 + 5" as a basis for the group of regular degrees of the supra-diatonic scale and then to adopt the initial section of this series which forms the group of regular degrees of the scale "7 + 5" as a pattern for that new section of natural Fifths which is destined to constitute the group of auxiliary degrees of the supra-diatonic scale. This entire operation is shown in the following schema:

Series of natural Fifths which forms the Supra-diatonic scale ("12 + 7")

F-C-G-D-A-E-B-F♯-C♯-G♯-D♯-A♯-E♯-B♯-F♯♯-C♯♯-G♯♯-D♯♯-A♯♯

| Section which forms the twelve regular degrees. | Section which forms the seven auxiliary degrees |

This extended series of natural Fifths does not yet give, however, a lucid idea of the acoustical structure of the supra-diatonic scale. First and foremost it should be pointed out that the very possibility of such an extension is rather foreign to the average musical mind accustomed at present to think of all tonal relations in their equally tempered form. For instance, the section of the above series which forms the seven auxiliary degrees (E♯—B♯—F♯♯—C♯♯—G♯♯—D♯♯—A♯♯) of the supra-diatonic scale will impress the average musician as being no more than an exact duplicate of some regular degrees (F-C-G-D-A-E-B) of the same scale which, of course, is not actually the case.

Furthermore, somewhat confusing may appear the exclusive application of the literal designations of the *diatonic scale* ("7 + 5") in all three series of natural Fifths given above. As a result, the group of regular degrees of the supra-diatonic scale (to cite but one instance) contains a few chromatically altered notes; this, as we know, conflicting with the very notion of a *regular* degree. These designations, however, are used here simply as being more familiar and, consequently, at present more advantageous (in spite of their inadequacy) for a general comprehension of the subject. The necessary substitutions of independent and new letters for the temporarily altered notes are given further on.

Finally, it may be added that if one could at once imagine how the whole series of natural Fifths of the supra-diatonic scale will be arranged when comprised within the compass of an octave, even then one would not have a *full* conception of the actual structure of this scale. This is because the Pythagorean intonation which results from the construction of the supra-diatonic scale by natural Fifths deviates too perceptibly from the just (i.e. normal) intonation of the same scale, as will be observed later.

Thus the functions of the Pythagorean intonation are confined here solely to the general determination of the number and relative position of the regular and auxiliary degrees of the supra-diatonic scale ("12 + 7") which only *after* this determination may be "retuned," as necessary, either to its just intonation or to its equally tempered intonation. Of these two intonations the latter (which I shall name with reference to the new scale *supra-tempered intonation*) would be the most suitable for practical purposes by reason of its simplicity. Requiring a certain acoustic compromise, the supra-tempered intonation will yield us, in return, the greatest advantages, especially in modulation, preserving at the same time the specific characteristics of the supra-diatonic scale.

The nature of the supra-tempered intonation, as well as of the Pythagorean intonation referring to the same scale, will be properly understood below with the aid of parallel calculations and diagrams. However, the interrelation between all three scales, already pointed out, obliges us to a preliminary and analogous demonstration of the two relatively similar intonations in regard to the diatonic and infra-diatonic scales. We shall immediately enter upon this demonstration, starting with the diatonic scale ("7 + 5") as the most familiar to us.

Should we give the commonly known circle of Fifths numbers expressing the dimension of every Fifth (350 ctn.) and then add up all these numbers, subtracting an octave (600 ctn.) from the total each time it exceeds the latter quantity, we would obtain a drawing represented on the left of the following example, the inner numbers indicating the exact position of all twelve degrees of the equally tempered scale ("7 + 5") within the compass of an octave:

EXAMPLE 7:

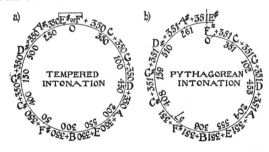

The drawing on the right of this example differs from the "circle" near it in that its outer numbers express the dimension of *natural* Fifths (351 ctn.) which being added up in the same manner will give a surplus of 12 ctn. (the "Pythagorean comma"), preventing the terminal points E♯ and F from contacting.

Inasmuch as in the latter case we dealt exclusively with natural intervals, it may be rightly inferred that a "circle" of Fifths does not exist in the nature of sounds and that only artificial intervention (Temperament) which evenly flattens every one of the twelve natural Fifths $\frac{1}{12}$ of the indicated Pythagorean comma, i.e., 1 ctn. can lead to contact of the terminal points E♯ and F, and to equality of all the tempered Fifths thus produced.

A similar artificial operation may be effected with the scale "5 + 2," with the sole difference that the flattening of its generating natural Fifths will be comparatively greater, *first,* because their general number is smaller (seven instead of twelve) and *secondly* because the surplus which, in this instance, prevents the terminal points (F♯ and F) of the corresponding series of Fifths from contacting, considerably exceeds the Pythagorean comma, reaching the number of 57 ctn. The similar and equal flattening of every one of the seven natural Fifths by $\frac{1}{7}$ of the indicated surplus (I shall name this surplus of 57 ct. *infra-comma*) i.e. by 8.14 ctn. will make the dimension of an infra-tempered Fifth 342.86 ctn. This is illustrated by the two following drawings (*a* and *b*) executed similarly to the preceding ones and showing respectively the position of all seven degrees of the scale "5 + 2" in its infra-tempered and Pythagorean intonations:

EXAMPLE 8:

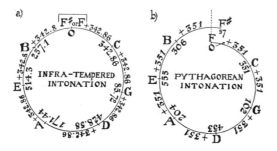

Arranging the inner numbers of every one of these drawings in progressive order and graphically representing the intervals formed by them, we shall obtain a comparative diagram of the Siamese and the Chinese scale as represented above (Ex. 2) although in a different infra-mode ("F-f" instead of "C-c").

The direct inference from the above exposition is that the principle of temperament applied in connection with the scales "7 + 5" and "5 + 2" automatically divides an octave into twelve and seven equal parts respectively. Hence it follows that the tempered and infra-tempered form of these two scales could be theoretically obtained not only by the method of flattening the natural Fifths but also by the method of directly dividing an octave into the general number of its component degrees. But while the former method only requires knowledge of the surplus between the two terminal points of the corresponding series of natural Fifths, the latter method presupposes knowledge of the relative position (in any non-tempered intonation) of the regular and auxiliary degrees of the scale subjected to temperament.

Both these methods can also be applied, under similar conditions, to the supra-diatonic scale ("12 + 7") but since the relative position of its regular and auxiliary degrees is so far unknown, it is evident that we shall have to resort to the "flattening-the-Fifths" method in order to obtain the supra-tempered form of this scale. The two following drawings executed similarly to the preceding ones bear witness to the fact that the surplus between the terminal points of the series of nineteen natural Fifths equals 69 ctn. (it may be named *supra-comma*) and that flattening every Fifth $\frac{1}{19}$ of this surplus brings the dimension of a supra-tempered Fifth to 347.4 ctn.

EXAMPLE 9:

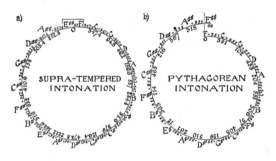

Should we arrange the inner numbers of every one of these drawings in progressive order and graphically represent the intervals they form, we shall obtain a comparative diagram of the Pythagorean and supra-tempered intonation of the scale "12 + 7," but, unlike the preceding scales, in two different supra-modes. The identical supra-modes would be obtained, in this instance, only by the "dividing-the-octave" method of temperament, which is now easily applied since the relative position of the regular and auxiliary degrees of the new scale in its Pythagorean intonation is already known. In the following diagram (Ex. 10) the result of dividing the octave into nineteen equal parts is represented by the lower solid lines, while the result of the equal flattening of the natural Fifths is represented by the upper solid lines. The Pythagorean intonation of the same supra-diatonic scale is represented by the middle row of dotted lines.

Two different supra-modes resulting from the two different methods of temperament of the scale "12 + 7" are, of course, both equally correct, for the distinction between them does not presuppose an actual change in structure of the supra-diatonic scale on which they rest.

It is unnecessary to dwell here on the purely acoustical side of the earlier noted interrelation between the different groups of degrees of the three scales discussed —an interrelation which, being totally preserved in the Pythagorean intonation when all

EXAMPLE 10:

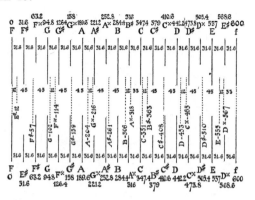

three series of natural Fifths are comprised within the compass of an octave, shows certain acoustic deviations when even one of these scales becomes equally tempered. I only think it worth while to remark, in this connection, that the comparative insignificance of those acoustic deviations in the equally tempered scale "7 + 5" is the reason for the generally known possibility of performing without perceptible error in intonation, any typical infra-diatonic melody (Chinese, Scotch, etc.) on the five black keys of our tempered pianoforte. With a somewhat more perceptible error in intonation one could also perform, starting from the interrelation referred to, any typical diatonic melody on the seven black keys of the future supra-tempered pianoforte. But under the conditions of Pythagorean intonation all the melodies would remain absolutely unaltered in their acoustic structure and would display no deviations whatever when performed on the "black keys" of a more complex pianoforte, in each instance.

Similar phenomena would also take place should still more complicated scales (to which theoretically there is no limit) be constructed in conformity with the earlier established principle. As in the three scales demonstrated above, the correlated groups of degrees of all subsequently constructed scales would coincide, as regards their acoustic structure, in the Pythagorean intonation and would show some acoustic deviation when equally tempered.

From this angle the infra-diatonic, diatonic and supra-diatonic scales may be regarded as three consecutive links in one common and theoretically infinite chain of "organic" scales, which gradually become more complex in tonal constitution and proportionately more subtle from the point of view of their minimum intervals. The concatenation of these links is due to the simple fact that every one of their corresponding series of natural Fifths actually represents a mere section of the subsequent series which, in turn, comprises all the preceding series and may be regarded as their natural extension. This mutual linking of quantitatively different series of natural Fifths is certainly preserved when comprised within an octave, and in the latter case may be demonstrated in the form of a common and continuous spiral which, combining their three corresponding representations (Ex. 7b, 8b, 9b) leaves them acoustically undisturbed, as shown in the following illustration:

EXAMPLE 11:

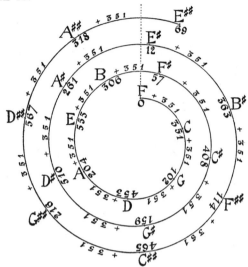

Hence it follows that the formation of these as well as all subsequent "organic" scales in the Pythagorean intonation only calls for a continuation, each time, of their uniting spiral with the preservation, of course, of their common principle of division of all scale-tones into regular and auxiliary degrees. On the other hand, the formation of the same scales in incompatible infra-tempered, tempered, supra-tempered, etc. intonations, requires each time a construction of separate and closed circles, every one of which acoustically excludes all the rest:

EXAMPLE 12:

Thus, if equal temperament brings dissimilar acoustic results when applied to different scales, and if, consequently, the formation of every scale in this artificial form predetermines a break with the preceding scale, then it is evident that by attempting to remain on the acoustic plane of one of the above "circles" while intending to build up a new and more complex scale (i.e. attempting to avoid the necessary break), one can never succeed in producing a real "organic" formation of the latter. Any efforts to increase, under these limiting conditions, the tonal material of the circles in question, i.e. practically the scales they represent, would inevitably result in a purely mechanical insertion therein of some number of new tones having no organic connection whatever with the initial series of tones.

It is hardly necessary, I think, to give proofs to the effect that such a mechanical complication (should it ever be adopted) would turn out to be, from the viewpoint of musical evolution, totally unjustified and, in practical application, nonsensical. Musical art would gain nothing, or at best, almost nothing, from this sort of tonal complication, for no scale can ever be creatively used in music without marked and mutual coherence of its component elements.

And yet this mechanical complication is the very direction to which turn the efforts of those modern theorists who, starting from the inviolability of the equally tempered intonation of the scale "7 + 5," propose to supply it with quarter tones or sixth tones, etc., as if the whole problem merely consisted in determining the acuteness of the musical ear in regard to various "microtonic" subdivisions. These theorists chiefly lose sight of the fact that the equally tempered intonation of the scale "7 + 5" can be in no way regarded as an infallible acoustic principle by which one must be guided for all possible future complications in our tonal system. This artificial intonation represents no more than one specific instance of adjustment of one of the scales to practical use and therefore only fits the scale for which it is introduced. To adopt this intonation as a starting point for all subsequent tonal complications is to convert a particular instance into a general rule, i.e. consciously to admit an error which, in practice, would soon crop out with fatal certainty in the way of very little promising artistic results.

THE SUPRA-DIATONIC SYSTEM

Having explained the formation of the supra-diatonic scale ("12 + 7") let us now analyze all its specific characteristics and, finally, inquire to what extent we believe it may be adopted in musical art, because of these characteristics, as an historically legitimate successor of the diatonic scale ("7 + 5").

For the sake of clarity I shall precede the examination of the supra-diatonic scale ("12 + 7") by a keyboard illustration (as was done before for the infra-diatonic scale) representing its twelve regular and seven auxiliary degrees by the same number of white and black keys respectively. [See Ex. 13 on the following page.]

In the first place it should be noted that this new scale is shown here in a different supra-mode ("C-c") as compared with those of its previous representations. This change, immaterial as far as the basic structure of the supra-diatonic scale is concerned, will greatly facilitate our further discussion.

EXAMPLE 13:

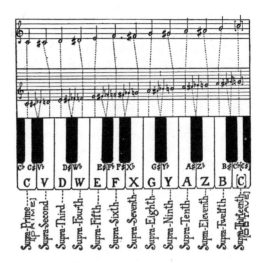

One more substitution observed in the above illustration concerns the names of the five newly introduced (in comparison with the diatonic scale) regular degrees which up to this point have been designated by the chromatically altered notes (C♯, D♯, F♯, G♯, A♯) of the scale "7 + 5." In the new scale they are no longer "derivatives" or auxiliary degrees, as in the diatonic scale, and therefore should be symbolized on a par with the seven other regular degrees of the supra-diatonic scale by means of independent denotations. The last five letters of the alphabet are used here for that purpose, namely: V (instead of C♯), W (instead of D♯), X (instead of F♯), Y (instead of G♯) and Z (instead of A♯).

The denotations of the seven auxiliary degrees of the supra-diatonic scale, for which we have used heretofore some other chromatically altered notes (B♯, C♯♯, D♯♯, E♯, F♯♯, G♯♯, A♯♯) of the scale "7 + 5," should be replaced by new supra-chromatically altered notes generated by their respective regular degrees. The new signs of alteration will be named here *supra-sharps* and *supra-flats* (being also slightly changed in their graphic notation) and will respectively raise and lower a regular degree of the new scale a half step, which, of course, is considerably smaller than a half step of any of the preceding scales. Inasmuch as the new scale is considered here in its supra-tempered intonation, the supra-sharps and supra-flats derived from the contiguous regular degrees will coincide as indicated above in front of every black key which serves for both these supra-chromatic alterations.

As to the general method of notation for the supra-diatonic scale, it is apparent that our customary five-line system is formally inappropriate for this purpose, as the tonally increased scale requires a greater number of stave lines on and between which its twelve regular degrees, with their derivative supra-chromatic alterations, may be easily placed. Should we desire to create a new stave containing—similarly to the two preceding scales

—two complete octaves, preserving at the same time the notation of the two terminal C's (c′ and c‴) we would have to increase the original number of lines up to ten, as shown in the above keyboard illustration. The use of heavier lines in the new stave is solely for the sake of facilitating visual perception of the unusual number of lines and has no other meaning whatever.

The chain of whole steps and half steps, formed by the supra-diatonic scale, as well as their characteristic arrangement, establishes a close connection between it and the two preceding and organically evolved scales, and, on the other hand, radically opposes it to the modern chromatic scale in so far as the latter is adopted by certain contemporary composers as a perfectly independent basis for their musical and theoretical constructions, and it is sometimes named, in such case, duodecuple or semitonal scale. Taking into consideration, however, the fact that the duodecuple scale (when quite unambiguously applied as such) tonally lacks those "organic" characteristics generally expressed by Mode and Tonality, I shall henceforth call it an *atonal scale,* and shall, at times, designate the series of its twelve independent and equidistant degrees by the figure "12."

The specific succession of whole steps and half steps is what imparts to the supra-diatonic scale that live and individual character by which, no doubt, it will be just as easily "recognized" in musical compositions in which it is used as are the diatonic and infra-diatonic scales in music that is based on them. But this character is certainly lacking in the anemic and neutralized atonal scale ("12") since its component intervals are rigorously levelled in comparison to the series of supra-diatonic whole steps and half steps. It is this characteristic order of intervals of the supra-diatonic scale that enables us to form upon it twelve supra-modes, differentiated from one another by the formula of arrangement of the unchangeable number of whole steps and half steps (i.e. in the same way as are distinguished in each of the preceding scales their modes and infra-modes) namely:

EXAMPLE 14:

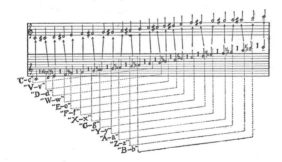

To facilitate the reading of the unfamiliar ten-line system, I have attached to this example the acoustically inadequate and merely approximate notation of the chromatic or, in the above sense, atonal scale ("12"). The latter precludes, of course, the formation upon it of any sort of "modes" as, in contradistinction to the supra-diatonic scale, the formula of arrangement of its component intervals remains, by reason of their equality, unaltered through all their possible permutations.

Conformably to the common number of degrees of the scale "12 + 7" every one of its supra-modes may be freely transposed—under the condition of equal temperament— into nineteen different keys consecutively arranged by Fifths. The following example represents a full set of keys (the enharmonically coinciding keys are excluded) of the supra-mode "C-c":

EXAMPLE 15:

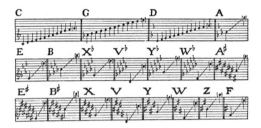

It is understood that the structure of the atonal scale ("12") which does not allow the formation of different "modes," strictly speaking does not permit either the formation of different "keys."

Turning now to the question of intervals of the supra-diatonic scale, we shall at once observe that while their quantitative determination (consisting of the ordinary reckoning up of their whole steps and half steps) presents no difficulty at all, their qualitative determination (which consists of hearing them as consonances and dissonances for an ear that will adjust itself, in the future, to the new scale) seemingly meets invincible obstacles. At any rate it is obvious that the qualitative determination of intervals entirely precludes an experimental approach to this problem, as does in chemistry, for instance, the determination of the properties of those elements which are but theoretically predicted and not yet actually found in Nature. However, just as in chemistry it is sometimes possible to apply for this purpose some other (deductive) method which starts from a certain regularity, manifested by the various properties of neighbouring elements (in the Periodic System) *actually found,* so one may avail himself of a similar method for the qualitative determination of the intervals of the supra-diatonic scale, starting from the undoubted regularity manifested in a specific opposition of consonances and dissonances in each of the two preceding scales.

Added to this there is a circumstance which greatly facilitates this problem. It rests on the fact that the indicated regularity governs not only the intervals of those scales but also their chords which are specifically opposed as concords and discords, depending on the combination of intervals they respectively contain. It is quite clear that to find, for instance, the common consonant chord of the supra-diatonic scale also means automatically to find all the latter's consonant intervals which, as in the preceding scales, should all be contained in this chord and in its inversions. Accordingly, those intervals which are not included in this consonant chord would have to be considered as dissonances. And any chord containing even one of these dissonant intervals would have to be classed as a dissonant chord of the supra-diatonic scale.

The most characteristic constructive feature of all infra-diatonic and diatonic chords appears to be, as already mentioned, their formation by intervals, covering in every instance the space occupied by *three* contiguous regular degrees of their respective scales. So, in the former instance those formative functions are filled by infra-Thirds, while in the latter case they are filled by Thirds. Hence, it will be plausible to conjecture that the functions of intervals forming the chords of the new scale will be filled by supra-Thirds.

Admitting this principle of chord-formation in the supra-diatonic scale—a principle thus formally identical in all three scales—it is now necessary to determine the *number* of tones which being arranged by supra-Thirds will form the new consonant chord. It will be recalled that the number of tones constituting the consonant chords of the two preceding scales is not the same and increases in inverse ratio to the acoustical contraction of their formative intervals. So the consonant chord of the infra-diatonic scale represents a *Dyad* C-F, i.e. a harmonic combination of two notes a perfect infra-Third apart. In the diatonic scale we already have, as a consonant chord, the *Triad* C-E-G, i.e. a harmonic combination of three notes arranged by Thirds, every one of which, of course, is acoustically smaller than the former infra-Third. Hence it will be logical to infer that the new consonant chord formed by supra-Thirds, i.e. by intervals still smaller than Thirds, would have to contain a greater number of tones. But how shall we find this number?

We can easily determine the *minimum* tonal constitution of this new consonant chord which, according to the above principle, ought to contain at least four notes. Similarly, it is not difficult to determine the possible *maximum* tonal constitution of this new consonant chord, since the even number of the (twelve) regular degrees of the supra-diatonic scale does not allow a chord-formation by supra-Thirds exceeding half that number, i.e. six. Besides these two chords there remains only one more which being formed by supra-Thirds would contain five notes. Consequently, there are altogether three chords which seem to have equal chances of being considered as consonant chords of the supra-diatonic scale, namely:

1) TETRAD (c-d-e-x)

2) PENTAD (c-d-e-x-y)

3) HEXAD (c-d-e-x-y-z)

In order to decide which one is the real consonant chord of the supra-diatonic scale, let us make a table of the intervals comprised in the simplest of these three chords, i.e. the *Tetrad*. In so far as the latter is assumed to be a consonant chord, all the intervals it contains, as well as their inversions, must also be considered as consonances, namely:

POSITIONS		INVERSIONS	
Supra-Thirds	C-D . . (1½ steps) D-E . . (1½ ") E-X . . (2 ")	Supra-Elevenths	D-c . . (8 steps) E-d . . (8 ") X-e . . (7½ ")
Supra-Fifths	C-E . . (3 ") D-X . . (3½ ")	Supra-Ninths	E-c . . (6½ ") X-d . . (6 ")
Supra-Seventh	C-X . . (5 ")	Supra-Seventh	X-c . . (4½ ")

If we now make another table of all those intervals that would be added thereto by the notes Y and Z characteristic of the *Pentad* and *Hexad* respectively, we shall not find among them a single interval not already represented in the above table. In other words, neither the *Pentad* nor the *Hexad* contains any other intervals, aside from those which we assumed above as consonances; therefore, by the same token, they may be considered as consonant chords of the supra-diatonic scale. But inasmuch as, according to this proposition, the Tetrad and the Pentad differ from the Hexad, not in quality but merely in quantitative tonal constitution, they cannot be considered as independent chords, in the musical sense, but simply as incomplete forms of the *Hexad* including them, which consequently *represents the sought-for consonant chord of the supra-diatonic scale in its complete form.*

Knowing the structure of this chord, it is not difficult now to obtain a full set of intervals of the supra-diatonic scale with the indication not only of their dimension but also of their quality. In the following table the Roman numerals show the regular degrees of the new scale and the Arabic numerals the number of whole steps and half steps each interval contains; the letter C signifies *consonance*, the letter D *dissonance*, the letter P *perfect* and the letter I *imperfect* (see table opposite page).

The first thing that attracts our attention in this table is the somewhat unusual subdivision (absent in the former scales) of the *dissonant* intervals into perfect and imperfect. In this the writer was guided by the commonly known subdivision of *consonant* intervals of the diatonic scale, in which the term *perfect* is applied to those consonances which are characterized, within the groups of intervals that contain them, by one constant dimension—their deviations, encountered on some degrees of these groups and named augmented and diminished intervals, thus becoming automatically qualified as dissonances—whereas the term *imperfect* is applied to those consonances which are characterized within their groups by two different dimensions known as major and minor.

In the supra-diatonic scale we for the first time come across a very similar subdivision among the dissonances which results from the existence of certain intervals, within some of their groups, equal in dimension to the previously established consonances of this scale. These intervals representing "deviations" from dissonances are accordingly designated by the terms "augmented" and "diminished." The rest of the intervals of these groups in which these deviations occur are thus characterized by one constant dimension and therefore are named *perfect dissonances*. Contrarily to the latter the qualification of

	I	II	III	IV	V	VI	VII	VIII	IX	X	XI	XII
Supra-Seconds (I.D.)	major 1	minor ½	major 1	minor ½	major 1	major 1	minor ½	major 1	minor ½	major 1	minor ½	major 1
Supra-Thirds (I.C.)	minor 1½	minor 1½	minor 1½	minor 1½	major 2	minor 1½	minor 1½	minor 1½	minor 1½	minor 1½	minor 1½	major 2
Supra-Fourths (P.D.)	perf. 2½	dim. 2	perf. 2½	perf. 2½	perf. 2½	perf. 2½	dim. 2	perf. 2½	dim. 2	perf. 2½	perf. 2½	perf. 2½
Supra-Fifths (I.C.)	minor 3	minor 3	major 3½	minor 3	major 3½	minor 3	minor 3	minor 3	minor 3	major 3½	minor 3	major 3½
Supra-Sixths (P.D.)	perf. 4	perf. 4	perf. 4	perf. 4	perf. 4	perf. 4	dim. 3½	perf. 4	perf. 4	perf. 4	perf. 4	perf. 4
Supra-Sevenths (I.C.)	major 5	minor 4½	major 5	minor 4½	major 5	minor 4½	minor 4½	major 5	minor 4½	major 5	minor 4½	major 5
Supra-Eighths (P.D.)	perf. 5½	perf. 5½	perf. 5½	perf. 5½	perf. 5½	perf. 5½	perf. 5½	perf. 5½	perf. 5½	perf. 5½	perf. 5½	augm. 6
Supra-Ninths (I.C.)	major 6½	minor 6	major 6½	minor 6	major 6½	major 6½	minor 6	major 6½	minor 6	major 6½	major 6½	major 6½
Supra-Tenths (P.D.)	perf. 7	perf. 7	perf. 7	perf. 7	augm. 7½	perf. 7	perf. 7	perf. 7	perf. 7	augm. 7½	perf. 7	augm. 7½
Supra-Elevenths (I.C.)	major 8	minor 7½	major 8	major 8	major 8	major 8	minor 7½	major 8	major 8	major 8	major 8	major 8
Supra-Twelfths (I.D.)	minor 8½	minor 8½	major 9	minor 8½	major 9	minor 8½	minor 8½	major 9	minor 8½	major 9	minor 8½	major 9

imperfect dissonances is assigned to those intervals that are characterized, within their corresponding groups, by two different dimensions and further designated by the terms "major" and "minor."

Another and still more puzzling phenomenon in the new grouping of intervals of the above table seems to be the classing of Fourths and Fifths among the *dissonances* of the supra-diatonic scale in which they exist under the names of supra-Sixths and supra-Eighths. The explanation of this imaginary paradox lies in the fact that acoustically pure Fourths and Fifths simply do not exist in the just intonation of the supra-diatonic scale (also another imaginary paradox) and that their seeming synonyms—the supra-Sixths and supra-Eighths—are merely approximate and do not coincide with them.

I shall omit here all those rather complicated acoustic considerations upon which I have based the just intonation of the supra-diatonic scale, and confine myself to a demonstration of ready-made results. The latter are given in the following diagram in which the just intonation of the new scale (indicated by lower solid lines) is represented together with the Pythagorean intonation (upper solid lines) and with the supra-tempered intonation (middle solid lines). I have left out of this diagram, for the sake of simplicity, the auxiliary degrees of the supra-diatonic scale. The dotted lines (without their corresponding figures) represent, for comparison, the twelve equidistant degrees of the atonal scale ("12"):

EXAMPLE 16:

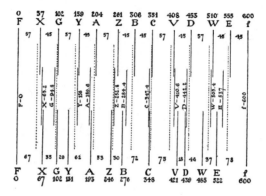

This diagram is at present of threefold importance. *First,* it confirms the absence of acoustically pure Fourths and Fifths in the just intonation of the supra-diatonic scale; *secondly,* it discloses the impracticableness of the Pythagorean intonation of this scale whose characteristic and musically indispensable succession of whole steps and half steps is too perceptibly distorted in this case, as compared with the just (i.e. normal) intonation, and *thirdly,* it shows that the acoustic deviations of the supra-tempered from the just intonation do not exceed (as a rule) those deviations which we have encountered in the infra-tempered scale actually used by the Siamese (See Ex. 2). The latter circumstance predetermines, to a certain extent, the possibility of practical use, in the future, of the supra-tempered intonation.

SUPRA-TONALITY VS. ATONALITY

The deductive method used above for finding the principle of harmonic construction of the supra-diatonic scale is, of course, very limited in its application, as it ends precisely where begins the field of tonal *functions* of the chords, formed in accordance with this principle. Aside from the fact that the application of the same method in order to find these tonal functions would be most uncertain, the results thus obtained (even if correct) in any case would have no significance for the musical ear in its present state. This is because the latter would inevitably apprehend those chordal functions now on the externally approximative plane of the atonal scale ("12") whose inherent inadequacy, in relation to the supra-diatonic scale, has already been sufficiently disclosed.

Indeed, even the very structure of the supra-diatonic Hexad, not to speak of its functions, we would apprehend quite incorrectly should we attempt actually to produce this chord through the material furnished by the atonal scale ("12"). The reason is that the whole-tone or whole-step *chord* (sometimes inaccurately termed a *scale*) which is included in the atonal scale and which externally approximates the supra-diatonic Hexad, exclusively consists of equal intervals, whereas this Hexad, irrespective of its intonation, contains two different kinds of supra-Thirds, as demonstrated by the following comparison:

Whole-step
Chord

| C | whole step | D | whole step | E | whole step | F♯ | whole step | G♯ | whole step | A♯ | whole step | c |

Supra-diatonic
Hexad

| C | minor supra-Third | D | minor supra-Third | E | MAJOR supra-Third | X | minor supra-Third | Y | minor supra-Third | Z | minor supra-Third | c |

It is difficult fully to realize the musical importance of this distinction without having at hand the true tonal embodiment of the supra-diatonic scale. But at the same time it will not be far-fetched to surmise that these two chords differ actually no less, for instance, than the characteristic major or minor Triad of the diatonic scale differs from an artificially decolored "neutral" Triad which becomes such as a result of an equalization of both its component Thirds within the span of the same interval of a perfect Fifth.

Despite all the inadequacy of the above two chords, however, the mere fact that the first flashes of modern music (in the sense used before) manifested themselves in the use of the whole-step harmonic combination as an independent chord not necessarily requiring resolution—usually ascribed to Debussy—is most significant. There is scarcely any doubt that this use resulted from an intuitive, though not perfectly clear perception of the fundamental harmony of the supra-diatonic scale unknown so far.

This point of view is particularly corroborated by the fact that subsequent evolution of the whole-step chord, which fairly soon revealed its musical paucity, proceeded in the direction of improvement towards the structure of the supra-diatonic Hexad. It must, of course, be fairly well understood that under the conditions of our present twelve-tone system, this improvement could be effected only in a very crude manner, since an expansion of any one of the intervals constituting the whole-step chord (for the purpose of likening it to the major supra-Third of the new Hexad) inevitably causes a contraction of one of its adjacent intervals. That is to say, a transformation of any whole step of this chord into a sesqui-step automatically transforms one of its adjacent whole steps into a half step, this phenomenon having no equivalent in the supra-diatonic Hexad.

It is this very kind of expansion of a whole step into a sesqui-step that is met with for the first time in the so-called "synthetic" chord which was intuitively found by Scriabin and which, by the way, was considered and emphatically maintained by him as an indubitable consonant chord. Judging from the position of the newly-formed sesqui-step in this chord, Scriabin inwardly perceived the Hexad of the supra-diatonic scale (assuming that it was a tonic chord) whether in the supra-mode "Z-z" or in the supra-mode "F-f," as will be seen from a general comparison of all these harmonic formations. [See following page.]

The changed position of the characteristic sesqui-step in later compositions of Scriabin's (for instance in the opening measures of his "Prometheus") shows that this composer gradually fathomed through his creative intuition certain other supra-modes of the new scale.

Supra-diatonic
Hexad

Scriabin's
Chord

Supra-diatonic
Hexad

It will be opportune to observe here that the commonly known theory of Scriabin's chord which *directly* deduces the latter from the Natural Harmonic Series (overtones) has little validity for the following reasons:

1. This theory is unable to explain the quantitative constitution of Scriabin's chord, i.e. it cannot give a foundation for its formation of no more and no less than six notes.

2. This theory is unable to explain the seemingly unimportant but in reality most essential elimination, from Scriabin's chord, of the perfect Fifth (G) which according to the same theory is supposed to be one of the very first items in the historic addition of overtones to the gradually more complicated consonant chord.

3. This theory is unable to explain Scriabin's expression of the thirteenth overtone by the note A instead of A♭ to which this overtone is about 9 ctn. nearer than to the former note in our present tempered system.

4. This theory is unable to explain all the subsequent versions of Scriabin's chord.

Although the progressive refining of the human harmonic sense in conformity with the gradual acoustic complication of the Natural Harmonic Series is, generally speaking, beyond dispute, yet in the course of historical development it does not proceed in as straight a line as the upholders of the theory seem inclined to believe.

The resources of the present twelve-tone system prevented Scriabin from fully cognizing the true structure of the supra-diatonic scale, but his foreseeing its fundamental harmony, especially the latter's most characteristic interval (the major supra-Third) which he approximately expressed by the notes F♯—A, seems little short of prophetic.

Scriabin's improvement of the whole-step chord, however, was the most that could be done with present tonal resources, in regard to the possible acoustic approach to fundamental supra-diatonic harmony. Moreover, this improvement (which incidentally led up to a rather noticeable harmonic variety) also proved to be the limit of normal harmonic development in the direction of supra-tonality in general—the limit resulting from the inadequacy, already disclosed, of the twelve-tone or atonal scale as compared with the supra-diatonic scale. Scriabin's chord thus appeared like a solitary isle in a foreign "atonal" environment. To build up, under these conditions, even the most rudimentary supra-diatonic system of Harmony was out of the question. Aside from the unfeasibility, strictly speaking, of the proper connection of Hexads formed according to Scriabin's principle, which somehow weakens their intertonal gravitation, the twelve-tone limit of the present musical system also precludes the possibility of the most ordinary modulation of these "approximative" supra-diatonic chords; it even limits, in a certain sense, their plain transposition.

Taking into consideration this inadequacy of the atonal scale ("12") there is nothing to be surprised at in the hypertrophic and, of necessity, purely "quantitative" harmonic complexity towards which modern music impetuously turned after Scriabin. It is easy to understand that without a strictly evolved harmonic system determining the tonal functions of the new chords, modern composers could not do more than superficially skim the "approximative" supra-diatonic Hexads, instead of exhausting their intrinsic resources. Continuing headlong in the same direction, they, naturally, very soon came to a "free" use of a quasi-consonant twelve-tone chord, seemingly not requiring any resolution,—a use for which scores of years would be required under normal conditions, i.e. were the adequate tonal material of the supra-diatonic scale actually accessible.

There can be no doubt that this hypertrophy and unduly rapid harmonic complication (and incidentally rhythmic complication, now so much favored, though musically less important) are also due in great part to the exceptional limitations, within the conditions of the atonal scale ("12"), of a melodic creation. That characteristic arrangement of whole steps and half steps of the supra-diatonic scale which is supposed to serve as a basis of construction for supra-diatonic melodies is neutralized in the atonal scale by its twelve equal semitones, which on account of this levelling, are deprived of any fundamental fulcrum and have neither beginning nor end in their succession.

Scriabin strove to avoid this embarrassing situation by creating his thematic material exclusively with notes which constitute his "synthetic" Hexad (that is, by the way, the reason why he qualified it simultaneously as a *chord* and a *scale*), taking advantage of its marked proximity to the supra-diatonic Hexad. As a result Scriabin obtained a rather close illusion of supra-diatonic melodies which, however, being limited to the six notes of his chord very often revealed a resemblance in structure hardly to be avoided.

The melodic design of Schönberg's composition is another and entirely different attempt at emancipation from bondage to the levelled intervals of the atonal scale. Not being confined, in contradistinction to Scriabin, to the six harmonic notes of the new and supposedly consonant chord for the construction of his thematic material, Schönberg most directly and openly confronted the inadequacy between these levelled "atonal" intervals and the characteristic whole steps and half steps of the supra-diatonic scale which, we assume, he subconsciously anticipated.

That the ear should be able to make some psychological correction in regard to the levelled intervals, especially in the case of "stepwise" progression of the melody, is out of the question. Schönberg's musical instinct, however, quite correctly told him that if one cannot expect of the ear this sort of correction in regard to such a small interval as a semitone (for instance e'—f'), it will be incomparably easier to effect this correction if the interval is augmented by a whole octave (e'—f'') or, which is almost the same, if its upper note is transposed a major Seventh lower (e'—f).

In this way every semitone in which one of the component notes leaps to the neigh-bouring octave, may already create, depending on its harmonic environment, the illusion either of a whole step or of a half step of the supra-diatonic scale. It is extremely probable that this circumstance may explain, at least in certain cases, that characteristic curve of Schönberg's melodic line which results in great part from the leaps of its component notes from one octave to another. Besides this, Schönberg attempts to enhance the illusion of supra-tonality by rather frequent melodic leaps at an interval of an augmented Fourth (major and minor supra-Sevenths)—in regard to which, as a characteristic con-sonance of the supra-diatonic scale, the ear can easily make the necessary psychological correction within the same octave—and, in general, by following the laws of so-called dissonant counterpoint which, as a rule, treats the dissonant intervals of the diatonic scale as if they were consonances, this being quite natural since the majority of diatonic dissonant intervals really are consonances in the supra-diatonic scale.

A further attempt at breaking through to the melodic plane of the supra-diatonic scale may be observed in the principle of polytonality so noticeable among the modern composers. Polytonality, as the construction of this term shows, signifies a simultaneous combination in a musical composition of two or more tonalities (in the sense of keys) of the diatonic scale. If this definition is correct, however, then polytonality is nothing but a fiction, because this very combination annihilates the specific characteristics of all the tonalities it represents, just as in the chemical combination of oxygen and hydrogen the specific characteristics of each of these elements are completely annihilated. In other words, polytonality is deprived of the feature of *plurality* of independently existing tonalities which, when combined, form some new and *single* whole with heretofore non-existing characteristics, as oxygen and hydrogen combined produce water, the character-istics of which have nothing in common with those of its component elements.

In exemplifying this statement I shall first avail myself, for the sake of clarity, of two keys of the infra-diatonic and not of the diatonic scale, i.e. of two infra-tonalities:

EXAMPLE 17:

The upper melody of this example is formed of notes of the infra-tonality "G," while the lower melody is formed of notes of the infra-tonality "C." Thus we seemingly have a simultaneous combination of two infra-tonalities and it is quite probable that should Chinese musicians, for instance, ever come across this way of composing by their future "modernists," they would qualify it as *poly-infratonality.*

But in reality we know that this poly-infratonality is pure fiction, because its two component infra-tonalities ("G" and "C") lose their specific characteristics by being merged in *one* diatonic tonality of C major (the small notes of the above example indicate the implicit harmony), and thus acquire the characteristics of the latter. And should we Occidental musicians come upon such a way of composing by Chinese "modernists," we would quite justly remark that their musical mind was beginning to turn to diatonic tonality, unfamiliar to them so far, and that their subconscious anticipation of it stimulated their "poly-infratonal" creation, this being merely an intuitive attempt to break through to the melodic plane of the diatonic scale.

An analogous correlation will be found between those Occidental composers of the future who will some day pre-eminently use the supra-diatonic scale, on the one hand, and our contemporary composers who so far have only subconsciously anticipated this new idiom, on the other. The former will quite justly explain all present experiments of the latter by the turning of their musical mind in the direction of supra-tonality, which embraces all the tonalities of the diatonic scale (thus depriving them of their specific characteristics) and which, being intuitively anticipated by our contemporary composers, stimulates their "polytonal" creativeness. Those contrapuntally combined melodies which in the opinion of modern composers are written in different tonalities, belong in reality to one and the same supra-tonality, as illustrated by the following example:

EXAMPLE 18:

This example, constructed similarly to the preceding one, does not appear, of course, as obvious as the latter, the reason being that the merging of two diatonic tonalities into one supra-tonality we can only grasp at present theoretically, whereas the merging of two infra-tonalities into one diatonic tonality (Example 17) we may also perceive in a practical way. There is no essential difference, however, between these two examples, since they demonstrate a perfectly identical interrelation between various organic scales which only gradually become more complex—an interrelation naturally resulting from their structural similarity.

Such being the case, it is not difficult to foresee that the similarity between all these scales will also crop out in their other aspects. Thus, for instance, we know that when the five auxiliary degrees of the Western tempered scale ("7 + 5") gradually acquired "independent" properties on a par with its seven regular degrees, they eventually transformed it into an atonal scale ("12") which, however, by reason of the absolute equality of its twelve component intervals turned out to be simply an inadequate reflection of the supra-diatonic scale. Likewise, if the two auxiliary degrees of the Siamese infra-tempered scale ("5 + 2") ever acquire "independent" properties on a par with its five regular degrees, they will thereby transform it into an infra-atonal scale ("7") which because of the absolute equality of its seven component intervals will turn out to be but an inadequate reflection of the diatonic scale.

Furthermore, the chords of the supra-diatonic scale arranged by supra-Thirds found their inadequate reflection, as we know, in the Western whole-step chords. In the same way the chords of the diatonic scale, arranged by Thirds, will some day find their inadequate reflection in the Siamese whole-step chords, as may be learned from the following comparison (*a* and *b*):

EXAMPLE 19:

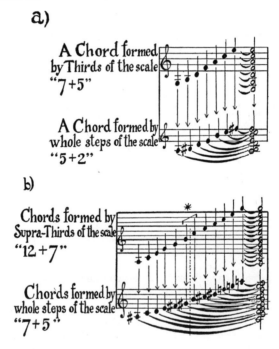

The musical limitation of the Western whole-step chords is too well-known to be commented on. But the Siamese whole-step chords will also prove musically limited

---

* The two supra-diatonic Hexads form here one continuous chain, being connected by an interval of a diminished supra-Fourth (marked by a bracket) which equals the major supra-Third. This connection permits the formation of dissonant chords of the new scale in a fashion similar to the formation of dissonant chords of the two preceding scales.

because they will be deprived (on account of their equal intervals) of those specific characteristics that are possessed by the diatonic chords inadequately reflected by them. Thus, the Siamese whole-step chord composed of three notes will appear, by reason of this equality of its component intervals, merely a "neutral" or decolored reflection of the characteristic diatonic Triad, in which even the simple reversal of position of its two Thirds produces two versions (major and minor Triads) as different as day and night.

Likewise all the other chords of the diatonic scale will be decolored in the Siamese whole-step reflection. Thus, we shall successively obtain but one "neutral" seventh-chord instead of the various versions of the diatonic seventh-chords, one "neutral" ninth-chord instead of different diatonic ninth-chords, etc.

It would not be surprising if the future Siamese "modernists," anticipating some day the structure of the diatonic scale and having at their command only the inadequate infra-atonal scale ("7"), should turn, like our contemporary modernists, to a purely external or quantitative harmonic complexity. They will be forced to it by the neutrality, already indicated, of the diatonic chords inadequately reflected, in their musical system, and, consequently, by the impossibility of fathoming the musical resources of those chords in their unaffected state. Above all, they will be impetuously urged to such complexity (and incidentally to a rhythmic complexity) by the total preclusion of genuine diatonic melody under the conditions of the infra-atonal scale ("7") which, instead of a characteristic succession of diatonic whole steps and half steps only offers a dull substitute of seven "neutralized" intervals.

It is quite possible that musical intuition will prompt our imaginary Siamese "modernists" to adopt certain artificial means (leaps by intervals larger than an octave, poly-infratonality, etc.), creating an illusion of the diatonic scale through the infra-atonal scale ("7"). However, all these temporary palliatives will be unable to conceal the musical paucity of the latter as compared with the wealth of resources of the former. And having nothing at their command aside from the "neutral" means of the infra-atonal scale ("7"), these Siamese composers, however gifted, will hardly be able to create anything except "neutral music."

But our modern Occidental composers are in the very same tragic position when they actually avail themselves of the atonal scale ("12") as a medium of expression for their, as yet, dimly sensed "supra-diatonic" creative ideas. Like our imaginary Siamese modernists, they can only construct "neutral," that is, mechanically levelled, harmonic combinations instead of organic supra-diatonic chords; they have at their command but twelve neutral semitones instead of characteristic supra-diatonic whole steps and half steps; they possess a lifeless equalized scale having neither beginning nor end, a scale which precludes the formation of different modes and keys; a scale which does not permit any sort of modulation, etc. Hence it is not difficult to understand why there are so few chances that those modern composers who are unambiguously applying the atonal principle in composition will be able to produce, even when highly gifted, anything more than the inevitable "neutral music."

Being at present compelled to use this neutralized atonal scale ("12") instead of the live supra-diatonic scale ("12 + 7"), modern composers are in the same position as would be, for instance, portrait painters compelled to use a mechanically levelled lay figure instead of an expressive living model. And as a portrait painted from such a wax figure would of course prove to be utterly emotionless, quite natural must be considered the lack of emotional characteristics in music wholly based on the atonal scale ("12") which is already *a priori* deprived of those characteristics. It was probably the subconscious perception of this negative feature of the atonal scale that brought forth recently the so-called "anti-emotional" theory in musical esthetics, advanced, I believe, by Stravinsky.

It seems almost superfluous to add that the lifelessness of the atonal scale could never be avoided by some multiple increase of its twelve component tones within an octave, be it a duplication or a triplication, etc. Indeed, the combination "12 + 12" (to take but one instance of such an increase) which is obtained by doubling all the tones of the atonal scale, would be just as absurd from the viewpoint of the supra-diatonic scale ("12 + 7") as the combination "7 + 7," obtained by doubling the infra-atonal scale, from the viewpoint of the diatonic scale ("7 + 5").

Nevertheless, one may be assured that the initial step of future Siamese modernists aiming to increase the contents of their meager infra-atonal scale ("7") would be none other than this nonsensical duplication ("7 + 7") as the simplest and following the line of least resistance. This duplication would in no way change the state of affairs in their music since, properly speaking, it would not create a single new scale, but would merely produce, in the end, a mechanical aggregation of two infra-atonal scales, one of them being tuned a quarter step (42.86 ctn.) higher or lower than the other. But exactly in the same way, the state of affairs in our own modern music will never be changed by the mechanical aggregation of two atonal scales ("12 + 12") tuned a quarter step (25 ctn.) apart. And as in Siamese music of the future it would be most logical under the conditions assumed to turn immediately from the infra-atonal ("7") to the diatonic scale ("7 + 5"), so in our modern music to turn immediately from the atonal ("12") to the supra-diatonic scale ("12 + 7") must be considered the straightest and most logical path of all.

The radicalism of such a step which presupposes a definite acoustical break with the scale previously applied, will meet, of course, with the most serious practical obstacles. I have taken them into account when dealing with the whole problem, and although this particular question cannot be finally solved in a theoretical way, yet it is hardly to be doubted that these obstacles are not of an invincible nature and that they will eventually be surmounted.

ADDENDUM II

TONALITY AND ATONALITY AS SYNTHESIZED BY SUPRA-TONALITY*

A comparison of the three musical concepts in this title with the three "evolutionary stages" constituting the Hegelian dialectic triad—Thesis, Antithesis, Synthesis—is too inviting not to be made here. Indeed there is much more than a similarity merely of form between these two groups of entities, although it is not always obvious.

It can hardly be denied that Tonality and Atonality actually represent a certain Thesis and an Antithesis in the history of music, at least of our Western music. But the prediction that they will eventually be synthesized by Supra-Tonality must be substantiated by something more than assertion or philosophic comparison. Proof is necessary, above all historical proof. For if adoption of the dialectic method in considering the process of musical evolution is correct, then the initial link of this dialectic chain, i.e. Tonality, which serves as a Thesis, must apart from that and in itself represent the Synthesis of a certain pre-existing and less complicated Tonality, which we may therefore call "Infra-Tonality," anthithesized by a pre-existing, less complicated Atonality, which we will accordingly call "Infra-Atonality."

In other words, the proposition to be demonstrated is that, strictly speaking, our prediction, which may be diagrammatically represented as

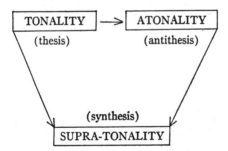

had an historical precedent which may be similarly represented as

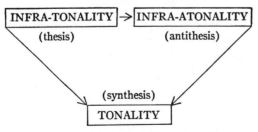

---

* The Future of Tonality was the original title of this article which is reprinted here by courtesy of Modern Music (Supplement to the Issue of November-December, 1930).

the natural interconnection of these two schemes forming one continuous evolutionary chain with Tonality as a connecting center:

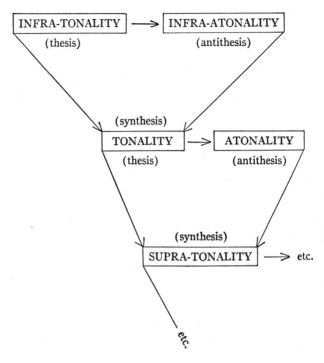

This chain could, of course, be theoretically extended *ad infinitum*, Supra-Tonality being antithesized by Supra-Atonality and both of them synthesized by some still more complicated "Hyper-Supra-Tonality," and so on. But for our immediate purposes the above section of this infinite chain will suffice, let alone the fact that too remote predictions would have, at present, no practical meaning.

WHAT IS TONALITY?

With this limitation, our problem is now fairly well formulated and apparently contains three unknown and two known quantities, the former group being Infra-Tonality, Infra-Atonality and Supra-Tonality, and the latter Tonality and Atonality. A definition, as exact as possible, of these two known quantities is naturally the first step toward the solution of our problem. What *is* Tonality? What *is* Atonality?

There are a good many definitions of Tonality, all more or less correct but none completely covering this rather vague concept. Without claiming to fill the gap or fully to express this notion in a single comprehensive and universal formula, I shall offer my own which at least will more adequately serve our purpose:

Tonality is a principle which organically and tonocentrically unites the melodic and harmonic functions of a certain number of systematically arranged sounds as most simply represented in a musical scale.

To expand this definition and describe the two functional aspects in reference to our present (diatonic) system which is governed by the above principle, we may add that the tonal center represents a single note (Tonic) from the melodic point of view, and a chord of three notes arranged by Thirds (tonic Triad) from the harmonic point of view. Again, that in the melodic aspect this system manifests a characteristic distribution of its seven regular (diatonic) degrees within an Octave, forming various chains of whole steps and half steps (Modes) which, by the aid of the additional set of five auxiliary (chromatic) degrees interpolated between the former, can be freely transposed into twelve different keys. Finally, that from the harmonic viewpoint this system divides all its possible tonal combinations into two distinctly opposed groups of consonances and dissonances, the latter inevitably "requiring" resolution into the former.

ATONALITY DEFINED

So much for Tonality. As regards Atonality it is easy to form a concept since, as the structure of the term shows, it appears to be simply a negation of Tonality, i.e. a negation of whatever this latter notion affirms. Thus, Atonality negates any principle of gravitation of the scale-tones toward some uniting "autocratic" center. It further negates the division of all scale-tones into two different groups labeled diatonic and chromatic or, in a more general sense, regular and auxiliary groups of degrees, all of them becoming equally "regular" in their functions, thereby precluding, to be exact, the possible formation of any "Modes" and "Keys." Atonality likewise negates the division of all harmonic combinations into consonances and dissonances, the latter also becoming some sort of "consonances," at least in the sense that, like the former, they no longer require resolution. In other words Atonality somehow disorganizes the musical system as a system, bringing it to a certain anarchic state.

The only thing that is completely preserved by Atonality in this general negating, is the actual tonal material of the previously used system (twelve tones within an octave in our instance), in which not even intonation is modified in the slightest degree. Moreover, as we shall see later, it is largely due to the equally tempered (i.e. artificial) intonation of the negated system that Atonality could have been carried to such an extreme as outlined above. This leads us to the conclusion that Atonality, in its extreme form, inevitably possesses some artificial characteristics that would never have appeared under the condition of just (i.e. natural) intonation.

I have purposely described the principles of Tonality and Atonality in most sharply defined terms so as to bring out more clearly their inward opposition to each other. But it should be borne in mind that the one does not suddenly follow the other in the process of historical evolution. There are a number of intermediate phases. The seeds of Atonality are inherent in Tonality and may easily be detected in many of its particular forms. Similarly the seeds of Supra-Tonality should be easily detected in Atonality which, historically, is followed by the former and synthesized jointly with Tonality.

It should not be a matter of surprise, therefore, if, in certain individual cases, a composer historically belonging, let us say, to the period of Atonality, or even to the early part of it,* suddenly manifests certain characteristics of Supra-Tonality so strikingly as to give the impression of arriving at the latter rather prematurely, and thus seemingly to refute the above dialectic chain or, at least, to interweave its evolutionary "stages" in too haphazard a manner; just as it should cause no surprise if another composer of the same period, or even of the latest part of it, suddenly reinstates the principle of (diatonic) Tonality and thus seemingly reverses the historical process. It must be remembered, too, that historical laws do not apply to individuals, at least not very rigidly, but to the masses in a given field, and that the line of historic evolution, whose definite direction, however "curved" in isolated instances, is easily detected when observed from a distance, so to speak, may make a very uncertain and chaotic impression when examined too closely.

SUPRA-TONALITY NO COMPROMISE

Formally representing a negative entity, Atonality possesses, none the less, certain constructive features; just as Tonality, formally representing a positive entity, may have certain negative characteristics. Supra-Tonality synthesizes only what is constructive in both Tonality and Atonality. But from this it should not be hastily and erroneously inferred that Supra-Tonality merely compromises Tonality and Atonality, that it is practically a sort of "happy medium" between them. Supra-Tonality is not to be found *between* Tonality and Atonality but *above* them; it does not *compromise* these two principles but *synthesizes* them, which is a different thing altogether. As a mere compromise Supra-Tonality would prove to be no more than "sand-papered" Atonality— which it is not. Thus Atonality, as already remarked, does not at all change the tonal medium of the old system (twelve tones within an octave) but only *its own attitude* toward that medium. Supra-Tonality creates a new and more complicated tonal medium which is technically modeled on the old and less complicated one.

It is easy to prove that in contradistinction to a compromise between Tonality and Atonality, their synthesis (i.e. the synthesis of their constructive elements, as already stated) calls for a complication of the old tonal medium. But first we apparently have to determine what their "constructive" parts are.

---

* The beginning of the period of Atonality does not coincide, of course, with the time of introduction of the term, which probably did not come into use before 1909, i.e. before Atonality had attained practically its full growth (as in the *Three Piano Pieces*, Op. 11, by Schönberg, for instance) and, therefore, was easily recognized as such. And inasmuch as Atonality is regarded as the *negation* of Tonality in the broad sense of the word (not merely as its final phase), its inception from the historical point of view must go back to the time when music first touched the borderland of (diatonic) Tonality, whose heretofore infallible absolutism began to inspire certain doubts. As a matter of fact, the sources of Atonality can already be traced through the chromatic harmony of Wagner's *Tristan* (1857), as correctly remarked by A. E. Hull (*Dictionary of Modern Music and Musicians*, page 19); and since some tentative attempts in this direction have been made at even earlier periods (Liszt), it will be proper to assume the beginning of the second half of the nineteenth century as the approximative line of demarcation between Tonality and Atonality, if they are regarded as two schematic evolutionary stages of the dialectic chain demonstrated in the text. Such is their correct classification in historical perspective, although it may appear rather unconventional from the purely musical standpoint which usually does not take into account the periods of incubation of various historical phenomena but only their full-fledged phases.

CONSTRUCTIVE ELEMENTS

In Tonality, these play a vital part in what may be generally defined as the "organization of the sound," and are actually manifested in the existence of a "tonocentric" system with a variety of modes and keys, with a division of all the scale-tones into two different groups of regular and auxiliary degrees and of all the harmonic combinations into two polar groups of consonances and dissonances, their interaction creating a genuine "dynamism" in the musical work. All this is lacking in Atonality, whose twofold advantage over Tonality (and this is what constitutes its constructive elements) is that it increases the number of "regular" scale-degrees (twelve instead of seven) and the number of chords not requiring resolution. Their limitation in Tonality represents its negative part.

It becomes immediately evident that the synthesis of the "constructive" elements of Tonality and Atonality by Supra-Tonality inevitably predetermines a more complicated tonal medium, since the synthesized scale must contain two functionally different sets of degrees (regular and auxiliary) on the one hand, and on the other, an *increased* number of regular degrees (which naturally calls for a proportionate increase of auxiliary degrees). This scale is shown in explanatory keyboard form (page 334) above the similar representation of our familiar diatonic scale (whose complete constitution, comprising both the regular and the auxiliary degrees, will henceforth be expressed by the formula "7 + 5") and apparently contains twelve regular and seven auxiliary degrees (formula "12 + 7"). Its structural similarity to the diatonic scale and, at the same time, the increased number of its component tones within an octave (which, of course, makes its characteristic "whole steps" and "half steps" acoustically much smaller than those of the diatonic scale) allows us to attach to it the name of supra-diatonic scale.

HISTORICAL PROOF

In order to explain how the supra-diatonic scale, which represents the material embodiment of the principle of Supra-Tonality, is evolved in this particular manner, we must turn far back in history. First of all, proofs must be produced of the existence of some sort of scale which might be considered the parallel material embodiment of the principle of Infra-Tonality. As such, this scale must obviously bear the same relation to the diatonic scale as the supra-diatonic scale does, but in reverse order. In other words, it must be structurally similar to the diatonic scale, and, at the same time, proportionately *less* complicated in its general tonal constitution, just as the supra-diatonic scale, structurally similar to the diatonic scale, is *more* complicated in its general tonal constitution. This less complicated or "infra-diatonic" scale must have two functionally different sets of degrees, regular and auxiliary. The former of these should be arranged in such a way as to form a characteristic chain of "whole steps and half steps," their acoustical dimension being, of course, much greater than what we are familiar with in the diatonic scale, since the general number of scale-tones within an octave is smaller in the former instance. It is precisely from the relation of the number and arrangement of the regular and auxiliary degrees of the infra-diatonic scale to the number and mutual arrangement of the regular and auxiliary degrees of the diatonic scale that the structure of the supra-diatonic scale must be evolved.

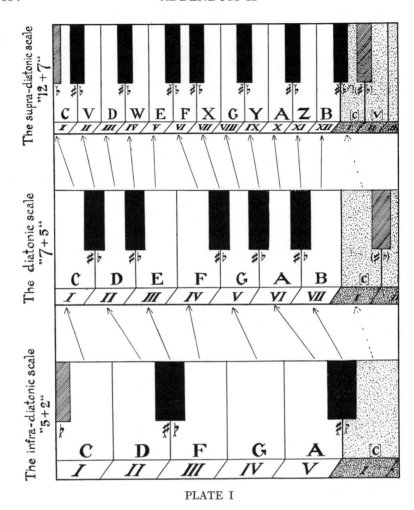

PLATE I

The shaded keys belong to the adjacent octaves. The last five letters of the alphabet, V, W, X, Y, Z are adopted for the increased number of the regular degrees of the supra-diatonic scale.

A small sign placed at the top of the sharp and flat transforms them into supra-sharp and supra-flat, and placed at the bottom transforms them into infra-sharp and infra-flat. These new alterations perform the same functions in their respective scales as the sharp and flat in the diatonic scale.

This historical method as applied to the evolution of a scale containing a greater number of tones within an octave and, consequently, more subtle intervals between them, in comparison with those of present musical practice, is the only one which leads to a *single* solution of the most pressing problem of our day. The writer emphatically opposes it to all other methods applied heretofore and especially to those very arbitrary ones which consist in a purely "mechanical" splitting of the existing equally tempered semitones into quarter tones or eighth tones or even smaller fractions, obviously lead-. ing to as many solutions of the problem as there are "splittings" of the semitones, to which there is practically no limit. By heedlessly ignoring all the historical factors, the upholders of these methods forget a very simple thing, viz. that the splitting of a semi- tone, let us say, into quarter tones, which results in the duplication of our present twelve tones into twenty-four within an octave, presupposes (if one is to be logical) the exist- ence of a six-tone system prior to our twelve-tone system, and that of a three-tone system preceding them all, thereby ineptly barring from musical evolution the heptatonic (diatonic) and pentatonic scales, practically the only ones bearing a stamp of *univer- sality* that is scarcely disputed.

In dealing with the evolution of musical scales, universality is the main, if not the only consideration in seeking "live" scales that actually play a part in the historical pro- cess under investigation. We cannot afford to pay too much attention to a multitude of scales of purely "local" significance (however interesting and curious), which usually turn out to be "variations" (obvious or diguised) of one of the universal types of scales, akin to those variations through which a number of seemingly different phenomena are similarly explained in biological science.

"LIVE" SCALES

There is of course no doubt of the relative universality of the Western diatonic scale. Modern musical science also accepts to the same extent the historic universality of the pentatonic scale which may be found in the past or present musical practice of almost every country. In Europe particularly, despite the difficulty of obtaining authentic information, the pentatonic scale is now known to have been used in Scandinavia, the British Isles (strongest evidences), Northern France (Brittany), Germany (Nithart's *Minnegesänge*), a good many parts of Russia (European and Asiatic), some parts of Finland, Rumania, Bulgaria, and possibly Spain (whose folksongs are considered by Riemann as an example of a *Zwischenstadie* between the pentatonic and the definite heptatonic scale). Even the old Gregorian chants are not devoid of pentatonic ele- ments. Ancient Greece (one of their sources, besides Hebrew cantillations, which are also full of "pentatonisms") experienced at one time the practical use of the pentatonic scale (eighth century B. C., according to Plutarch), in spite of the parallel existence of heptatonic and other scales in her musical theory.*

THE UNIVERSAL PENTATONIC

We may therefore surmise with a fair amount of safety: First, that the countries omitted in this list are but "missing links" in what was once a general use of the penta- tonic scale in the musical practice of Europe (the use of this scale in non-European

---

* The following studies contain some information on the use of the pentatonic scale in European countries: *Folkloristische Tonalitätstudien; Pentatonik und tetrachordale Melodie im schottischen, irischen, walisischen, skandinawischen und spanischen Volksliede und im Gregorianischen Gesänge* von Hugo Riemann (Leipzig, 1916) ; *Eine pentatonische Bibelweise in der deutschen Synagoge* (um 1518) von Herbert Loewenstein, in *Zeitschrift für Musikwissenschaft* (Juni-Juli, 1930) ; *Die Rassen der Erde im Spiegel der vergleichenden Musikforschung* von Peter Panoff, in *Die Musik* (August, 1931).

countries is too well-known to be mentioned here). Second, that only the pentatonic scale, if any, could serve as the possible embodiment of the principle of "Infra-Tonality," if we believe that the latter has ever had any existence at all. Let us therefore closely examine this scale and see whether it has some of the characteristics of the diatonic (even though on a "lower plane") and, if so, whether the development of the pentatonic into the diatonic scale could proceed historically along lines similar to those which we are all witnessing to-day in the development of the diatonic into the supra-diatonic scale, predicted above.

The most widely known form of the pentatonic scale, to which all its "variations" can be easily reduced, is the one usually expressed by the five notes C, D, F, G, A of our present musical system. Each of these notes may naturally serve as the Tonic of the pentatonic scale, thereby producing its various "modal" versions. As a matter of fact, these are found in the music of different countries where the pentatonic scale is or was used. The five notes represent the *complete* set of "regular" degrees of this scale. However, judging from the musical practice of some nations, it also has a pair of "auxiliary" degrees interpolated between its regular ones, similar to the chromatic (auxiliary) degrees of our present system interpolated between its diatonic (regular) ones. The two auxiliary degrees of the pentatonic scale, which can be very closely expressed by the notes E and B of our diatonic (perfectly accurate under the condition of Pythagorean intonation of both scales), are rigidly distinguished from the five regular degrees, their functions being practically the same as those of the auxiliaries within the diatonic scale. Considering the striking structural similarity between the less complicated pentatonic scale (complete formula "5 + 2") on the one hand, and the comparatively more complicated diatonic scale (complete formula "7 + 5") on the other, I have found it advisable to attach the name *infra-diatonic scale* to the former. This is pictured in a manner similar to the latter, in the convenient form of a keyboard with white and black keys representing its five regular and two auxiliary degrees respectively (Plate I).

To achieve simplicity all three keyboards of this illustration are drawn for the equally tempered intonation of the infra-diatonic, diatonic and supra-diatonic scales, which assumes that the Octave is divided into seven equal parts in the first instance ("5 + 2"), twelve equal parts in the second ("7 + 5"), and nineteen equal parts in the third ("12 + 7"). Without making any predictions as to the practicability of equally tempered intonation for the supra-diatonic scale (which will be called *supratempered intonation,* for distinction), it is worth mentioning that the diatonic scale ("7 + 5") is not the only one to which the principle of Equal Temperament has been applied. The same principle is used in the infra-diatonic scale ("5 + 2") of the Siamese who, through their *infra-tempered intonation,* adopted recently, as time goes in the Orient, now have the most powerful technical means for the exhaustive exploitation of the musical resources latent in this scale—a potential possibility that has never really been within the reach of any other nation without that intonation at hand.

EFFECTS OF TEMPERAMENT

We are all familiar with the magnificent results which were obtained in European music through the application of the principle of Equal Temperament to the diatonic scale ("7 + 5"). That is why we may safely approve the Siamese idea of tempering the infra-diatonic scale ("5 + 2") and encourage the idea of tempering in the future the supra-diatonic scale ("12 + 7"). But at the same time we must not close our eyes to a considerable drawback in the principle of Equal Temperament, of which few people are fully aware. It does *not* reside, as some will probably think, in the much discussed discrepancy between the equally tempered and just intonation of one and the same scale—a difference which, as repeatedly proved, is perfectly negligible from a practical point of view. The drawback is much more serious and will be better understood in connection with the following explanation of the method by which the supra-diatonic scale is evolved.

Even a superficial glance at the keyboard illustration (Plate I) in which our newly conceived pentatonic (infra-diatonic) scale plays a basic part, at once conveys the idea of the historic evolution of each "regular" set of degrees of the two subsequent scales. Indeed, it is more than natural to assume that the pair of auxiliary degrees of the infra-diatonic scale, represented therein by two black keys and originally mere "embellishments" of the five regular degrees, gradually came to be used on a par with the latter and with them eventually formed the set of seven regular degrees of the diatonic scale (this process is indicated by arrows). The diatonic scale, as known, was long used without any auxiliary degrees. Considerably later they formed a separate group of five notes, until recently rigidly distinguished in their functions from the group of seven regular degrees. Now we see the strongest tendency on the part of some composers to use the five auxiliary degrees of this scale on a par with its seven regular degrees, jointly forming the *number* (twelve) of the regular degrees of the supra-diatonic scale. This fact inspires the conviction that certain modern composers dimly anticipate the structure of the supra-diatonic scale in spite of the fact that the characteristic *arrangement* of its twelve regular degrees "by whole steps and half steps" differs greatly from the characterless arrangement of the twelve-degree set of equal intervals "independently" used by these composers under the name of duodecuple (practically our chromatic) scale.

A FORCED ARRANGEMENT

In order to understand the reason for the disparity between these two scales, which apparently were without precedent when the gradual transformation of the infra-diatonic into the diatonic scale took place, we must plainly realize that the arrangement of the twelve degrees by equal intervals was not the result of a free choice on the part of modern composers but was *forced* upon them by the existing musical instruments with fixed, equally tempered intonation or by the habits acquired through their general use. The unknown composers of the past would have faced the same experience had they had at their disposal musical instruments with fixed infra-tempered intonation, while inwardly anticipating the structure of the diatonic scale. Would they not have been forced to work with seven "independent" degrees arranged by equal intervals instead of the seven regular degrees of the diatonic scale arranged by characteristic whole steps and half steps? And would they not have tried in vain to express, by the aid of these equal intervals, diatonic melodies which can never be recognized by the ear unless they are based on the familiar distribution of whole steps and half steps—just as our modern composers are vainly trying to squeeze into the twelve equal intervals of the duodecuple scale the supra-diatonic melodies unconsciously created by them?

In the light of this disparity between the scale which, we assume, is inwardly heard by the composers of to-day, and the scale they are compelled to use for technical reasons, the destructive side of Equal Temperament becomes most conspicuous. The happy invention to which we are indebted for the splendid musical development of the last few centuries and even for the very existence of the greatest musical works, becomes something little short of a calamity when the tonal foundation of music in itself shows certain tendencies towards growth. This is being artificially halted by the old and threadbare, equally tempered intonation or is misdirected by those who believe that the existing equally tempered scale will give rise to a somewhat renovated if not entirely new intonation, when duplicated a quarter tone higher or lower. It is like believing that two old, worn-out garments placed side by side will create the impression of a new one.

The fundamental error of the "quarter-tonists" is that they unwittingly postulate the whole tone (and, especially, the equally tempered whole tone) to be a certain standard acoustic *unit,* from which all other fractional musical intervals must derive. In reality, however, the whole tone is a purely conventional concept and has no more the characteristic of a *unit* than any other (smaller or larger) interval. And even if, in a relative sense, the whole tone may be considered as a *musical* unit for the diatonic scale, this certainly does not hold good for a single other scale which may have, and indeed, has, its own musical unit incompatible with the former. The adoption of a whole tone as an *absolute* unit, for the sole reason that it may conventionally serve as such for the diatonic scale, now in use, strongly reminds one of those pre-Copernican astronomers who believed the Earth to be the center of the Universe only because they happened to be inhabitants of this celestial body.

THE AUXILIARY DEGREES

The destructive side of Equal Temperament, demonstrated above from the melodic aspect of the scale, manifests itself still more obviously from the harmonic point of view. But prior to this part of our analysis we have to complete the foregoing explanation of the evolutionary process of the scales discussed by pointing out the law of distribution of their auxiliary degrees, on which the entire arrangement (and not merely the number) of scale-tones largely depends. This law is just as simple as the one which concerns the evolution of the regular degrees of these scales, and is visually expressed in the other keyboard illustration, Plate II, in which our three keyboards are again represented but in reverse order; thus the one referring to the infra-diatonic scale is placed at the top instead of the bottom, and so on.

Every musician undoubtedly knows from experience that any "pentatonic" tune— Chinese, Scotch, etc.— may be easily performed on the five black keys of our pianoforte without touching the white keys at all. This is due to the fact that the number and arrangement of the regular degrees of the infra-diatonic scale are identical with the number and arrangement of the auxiliary degrees of the diatonic scale, as indicated by the arrows in the illustration (the difference in pitch and intonation is of no concern here, since each of these two factors can always be identified in both scales, if desired).

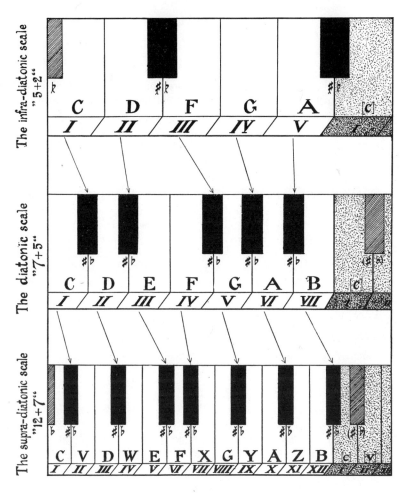

PLATE II

(See explanatory note under Plate I, page 334)

It is then perfectly apparent that in order to establish a similar relationship between the respective sets of degrees of the diatonic and supra-diatonic scales it is necessary to distribute the latter's auxiliary degrees in such a manner that any diatonic tune may easily be performed on the seven black keys of the new keyboard, without touching its twelve white keys at all. This is exactly what we have done with the supra-diatonic scale ("12 + 7"), the rather complicated mathematical procedure involved being omitted here for simplicity. Owing to this principle (demonstrated by the two keyboard illustrations), it now bears the very same relation to the diatonic scale ("7 + 5") as the latter does to the infra-diatonic scale ("5 + 2").*

With the structure and interrelation of all three scales clearly explained, let us now see how the new principle of evolution works out in the field of harmony and how it explains the most outstanding tendencies of chord-formation in the three respective stages of musical development. Three genuine methods of chord-formation are known which it is fairly safe to accept as characteristic and which may be roughly outlined as follows:

First Stage. The Infra-Diatonic Scale ("5 + 2"):

> Principally, harmonic combinations of perfect Fourths and their progressions, especially prevalent in Far-Eastern countries and among peoples of Celtic origin. The Celts introduced this method to Europe where it endured for a long time, partly because of dogmatic reasons (theoretical conformity with Greek authorities) and partly for musico-psychological ones (discussed later). Thus it was erroneously applied to music based mostly on the diatonic scale ("diaphonized" Gregorian chants). Feeble attempts to form more complicated chords "by Fourths" (Chinese).
>
> Intermediate Stage: Gradually increasing use of Thirds and other intervals.

Second Stage: The Diatonic Scale ("7 + 5"):

> Familiar construction of chords "by Thirds."
> Intermediate Stage: Gradually increasing use of chromatically altered chords.

Third Stage. The Supra-Diatonic Scale ("12 + 7"):

> Formation of chords by various intervals which, however, could be reduced to a whole-step harmonic combination (inaccurately termed "whole-tone *scale*"), when brought within the compass of an octave. Further harmonic development connected with this stage will be touched upon later.

These three methods of chord-formation taken separately and outside of their connection with the three tonal systems seem different and even contradistinctive. But glance at the three keyboards represented above and you will soon observe that these

---

* It may be of some interest to the reader to note that besides the double interrelation between all scales which has been marked by arrows in the two keyboard illustrations (Plate I and II), there exists one more interrelation automatically resulting from the former. It consists in that the number of minimum intervals (half steps) found among the regular degrees of any scale is equal to the number of whole steps (or auxiliary degrees which predetermine them) found among the regular degrees of the scale which precedes it in historical evolution. Thus, there are two minimum intervals (half steps) among the regular degrees of the diatonic scale, and the same number of whole steps is found among the regular degrees of the infra-diatonic scale. Again, there are five minimum intervals among the regular degrees of the supra-diatonic scale, and the same number of whole steps is found among the regular degrees of the diatonic scale. All these three forms of interrelation will hold good for any pair of contiguous scales constructed according to our principle, irrespective of their complexity.

three methods, unexpected as it may seem, are subject to the same principle of chord-formation "by Thirds," provided that the interval of a "Third" is everywhere (and not only in the diatonic scale) understood in its direct "numerical" sense, whatever its actual acoustic dimension may be, i.e., concretely speaking, as an interval between the first and the third regular degree or, which comes to the same thing, between the second and the fourth regular degrees, etc. of any scale. From this point of view, intervals like C-F or D-G, for instance, which play the principal part in the harmonic formations of music based on the infra-diatonic scale (first "stage") are *not* "Fourths" in it any more, but "Thirds," since F is the third and not the fourth regular degree in relation to note C of this scale, and so is note G in relation to D. The same is true of intervals such as C-D or D-E, which play the principal part in harmonic formations of music based (presumably) on the supra-diatonic scale (third "stage") and which are *not* "Seconds" or "whole steps" in it any more, but "Thirds," since note D is the third and not the second regular degree in relation to note C of this scale, and so is note E in relation to D. All of which apparently leads to a quite elastic "relative" meaning of the term "Third" (as well as of the other numerical designations of intervals), when considered in different scales, and makes it practical to name it, for distinction, "infra-Third" and "supra-Third," when referring to the infra-diatonic and supra-diatonic scales respectively.

The essential point of this discussion, of course, lies in the fact that the formal method of harmonic construction is the same in every one of our three principal "stages" of musical development. The chords are formed "by infra-Thirds" in the first instance, "by Thirds" in the second, and "by supra-Thirds" in the last—a fact which brings additional proof of similarity between the three scales in question. A still more important consequence follows from this generalized method of chord-formation which deserves special attention. It concerns the harmonic combinations of the supra-diatonic scale which, being formed "by supra-Thirds" (C-D-E-X-Y-Z, for instance), are considered as based on the whole-step chord (C-D-E-F♯-G♯-A♯) from the standpoint of the diatonic scale. Now glance again at the first of our two keyboard illustrations (Plate I) and you will see that the very same interrelation exists between the diatonic and infra-diatonic scales. Any chord constructed "by Thirds" in the former of these two scales (C-E-G, for instance) could not be regarded otherwise than as based on the "whole-step chord" (C-D infra-sharp-G) from the standpoint of the latter.

THE EVILS OF NEUTRALITY

Now here is another point where the drawback of Equal Temperament manifests itself sharply. If we consider the infra-diatonic scale in the equally tempered form, when comparing its "whole-step chord" with the diatonic chord constructed "by Thirds," we shall at once discover that the combination C-D infra-sharp-G does not adequately represent the combination C-E-G, since the two whole steps of the former harmonic combination (C-D infra-sharp, and D infra-sharp-G) are equal to each other, under the condition of Equal Temperament, jointly forming the so-called "neutral Triad," while the two Thirds (C-E and E-G) of the latter harmonic combination always remain of different dimensions, irrespective of the intonation of the diatonic scale. It is precisely the same relation that exists between the whole-step chord C-D-E-F♯-G♯-A♯

and the chord of six notes (Hexad) constructed by supra-Thirds C-D-E-X-Y-Z, of which the former does not adequately represent the latter in the equally tempered intonation of the scale "7 + 5." This is because all the whole steps, being tempered, become absolutely equal to each other, while among the series of supra-Thirds there is one (E-X) which is apparently larger than all the rest. In this way the whole-step combination of six notes of the scale "7 + 5" represents a "neutral Hexad" to the same extent as the whole-step combination of three notes of the scale "5 + 2" represents a neutral Triad. Now imagine a composer who inwardly creates plain "diatonic" music and at the same time has at his command "infra-tempered" musical instruments for its reproduction (i.e. instruments with seven equidistant tones within an octave instead of the characteristic "modal" distribution of the same number of tones, and with the possibility of forming only "neutral" Triads instead of diatonic major and minor Triads). By analogy you will realize fairly well the problem of our modern composer who inwardly creates "supra-diatonic" music and, at the same time, is compelled to use the present tempered system and instruments for its notation and reproduction.

Needless to say, no harmonic complication of any sort to which our modern composers have turned after the "neutrality" of the whole-step chord revealed its musical paucity, will ever conceal the basic disparity between the scale in which they create and the scale in which their music is misrepresented. And, of course, it is the resulting impossibility on the part of the modern composer to express himself adequately and in comparatively simple terms in the new "supra-diatonic" language and to create at least a rudimentary musical grammar for it under existing conditions, which drives him to hypertrophic and groundless harmonic complication and to the proclamation of Atonality, in its most acute form, already long outgrown by him. Thus artificial, equally tempered intonation, former ally of the composer, has now turned against him, and bars the entrance to the realm of Supra-Tonality, holding his creative development at a standstill.

Inasmuch as the "atonal" period in European music appears to be an integral part of a natural historic process, it would certainly have occurred without the existence of Equal Temperament. But then it would never have acquired such an extreme form and would probably have passed into the "supra-tonal" period without any particular commotion. Such was the case with the "infra-atonal" period in European music which, generally speaking, passed into the "tonal" period (diatonic scale) so gradually that its very existence or, at all events, its proper nature, was not fully realized until the present. Now we face the difficult task of proving the historical existence of Infra-Atonality in order to support our "dialectic" construction, of which it is apparently one of the fundamental pillars.

INFRA-ATONALITY

It must be admitted that conditions for our demonstration are far from favorable. The scarcity of genuine material about the period in question, and the comparative primitiveness and insignificance (from our present standpoint) of the possible "revolts" and "anarchic" tendencies supposedly characteristic of the "infra-atonal" music of the remote past are the chief handicaps. Furthermore, the distinctive characteristics of Infra-Atonality will undoubtedly appear somewhat dulled, because Equal Temperament has never been applied to the infra-diatonic scale in the Western world. For these reasons, the utmost concentration will be required of the reader in following the brief analysis of Infra-Atonality and its period in European music, which we shall now give.

Infra-Atonality is the negation of Infra-Tonality—so much is clear. Regarding the latter principle we know so far only that it is embodied in the infra-diatonic scale ("5 + 2") which, like the diatonic scale, contains two functionally different groups of degrees (regular and auxiliary). From the melodic aspect the tonal center of this scale is, of course, represented by a single note (Tonic), identical with the tonal center of the diatonic scale. But these two outwardly identical tonal centers imply two entirely different constructions from the harmonic aspect of their respective scales. The tonal center of the diatonic scale is harmonically represented by a *Triad*, i.e. a chord of three notes arranged "by Thirds." The tonal center of the infra-diatonic scale must naturally be represented by a less complicated chord which, considering its subordination to the principle of construction "by infra-Thirds," can be expressed only by a *Dyad*, i.e. a chord of two notes, an infra-Third apart, like C-F or D-G, etc.—a fact which immediately explains the abundance of Fourths (infra-Thirds) in primitive "infra-diatonic" harmonizations. These infra-Thirds are already *complete consonant chords* from the standpoint of the infra-diatonic scale and, under the condition of two-part harmony, permit hardly anything but parallel progressions. The only infra-Third (F-A) which is qualitatively smaller than the rest must be regarded as a "diminished Dyad" in the infra-diatonic scale and consequently as a discord, similar to the diminished Triad in the diatonic scale. This point of view fully accounts for the fact, so long a puzzle, that a major Third was deemed a dissonance in medieval Europe. Besides being a "diminished Dyad" in the infra-diatonic scale, not completely abandoned at that period, it is dimensionally equal to a whole step (from the standpoint of this scale) which, like a whole step of the diatonic scale, could not be considered a consonance.

STAGES OF REVOLT

The initial flashes of "revolt" against Infra-Tonality (beginning of the "infra-atonal" period) naturally touched first the melodic aspect of the infra-diatonic scale in which the functional distinction between its two groups of regular and auxiliary degrees ("5 + 2") gradually disappeared. But the abolition of this distinction did not instantly transform the infra-diatonic scale into the diatonic scale, in the full sense of the word, as may at first appear. The musical psychology of medieval Europe remained for a long time "infra-tonal" in spite of the disappearance of this distinction, which is proved by the habits of harmonic thinking of the composers of that period who, until the end of the twelfth century, continued to look upon the interval of a Third as a dissonance. The Pythagorean intonation, then in use, which is the "just" intonation of the infra-diatonic scale, may serve as additional proof of this statement.

The further progress of Infra-Atonality already involves the harmonic aspect of the infra-diatonic scale and here, for almost two centuries, we find musical art fighting its way through an intermediate "anarchic" stage which (taking into account the non-existence of infra-tempered intonation at that time) it may not be too far-fetched to compare to our present musical period with its manifold methods of composition all of them ready for a certain new and dimly anticipated homogeneous language. The first step taken by medieval composers in the "negation" of the old harmonic principles concerned the interval of a Third (both major and minor) which gradually ceased to be a dissonance. It was formally proclaimed an "imperfect" consonance by Franco of Cologne who, however, did not find it possible (as might naturally be expected) to adopt the same attitude towards the interval of a Sixth, which represents simply an inversion of the former and, therefore, is harmonically identical with it from the musical (though not the acoustical) point of view. This fact rather unambiguously suggests to us that the harmonic thought of that time, while "negating" what was characteristic of *Infra-Tonality*, had no definite "feeling" yet for what is characteristic of Tonality as embodied in the diatonic scale.

PRACTICE IN FAUX-BOURDON

In Faux-bourdon we already come across the application of the Sixth on a par with the Third. Both being used in harmonic combination yielded practically all the elements found in the diatonic Triad. But the Triad when brought to its root position represents a whole-step chord from the standpoint of the infra-diatonic scale, as has been already demonstrated. With this in mind one cannot help finding in the practice of Faux-bourdon an obvious similarity with the initial steps of "negation" of our diatonic system by modern composers, also manifested in the use of harmonic formations reducible to a whole-step chord from the standpoint of the diatonic scale. And as the latter whole-step chord did not appear suddenly in our modern music but was historically preceded by the use of less complicated chords which already contained certain of its elements (the chords of the Ninth, for instance, when inverted), similarly the former whole-step chord was historically prepared by still more primitive harmonic combinations (progression of Thirds in the Gymel and prior to that, though but occasionally, in the so-called "irregular" Organum), which practically constituted its integral elements.

The Faux-bourdon, which (in its strict form) represents a series of inverted Triads ensuing from and returning to a fundamental Triad with the Third omitted, seems to be so close to rudimentary chord-formation and, loosely speaking, even to chord-progression as prescribed by regular diatonic harmony, that one might naturally expect the latter immediately to follow the former in the process of historical evolution. But this was not the case. It is true that the composers who availed themselves of the principle of Faux-bourdon definitely departed from the principle of Infra-Tonality (particularly "negating" its tonal center, as expressed by the interval of a Fourth) but they apparently were still very far in their harmonic contemplation from the Tonality of the diatonic scale. This is proved by the fact that, from the time Faux-bourdon was in use, it took about a whole century (the thirteenth) before the correct division of consonances and dissonances, as well as the rudimentary rules of part-progression relating to "diatonic" Tonality, were outlined by Philippe de Vitry. That luminous exponent of "Ars Nova," after strenuous efforts made by his predecessors and, no doubt, by himself too, finally discovered the right track to further harmonic development.

As to the character and the most diverse forms of these efforts, they are so typical of a transitional stage and so closely resemble the efforts of our own contemporary composers that, in view of our "dialectic" construction, the formal similarity of these two widely separated historical periods (Atonality and Infra-Atonality) is hardly open to doubt. Indeed, on investigating the history of the medieval *descant*, we find a multitude of polyphonic methods tentatively established by different composers. The moderately inclined groups were earnestly seeking new, more or less definite rules of simultaneous combination of parts; while the "radicals," deriving their ideas from the old art of improvisation by a descanting voice around a given *tenor*, gradually took more liberties in handling the different and quantitatively increased parts. Eventually they discarded the necessity of any rules for the intervals, however dissonant, to be employed between them. The sole exception was at the beginning and end of each line of the composition for which some consonant harmony (often just a plain unison) was required.

From the harsh sonorities of this "infra-dissonant counterpoint" the attention of the listener was supposed to be diverted by the decided motion and rhythmical variety of the combined parts for which, preferably, popular tunes served as the principal musical material. The tunes selected, differing widely from every angle, including their French texts intentionally left untouched, were forcibly compressed within the official triple time-division of the tenor part, composed of short and constantly reiterated phrases of a certain plainsong which preserved its original Latin. Thus there arose a curious combination not only of different texts but also of different languages, producing what must have been a rather colorful "verbal orchestration"—a device which even our sophisticated modernists seem to have overlooked so far. The metrical conformity to which the combined melodies were artificially forced could certainly not change their intrinsic and often dissimilar rhythms (in the broad sense of the word); therefore it would not be too daring to conjecture that these "radical" *motets* of 700 years ago contained, above all, a good many outwardly disguised elements of *polyrhythm*.

As to the general tonal basis of these compositions it perhaps did not venture, as a rule, beyond the conventional series (or its equivalent) of the heptatonic scale C-D-E-F-G-A-B which, at the period referred to, undoubtedly also served as material for the melodies themselves, subjected to simultaneous combination. Long before that, naturally, far less complicated (probably "pentatonic") and more homogeneous (at one time identical) melodies used to be combined in a similar "improvising" manner. In this connection there seem to be valid reasons to believe that the well-known statement of Gerald de Bari (twelfth century) concerning the polyphonic singing of the Welsh choruses in which "one may sometimes hear as many parts as there are performers," points to one of the earliest attempts to combine different melodic lines based on the infra-diatonic scale, then still in use. But even if, with Riemann, we make the safest supposition, namely, that all these choral parts were confined to the very same series of notes of the infra-diatonic scale (of which, however, there are no indications in Gerald's statement) it would of course be quite logical to conjecture further that there existed a few intermediate links between these two forms of polyphonic improvisation (since history knows no sudden leaps) and, consequently, that the combined parts were sometimes based on slightly different series of five notes, all of them, however, remaining within the limits of the seven diatonic degrees.

Thus, supposing one of the parts to be based on the series C-D-F-G-A, while the other part was based on the series G-A-C-D-E, from the standpoint of the diatonic scale there would be nothing unusual in their combination, certainly less complicated than the combination of two or more parts based on the series of seven notes each, as practiced by the "radicals" in the immeasurably more developed form of descant described above. But from the standpoint of the infra-diatonic scale, the combination of these two five-tone series, which unquestionably must have been used prior to that "radical" form of descant, appears as something altogether different and rather out of the ordinary. This is because the note E found in the second of these series (G-A-C-D-E) does not exist in the regular degrees of the infra-diatonic scale, and in fact is merely a designation borrowed from the diatonic scale, equivalent to one of the auxiliary degrees (F♭) of the former. Therefore the two five-tone series above, which belong to one key from the standpoint of the diatonic scale, represent in reality two different keys of the infra-diatonic scale, one of which has no infra-chromatic alterations at all (C-D-F-G-A), while the other, built a Fifth above, contains one such alteration (G-A-C-D-F♭). And if we suppose that there existed, in medieval musical practice, a three-part vocal improvisation based on the infra-diatonic scale, the third part comprising no other notes than D-E-G-A-B (which is not at all improbable since this series still belongs to one and the same key from the standpoint of the diatonic scale), then we would have three keys of the infra-diatonic scale combined together, the last indicated series containing, in reality, two infra-chromatic alterations (D-F♭-G-A-C♭).

INFRA-POLYTONALITY

It seems needless to add that the combination of different keys of the infra-diatonic scale, by which the predominance of a single infra-tonal center is negated, evidently represents an application (though unconscious, as everything else with medieval composers) of the principle of "Infra-Polytonality," as we may appropriately term it. But through the multiplicity of infra-tonal centers, Infra-Polytonality imperceptibly strives at the same time to affirm a single tonal (diatonic) center, since the above combination of keys of the infra-diatonic scale, as we have seen, is easily disposed within the limits of a single key of the diatonic scale. Therefore, Infra-Polytonality, apparently representing one of the intermediate phases between Infra-Tonality and diatonic Tonality, should be regarded simply as a particular form of Infra-Atonality which, in general, not only negates the principle of Infra-Tonality but also manifests a definite tendency towards diatonic Tonality in the process of evolution.

The various forms of descant practiced during the medieval "infra-atonal" period could of course be more specifically analyzed and parallel comparisons made with the individual creative output of the modern "atonal" period which, according to our basic premise, is merely repeating (in principle) the former, though on a "higher plane." It will be sufficient for our present discussion, however, to offer but a single comparison of this kind in order to dispel any doubts regarding the possibility of such an historic parallelism.

I have selected for this purpose a rather peculiar form of descant, briefly described by Simon Tunsted (fourteenth century), in which the cantus firmus, doubled (occasionally with embellishments) by two or three voices at the Fifth, Eighth and Twelfth, evidently produces a primitive and typical infra-diatonic harmony, the interval of a Fourth (between the Fifth and the Eighth) probably serving as the nucleus of a Diaphony. At the same time an experienced descanter, while leading his own part against these rigid progressions, intentionally avoids the concords (from the standpoint of that harmony) in order to deceive the ear and to convey the impression that all the rest of the singers, who constitute the principal body of the ensemble, are also descanting and not merely performing their regular task. The work which, in our modern times, follows the same principle on a "higher plane" is Stravinsky's *Les Noces*. The principal choral body of this composition is garbed—as a rule—in primitive diatonic harmonies, while the pianoforte ensemble (the instrumental "descanter" in this case, only with all the notes written down) intentionally avoids the concords and certainly deceives the ear, which receives the impression that the vocalists are also carrying out their parts according to non-diatonic formulas.

There is reason to believe that the form of descant referred to, although quoted from a fourteenth century treatise (regarded now as a compilation rather than as an original work), was already in practical use as early as the beginning of the twelfth century and perhaps was one of those which then evoked the characteristic criticism of John Cotton with his well-known comparison of the descanters to far-gone drunkards who after long wandering do indeed reach home but can never explain later, even to themselves, how and by what route they managed to do so. Similar criticisms were doubtless made throughout the entire period of descant and perhaps even grew in severity as may be judged from the much later attacks by Johannes de Muris, a writer of the fourteenth century. This famous theorist accused the descanters of his day of not knowing and not wanting to apply any musical rules—hence of being unable to distinguish good harmonic combinations from bad, thereby inflicting atrocious torture upon the ears of their listeners.

"JUST A LUCKY ACCIDENT"

"What a rudeness," he said, "what a brutality not to distinguish an ass from a man, a goat from a lion, a sheep from a fish; the descanters sing without any knowledge of harmony, their voices totter around the *tenor* without any system and if they sometimes produce a concord it is just a lucky accident, similar to that of a stone which hits the target about once in a hundred times, when flung at random by an unskilled hand."

It is noteworthy that in spite of living at a time when the application of the "tonal" principles of the "Ars Nova" was already in full swing, the author of the above quotation still adhered *psychologically* to the old "infra-tonal" conceptions, in that he considered the Octave, the Fifth and the Fourth as having a *nobler* effect on the human mind than the Third and Sixth (he once even spoke of a minor Sixth as still being a dissonance), not to mention the rest of the intervals. On the other hand the same "Ars Nova" which, from all evidence, had not yet succeeded in thoroughly eradicating conservative "infratonal" propensities, could not at one stroke put an end to the radical art of the descanters which progressed by the power of historic inertia as far as the middle of the sixteenth century, under the name of *Contrapunto alla mente* and, moreover, was even practiced on holy days in the Papal chapel, notwithstanding its prohibition by the notorious bull of Pope John XXII in 1324. Which shows how gradual was the entire evolutionary process beginning with the first symptoms of rebellious Infra-Atonality and ending with the definitive establishment of diatonic Tonality.

TEMPERING INFRA-TONALITY

Musical development would have been quite different, however, had the principle of Equal Temperament been applied to the infra-diatonic scale ("5 + 2") in early medieval music, just as it is now being applied by the Siamese. It is not difficult at all to guess, in the first place, that the European music which was based on the infra-diatonic scale would then have reached a much higher level because infra-tempered intonation (Octave divided into seven equal intervals) would immediately release the great and extraordinarily productive potentialities of modulation (including the possibility of construction of a complete and closed system of harmony) which, as we know from experience with our own diatonic scale ("7 + 5"), cannot be effected in all its manifold aspects under the condition of just intonation. We may safely take it for granted that Infra-Tonality would have been well-nigh exhausted before showing even the slightest tendency towards negation, i.e. Infra-Atonality. But when the time came for the latter principle, we may be sure that it would soon have eclipsed in acuteness, the most daring harmonies and polyphonic experiments of the "radical" descanters, described above. Indeed, even beginning with the first few feeble "revolts" in connection with the melodic aspect of the old infra-diatonic system, Infra-Atonality, when armed with Equal Temperament, would have brought forth something entirely different from what actually took place in the history of medieval music. The two auxiliary degrees of the infra-diatonic scale used on a par with its five regular degrees would in no wise yield to the composer the tonal material of the diatonic scale, but merely a series of seven equidistant tones within an octave, upon which none of the newly composed tunes, based on seven "regular" degrees, could be adequately performed. This circumstance would naturally have turned composers (sooner than was actually the case) to the exploitation of the harmonic aspect of the new scale which, however, would not have justified their expectations, as we shall now see.

STEPS TOWARD "ARS NOVA"

Let us suppose that these medieval composers would first come to the use of the Gymel and the Faux-bourdon—a natural inference since the harmonic combinations involved in these two principles are Thirds (original or inverted) from the standpoint of the diatonic scale, and whole steps from the standpoint of the old infra-diatonic scale. In the actual march of events these harmonic combinations, as we know, gave composers a fairly approximate idea of what the real diatonic harmonies they were seeking sounded like. This, in turn, led some of them to the difficult task of delving more deeply into the matter, notwithstanding the gradually increasing vagaries of their impatient "radical" brethren, which in the long run resulted in the firm establishment of the principles of the "Ars Nova" and further in a development of polyphonic art unparalleled in the history of music.

But all these results could never materialize with the Octave divided into seven equal intervals as required by infra-tempered intonation. In the first place the "Thirds" of the Gymel and Faux-bourdon would actually be "neutralized" by this intonation, since the whole steps of the infra-diatonic scale, by the use of which these Thirds are produced, would themselves be rigidly equalized. In other words, composers could not then obtain a series of major and minor Thirds (Gymel) or a series of major and minor inverted Triads (Faux-bourdon) but merely a sort of *neutral* Thirds and *neutral* inverted Triads acoustically occupying some middle position between the former. These neutral intervals and chords would certainly convey to the composers a very poor idea, if any, of the characteristic diatonic intervals and chords, which they dimly anticipated at that time, and would most probably have altogether perverted their dawning conceptions of consonance and dissonance, so closely connected with that anticipation. At all events we may be perfectly sure that no composer or theorist, not even a dozen Philippe de Vitrys, could ever have evolved the principles of the "Ars Nova" had he had at his command seven equal intervals within an octave instead of the characteristic series of whole steps and half steps of the diatonic scale, and "neutral" Thirds, Sixths, Seconds and Sevenths instead of these intervals properly and characteristically distinguished, in each instance, as "major" and "minor."

HYPOTHETICAL PROGRESS

This state of affairs would most certainly have given the upper hand, perhaps even complete hegemony, to the radical group of composers who, no longer finding any resistance in their path, would have accelerated the otherwise slow historical process, very soon coming to the "free" use of complicated harmonic combinations, simultaneously involving the seven equidistant tones of their scale. They would have been driven inevitably to this harmonic complication by the inadequate intonation of "neutral" intervals which, however, would soon follow them like a shadow in all their experiments until they reached the above limit. This would have been the *non plus ultra* of Infra-Atonality, with utter negation of all former principles but without the establishment of any new ones, and in particular, acute negation of the infra-tonal as well as of the tonal center, which is to be expected since the latter "center" could be represented in their system only by the caricature of a "neutral" Triad. And after that? It is immediately evident that the only, and rather empty possibility left to these medieval radicals would be to treat the scale-tones *not* as members of a certain system but simply as a group of disconnected units serving for the production of new sonorities as sonorities which, when combined with variety of rhythm and timbre, would probably give rise to some amusing and, at times, even clever inventions. But all these potentialities could hardly satisfy a composer craving for something deeper, a man convinced that he had within him a message to give to the world. Imagine a Palestrina or a Beethoven compelled to such musical externalism or, at best, to a choice between that and the most outrageous misrepresentation of his ideas by the "infra-atonal" medium with its seven equidistant tones and "neutral" harmonic formations. The position of such composers would certainly be little short of tragic. One can also understand that no mechanical increase of the number of tones within an octave (which would give, for instance, fourteen tones instead of seven in the case of duplication) could save the situation. It would, if anything, lead to still greater confusion.

Not a single composer or theorist of our day will doubt that under such conditions, the only way to remove the "infra-atonal" music of medieval composers from the impasse to which infra-tempered intonation, long outgrown, would lead them, would be to distemper their seven-tone scale and then to re-temper it jointly with the five auxiliary (chromatically altered) tones after the latter should gradually appear in the process of evolution. This operation would call for a division of the octave into twelve equal intervals (instead of seven, as heretofore) which, as we know at present, does not perceptibly affect the characteristic qualities of the diatonic scale and of its harmonic structures, and at the same time places at the disposal of the composer all the marvelous advantages already mentioned. However, this new division of an Octave (tempered intonation) is only *relatively* better than the old one and by no means represents a final form for all future musical systems to come. It is good only for the diatonic scale which brought it to life and it becomes obsolete as soon as this scale shows definite signs of wear. Moreover, it then constitutes a dangerous obstacle to musical creation, similar to the old division of an Octave (infra-tempered intonation), when outgrown, and the only way to evade this periodically recurrent evil is to break it up inexorably and then to substitute for it a still more subtle division of the Octave (supra-tempered intonation) corresponding to the general number of tones the new scale comprises.

The modern composer who, we assume, could easily solve the above problem for the medieval composer (supposedly enchained by infra-tempered intonation) must fully realize that he himself is now facing an identical problem, although on a "higher plane." There is no need to repeat, or to dwell on the consecutive phases through which the modern composer (himself actually enchained by tempered intonation) has passed during the present "atonal" period, since they are similar and parallel to those of the "infra-atonal" period already described. It is only worth while to point out one interesting and significant phase which occurred in the evolution of modern music immediately after the whole-step harmonic constructions of Debussy and his followers were widely used.

I have said that a complete whole-step chord which consists of six notes arranged by *equal* intervals represents but an inadequate reflection of the supra-diatonic Hexad, since one of the latter's component intervals (E-X) is *larger* than all the rest. This disparity between the supra-diatonic Hexad and the whole-step chord (which obviously is a "neutral" Hexad in relation to the former) could not, of course, be avoided under the conditions of our present twelve-tone tempered system. Now the reader may claim and justly so, that this disparity would not have passed absolutely unnoticed by the modern composer if our construction and prediction of the supra-diatonic scale were correct. He would already have made some effort to remedy this fault, however short he might fall of success.

It is, then, extremely significant to point out that an effort of this kind was actually made by Scriabin, who at the time could not have had the slightest idea of the construction of the supra-diatonic scale and its basic Hexad. Guided by intuition only, he did the most that could be done under the given conditions. In fact he *enlarged* one of the six equal whole steps of the "neutral Hexad" by transforming it into a sesqui-step (F♯-A instead of F♯-G♯) and thus obtained a chord which could be expressed by the notes C-D-E-F♯-A-B♭ (when brought within an octave) approximating in structure the supra-diatonic Hexad Z-C-D-E-X-Y as well as F-G-A-B-V-W. Later (in *Prometheus,* for instance) he applied the same method to another whole step, transforming it from A♭-B♭ into A♭-B and thereby obtaining a chord C-D-E-F♯-A♭-B (when transposed to the key of C.) This shows only that Scriabin inwardly heard the supra-diatonic Hexad on different degrees of its particular scale or (if we have to assume it each time as a tonic chord) in different modes.

The obvious drawback of Scriabin's chord is that the transformation of any whole step of the "neutral Hexad" into a sesqui-step, in order to make it resemble the "large" interval (E-X) of the supra-diatonic Hexad, automatically affects one of the adjacent whole steps, which is thereby transformed into a half step. This new, though lesser disparity between the two chords in question is inevitable under the conditions of our present tempered system and represents one of the negative factors which prevent the further evolution of even a most rudimentary system of supra-diatonic harmony. It explains, in turn, all the subsequent phases through which modern methods of composition have passed since Scriabin. The impossibility of establishing any new harmonic rules on the one hand, and the inadequate intonation of the existing tonal system on the other, prematurely accelerated the historic process and soon led to a "free" use of the twelve-tone chord, as exemplified by Schönberg and his group, or to polyphonic constructions based upon it—Polytonality, which represents but a particular instance of Atonality that has already reached its apex.

With no other path in sight, as far as harmonic and polyphonic complication is concerned, and with the still existing form of tempered intonation, the modern composer is now compelled to choose between "musical externalism" (aiming at nothing but variety of purely "sensory" effects) and the misrepresentation of his ideas by the inadequate tonal system. To avoid turning back or compromising by mixing the old creative formulae with the new, as many do at present, only one way out is possible: to break with the old tonal system and accept a new one logically evolved therefrom.

BREAKING WITH THE OLD

This is not the *easiest* way out—far from it. That, however, is rather to be expected, since the easiest way is not necessarily the right way in matters of art. Even with the new system already at hand, the actual "transplantation" of the composer to unfamiliar "supra-tonal soil" represents a problem far more difficult than appears at a casual glance. It is not only the matter of a new musical instrument, on which anyone could immediately create "supra-tonal symphonies." The composer must first accustom himself to new acoustic relations, probably a slow process on account of the obstacles to be surmounted. The previous tonal system, especially its tempered intonation (rather solidly rooted in every musician's mind at the present time), are his two old partners, to get rid of whom is not simple. Even the pure intonation of the familiar diatonic scale, oddly enough, strikes his ear now as sounding somewhat "false," until he gets used to it. So it is natural to expect that the new scale, be its intonation pure or supra-tempered, will at first displease him. Therefore special methods of ear-accommodation will have to be found. The establishment of new and, at least, rudimentary rules of harmony and counterpoint (presupposing, of course, an entirely new classification of consonances and dissonances) would probably represent the next and no less complicated problem to be tackled before any "supra-tonal" musical compositions could be created at all, before even the simplest class-room harmonizations based on the supra-diatonic scale could be properly executed. These rules, when definitely established and codified, will serve as the educational background of composers intending to create "supra-tonal" music, and will have to be thoroughly mastered at the very outset of their career, no matter whether they strictly follow or intentionally and judiciously transgress them later on.

So in practically every way, and from the very bottom up, modern composers, especially the young generation, are to be re-trained and concurrently re-disciplined after the relaxing effect of "all-permitting" Atonality which is now historically doomed and bound to vanish with the sure advent of organized Supra-Tonality, just as "all-permitting" Infra-Atonality gradually yielded towards the close of the Middle Ages before victorious and organized Tonality. These composers have to become fully aware of the fact that we are now passing through a period of some sort of *New Medievalism* in tonal art (perhaps, too, in other departments of life and culture). This inescapable evolutionary stage, however, may be lived through perhaps with comparative ease, even though not with race-track speed, if actual and conscious efforts based on scientifically positive methods (not mere "creative experimentation") should be exerted towards the practical exploitation of the new scale, whose introduction in music is now urgently dictated by the inexorable laws of historical logic. It is, of course, not difficult to fore-see that a great number of problems—technical, acoustical, theoretical, psycho-physiological, pedagogical, etc.—besides those briefly outlined here, would immediately arise and would have to be scrupulously worked out. It is hardly necessary to add that no single person is in a position to undertake this gigantic task. A special institution equipped with the necessary means and guided by experts in all its branches will have to be established for that purpose. And the sooner the better, before musical creative art with its vital and inwardly stirring forces becomes self-poisoned for lack of a natural outlet.

CENTITONES AND VIBRATION-RATIOS

GLOSSARY OF TECHNICAL TERMS

INDEX

PARALLEL TABLE OF CENTITONES AND THEIR EQUIVALENT VIBRATION-RATIOS

FOR ALL INTERVALS (WITHIN THE COMPASS OF AN OCTAVE)

ENCOUNTERED IN THE PRESENT VOLUME

Pages On Which The Intervals Occur	Centi-tones	Ratios	Pages On Which The Intervals Occur	Centi-tones	Ratios
190	0	$=\dfrac{1}{1}$	190	6	$=\dfrac{2517}{2500}$
190	0.6	$=\dfrac{61875}{61789}$ [6 mtn.]	190	6.8	$=\dfrac{3046}{3025}$
16, 119, 190	1	$=\dfrac{149819}{149645}$	190	7*	$=\dfrac{15749}{15625}$
31, 118	1.8	$=\dfrac{19383245667680019896796723}{19342813113834066795298816}$ [18 mtn.]	179	7*	$=\dfrac{512}{507}$
17, 190	2	$=\dfrac{62500}{62359}$	190	7.2	$=\dfrac{3750}{3719}$
204, 212	3*	$=\dfrac{364}{363}$	178	8	$=\dfrac{363}{360}$
190	3*	$=\dfrac{5625}{5606}$	122, 190	8.14	$=\dfrac{125000}{123833}$ [8.2]
190	3.2	$=\dfrac{27573}{27500}$	190	8.4	$=\dfrac{13887}{13750}$
190	3.4	$=\dfrac{12500}{12447}$	190	10.4	$=\dfrac{8125}{8034}$
126, 129	3.6	$=\dfrac{7500}{7469}$	184, 192, 215	11	$=\dfrac{81}{80}$
190	3.8	$=\dfrac{3025}{3012}$	191	11.2	$=\dfrac{2500}{2469}$
191	4.6	$=\dfrac{6875}{6838}$	27, 117, 120, 369	12	$=\dfrac{531441}{524288}$
190	5	$=\dfrac{28284}{28125}$	179	14	$=\dfrac{65}{64}$

* The representation of *different* ratios by the *same* number of centitones is due to approximations.

356 CENTITONES AND VIBRATION-RATIOS

Pages On Which The Intervals Occur	Centi-tones	Ratios
190	15	$\frac{33839}{33075}$
190	16.3	$\frac{37500}{36803}$
189, 205, 213, 271	18	$\frac{1210}{1183}$
178	19	$\frac{45}{44}$
190, 191	20.4	$\frac{2561}{2500}$
179, 205, 213	21	$\frac{40}{39}$
192	24	$\frac{36}{35}$
190	24.5	$\frac{56250}{54689}$
14	25	$\frac{1029302}{1000000}$
177, 205, 213	27*	$\frac{33}{32}$
190, 191	27*	$\frac{14183}{13750}$
185, 205, 213, 271	29	$\frac{121}{117}$
189, 205, 213, 271	30	$\frac{91}{88}$
127, 191, 213, 223, 292	31.6	$\sqrt[19]{2} = \frac{10372}{10000}$
205, 213	32*	$\frac{28}{27}$
205, 213	32*	$\frac{27}{26}$

Pages On Which The Intervals Occur	Centi-tones	Ratios
190, 191	32.6	$\frac{84375}{81268}$
128	33	$\frac{134217728}{129140163}$
189, 205, 213, 271	35*	$\frac{126}{121}$
220	35*	$\frac{25}{24}$
189, 205, 213, 271	37	$\frac{1331}{1274}$
205, 213	40	$\frac{22}{21}$
205, 213	43	$\frac{21}{20}$
29, 49, 108, 142	45	$\frac{256}{243}$
189, 205, 213, 271	46	$\frac{637}{605}$
14, 17, 18, 108, 120, 227	50	$\sqrt[12]{2} = \frac{105946}{100000}$ $\left[\text{about } \frac{89}{84}\right]$
189, 205, 213, 271	53	$\frac{484}{455}$
108, 177, 205, 213, 220	56	$\frac{16}{15}$
29, 120, 122	57	$\frac{2187}{2048}$
177, 205, 213	59	$\frac{15}{14}$
189, 205, 213, 271	62	$\frac{130}{121}$
127, 189, 213	63.2	$\sqrt[19]{2^2} = \frac{10757}{10000}$

* The representation of *different* ratios by the *same* number of centitones is due to approximations.

Pages On Which The Intervals Occur	Centitones	Ratios
177, 199 227, 231	64	$=\dfrac{14}{13}$
220	67*	$=\dfrac{27}{25}$
189, 205 213, 271	67*	$=\dfrac{121}{112}$
126	69	$=\dfrac{1162261467}{1073741824}$
177, 205 211, 213	70	$=\dfrac{13}{12}$
189, 205 213, 271	72	$=\dfrac{99}{91}$
189, 205 213, 271	73	$=\dfrac{1183}{1089}$
177, 205 211, 213	75	$=\dfrac{12}{11}$
189, 205 213, 271	78	$=\dfrac{1456}{1331}$
177, 199 227, 231	83	$=\dfrac{11}{10}$
45, 123 191, 258	85.7 [85.72]	$=\sqrt[7]{2}=\dfrac{110409}{100000}$
30, 139	90	$=\dfrac{65536}{59049}$
108, 177 199, 215	91	$=\dfrac{10}{9}$
127, 185, 189 213, 231	94.8	$=\sqrt[19]{2^3}=\dfrac{11157}{10000}$
368	96.5	$=\dfrac{1118034}{1000000}$
14, 18, 29 45, 108, 120	100	$=\sqrt[12]{2^2}=\dfrac{112246}{100000}\left[\text{about }\dfrac{449}{400}\right]$
206	101	$=\dfrac{1331}{1183}$
17, 29, 45 49, 108, 177	102	$=\dfrac{9}{8}$
206	104	$=\dfrac{44}{39}$
127	114	$=\dfrac{4782969}{4194304}$
117, 187 199, 231	115	$=\dfrac{8}{7}$
143	120	$=\sqrt[5]{2}=\dfrac{11487}{10000}$
220, 221	123*	$=\dfrac{144}{125}$
206	123*	$=\dfrac{15}{13}$
206, 237	126	$=\dfrac{140}{121}$
127, 185 213, 231	126.4	$=\sqrt[19]{2^4}=\dfrac{11571}{10000}$
189, 206 213, 271	131	$=\dfrac{121}{104}$
177, 206, 211	134	$=\dfrac{7}{6}$
206, 271	137	$=\dfrac{1274}{1089}$
206	142	$=\dfrac{33}{28}$
206	144	$=\dfrac{968}{819}$

* The representation of *different* ratios by the *same* number of centitones is due to approximations.

Pages On Which The Intervals Occur	Centi-tones	Ratios	Pages On Which The Intervals Occur	Centi-tones	Ratios
184, 186, 206, 211, 221, 231	145	$=\dfrac{13}{11}$	200	179	$=\dfrac{16}{13}$
30, 139, 193, 206, 215	147	$=\dfrac{32}{27}$	206	180	$=\dfrac{1638}{1331}$
18, 29, 120, 227	150	$=\sqrt[12]{2^3}=\dfrac{11892}{10000}\left[\text{about }\dfrac{44}{37}\right]$	206	182*	$=\dfrac{121}{98}$
206	155	$=\dfrac{1089}{910}$	220	182*	$=\dfrac{100}{81}$
177, 206, 211, 215, 270, 271	158*	$=\dfrac{6}{5}$	206	185	$=\dfrac{26}{21}$
127, 189, 213	158*	$=\sqrt[19]{2^5}=\dfrac{12001}{10000}$	127, 185, 189, 213, 374	189.6	$=\sqrt[19]{2^6}=\dfrac{12447}{10000}$
29, 30, 120	159	$=\dfrac{19683}{16384}$	30, 139	192	$=\dfrac{8192}{6561}$
206	161	$=\dfrac{728}{605}$	16, 21, 108, 177, 237, 270	193	$=\dfrac{5}{4}$
206	163	$=\dfrac{110}{91}$	14, 18, 29, 120	200	$=\sqrt[12]{2^4}=\dfrac{125992}{100000}\left[\text{about }\dfrac{63}{50}\right]$
206	166	$=\dfrac{40}{33}$	22, 29, 108, 120, 237	204	$=\dfrac{81}{64}$
45, 46, 123, 258, 260	171.4	$=\sqrt[7]{2^2}=\dfrac{121901}{100000}$	207, 212	206	$=\dfrac{33}{26}$
206	172	$=\dfrac{39}{32}$	200, 207, 211	209	$=\dfrac{14}{11}$
200	174	$=\dfrac{11}{9}$	127	216	$=\dfrac{43046721}{33554432}$
206	175	$=\dfrac{1183}{968}$	200	217	$=\dfrac{9}{7}$
206	177	$=\dfrac{27}{22}$	127, 213, 374	221.2	$=\sqrt[19]{2^7}=\dfrac{12909}{10000}$
			200	228	$=\dfrac{13}{10}$

* The representation of *different* ratios by the *same* number of centitones is due to approximations.

Pages On Which The Intervals Occur	Centi-tones	Ratios
207	236	$=\dfrac{21}{16}$
207, 271	239	$=\dfrac{637}{484}$
143	240	$=\sqrt[5]{2^2}=\dfrac{13195}{10000}$
189, 207, 211 213, 271	246	$=\dfrac{121}{91}$
17, 108, 119 177, 207	249	$=\dfrac{4}{3}$
14, 18 29, 119	250	$=\sqrt[12]{2^5}=\dfrac{133484}{100000}$ $\left[\text{about }\dfrac{303}{227}\right]$
281	251.7	$=\dfrac{13375}{10000}$
207, 211	252	$=\dfrac{1456}{1089}$
127, 189, 213	252.8	$=\sqrt[19]{2^8}=\dfrac{13389}{10000}$
46, 122, 258	257.1	$=\sqrt[7]{2^3}=\dfrac{1345901}{1000000}$
207	260	$=\dfrac{27}{20}$
29, 120	261	$=\dfrac{177147}{131072}$
207	263	$=\dfrac{819}{605}$
207	268	$=\dfrac{15}{11}$
207	271	$=\dfrac{1820}{1331}$
189, 201, 213 231, 271	276	$=\dfrac{11}{8}$
201	281	$=\dfrac{18}{13}$
220, 221	284	$=\dfrac{25}{18}$
127, 185 189, 213	284.4	$=\sqrt[19]{2^9}=\dfrac{13887}{10000}$
207	287	$=\dfrac{39}{28}$
207	290	$=\dfrac{169}{121}$
201	292	$=\dfrac{7}{5}$
178, 271	295	$=\dfrac{45}{32}$
18, 29, 120	300	$=\sqrt[12]{2^6}=\dfrac{141421}{100000}$ $\left[\text{about }\dfrac{140}{99}\right]$
29, 120, 269	306	$=\dfrac{729}{512}$
201	308	$=\dfrac{10}{7}$
192, 208	310	$=\dfrac{242}{169}$
208	313	$=\dfrac{56}{39}$
127, 213	316	$=\sqrt[19]{2^{10}}=\dfrac{14402}{10000}$
127	318	$=\dfrac{387420489}{268435456}$
201	319	$=\dfrac{13}{9}$
201	324	$=\dfrac{16}{11}$

Pages On Which The Intervals Occur	Centitones	Ratios	Pages On Which The Intervals Occur	Centitones	Ratios
192, 208	329	$=\dfrac{1331}{910}$	202	372	$=\dfrac{20}{13}$
208	332	$=\dfrac{22}{15}$	127, 213	379	$=\sqrt[19]{\dfrac{12}{2}}=\dfrac{15493}{10000}$
191, 208	337	$=\dfrac{1210}{819}$	202	383	$=\dfrac{14}{9}$
30, 139	339	$=\dfrac{262144}{177147}$	192, 202 208, 211	391	$=\dfrac{11}{7}$
194, 208 215, 237	340	$=\dfrac{40}{27}$	208, 212	394	$=\dfrac{52}{33}$
46, 122, 134 258, 262, 367	342.8	$=\sqrt[7]{\dfrac{4}{2}}=\dfrac{1485996}{1000000}$	139	396	$=\dfrac{128}{81}$
126, 134, 189 213, 374	347.4	$=\sqrt[19]{\dfrac{11}{2}}=\dfrac{14938}{10000}$	18, 29, 120	400	$=\sqrt[12]{\dfrac{8}{2}}=\dfrac{15874}{10000}\left[\text{about }\dfrac{100}{63}\right]$
189, 191, 208 211, 213, 271	348	$=\dfrac{1089}{728}$	179, 202 220, 271	407	$=\dfrac{8}{5}$
281	348.3	$=\dfrac{14954}{10000}$	29, 120	408	$=\dfrac{6561}{4096}$
14, 16, 18 22, 29, 120	350	$=\sqrt[12]{\dfrac{7}{2}}=\dfrac{14983}{10000}\left[\text{about }\dfrac{433}{298}\right]$	127, 185 189, 213	410.6	$=\sqrt[19]{\dfrac{13}{2}}=\dfrac{16068}{10000}$
11, 15, 108 117, 120, 177	351	$=\dfrac{3}{2}$	209	415	$=\dfrac{21}{13}$
191, 208, 211	354	$=\dfrac{182}{121}$	209	418	$=\dfrac{196}{121}$
143	360	$=\sqrt[5]{\dfrac{3}{2}}=\dfrac{15157}{10000}$	209	420	$=\dfrac{1331}{819}$
192, 208	361	$=\dfrac{968}{637}$	179, 189, 202 213, 231, 271	421	$=\dfrac{13}{8}$
127	363	$=\dfrac{1594323}{1048576}$	209	423	$=\dfrac{44}{27}$
208	364	$=\dfrac{32}{21}$	209	425	$=\dfrac{1936}{1183}$

Pages On Which The Intervals Occur	Centitones	Ratios
202	426	$= \dfrac{18}{11}$
209	428	$= \dfrac{64}{39}$
46, 123 253, 367	428.5	$= \sqrt[7]{2^5} = \dfrac{164067}{100000}$
209	434	$= \dfrac{33}{20}$
209	437	$= \dfrac{91}{55}$
189, 209 213, 271	439	$= \dfrac{605}{364}$
30, 139	441	$= \dfrac{32768}{19683}$
108, 209, 211 213, 220, 258	442	$= \dfrac{5}{3}$
127, 139, 213	442.2	$= \sqrt[19]{2^{14}} = \dfrac{16665}{10000}$
209	445	$= \dfrac{1820}{1089}$
18, 29, 120	450	$= \sqrt[12]{2^9} = \dfrac{168179}{100000} \left[\text{about } \dfrac{37}{22}\right]$
29, 108 120, 209	453	$= \dfrac{27}{16}$
203, 209, 211	455	$= \dfrac{22}{13}$
209	456	$= \dfrac{819}{484}$
209	458	$= \dfrac{56}{33}$
209	463	$= \dfrac{1089}{637}$
127	465	$= \dfrac{14348907}{8388608}$
209, 211	466	$= \dfrac{12}{7}$
209	469	$= \dfrac{208}{121}$
127, 213	473.8	$= \sqrt[19]{2^{15}} = \dfrac{17284}{10000}$
209	474	$= \dfrac{121}{70}$
209	477	$= \dfrac{26}{15}$
143	480	$= \sqrt[5]{2^4} = \dfrac{17411}{10000}$
189, 203 213, 271	485	$= \dfrac{7}{4}$
209, 231, 237	496	$= \dfrac{39}{22}$
139, 178, 192 203, 220	498	$= \dfrac{16}{9}$
209	499	$= \dfrac{2366}{1331}$
18, 29, 120	500	$= \sqrt[12]{2^{10}} = \dfrac{178179}{100000} \left[\text{about } \dfrac{98}{55}\right]$
127, 185 189, 213	505.4	$= \sqrt[19]{2^{16}} = \dfrac{17927}{10000}$
192, 203, 271	509	$= \dfrac{9}{5}$
29, 120	510	$= \dfrac{59049}{10000}$

Pages On Which The Intervals Occur	Centitones	Ratios	Pages On Which The Intervals Occur	Centitones	Ratios
46, 123 258, 367	514.3 =	$\sqrt[7]{2^6} = \dfrac{181145}{100000}$	210	554	$\dfrac{1210}{637}$
203	517 =	$\dfrac{20}{11}$	29, 108 120, 269	555 =	$\dfrac{243}{128}$
189, 210 213, 271	522 =	$\dfrac{1331}{728}$	210	557 =	$\dfrac{40}{21}$
210, 211	525 =	$\dfrac{11}{6}$	210	560 =	$\dfrac{21}{11}$
210	527 =	$\dfrac{2178}{1183}$	210	563 =	$\dfrac{2548}{1331}$
210	528 =	$\dfrac{182}{99}$	210	565 =	$\dfrac{121}{63}$
210, 211	530 =	$\dfrac{24}{13}$	127	567 =	$\dfrac{129140163}{67108864}$
210	533* =	$\dfrac{224}{121}$	210	568* =	$\dfrac{52}{27}$
220	533* =	$\dfrac{50}{27}$	210	568* =	$\dfrac{27}{14}$
203	536 =	$\dfrac{13}{7}$	127, 213	568.6 =	$\sqrt[19]{2^{18}} = \dfrac{19284}{10000}$
127, 189, 213	537 =	$\sqrt[19]{2^{17}} = \dfrac{18593}{10000}$	210	570 =	$\dfrac{176}{91}$
210	538 =	$\dfrac{121}{65}$	210	571 =	$\dfrac{234}{121}$
210	541 =	$\dfrac{28}{15}$	210	573 =	$\dfrac{64}{33}$
108, 210 258, 271	544 =	$\dfrac{15}{8}$	210	579 =	$\dfrac{39}{20}$
210	547 =	$\dfrac{455}{242}$	210	582 =	$\dfrac{1183}{605}$
18, 29, 120	550 =	$\sqrt[12]{2^{11}} = \dfrac{188774}{100000}$ $\left[\text{about } \dfrac{168}{89}\right]$	17, 177	600 =	$\dfrac{2}{1}$

* The representation of *different* ratios by the *same* number of centitones is due to approximations.

GLOSSARY OF TECHNICAL TERMS

ACOUSTIC COMPROMISE. Acceptance, by the ear, of a certain degree of acoustic inaccuracy in various artificial intonations (q.v.) which yields, in return, some practical advantages without detriment to the music itself.

ARTIFICIAL INTONATION. The one which is mostly used for practical convenience and which is acoustically inaccurate from the standpoint of pure or natural intonation. (Compare with TEMPERED INTONATION).

ATONAL SCALE. An artificial scale which contains twelve equidistant and musically independent degrees deprived of any "intertonal gravitation" (q.v.) between themselves and jointly to a common center, known as the Tonic. It serves as a basis for "atonal" music (whence the name), i.e. the one that is free from any of the characteristics of "mode" and "tonality." [It was known, heretofore, under the name of "semitonal" or "duodecuple" scale, the latter term having been introduced by A. E. Hull].

ATONALITY. Literally, negation of tonality. In a more specific sense, a method of composition which regards every scale-degree as being perfectly independent from all the rest and, especially, from any preselected Tonic, in so far as the factor of "intertonal gravitation" (q.v.) is concerned.

AUXILIARY DEGREES. Identical to chromatic (or infra-chromatic or supra-chromatic) degrees as opposed to diatonic (or infra-diatonic or supra-diatonic), i.e. to "regular" degrees that form the main body of any organic scale (q.v.)

CENTITONE (ctn.) One hundredth part of an equally tempered whole tone (or $\frac{1}{600}$ of an octave).

CHROMATIC ALTERATION. Raising or lowering of a diatonic scale-degree by means of a sharp or flat.

CHROMATIC MODE. A term introduced in this volume for the twelve-tone chromatic scale in which the original inequality of its component intervals stays fundamentally unimpaired owing either to just or to an appropriately tempered intonation. Such a mode is structurally identical with a supra-diatonic mode (supra-mode) in the nineteen-tone Temperament system.

CHROMATIC SCALE. Identical to atonal scale (q.v.) when considered as a perfectly independent basis for musical composition. Otherwise merely a progression of notes by half steps in which, consequently, none of the chromatic degrees (besides the diatonic ones) is missing.

CHROMATIC SEMITONE. A term commonly accepted for semitones, which are represented by two *similar* literal designations in each instance, like C-C♯, D-D♯, etc. (Compare with DIATONIC SEMITONE).

COMMA OF DIDYMUS. Difference (11 ctn.) between the Pythagorean and acoustically pure major Third (204 ctn. and 193 ctn. respectively), or, which comes to the same thing, between the justly intoned major and minor whole tones (102 ctn. and 91 ctn. respectively).

COMMON CHORD. Consonant chord in a given scale. It is a *Monad* in the sub-infra-diatonic scale, a *Dyad* in the infra-diatonic scale, a *Triad* in the diatonic scale, and a *Hexad* in the supra-diatonic scale.

CONSONANCE. An interval or any harmonic combination which requires no resolution within a given scale. (Compare with DISSONANCE and FALSONANCE).

DECIMAL SYSTEM. Applied for the first time in this book for the purpose of expressing the dimension of musical intervals in simple and easily understood terms. It is worked out similarly to the metric system, with the assumption of an equally tempered whole tone as a basic measuring unit which is divided into tenths, hundredths and thousandths parts, termed *decitones, centitones* and *millitones,* respectively.

DECITONE (dtn.) One tenth part of an equally tempered whole tone (or $\frac{1}{60}$ of an octave).

DEGREE. In relation to a scale (i.e. as a scale-degree), the same as a scale-tone or a scale-note. In this connection, however, the reservation has to be made that any given scale-degree is, to a certain extent, rather flexible with regard to its pitch, permitting various "shadings" of intonation and, therefore it may represent in practice a good many different, though proximate "tones" in the strictly acoustical sense of this term (i.e. as musical sounds with definitely fixed vibration-numbers).

DIALECTIC TRIAD. In Hegel's philosophical system, an "evolutionary" formula to which the laws of logical thinking as well as of the various historic and other manifestations in actual life are subject. It comprises three consecutive stages—Thesis, Antithesis, Synthesis—of which the first two (Thesis and Antithesis) respectively representing the positive and negative (i.e. strictly contradictory) principles, eventually meet and complete each other in the third and much broader one (Synthesis). The latter, however, serves as the starting point, i.e. Thesis, of a new "Triad," being contradicted by its own Antithesis and both of them again meeting in a still broader Synthesis, etc.

DIATONIC SCALE. According to the definition given in this book, the complete form of this scale comprises seven regular and five auxiliary degrees (formula "7 + 5"), the former set (seven degrees) representing what has been heretofore known as the diatonic scale proper, and the latter set being identical in construction with the five regular degrees of the infra-diatonic scale.

DIATONIC SEMITONE. A term commonly accepted for semitones, which are represented by two *different* literal designations in each instance, like C-Db, D-Eb, E-F, etc. (Compare with CHROMATIC SEMITONE).

DICHORD. A scale of two tones a perfect Fourth apart. The term is derived from one of the ancient Greek Lyres of two strings tuned in accordance with this interval.

DISSONANCE. An interval or harmonic combination which requires resolution within a given scale. (Compare with CONSONANCE and FALSONANCE).

DISSONANT COUNTERPOINT. The one in which, contrary to the familiar "consonant" counterpoint, all the basic intervals are dissonances, the consonances playing merely a secondary rôle and tending to the former.

DUODECUPLE SCALE. Same as ATONAL SCALE (q.v.)

DYAD. A common chord (q.v.) of the infra-diatonic scale. It consists of two notes an infra-Third apart. A perfect (consonant) Dyad contains one and a half steps; a diminished (dissonant) Dyad contains one whole step.

EQUAL TEMPERAMENT. See TEMPERAMENT.

EQUALLY TEMPERED INTONATION. See TEMPERED INTONATION.

FALSONANCE. An interval or harmonic combination which, irrespective of its individual "harmoniousness" or "inharmoniousness," is foreign to a given scale, and, as a rule, excluded by the just intonation of the latter (compare with CONSONANCE and DISSONANCE).

FIXED INTONATION. The one embodied in musical instruments with a definite number of tones for the entire scale whose pitch cannot be changed at the will of the performer. (Compare with VARIABLE INTONATION).

FUNDAMENTAL INFRA-MODE. Same as *fundamental mode* (q.v.) but considered with reference to the infra-diatonic scale (i.e. infra-mode "F-f").

FUNDAMENTAL MODE. A term provisionally given in this volume to the mode "F-f" of the diatonic scale (familiarly known as the Lydian mode), the only one that can be formed throughout either by ascending Fifths or descending Fourths.

FUNDAMENTAL SUPRA-MODE. Same as *fundamental mode* (q.v.) but considered with reference to the supra-diatonic scale (i.e. supra-mode "F-f").

HALF STEP. Minimum interval in a given scale. When tempered, it is equal to a semitone in the diatonic scale, but differs, dimensionally, in any other scale.

HARMONIC DUALISM. A theory (upheld in this book) that the notions of consonance and dissonance, however "relative" and mutable in the process of historical evolution, will never disappear from musical art, since they represent but outward manifestations of the basic polarity which is characteristic of human emotion and which, therefore, is profoundly and unalterably rooted in the human *psyche.*

HARMONIC INTONATION. A system of tuning which serves as a theoretical norm for simultaneous harmonic combinations in a given scale. (Compare with MELODIC INTONATION and JUST INTONATION).

HARMONIC MONISM. A theory that the division of intervals into consonances and dissonances is groundless in every respect and that these two notions, even psychologically, differ merely in degree and not in essence.

HEPTATONIC SCALE. Literally, a seven-tone scale. In a more limited sense, the familiar diatonic scale.

HEXAD. A chord composed of six tones. In this book the term mostly implies the common chord of the supra-diatonic scale. (See SUPRA-DIATONIC HEXAD).

HYPERTONIC DYAD. A common chord of the infra-diatonic scale formed on the second (regular) degree of the latter.

IMPERFECT INFRA-MODE. A name given in this volume to the infra-mode "F-f" of the infra-diatonic scale for the reason that its tonic Dyad (F-A) represents a discord, namely a *diminished* Dyad. No confusion should arise from the fact that, on another occasion, it has been termed *fundamental infra-mode* (q.v.) The latter name is purely provisional and points merely to the *acoustic* principle according to which this infra-mode is constructed, while the former name (imperfect) applies to the *musical* value of the same infra-mode.

INFRA. A prefix indicating that the term to which it is attached must be considered with reference to the infra-diatonic system.

INFRA-ATONAL SCALE. Same as *atonal scale* (q.v.) but with seven instead of twelve equidistant and musically "independent" tones within an octave.

INFRA-ATONALITY. Same as *atonality* (q.v.) but considered with reference to the *infra-atonal scale* (q.v.) Literally, negation of infra-tonality.

INFRA-CHROMATIC ALTERATION. Same as *chromatic alteration* (q.v.) but considered with reference to the degrees of the infra-diatonic scale.

INFRA-CHROMATIC DEGREES. See AUXILIARY DEGREES.

INFRA-CHROMATIC SCALE. Identical to infra-atonal scale (q.v.) when considered as a perfectly independent basis for musical composition. Otherwise merely a progression of notes by half steps in which, consequently, none of the infra-chromatic degrees (besides the infra-diatonic ones) is missing. Bears the same relation to the scale "5 + 2" as the chromatic scale to the scale "7 + 5."

INFRA-COMMA. Difference (57 ctn.) between seven natural Fifths and four Octaves.

INFRA-DIATONIC DEGREES. See REGULAR DEGREES.

INFRA-DIATONIC SCALE. A diatonic scale of a "lower order." In its complete form it contains five regular and two auxiliary degrees (formula "5 + 2"), the former set being identical with the "pentatonic" scale (e.g. C, D, F, G, A) and the latter set closely approaching the notes E and B of the diatonic scale.

INFRA-FIFTH. The fifth degree of the infra-diatonic scale. Also an interval between the first and the fifth degree as well as any of its quantitative equivalents found in this scale (like C-A or D-C etc.)

INFRA-FIFTH-CHORD. A chord of three notes arranged by infra-Thirds. In the root position its two extreme notes form the interval of an infra-Fifth, whence the name.

INFRA-FLAT. A sign of alteration which lowers any degree of the infra-diatonic scale a half step.

INFRA-FOURTH. The fourth degree of the infra-diatonic scale. Also an interval between the first and the fourth degree as well as any of its quantitative equivalents found in this scale (like C-G or D-A, etc.)

INFRA-MODE. Same as *mode* (q.v.) but considered with reference to the infra-diatonic scale. The various infra-modes are designated by their extreme notes (like "C-c," "D-d," "F-f," etc.) which become such as a result of these infra-modes being placed exclusively upon white keys, i.e. without containing any black keys at all. They are sometimes referred to as *principal infra-modes,* as distinguished from *altered infra-modes* which cannot be placed upon white keys exclusively, and which contain at least one infra-chromatic alteration.

INFRA-NINTH-CHORD. A chord of five notes arranged by infra-Thirds. In the root position its two extreme notes form the interval of an infra-Ninth, whence the name.

INFRA-PRIME. The first degree of the infra-diatonic scale. Also a unison of two parts in this scale.

INFRA-POLYTONALITY. Simultaneous combination of two or more infra-tonalities (in the sense of keys) in a musical composition.

INFRA-SECOND. The second degree of the infra-diatonic scale. Also an interval between the first and the second degree as well as any of its quantitative equivalents found in this scale (like C-D or D-F, etc.).

INFRA-SEVENTH-CHORD. A chord of four notes arranged by infra-Thirds. In the root position, its two extreme notes form the interval of an infra-Seventh, whence the name.

INFRA-SHARP. A sign of alteration that raises any degree of the infra-diatonic scale a half step.

INFRA-SIXTH. The sixth degree of the infra-diatonic scale. Also an interval between the first and the sixth degree as well as any of its quantitative equivalents found in this scale (like C-c, or D-d, etc.)

INFRA-TEMPERED FIFTH. (Not to be confused with *infra-tempered infra-Fifth*). A *diatonic* Fifth reduced to 342.8 ctn. in the infra-tempered scale (q.v.)

INFRA-TEMPERED INFRA-FIFTH. The interval of an infra-Fifth equally tempered (minor = 428.5 ctn., major = 514.3 ctn.)

INFRA-TEMPERED INTONATION. The one which results from the division of an octave into seven equal intervals, thereby automatically equalizing all half steps as well as all whole steps of the infra-diatonic scale.

INFRA-TEMPERED SCALE. The infra-diatonic scale ("5 + 2") equally tempered. At present used only in Siamese music.

INFRA-THIRD. The third degree of the infra-diatonic scale. Also an interval between the first and the third degree as well as any of its quantitative equivalents found in this scale (like C-F or D-G, etc.)

INFRA-TONALITY. Same as *Tonality* (q.v.) but considered with reference to the infra-diatonic scale.

INTERTONAL GRAVITATION. The one that exists between the various degrees of a given scale to each other and to their common Tonic, and that constitutes the basic characteristic of the principle of *Tonality* (q.v.)

JUST INTONATION. The one that results from the common (consonant) chords of a given scale being identically tuned in accordance with a certain preselected group of acoustically pure intervals (specific for each scale), as found in the Natural Harmonic Series.

LÜ. A sort of stopped pipe used for acoustical experiments by the Chinese. A set of such pipes forms the Chinese pan-pipes known as the *Hsiao*.

MAGADIZED OCTAVES. Same as parallel Octaves. The term derives from *magadis,* an ancient Greek Lyre of 20 strings on which it was possible to play in Octaves (magadization).

MEANTONE TEMPERAMENT. The one which historically preceded Equal Temperament in musical practice and whose main characteristics are that it preserves the acoustical purity of major Thirds ($\frac{5}{4}$ or 193 ctn.) and establishes an artificial and uniform dimension for whole tones equalling half a major Third (96.5 ctn.), thus representing a *mean* value (hence the name) of a major and minor whole tone ($\frac{9}{8}$ or 102 ctn. and $\frac{10}{9}$ or 91 ctn., respectively). With twelve tones to an octave only six major and three minor keys of the diatonic scale could be used in Meantone Temperament, any further extension in modulation and transposition requiring a correspondingly increased number of "extra" tones, in order to avoid an intolerable effect in tuning.

MELODIC INTONATION. A system of tuning conventionally assumed as a theoretical norm for strictly melodic progressions in a given scale. (Compare with HARMONIC INTONATION).

MILLITONE (mtn.) One thousandth part of an equally tempered whole tone ($\frac{1}{6000}$ of an octave).

MODE. A modification of a given scale (of the diatonic scale, in a more particular sense) characterized by a specific arrangement of its component whole steps and half steps. The various modes of the diatonic scale, familiarly known by their Greek names (like *Ionian, Dorian, Phrygian,* etc.) are also designated in this volume by their extreme notes (like "C-c," "D-d," "E-e," etc.) which become such as a result of these modes being placed exclusively upon white keys, i.e. without containing any black keys at all. They are sometimes referred to as *principal modes,* as distinguished from *altered modes* which cannot be placed upon white keys exclusively, and which contain at least one chromatic alteration.

MONAD. A common chord of the sub-infra-diatonic scale (q.v.) In close position it represents a unison of two parts in this scale.

NATURAL FIFTH. An interval formed in the Natural Harmonic Series by the overtones 2 and 3, and therefore expressed by the ratio $\frac{3}{2}$. It equals 351 ctn. (in round numbers).

NATURAL HARMONIC SERIES. Partial tones (Harmonics, Overtones) produced by a sounding body simultaneously with its fundamental tone (Generator) and forming a series whose vibration-ratios can be mathematically expressed by ordinary numbers as 1, 2, 3, 4, 5, 6 etc.

NEUTRAL HEXAD. A chord of six notes comprising six equal intervals (neutral supra-Thirds) within the span of an Octave. It is a whole-step chord from the standpoint of the diatonic (tempered) scale.

NEUTRAL TRIAD. A chord of three notes comprising two equal intervals (neutral Thirds) within the span of a perfect Fifth. It is a whole-step chord from the standpoint of the infra-tempered scale (q.v.)

"ORGANIC" SCALE. In this book, a scale which bears an unambiguous stamp of universality in so far as its practical use in the world's music is concerned, and which therefore, from all evidences, spontaneously develops in accordance with some inherent "organic" laws of our musical consciousness. Such are, beyond any doubt, the pentatonic (infra-diatonic) and heptatonic (diatonic) scales. It is the author's aim to prove that such is also gradually becoming the supra-diatonic scale.

PENTATONIC SCALE. Literally, a five-tone scale. In a more limited sense, the so-called "Chinese" or "Scotch" scale, represented by the five black keys of our piano. This particular form comprising no intervals smaller than a whole tone is sometimes referred to as a *tonal pentatonic scale,* as distinguished from a *semitonal pentatonic scale* which contains half tones.

PENTATONISM. Melodic expression more characteristic of the pentatonic than of any other scale.

PIEN. A Chinese term equivalent to "flat" in Occidental music. Riemann uses the term *pien-tone* for auxiliary degrees of the pentatonic (infra-diatonic) scale.

POLYRHYTHM. Simultaneous combination of two or more different time-divisions in a musical composition.

POLYTONALITY. Simultaneous combination of two or more tonalities (in the sense of keys)in a musical composition.

POSITION. In relation to intervals or chords, the same as *Root position* unless otherwise specified.

PYTHAGOREAN COMMA. Difference (12 ctn.) between twelve natural Fifths and seven Octaves.

PYTHAGOREAN INTONATION. In a strict sense, the intonation, based on the principles of ascending and descending natural Fifths (twenty-six in all), as worked out by Pythagoras for the diatonic scale. In a more general sense (used in the present volume) the intonation resulting from *any* number of natural Fifths brought within the compass of an octave, and, therefore, applicable to any scale formed upon this principle.

"RECTIFIED" CHORD. Any chord within our twelve-tone tempered system that approximates the supra-diatonic Hexad more closely than does the whole-step chord. One of the instances of such approximation is Scriabin's chord (q.v.).

REGULAR DEGREES. Identical to diatonic (or infra-diatonic or supra-diatonic) degrees as opposed to chromatic (or infra-chromatic or supra-chromatic), i.e. to "auxiliary" degrees that fill "embellishing functions" in any organic scale, and also serve as a medium for modulation.

SALENDRO SCALE. It is sometimes transliterated as *Slendro* scale, a term said to be derived from *Sailendra,* the name of Hindu princes of Sumatra who supposedly introduced this scale in Java in approximately the eighth century of our era. The scale itself originates from the division of an octave into five equal intervals. At present used (among other scales) only in Javanese music. [See SUB-INFRA-ATONAL SCALE].

SCALE-DEGREE. See DEGREE.

SCALE "2 + 3." See SUB-INFRA-DIATONIC SCALE.

SCALE "5." See SUB-INFRA-ATONAL SCALE.

SCALE "5 + 2." See INFRA-DIATONIC SCALE.

SCALE "7." See INFRA-ATONAL SCALE.

SCALE "7 + 5." See DIATONIC SCALE.

SCALE "12." See ATONAL SCALE.

SCALE "12 + 7." See SUPRA-DIATONIC SCALE.

SCRIABIN'S CHORD. Consisting of six notes (C-D-E-F♯-A-B♭, when brought within an octave), it approximates the supra-diatonic Hexad more closely than any other chord formed within the limit of our twelve-tone tempered system. It is therefore sometimes called in this book *approximative Hexad* or *approximatively rectified Hexad,* or *approximatively rectified whole-step chord,* the latter harmonic formation also bearing, in its original form, a certain resemblance (though not as "approximate") to the genuine supra-diatonic Hexad. Scriabin himself termed it (without any substantial reason) the *synthetic chord* and erroneously considered it as a "scale" in its close position, given above. He arranged it predominantly by Fourths when used for harmonic purposes.

SEMI-SESQUITONE TEMPERAMENT. The one introduced in musical practice by Scotch bagpipers, and which artificially divides each sesquitone (one tone and a half) of the pentatonic scale in two equal three-quarter tones.

SEMITONAL SCALE. See ATONAL SCALE.

SEMITONE. In this volume, invariably refers to an *equally tempered* semitone (viz. one-twelfth of an octave) unless otherwise indicated.

SERIES OF NATURAL FIFTHS. A chain of consecutively connected natural Fifths (like C-G-D-A-E, etc.) which produces the Pythagorean intonation (q.v.) of a given scale, when brought within the compass of an octave.

SESQUI-STEP. An interval consisting of one whole step and a half. It is equal to a sesqui-tone in the diatonic scale but differs dimensionally in any other scale.

SIAMESE SCALE. See INFRA-TEMPERED SCALE.

SINEAN. In a broad sense anything pertaining to Chinese culture. In ethnology the name *Sinean* (or Sinaic) is applied to one of the three branches of the Yellow Race, the two others being the Mongolian and the Hyperborean.

SPRECHSTIMME. Literally "speaking voice." In music, a voice that carries its part in a sort of melo-recitative declamatory style and, in contradistinction to "singing voice" *(Gesangstimme)*, is not supposed to keep inflexibly to the pitch, but as Schönberg puts it, merely starts with it and at once departs from it by going lower or higher.

STEPWISE PROGRESSION. The progression of a melody by contiguous scale-degrees, whether they form whole steps or half steps or any combined order of both.

SUB-INFRA. A double prefix indicating that the term to which it is attached must be considered with reference to the sub-infra-diatonic system.

SUB-INFRA-ATONAL SCALE. Same as *atonal* scale (q.v.) but with five instead of twelve equidistant and musically "independent" tones within an octave. (Compare with SALENDRO SCALE).

SUB-INFRA-ATONALITY. Same as *atonality* (q.v.) but considered with reference to the sub-infra-atonal scale (q.v.). Literally, negation of sub-infra-tonality.

SUB-INFRA-CHROMATIC ALTERATION. Same as *chromatic alteration* (q.v.) but considered with reference to the degrees of the sub-infra-diatonic scale.

SUB-INFRA-CHROMATIC DEGREES. Auxiliary degrees of the scale "2 + 3."

SUB-INFRA-CHROMATIC SCALE. Identical to supra-atonal scale (q.v.) when considered as a perfectly independent basis for musical composition. Otherwise merely a progression of notes by half steps in which, consequently, none of the sub-infra-chromatic degrees (besides the sub-infra-diatonic ones) is missing. Bears the same relation to the scale "2 + 3" as the chromatic scale to the scale "7 + 5."

SUB-INFRA-COMMA. Difference (45 ctn.) between five natural Fifths and three Octaves.

SUB-INFRA-DIATONIC DEGREES. Regular degrees of the scale "2 + 3."

SUB-INFRA-DIATONIC SCALE. A diatonic scale of the "lowest order." In its complete form it contains two regular and three auxiliary degrees (formula "2 + 3"), the former being placed a perfect Fourth or Fifth apart (like C-F or F-C) while the latter group coincides with the notes D, G, A of the infra-diatonic scale, and closely approaches the same notes of the diatonic scale under the condition of just intonation of all these scales.

SUB-INFRA-FLAT. A sign of alteration which lowers any degree of the sub-infra-diatonic scale a half step.

SUB-INFRA-FOURTH-CHORD. A chord of two notes which, in its root position, forms the interval of a sub-infra-Fourth, whence the name.

SUB-INFRA-MODE. Same as *mode*, (q.v.) but considered with reference to the sub-infra-diatonic scale. The two possible sub-infra-modes are named after their extreme notes (viz. "F-f" and "C-c") which become such as a result of these sub-infra-modes being placed exclusively upon white keys, i.e. without containing any black keys at all. They are sometimes referred to as *principal sub-infra-modes*, as distinguished from *altered sub-infra-modes* which cannot be placed upon white keys exclusively and which contain at least one sub-infra-chromatic alteration.

SUB-INFRA-PRIME. The first regular degree of the sub-infra-diatonic scale. Also a unison of two parts in this scale.

SUB-INFRA-SECOND. The second regular degree of the sub-infra-diatonic scale. Also an interval between the first and the second degree, as well as any of its quantitative equivalents found in this scale.

SUB-INFRA-SHARP. A sign of alteration that raises any degree of the sub-infra-diatonic scale a half step.

SUB-INFRA-TEMPERED FIFTH. A *diatonic* Fifth extended to 360 ctn. in the sub-infra-tempered scale.

SUB-INFRA-TEMPERED INTONATION. The one which results from the division of an Octave into five equal intervals, thereby automatically equalizing all half steps of the sub-infra-diatonic scale.

SUB-INFRA-TEMPERED SCALE. The sub-infra-diatonic scale ("2 + 3") equally tempered.

SUB-INFRA-THIRD. The third regular degree of the sub-infra-diatonic scale. Also an interval between the first and the third degree, as well as any of its quantitative equivalents found in this scale.

SUB-INFRA-TONALITY. Same as *Tonality* (q.v.) but considered with reference to the sub-infra-diatonic scale.

SUPRA. A prefix indicating that the term to which it is attached must be considered with reference to the supra-diatonic system.

SUPRA-ATONAL SCALE. Same as *atonal* scale (q.v.) but with nineteen instead of twelve equidistant and musically "independent" tones within an octave.

SUPRA-CHROMATIC ALTERATION. Same as *chromatic alteration* (q.v.) but considered with reference to the degrees of the supra-diatonic scale.

SUPRA-CHROMATIC DEGREES. See AUXILIARY DEGREES.

SUPRA-CHROMATIC SCALE. Identical to supra-atonal scale (q.v.) when considered as a perfectly independent basis for musical composition. Otherwise merely a progression of notes by half steps in which, consequently, none of the supra-chromatic degrees(besides the supra-diatonic ones) is missing. Bears the same relation to the scale "12 + 7" as the chromatic scale to the scale "7 + 5."

SUPRA-COMMA. Difference (69 ctn.) between nineteen natural Fifths and eleven Octaves.

SUPRA-DIATONIC DEGREES. See REGULAR DEGREES.

SUPRA-DIATONIC HEXAD. A chord of six tones arranged by supra-Thirds. It is the common (consonant) chord of the supra-diatonic scale in its complete form.

SUPRA-DIATONIC SCALE. A diatonic scale of a "higher order." In its complete form it contains twelve regular and seven auxiliary degrees (formula "12 + 7"), the former set bearing a remote resemblance to our chromatic scale and the latter set closely approaching our diatonic scale (in the strict sense).

SUPRA-EIGHTH. The eighth regular degree of the supra-diatonic scale. Also an interval between the first and the eighth degree, as well as any of its quantitative equivalents, found in this scale (like C-G or V-Y or D-A etc.)

SUPRA-ELEVENTH. The eleventh regular degree of the supra-diatonic scale. Also an interval between the first and the eleventh degree, as well as any of its quantitative equivalents, found in this scale (like C-Z or V-B or D-C, etc.)

SUPRA-FIFTH. The fifth regular degree of the supra-diatonic scale. Also an interval between the first and the fifth degree, as well as any of its quantitative equivalents, found in this scale (like C-E or V-F or D-X, etc.)

SUPRA-FLAT. A sign of alteration that lowers any degree of the supra-diatonic scale a half step.

SUPRA-FOURTH. The fourth regular degree of the supra-diatonic scale. Also an interval between the first and the fourth degree, as well as any of its quantitative equivalents, found in this scale (like C-W or V-E or D-F, etc.)

SUPRA-MODE. Same as *mode* (q.v.) but considered with reference to the supra-diatonic scale. The various supra-modes are named after their extreme notes (like "C-c," "V-v," "D-d," etc.) which become such as a result of these supra-modes being placed exclusively upon white keys, i.e. without containing any black keys at all. They are sometimes referred to as *principal supra-modes,* as distinguished from *altered supra-modes* which cannot be placed upon white keys exclusively and which contain at least one supra-chromatic alteration.

SUPRA-NINTH. The ninth regular degree of the supra-diatonic scale. Also an interval between the first and the ninth degree, as well as any of its quantitative equivalents, found in this scale (like C-Y or V-A or D-Z, etc.)

SUPRA-PRIME. The first regular degree of the supra-diatonic scale. Also a unison of two parts in this scale.

SUPRA-SECOND. The second regular degree of the supra-diatonic scale. Also an interval between the first and the second degree, as well as any of its quantitative equivalents, found in this scale (like C-V or V-D, etc.)

SUPRA-SEVENTH. The seventh regular degree of the supra-diatonic scale. Also an interval between the first and the seventh degree, as well as any of its quantitative equivalents, found in this scale (like C-X or V-G or D-Y, etc.)

SUPRA-SHARP. A sign of alteration that raises any degree of the supra-diatonic scale a half step.

SUPRA-SIXTH. The sixth regular degree of the supra-diatonic scale. Also an interval between the first and the sixth degree, as well as any of its quantitative equivalents, found in this scale (like C-F or V-X or D-G, etc.)

SUPRA-TEMPERED INTONATION. The one which results from the division of an Octave into nineteen equal intervals, thereby automatically equalizing all half steps as well as all whole steps of the supra-diatonic scale.

SUPRA-TEMPERED FIFTH. (Not to be confused with *supra-tempered supra-Fifth*). A *diatonic* Fifth reduced to 347.4 ctn. in the supra-diatonic scale.

SUPRA-TEMPERED SCALE. The supra-diatonic scale ("12 + 7") equally tempered.

SUPRA-TEMPERED SUPRA-FIFTH. The interval of a supra-Fifth equally tempered (major = 221.2 ctn., minor = 189.6 ctn.)

SUPRA-TENTH. The tenth regular degree of the supra-diatonic scale. Also an interval between the first and the tenth degree, as well as any of its quantitative equivalents, found in this scale (like C-A or V-Z or D-B, etc.)

SUPRA-THIRD. The third regular degree of the supra-diatonic scale. Also an interval between the first and the third degree, as well as any of its quantitative equivalents, found in this scale (like C-D or V-W or D-E, etc.)

SUPRA-THIRTEENTH. The thirteenth regular degree of the supra-diatonic scale. Also an interval between the first and the thirteenth degree, as well as any of its quantitative equivalents, found in this scale(like C-c or V-v or D-d, etc.)

SUPRA-TONALITY. Same as *Tonality* (q.v.) but considered with reference to the supra-diatonic scale.

SUPRA-TWELFTH. The twelfth regular degree of the supra-diatonic scale. Also an interval between the first and the twelfth degree, as well as any of its quantitative equivalents, found in this scale (like C-B or V-C or D-V, etc.)

SYNTHETIC CHORD. See SCRIABIN'S CHORD.

TEMPERAMENT. A principle of artificial tuning which, at the cost of a certain acoustic compromise (q.v.) makes it possible to limit a given musical system to a much smaller number of tones than would be required under the condition of acoustically natural or pure tuning. *Equal* Temperament (which is invariably implied by this term in this volume) represents one of many particular instances of this principle and has an advantage over all the rest in that it requires a minimum number of tones, for a given musical system, with maximum results. (See also TEMPERED INTONATION).

TEMPERED FIFTH. A diatonic Fifth reduced to 350 ctn., its "natural" dimension being equal to 351 ctn.

TEMPERED INTONATION. The one which results from the application of the principle of Temperament (q.v.) to a given scale. *Equally* tempered intonation (which is invariably implied by this term in this volume) results from the division of an Octave into the same number of equal intervals as the number of both regular and auxiliary degrees of this scale, thereby automatically equalizing all its component half steps as well as all its whole steps. In a more specific sense *tempered intonation* (as distinguished from infra-tempered and supra-tempered intonations) implies, in this book, the equally tempered intonation of the diatonic scale ("7 + 5") that results from the division of an Octave into twelve equal intervals.

TONAL CENTER. The general point of gravitation in a given scale. It is the Tonic from the melodic point of view, and the tonic consonant chord (like Monad, Dyad, Triad or Hexad) from the harmonic point of view.

TONALITY. A principle which organically and tonocentrically unites the functions of a certain number of systematically arranged sounds (as most simply represented in a musical scale) in their melodic and harmonic aspects. Sometimes the term Tonality is used for the musical scale itself based on this principle, and, in a still more restricted sense, to designate the key of such a scale. In another and very particular connection, this term implies the *diatonic* tonality, as distinguished from the infra-tonality, supra-tonality, etc.

TONOCENTRIC SYSTEM. A musical system or a scale, based on the principle of Tonality (q.v.), in which all component tones gravitate, in a certain way, to each other, and most definitely to a common center, known as the Tonic.

TRICHORD. A scale of three tones corresponding to the notes C, F, G of the diatonic scale. The term is derived from one of the ancient Greek Lyres of three strings tuned in accordance with the intervals formed by the above notes.

ULTRA-DIATONIC SCALE. A diatonic scale of the "highest order,"—a definition which can be applied in practice, however, only provisionally, since there is no limit to the theoretical construction of scales according to the principle evolved in this book. The physiological limit of our ear in reference to musical intervals being still uncertain, it is impossible to establish the tonal constitution of this scale in a final and definite way.

VARIABLE INTONATION. The one embodied in musical instruments either without or with a few definitely fixed series of tones, the pitch of practically the entire scale being produced by the performer while playing. (Compare with FIXED INTONATION).

VIBRATION-FRACTION. A mathematically exact expression of a musical interval, its two component tones being represented in the form of a ratio of their respective vibration-numbers.

VIBRATION-NUMBER or VIBRATION-FREQUENCY. A number of sound-waves (vibrations of a sounding body) per second producing the pitch of a musical tone.

VIBRATION-RATIO. See VIBRATION-FRACTION.

WHOLE STEP. An interval composed of two "minimum" intervals or half steps (q.v.) in a given scale. When tempered, it is equal to a whole tone in the diatonic scale but differs dimensionally in any other scale.

WHOLE-STEP CHORD or WHOLE-STEP HARMONIC COMBINATION. One whose component notes, when brought close together, form a scale-like progression by whole steps in a given musical system.

WHOLE-STEP SCALE. A progression by whole steps in a given musical system. In reality, however, it is simply a chord formed by "Thirds" of another and more complicated system as compared to the former.

WHOLE TONE. In this volume, invariably refers to an *equally tempered* whole tone (viz. one-sixth part of an Octave) unless otherwise indicated. As such it is assumed as a basic measuring unit for the *decimal system* (q.v.) introduced by the author.

WHOLE-TONE SCALE. A progression of whole tones. It is identical to *whole-step scale* (q.v.) when the latter is considered within the diatonic system, but differs from it, acoustically, in any other system.

INDEX

[The asterisks placed after the numbers indicating the pages, refer to their respective Footnotes]

AALST, A. VAN (on Chinese music), 31**, 64, 65
ABORIGINES, African, American and Australian, 5
ACOUSTIC COMPROMISE, 117*, 260, 272
ACOUSTIC COMPUTATIONS, 17
ACOUSTIC LAWS, 25, 177, 179
ACOUSTICS AND ESTHETICS, 56**, 193*
AMALGAMATED SCALES (Chinese), 37
AMBROS, A. W. (harmonized a Chinese tune), 100
AMIOT, PÈRE (on Chinese music), 36, 64
ANARCHIC PERIOD OF TONAL REVOLUTION, 288
ANCESTORS (Chinese hymn in honor of), 73, 101*
ANTI-EMOTIONAL THEORY, 234, 266
ARCHITECTURE AND MUSIC, 289, 290
ARCHYTAS, 270
ARIEL, 217*, 220, 280*
ARS NOVA, 344, 347
ART, ephemeral and lasting, 290
ARTISTS AND SCIENTISTS (problem of melodic intonation), 222
ASIATIC NATIONS, 5, 55, 279
ATONAL SCALE, definition of the term, 160; precludes the formation of modes and keys, 160, 163; its intonation, 189; structurally identical to the chromatic (tempered) scale, 225; its esthetical failure, 266, 290, 291; illegitimate child of tempered intonation, 272; hastily erected on diatonic ruins, 287; its component tones have no functions, 291.
ATONALITY, a transitory stage, 8; chaotic world of, 239; its essence, 287, 331; beginning of, 332*
AUXILIARY DEGREES, see REGULAR DEGREES

BAGPIPE, 41**, 67*, 270**
BARDIC ART, 67*
BEATS, 168*, 215, 235*
BEAUMONT, A. G. (on Siamese music), 57***
BEETHOVEN, 349
BELLERMAN, H., 20**
BETT, H., 67*
BLAIKLAY, D. J. (traditional tuning of the Scotch bagpipe), 41**
BORREN, C. VAN DEN (origin of the Faux-bourdon), 69*
BOSANQUET, R. (53-tone harmonium), 32****

CADENCES, 217, 218
CAMBODIAN BAS-RELIEF (picturing Chinese musical instruments), 55*
CATEGORICAL IMPERATIVE (of musical consciousness), 235, 236
CELTIC MUSIC, scale foundation of, 40, 41, 68; folk songs, 47, 70*, 94, 95, 102, 103, 133; harmony, 67, 69, 73, 340; instruments, 67*
CENT, 20, 21
CENTITONE, definition of the term, 14
CH'IN (Chinese lute), 33, 64, 74, 81

CHINESE MUSIC, sacred, semi-sacred and popular, 78-81; folk songs, 38; theoretical speculations, 9, 25-27, 31, 32; symbolism, 25, 28, 31, 33, 71, 78; equal temperament, 30, 33, 34; reforms in the second century, B. C., 34; harmony and polyphony, 64; phonograms, 66, 78; orchestral score, 74; native harmonizations, 72, 74, 75; diatonic and infra-diatonic harmonizations, 98-100; amateurs and professionals, 81*; relation to Indo-Chinese music, 55*
CHOIR (a cappella); 56**, 193*
CHORD-FORMATION, by Thirds, 69, 145, 238, 340; by Fourths, 76, 230*, 340; in cluster-like fashion, 289; in the infra-diatonic system, 77; in the supra-diatonic system, 170; three characteristic methods of, 340
CHROMATIC HARMONY, 332*
CHROMATIC SCALE, 3, 28, 58, 160; its pure intonation, 271; its modal characteristics, 283
CHROMATICISTS, modern, 284
CHURCH MODES, 168*; see also MODES
CITHARA (Greek), its tuning, 151
CIVILIZATION, modern, 4, 266*
CLAVICYMBALUM UNIVERSALE, 279*, 284
COLOGNE, FRANCO OF, 71*, 344
COMBARIEU, J., 66, 68*
COMMA, 56**; of Pythagoras, 117, 204; of Didymus, 216; infra-comma, 122; supra-comma, 127; sub-infra-comma, 142
CONFUCIUS (hymn to), 38, 72, 73
CONSONANCES AND DISSONANCES, relativity of, 60; cardinal opposition of, 63, 169, 260, 331; attitude of modern composers towards the problem, 166, 234, 287; essential attributes of all organic scales, 174; acoustical and psychological considerations, 175**, 235*, 236; polarity of, 194, 235, 333; interbalance of, 197, 204, 211; their division specific in each scale, 198; definition and historic classification, 234*; their fields expand in *direct* ratio to each other in the process of evolution, 236; new division of, 286; connected with the law of tonal gravitation, 289, see also FALSONANCE
CONTRAPUNTO ALLA MENTE, 347
CORNU AND MERCADIER (experiments on intonation of bow instruments), 214
COTTON, JOHN (on medieval descanters), 347
COURANT, MAURICE (on Chinese music), 36, 66, 73, 81, 101*
CREATIVE EXPERIMENTS, 3, 352
CROWD, ancient Welsh fiddle, 67*
CULWICK, J. C. (on Irish melody), 47*

DARWINIANS AND SPENCERITES (controversy between), 150
DAWES, E., 55*

DEBUSSY, 104, 226, 230*, 238, 259, 350
DECIMAL SYSTEM, applied to intervals, 13
DECITONE, definition of the term, 14
DECLAMATORY ELEMENTS (in vocal intonation), 150; see also SPRECHSTIMME
DECORATIVE MUSIC, 289; its negative characteristics, 290
DEDUCTIVE METHOD, 169, 225
DESCANT, 79, 345; special form of, 347
DESCARTES, 215
DEVIATIONS (acoustic), 30, 55, 131, 134, 168*
DIALECTIC METHOD, V, 288*, 329
DIAPHONY, 66, 340, 347
DIATONIC, origin and definition of the term, 7*
DIATONIC SCALE, 107, 108; on the basis of twelve-tone and nineteen-tone temperament, 281*
DIATONICISM AND CHROMATICISM, 11
DICHORD (Greek), 151
DIDYMUS, 216, 217, 270
DILETTANTS, 239; modern, 288
DISSONANT COUNTERPOINT, 250, 253, 255, 345
DROBISCH, M. W., 19*
DUHAMEL, MAURICE (on Celtic scales), 47*
DUODECUPLE SCALE, 160, 337
DYAD, 77, 170, 180, 252, 259, 288, 343

EAR, 3, accommodation of, 56, 57, 122, 166, 176, 247, 277, 279, 352; its faculty of the psychological corrective, 56**, 168*, 190, 193, 245, 246; interval barely perceptible by, 118; its flexibility, 168
EASTLAKE, F. (on Chinese reed-organ), 65
EGGEN, ERIK, 281*
ELECTRIC TONE-PRODUCTION, 285
ELLIS, A. J., 20, 56*, 57, 214, 279*
EMOTIONS, 62, 149, 234-236, 278*; see also ANTI-EMOTIONAL THEORY
ENGEL, CARL, 6*, 40**
ERATOSTHENES, 270
ERIGENA, SCOTUS, 67*
EULER, LEONARD, 19*, 21**
EVOLUTION OF SCALES, 3, 4, 131, 136, 334
EXTERNALISM, musical, 289, 349

FABER, E. (on Chinese theory of music), 31**
FALSONANCE, 237, 285; see also CONSONANCES AND DISSONANCES
FAUX-BOURDON, its origin, 69; its strict form, 70**, 343, 348
"FEUERZAUBER" (Wagner), 57, 102
FIFTHS, series of natural, 27, 31, 51, 113, 114, 117, 126, 135, 142, 157**; ascending and descending, 138; series of tempered, 119, infra-tempered, 123, supra-tempered, 127, 157**; circles of, 119, 123, 127, 137, 143; re-demonstrated in proper notation, 158**; spirals of, 136, 139, 141
FIONN SAGA, 94
FISCHER, ERICH (Chinese phonograms), 66, 78
FLEISCHER, OSCAR (analyzed St. Stephen's hymn), 70*
FLUCTUATING NOTES, 150
FOGLIANO, LODOVICO, 270
FOLK-LORE (musical), 5; see also CHINESE, CELTIC, SCOTCH AND IRISH FOLK SONGS
FOLKLORISTIC SCALES, 6*, 56**

FORKEL, J. N., 216**
FORTUNATUS, VENANTIUS, 67*
FOURTH, formative unit in harmonic constructions, 76, 230*, 340; a dissonance in two-part diatonic harmony, 175**
FRASER, MARJORIE K. (collected Celtic songs), 95*

GAILHARD, ANDRÉ (describes a Chinese musical performance), 64***, 67*
GAMELAN (Javanese), 278
GAUDY (author of the Geometrical Scale in Musick), 21**
GENIUS, 278*
GERBERT, MARTIN, 70*
GIRALDUS CAMBRENSIS (Gerald de Barri), 67*, 345
GRAVITATION, tonal, 84, 236, 241, 244, 263, 291, and physical, 289
GREECE (ancient), 25**, 68; Rhapsodists, 151; three movements of the voice distinguished, 151*; magadized octaves, 152; pentatonic scales, 49, 151
GREEN, G. P., 35*
GREGORIAN CHANTS, 68**, 335, 340
GYMEL, 344, 348

HALF STEP AND HALF TONE, 44
HANDSCHIN, JACQUES, on Scotus Erigena, 67*; on nineteen-tone temperament, 280*
HARMONIC AND MELODIC INTONATION, 49, 51, 213, 269, 271; qualities of, 218; problem of, 222
HARMONIC EVOLUTION, 66, 340
HARMONIC MONISM AND DUALISM, 234
HARMONIC SENSE OF THE ORIENTALS, 62
HARMONY, its origin in Europe, 66, 340
HARMONY AND COUNTERPOINT (new), 286
HARMONY AND MELODY, 102
HARMONY AND SCALE, 63
HEBREW CANTILLATIONS, 335
HEGELIAN DIALECTIC TRIAD, 329, 364
HELMHOLTZ, H., 20* 40, 151, 175**, 214, 215, 235*, 279*
HERSCHEL, JOHN, 19
HEXAD, 170, consonant chord of the supra-diatonic scale, 172; its pure tuning, 182, 184, 196; principal and subsidiary Hexads, 182, 187, 188, 219; table of Hexads, 183; neutral Hexad, 263, 342, 350
HINDU MUSIC, in China, 37, Hindu Raga, 278
HISTORICAL METHOD, 4, 334
HOLDER, WILLIAM, 31****
HOMER, 151
HUCBALD, 70*
HUGHES, DOM ANSELM, 66, 67*, 70**
HYPOTHESES, 153

IMPROVISATION, medieval art of, 345
INDUCTIVE METHOD, 169
INFRA, 12
INFRA-ATONAL SCALE, 260, 264, 265
INFRA-ATONALITY, 329, 342
INFRA-CHROMATIC ALTERATIONS, 44, 49
INFRA-CHROMATIC SCALE, 56, 260

INFRA-DIATONIC SCALE, definition, 7; transposition by the Chinese, 27; evolution, 34, 151; nature and properties, 42; keyboard illustration, 43, 334; notation, 45; cycles of keys, 54; intervals, 58; harmonic laws, 63
INFRA-MODES, principal and altered, 47; fundamental, 51; character of, 88; imperfect, 101*
INFRA-POLYTONALITY, 253, 346
INFRA-TEMPERED INTONATION, 43-45, 123, 257, 258
INFRA-TONALITY, 23, 48, 344, 349
INNOVATORS (Chinese), 35
INTERRELATED SCALES, 7, 113, 130-134, 285*, 340*
INTERVALS, addition and subtraction of, 16; simple and compound, 20; acoustical character of, 22, 195, 204; musical quality of, 59, 166, 169, 184; deviated, 186, 204, 211; tables of infra-diatonic, 58, diatonic, 109, sub-infra-diatonic, 146, supra-diatonic, 173
INTONATION, variety of, 56**; shadings of, 280; Ptolemaic, 218; variable and fixed, 214, 239; see also INFRA-TEMPERED, SUB-INFRA-TEMPERED, SUPRA-TEMPERED INTONATIONS, JUST INTONATION, HARMONIC AND MELODIC INTONATION, PYTHAGOREAN INTONATION, TEMPERAMENT
IRISH FOLK SONGS, 40, 57; scale foundation of, 41*
INTUITION AND INTELLECTUALISM (in Art), 42

JAPANESE SCALES, 49
JAVANESE SCALES, 153, 278
JOYCE, P. W. (on Celtic linguistic expressions suggesting Harmony), 67*
JUST (NATURAL, PURE) INTONATION, 45, 58, 108; of the diatonic scale, 107, 178, 269, 271; of the infra-diatonic scale, 131, 180, 269; of the supra-diatonic scale, 189, 195, 213, 219, 271; of the chromatic scale, 271; definition of, 176; norms and oddities of, 195; relativity of, 212; melodic inconsistency of, 215; and Tonality, 222

KANT, 235
KEPLER, 215
KEYBOARD MODELS (nineteen keys to an octave), 154, 281, 283, 285
KEYS, five cycles of infra-diatonic, 54; seven cycles of diatonic, 109; two cycles of sub-infra-diatonic, 146; twelve cycles of supra-diatonic, 167
KING FANG (originator of the 53-tone system), 31
KNOSP, GASTON (on folk songs of the Annamites), 38*
KOCZIRZ, ADOLF, 279*
KOECHLIN, CHARLES, 216*
KORNERUP, THORVALD (on nineteen-tone temperament), 280*
KOWALENKOFF, VALENTIN (experiments on nineteen-tone temperament), 280*
KUBLAI-KHAN, 37

LAKER, KARL, 19*
LALOY, LOUIS (on Chinese auxiliary scale-degrees), 36
LEADING NOTE, natural tendency of the, 214
LEDERER, V., 66

LISZT, 332*
LOCRIAN MODE, 101*, 108
LOEWENSTEIN, HERBERT (on Hebrew Pentatonic), 335*
LOGARITHMS, 17, common and binary, 19*
LÜ (Chinese), 27-32
LUYTON, CARL, his nineteen-tone Clavicymbalum, 279*, 284
LYDIAN MODE, 51, 108, 178, 214

MASON, REDFERN (on Irish folk songs), 40
MASSARINI, RENZO, 250*
MEANTONE TEMPERAMENT, 279*, 281*, 368
MEDIEVALISM (new), 352
MELO-RHYTHMIC ORNAMENTS, 289
MELODIC LINE, tension of, 291
MERCATOR, NICHOLAS, his 53-tone temperament, 31****
MERSENNE, 21*, 215
METHOD, deductive, 169, 225; dialectic, V, 288*, 329; historical, 4, 334; inductive, 169
MIDDLE AGES, musical psychology, V, 340, 347; harmonization, 66; retuning the Thirds, 270; radical descanters, 345
MILLIOCTAVE, 19
MILLITONE, definition of the term, 14
MINIMUM INTERVAL, 125, 129, 145, 191, 220, 292, 340*
MIXOLYDIAN MODE, 101*, 108, 178
MODERN COMPOSERS, their chord-formation, 230*, 244, 245, 260, 261, 289, 340, 351; failed to evolve a new musical grammar, 239; diverted from actual channels of historic evolution, 273; compelled to use inadequately tuned instruments, 342; two fundamentally distinct types of, 290, 291
MODERN MUSIC, definition of, 4; functions of all scale-degrees equalized, 133, 331; quantitative harmonic complexity, 244, 245; creatively sterile, 266, 291; its psychological impetus, 284; constructive period, 287, 292; akin to medieval descant, 347; needs a natural outlet, 352
MODES, diatonic, 108, 331; harmonic major, 179, 194**; twelve-tone chromatic, 283
MONAD, 147, 181
MONGOLIAN SCALES, 37, 101*
MONRO, D. B. (on ancient Greek music), 151
MOTETS (medieval), 345
MOUHOT, HENRI, 55*
MOULE, A. C. (on Chinese musical instruments), 75
MOULE, G. E. (deciphered a Chinese orchestral score), 74
MÜLLER, HANS (on Hucbald), 70*
MUNCK, P. S., 281*
MURIS, JOHANN DE (on medieval descanters), 347
MUSICA ENCHIRIADIS, 70*
MUSICAL ART, organized, 6*; principally an es-thetico-psychological phenomenon, 193*; dualistically emotional, 236
MUSICAL DECORATORS, 290
MUSICAL NOTIONS, relativity of, 11, 44, 60, 212
MUSICAL PERCEPTION, 40
MUSICAL PROGRESS, 292

NATURAL HARMONIC SERIES, 107, 177, 179, 260
NEO-CONTRAPUNTISTS, 291
NEUTRAL INTERVALS, 265, 349; see also TRIAD and HEXAD for neutral chords
NEUTRAL MUSIC, 265
NEWMAN, ERNEST (on scale and harmony), 63*
NICOMACHUS (on practical use of the pentatonic scale in ancient Greece), 151
NINETEEN-TONE TEMPERAMENT, 217*; its vibration-ratios, 224; its history, 279*; its possible use for music based on the diatonic and supra-diatonic scales, 280; its advantage over the twelve-tone temperament, 283
NITHART'S "MINNEGESÄNGE," 335
"NORTHERN TONES" (Chinese), 35

ODINGTON, WALTER, 270
OETTINGEN, ARTHUR VON, 19*
OKTAVENZENTIMETER (K. Laker), 19*
OPELT, F. W. (originator of the nineteen-tone temperament), 280*
ORGANIC SCALES (and tonal systems), 61, 113, 135, 137, 140, 160, 193*, 261, 285*, 289
ORGANICA CANTILENA AND ORGANICUM MELOS (in ancient Celtic music), 67*
ORGANISTRUM, 67*
ORGANIZATION OF THE SOUND, 5*, 333, 352
ORGANUM, 66, 67, 68**, 69, 73, 102; irregular, 70*, 344
ORLOFF, I. E. (made a study on the significance of beats in modern music), 168*
OVERTONES, used as nuclei for the just intonations of different scales, 181, 196, 204; their rôle in harmonic evolution, 233; deprived of harmonic polarity; see also NATURAL HARMONIC SERIES
OWEN, H., 67*

PALESTRINA, 104, 349
PANOFF, P., 335*
PENTAD, 170
PENTATONIC MELODIES, 57, 58, 130; method for harmonization, 83-101; their frequent use in modern music, 230*
PENTATONIC SCALE, stage of musical development in general, 5; its comparative universality, 5*, 335; its complete form, 6; tonal and semitonal, 49; archaic Greek, 49, 151; of Southern India, 49; see also JAPANESE AND JAVANESE SCALES
PENTATONISMS, 335
PIEN, 35
PIERCE, E. H. (experiments on Just Intonation), 58*, 193*
PITCH, philosophic, 15; international, 223
PLAINSONG, 345
PLUTARCH (on pentatonic scale in ancient Greece), 151, 335
POLYRHYTHM, 345
POLYTONALITY, 250; a particular instance of Atonality, 351
POPE JOHN, XXII, 348
PRAETORIUS, M., 279*, 284*
PRE-DIATONIC SCALES, 49, 218
PRE-PENTATONIC FORMATIONS, 6*
PRIMITIVE SCALES, 5*
PRIMITIVE TUNES, 150
PROUT, EBENEZER, 216*

PTOLEMY, 215, 217, 270
PYTHAGORAS, 27*
PYTHAGOREAN INTONATION, 27*, of the diatonic scale, 107, 121; derives from the construction of scales by natural fifths, 115; used as a "common denominator," 116; applied to the infra-diatonic scale, 123, 131, 180, to the sub-infra-diatonic scale, 143, and to the supra-diatonic scale, 127, 155, 189; relative position of sharps and flats in, 138, 139, 214; unfit for practical purposes as the complexity of scales increases, 140, 190

QUARTER TONES (and smaller fractions), 4, 14, 56**, 138, 267, 335, 338

RAGA (Hindu), 278
RAMIS DE PAREJA, B., 270
RECTIFICATION OF THE WHOLE-STEP CHORD, 226-230
REGULAR AND AUXILIARY DEGREES, represented in all diagrams by long and short lines respectively, 18; functions of, 6, 35, 36, 40, 57**, 268, 336; interrelation of, 7, 114, 115, 130-134, 340*; historic evolution of, 132, 133, 151, 152, 268, 337, 338
RESOLUTION, property of, 198, 331
RESTRICTIONS FOR CREATIVE PURPOSES, 288, 292
RICHARDS, T. (on Chinese Harmony), 65
RIEMANN, HUGO, 19*, 66, 67*, 68**, 70*, 151, 335, 345
ROCKSTRO, W. S., 216**
RUSSIAN ORTHODOX CHURCH, music of, 193*

SABANEEV, LEONID, 56**
SCALE, intermediate agent between music and acoustics, 168*; universal and local, 5*, 335; see also AMALGAMATED SCALES, ATONÀL SCÀLE, CHROMATIC SCALE, DIATONIC SCALE, DUODECUPLE SCALE, HARMONY AND SCALE, INFRA-DIATONIC SCALE, INTERRELATED SCALES, JAPANESE AND JAVANESE SCALES, ORGANIC SCALES, PENTATONIC SCALE, PRE-DIATONIC SCALES, SUB-INFRA-DIATONIC SCALE, SUPRA-DIATONIC SCALE, TWELVE-TONE SCALE, WHOLE-TONE SCALE
SCALE-FORMATION, 62, 113
SCHÖNBERG, A., 244; melodic design of, 246, 249; on his own music, 250*; three piano pieces (op. 11), 332*; and his group, 351
SCHOPENHAUER, A., 63
SCOTCH MUSIC, scale foundation, 41*; folk songs, 57, 130; bagpipe, 41**; 270**
SCRIABIN, A., his chord, 229, 231, 239, 350; his scale, 246; "Prometheus," 232, 351; his seventh and eighth sonatas, 242*; his theory, 232, 233, 236; anticipated supra-diatonic harmony, 238
SÊ (Chinese lute), 64, 74
SEMI-SESQUITONE TEMPERAMENT, 41*, 270*
SESQUI-STEP, 45, 227, 241
SHARPS AND FLATS, their relative position in Just and Pythagorean intonations, 139, 214, 271, 283*
SHÊNG (Chinese reed-organ), 65; harmonic indications on its pipes, 66, 74, 75, 76, 80

SIAMESE MUSIC, based on seven-tone equally tempered scale, 7, 41, 42, 52, 71, 122, 123, 152, 191, 248, 336; five regular and two auxiliary degrees distinguished, 57**; instruments, 57*

SINOLOGY (modern), 25*

SMITH, H. (on harmonic sense of the Chinese), 65

SOULIÉ, G. (on Chinese harmony and poly-phony), 64

SPINOZA, VI

SPECULATION, scientifically undisciplined, 4

SPRECHSTIMME, 246, 371

ST. STEPHEN, hymn of, 70*

STAVE, one-line, 145; three-line, 46; ten-line, 159, 160

STRANGWAYS, A. H. Fox, 41, 150

STRAVINSKY, I., 230*, 266, 347

STUMPF, CARL (on Siamese music), 57

SUB-INFRA-DIATONIC SCALE, 136*, 140; initial link of the common spiral, 141; keyboard illustration, 144; intervals, 146; harmony of, 147

SUB-INFRA-MODE, 144; principal and altered, 145

SUB-INFRA-TEMPERED INTONATION, 142-144

SUB-INFRA-TONALITY, 149

SUPRA, 12

SUPRA-DIATONIC-SCALE, definition of, 7; anticipated by modern composers, 8, 246; formation of, 113, 114; acoustic structure of, 115; legitimate successor of the diatonic scale, 154; keyboard illustration, 154, 283, 334; twelve cycles of keys, 167; intervals, 166-173; chordal formations of, 172, 225, 241; experimental test of, 277

SUPRA-MODES, 8, 125, 129, 155; principal and altered, 161*; structurally identical to twelve-tone chromatic modes, 283

SUPRA-TEMPERED-INTONATION, 116, 128, 140, 176, 185, 189, 336; practical use of, 191, 212, 220, 277; method of computation, 223

SUPRA-TEMPERED PIANOFORTE, 131**

SUPRA-TONALITY, to supplant Tonality and Atonality, 8; theory of, 111; versus Atonality, 225; synthesizes Tonality and Atonality, 329

TEMPERAMENT, equal, 29; psycho-physiological considerations, 55; artistic factor, 58; practical expediency of, 122, 222; two methods of, 124, 128, 129, 157**; applied to different scales, 137; in the Orient, 32, 152; opinions on, 168*; constructive and destructive properties, 272, 337, 338; a convenient error, 287; meantone, 279*, 281*, 368; semi-sesquitone, 41*, 270*, see also INTONATION

TERMINOLOGICAL FORMATIONS, necessity of additional, 12

TETRACHORD, 44**, 214, 215; symmetrical and asymmetrical, 216, 217

TETRAD, 170

THIRD, 77, 110, 170, 179, 259, 288, 343; a dissonance, 71*, 343; formative unit in harmonic constructions, 77; chain of Thirds, 180

THOROUGH-BASS, 63

TONAL CENTER, 160, 263, 331; harmonic and melodic, 342

TONAL FOUNDATIONS, evolution of, 3

TONALITY, definition of, 5*, 330; an evolving phenomenon, 3; diatonic, 49, 287; rational and non-rational aspects of, 222; synthesized jointly with Atonality, 329; constructive elements of, 333

TONE (interval), see WHOLE TONE

TONE (sound), origin of the term, 7*; breadth of, 56**

TONE-PAINTING, decorative, 289

TONOCENTRIC SYSTEM, 333

TONOMETER, 14

TRIAD, 77, 110, 170, 179, 259, 288, 343; neutral, 226, 262, 265, 342

TRICHORD (Greek), 151

TSAI-YU (originator of the Equal Temperament system in China), 32, 33

TSCHAIKOWSKY, P., 102

TSAIU-YEN-SHIAU (originator of the Chinese 60-tone system), 31

TUNSTED, SIMON (theoretician of the fourteenth century), 347

TWELVE-TONE CHORD, 244, 351

TWELVE-TONE SCALE, Chinese, 25, 28, 52, 55; European, 160, 225; by Ariel, 220

ULTRA-DIATONIC SCALE, 136*, 141

"VERBAL ORCHESTRATION" (in medieval music), 345

VIBRATION-FRACTIONS, musical intervals expressed by, 15; involution and evolution of, 17

VIBRATION-NUMBER, 15

VITRY, PHILIPPE DE, 344

WAGNER, R., 57, 102, 332*

WEDELL, P. S., 281*

WELLS, WILLIAM S., 35*

WELSH MEDIEVAL POLYPHONY, 67*, 345

WHOLE-STEP CHORD, compared to the supra-diatonic Hexad, 226, 261, 350; on a tempered pianoforte, 256; stage of harmonic evolution, 340, 344; Siamese, 260; compared to the diatonic Triad, 262

WHOLE STEPS AND HALF STEPS, chain of, 47, 48, 160, 168*, 333; progression by, 245

WHOLE TONE, basic measuring unit, 13; not an absolute unit, 338; and whole step, 44

WHOLE-TONE SCALE, 8*, 14**, 225*, 340

WHOLE TONES AND HALF TONES (natural), incommensurability of, 120

WOOLDRIDGE, H. E., 68*

WÜRSCHMIDT, J. (on nineteen-tone temperament), 280*

YELLOW RACE, Sinean branch of the, 55, 371

ZARLINO, 215, 270